Derek Prime addresses crucial questions concisely, practically and, most of all, biblically. This is one of the best books to help us ground our faith in the solid truths of God's Word.

John Benton

Here are questions on the Christian faith answered from the Bible, clearly, succinctly and helpfully. 'Bible Answers' has for twenty-five years been a vital resource in teaching others. I have worn out more than one copy. Simple enough for the beginner and comprehensive enough for the serious student, this updated version should sit beside the Bible of every eager learner.

Bible Answers stands alone as an aid to Bible study. In this respect, instead of being introduced to the comments of the author, the reader is taken directly to the content of the Bible. Derek Prime has done us all a great service in providing this updated version. I cannot recommend it highly enough.

Alistair Begg

In an age of increasing Biblical illiteracy among Christians, here is an excellent resource book, which gives comprehensive answers to one hundred of the most common questions on the Christian faith and life. Bible Answers does not provide a substitute for reading the Bible but rather an incentive to study and use it, for each answer is supported by relevant Scripture references. A user-friendly guidebook for those starting out on the Christian pathway, and a useful reference book for seasoned travellers, written by a pastor and teacher with many years of experience.

Peter Grainger

What a mine of wisdom and knowledge this volume is! Derek Prime has done a unique service to the whole Christian Church by giving us a compendium of Biblical truth which is both thorough and accessible for the youngest Christian, and stimulating and educative for the most mature.

Its key characteristics are its complete commitment to the teaching of Scripture, and the constant reference to Scripture passages as the source of every statement made.

This book is a comprehensive introduction to the Christian faith, and those who work their way carefully through it profit immeasurably.

I could not be more enthusia

D1111948

Other Books by Derek Prime
available from Christian Focus Publications:

Active Evangelism   ISBN 978-1-85792-880-8

Bible Answers   ISBN 978-1-85792-934-8

Directions for Christian Living   ISBN 978-1-84550-614-8

Practical Prayer   ISBN 978-1-84550-309-3

Sarah and Paul (6 volume set for children, aged 7-10):

    Go back to School   ISBN 978-1-84550-157-0

    Have a Visitor   ISBN 978-1-84550-158-7

    Go to the Seaside   ISBN 978-1-84550-159-4

    Make a Scrapbook   ISBN 978-1-84550-160-0

    Go to the Museum   ISBN 978-1-84550-161-7

    Go on Holiday again   ISBN 978-1-84550-162-4

BIBLE ANSWERS

TO QUESTIONS ABOUT THE CHRISTIAN FAITH & LIFE

DEREK PRIME

CHRISTIAN
FOCUS

A word of explanation

This book was first published in two separate books in the United Kingdom entitled *Questions on the Christian Faith answered from the Bible* and *Bible Guidelines* and then together in one book in the USA as *Baker's Bible Study Guide*. They were based upon The Authorised Version of the Bible (The King James' Version) in the different editions that were published. Their going out of print has provided the opportunity for a revision of the material, especially in view of the many contemporary translations of the Bible, with special regard to the *New International Version (NIV),* copyright © 1973, 1978, 1984, by International Bible Society.

ISBN 978-1-85792-934-8

© Copyright Derek Prime 2001

Previously published in 2001 as a
hardback edition (ISBN 1 85792 6447)

This edition published in 2004,
reprinted in 2004, 2008 and 2011 as a paperback edition
by
Christian Focus Publications
Geanies House, Fearn
Ross-shire, IV20 1TW, Scotland

www.christianfocus.com

Cover design by Alister MacInnes

Printed and bound by
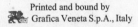 Grafica Veneta S.p.A., Italy

CONTENTS

Questions about the Christian Faith

Bible Guidelines

The Ten Commandments

Subjects arising, directly or indirectly, from the Ten Commandments

BIBLE REFERENCES

(Alphabetical list of the abbreviations used for the books of the Bible)

Acts	Acts	1 Kings	1 Kings
Amos	Amos	2 Kings	2 Kings
1 Chron.	1 Chronicles	Lam.	Lamentations
2 Chron.	2 Chronicles	Lev.	Leviticus
Col.	Colossians	Luke	Luke
1 Cor.	1 Corinthians	Mal.	Malachi
2 Cor.	2 Corinthians	Mark	Mark
Dan.	Daniel	Matt.	Matthew
Deut.	Deuteronomy	Micah	Micah
Eccl.	Ecclesiastes	Nahum	Nahum
Eph.	Ephesians	Neh.	Nehemiah
Esth.	Esther	Num.	Numbers
Ex.	Exodus	Obad.	Obadiah
Ezek.	Ezekiel	1 Pet.	1 Peter
Ezra	Ezra	2 Pet.	2 Peter
Gal.	Galatians	Philem.	Philemon
Gen.	Genesis	Phil.	Philippians
Hab.	Habakkuk	Prov.	Proverbs
Hag.	Haggai	Ps.	Psalms
Heb.	Hebrews	Rev.	Revelation
Hos.	Hosea	Romans	Romans
Isa.	Isaiah	Ruth	Ruth
Jas.	James	1 Sam.	1 Samuel
Jer.	Jeremiah	2 Sam.	2 Samuel
Job	Job	S. of Songs	Song of Songs
Joel	Joel	1 Thess.	1 Thessalonians
John	John	2 Thess.	2 Thessalonians
1 John	1 John	1 Tim.	1 Timothy
2 John	2 John	2 Tim.	2 Timothy
3 John	3 John	Tit.	Titus
Jonah	Jonah	Zech.	Zechariah
Josh.	Joshua	Zeph.	Zephaniah
Jude	Jude		

Using the Book

This book should be studied or referred to with the Bible at hand. The concern throughout has been to state what the Bible has to say in answer to each question. Where possible every statement has a Bible reference that should substantiate or illustrate it in some way.

The material has been set out in sections and sub-sections, both numerically and alphabetically, to make it easy for the book to be studied by sections, rather than read through hurriedly. Read without the Bible this book will appear heavy and solid. Read with the Bible it should become alive through the power of Bible-truth.

The endeavour has been made to avoid words that would not be familiar to the reader who is only just becoming acquainted with Biblical language and phraseology. But this is not always possible and the attempt sometimes means that the full force of an idea is lost. Where a word is unusual or has a particular significance in the Bible, a brief explanation of the word and its use will be found at the end of the book in the section entitled *Bible Definitions*.

Finding References

A few hints may be helpful for those not used to finding references in the Bible.

An example: 1 Thessalonians 2: 13.The name 'Thessalonians' refers to the book in the Bible. All Bibles have a list of books in the front and some have an alphabetical list as well. Look up 'Thessalonians' in this list and you will find the page number. The '1' before the name indicates that there is more than one book of this name. 'Thessalonians' has books '1' and '2'.

The figure immediately after the name is the number of the chapter in that book and the last figure is the number of the verse. In the Authorised or King James' Version the verses are all separated, but in the New International Version and other contemporary translations the chapters are usually in paragraphs but the equivalent verse number is placed in the margin, or within the text. A little practice will soon make you familiar with the layout of the Bible.

---

1. DEFINING CHRISTIANITY

Question: What is Christianity?

Answer: It is the only way to know God as He intends, and to live for Him.

1.   There is but one God.

(a)   There have been, and are, many so-called 'gods', but they are false (1 Cor. 8:4-6).

(b)   There is one God (Eph. 4:6).

(c)   Although God is revealed to us as a Trinity, He is one Lord – the only Lord (Deut. 6:4).

(d)   He is the Creator (Gen. 1:1ff).

(e)   He alone is supreme and sovereign: everything comes from Him, exists by His power and has His glory as its object (Rom. 11:36; Rev. 19:6).

(f)   He is the Judge of everyone's secret life (Gen. 18:25; Rom. 2:16).

2.   Men and women are not in a right relationship with God.

(a)   When first created, Adam and Eve were in a right relationship with God.   They possessed true knowledge, righteousness and holiness, for God made everything excellent and perfect (Gen.1:27, 31; Eccl. 7:29).

(b)   In such circumstances, they enjoyed fellowship with God (Gen. 3:8).

(c)   This right relationship was exchanged for a wrong relationship through Adam and Eve's disobedience, what we call the fall (Gen. 3).

(d)   Sin came into the world through Adam, and death through sin (Rom. 5:12); all human beings share in sin (Rom. 3:23).

(e)   Human sin constitutes a barrier to men and women's fellowship with God since He is holy and righteous (Isa. 59:2; 1 John 1:5).

(f)   Separated from God by their evil behaviour, men and women are far away from the life of God (Eph. 4:18; Col. 1:21).

(g)   In such a position they are incapable of knowing God and of living righteously (Ps. 14:1-3; Isa. 64:6; Rom. 7:18).

3. **Christianity proclaims what God has done through Jesus Christ to make possible men and women's reconciliation to God.**

(a) God takes no pleasure in the death of sinners (Ezek. 18:32; 33:11; 2 Pet. 3:9).

(b) He loves the world (John 3:16).

(c) He sent His Son into the world to save sinners (1 Tim. 1:15). This purpose involved His bearing the sin of sinners, and experiencing the death due to them (1 Pet. 2:24; Isa. 53:5,6).

(d) Through Jesus Christ God has made possible reconciliation, and men and women may be urged to be reconciled to Him through His Son's reconciling work (2 Cor. 5:18-21).

(e) On repentance and faith in the good news of Jesus Christ, men and women may enter into the benefits of this reconciliation (Mark 1:15; Acts 17:30; Rom. 5:1-5).

4. **Having been reconciled to God, men and women may know God.**

(a) God then gives to reconciled men and women such an understanding of our Lord Jesus Christ that they realise that to know Him is to know God (2 Cor. 4:6).

(b) He came to show us the Father (John 14:8, 9).

(c) He carefully gave God's words to men and women (John 14:24).

(d) Jesus Christ is uniquely the way for us to God (John 14:6).

(c) When we are reconciled to God, the Spirit of Christ is sent into our hearts that we may know God (John 14:16, 17; Rom. 8:15, 16; Eph. 1:17).

(f) This experience of knowing God was promised in the new covenant that God made known through the Old Testament prophets (Jer. 31:34).

(g) Knowing God means:

    (i) A growing appreciation of God's character and the kind of life He wants us to live (Eph. 1:17; Col. 1:10; 2 Pet. 3:18; 1 John 1:5; 1 John 4:8);

    (ii) Freedom and confidence to enter God's presence (Heb. 10:19-22);

    (iii) Fellowship with the Father and with His Son Jesus Christ (1 John 1:3).

5. **Having been reconciled to God, men and women may live for God.**

(a) They feel a constant urge to do so (Rom. 12:1; 2 Cor. 5:15).

(b) They possess a new dynamic that encourages them in this right and beneficial direction (2 Cor.5:17; Gal.2:19, 20; Phil. 2:13).

(c) The Holy Spirit, who now dwells within them, makes possible a new and better way of life (Rom. 8:9; Gal. 5:22-24).

(d) Living for God means:

    (i) Negatively, not to go on sinning (Rom. 6:11,13).

    (ii) But positively, to give our life to God (Rom. 6:11,13).

    (iii) To make it our ambition to please Him (2 Cor. 5:9).

    (iv) To live a life of simple and straightforward obedience to God's commandments (1 John 2:4, 5).

    (v) To strive more and more after holiness (1 Thess. 4:1-4).

6. **Men and women who know God and live for Him find themselves restored, in some measure, to the original condition of men and women before the fall.**

(a) Before the fall, men and women knew God and were righteous (Gen. 1:27; 2:15-17; 3:8,9).

(b) When we are 'in Christ' there is a new creation (2 Cor. 5:17).

(c) We are then brought to a true knowledge of God (Col. 3:10).

(d) Righteousness and holiness become the pattern of our life (Eph.4:24).

7. **Knowing God and living for Him are possible for us through Jesus Christ alone.**

(a) The key statement is John 14:6: 'I am the way and the truth and the life. No-one comes to the Father except through me.' Although there may be many ways to Christ, there is but one way to the Father.

(b) Truth about God may be gained by observing around us the natural world, providence and history. However, all such knowledge is incomplete and insufficient (Rom. 1:19, 20), since it falls short of a personal and intimate knowledge of God.

(c) Life lived by men and women without Christ is not pleasing to God (John 15:5; Eph. 2:3, 12).

(d) Only through Jesus Christ is the right relationship with God possible that we so desperately need (Acts 4:12).

(e)   To Jesus Christ alone can we turn for the true knowledge of God and eternal life (Matt.11:27; John 6:68; 17:3).

8.   It is easy to appreciate why true Christianity is so vigorous and active.

(a)   Without saving faith in Jesus Christ, men and women are dead towards God, without hope and without God in the world, lost and condemned (Eph. 2:1, 12; John 3:18).

(b)   Christianity is unique (John 14:6). The Incarnation, the perfect life of Jesus Christ, the 'once-for-all' character of His death as a sacrifice for sins, His Resurrection, His Ascension, and His promised return are all unique facts. They are unique not only in history but also in their continuing consequences (Acts 2:39). Nowhere are higher conceptions of God to be found. No one is a more sufficient Saviour than Jesus Christ (Acts 4:12; Heb. 7:25).

(c)   While Christians should not be intolerant of followers of other religions, they cannot accept that these religions are in any way approved by God or are properly satisfying to the human soul (1 Thess. 1:9; 1 John 4:1-3).

(d)   By reason of men and women's serious need and the compelling love of God Christianity must be vigorous and active (Matt.9:36-38; Mark 16:15, 16): truth opposes error; holiness cannot compromise with sin; God's love in the hearts of reconciled men and women compels them to proclaim the Christian gospel (2 Cor. 5:14, 20).

(e)   Christianity is worth dying for (Acts 20:24; 2 Tim. 1:8-12).

---

2. LEARNING THE TRUTH ABOUT CHRISTIANITY

Question: Where are we to learn the truth about Christianity?

Answer: From the Bible alone.

1.   Christianity presents us with unique historical facts and spiritual truths that are to be understood and believed (1 John 1:1-4).

For example:

(a) The deity of Christ (John 20:31);
(b) His Incarnation (1 John 4:2, 3; 2 John 7; John 1:14);
(c) His atoning death for our sins (1 Cor. 15:3; 1 John 2:2; 4:10);
(d) His resurrection (John 20:26-29; 1 Cor. 15:4; Acts 2:32);
(e) His ascension (Acts 7:55, 56; Heb. 1:3; 2:9);
(f) His second coming (1 Thess. 1:10).

2. **The record of these historical facts and the witness to these spiritual truths are found in the Bible** (Luke 1:1-4).
For example:

(a) The deity of Christ (John 1:1-14; Matt. 16:13-20);
(b) His Incarnation (Matt. 1:18-25; Luke 1:26-38; 2:1-7);
(c) His atoning death for our sins (Matt. 27:26-61; Mark 15:15-41; Luke 23:27-49; John 19:13-37);
(d) His resurrection (Matt. 28:1-10; Mark 16:1-13; Luke 24:1-48; John 20:1-29; 1 Cor. 15:4-8);
(e) His ascension (Mark 16:19; Luke 24:51; Acts 1:9-11);
(f) His second coming (Matt 24:3-31; 1 Thess. 5:1-3; 2 Thess. 1:7-10).

3. **The authoritative significance or interpretation of any fact or truth of Christianity is what the Bible gives** (John 20:30, 31;   1 Cor. 10:11).

(a) Many of the truths of Christianity need explanation in detail (Luke 24:27; Acts 18:26).
(b) Human understanding, unaided, cannot provide the satisfactory explanation (Matt. 16:17; 1 Cor. 2:14).
(c) The Scriptures were given by God to provide us with the illumination and instruction we need (Psa. 119:130; Matt. 21:42; Rom. 15:4) - the basis on which the gospel is preached is the statements of the Scriptures (Luke 24:44-47; Acts 10:43; 17:2; 18:28; 1 Cor. 15:3,4).
(d) The Holy Spirit uses the Scriptures to explain truths to which we would otherwise be blind (Luke 24:27).
(e) When we fail to understand what the Scriptures say on a subject, we soon make mistaken judgments on spiritual matters (Mark 12:24; Matt. 22:29).

4. **The Bible alone must be our authority in all matters of faith and conduct.**

(a) The Bible is authoritative (Matt. 22:31).

(b) It is inspired by God (2 Tim. 3:16; 2 Pet. 1:19-21).

(c) The revelation the Bible provides is final – anything that goes against it is false (Isa. 8:20; Gal. 1:8,9).

(d) The revelation God has given in the Bible - through prophets, apostles and through the Lord Jesus Christ – is the foundation of the Church (Eph. 2:20).

(e) All that is taught must be examined and tested in the light of what the Bible says (Acts 17:11).

(f) What the Bible says must be the deciding factor in any decision that has to be made (Matt. 4:1-11; Acts 15:14, 15).

(g) The Bible teaches us all that is right and true and equips us to live in a way that pleases God (2 Tim. 3:15-17).

(h) If we fail to recognize the Bible's supreme authority in matters of faith and conduct, we find ourselves breaking God's commandments by paying attention to lesser authorities (Matt. 15:1-9).

(i) Hollow and delusive speculations based upon traditions of human teaching quickly capture our attention if we neglect the Bible's authority (Col. 2:8).

5. **Everything points logically to the supreme authority of the Bible whenever Christianity is under consideration.**

(a) The Lord Jesus Christ came to fulfil the promises made by God in the Old Testament Scriptures (Luke 24:27, 44).

(b) The New Testament came into being because of the saving work of Jesus Christ (Mark 1:1; Luke 1:1-4; 1 Cor. 11:25; Rev. 1:19).

(c) The Spirit of Christ who caused the Old Testament Scriptures to be written also caused the New Testament Scriptures to be written (John 14:26; Heb. 2:4; 1 Pet. 1:10,11).

---

3. THE BIBLE

Question: What is the Bible?

Answer: The Bible is composed of the books of the Old and New Testaments, all uniquely inspired by God the Holy Spirit. It contains everything that we are to believe and do, so that our souls may be saved and our lives equipped to serve God.

1. **The Bible is a collection of books – a library.**
(a) The Old Testament is made up of the Law of Moses, the Prophets, and the Book of Psalms (Luke 24:44).
(b) What we call historical books the Jews reckoned among their prophetic or inspired writings: 'the Psalms', as the first and longest item, was a way of referring to the final section of these inspired 'Writings'. The historical books record God's dealings with His people, and provide the contemporary background of the prophets' ministries.
(c) God's very words were entrusted to the Jews in the Old Testament Scriptures (Rom. 3:2).
(d) The New Testament has four parts: first, the four gospels, which record the earthly ministry of Jesus; second, the Acts of the Apostles, which describes the establishment and growth of the early Church; third, the letters which convey the teaching of the apostles to the early churches; and, fourth, the Book of the Revelation (sometimes called 'the Apocalypse' meaning 'an unveiling') which is a prophetic book, looking very much into the future.
(e) The books of the Bible should be read as books rather than as collections of verses or texts.
(f) The books of the Bible have come together from a variety of backgrounds:
    (i) They were written by kings (e.g. David wrote many of the Psalms), prophets (e.g. Isaiah), apostles (e.g. Paul), historians (e.g. The Books of Kings), and others (e.g. Luke and his gospel and the Acts).

(ii) They were written in several languages, although mainly in Hebrew (the Old Testament) and Greek (the New Testament).

(iii) They were written over a period of more than a thousand years.

(iv) They originated from places as far apart as Babylon and Rome.

(v) They were written by as many as forty different individuals.

2.   The books of the Bible have to do with either the Old or the New Covenant, or Testament.

(a) The books of the Old Testament relate particularly to the covenant God made with the children of Israel in the desert before they entered the promised land (Ex. 19:5).

(b) The essential message of the Old Testament (or covenant), with its demand for obedience to God's decrees and laws, was 'Do this and you will live' (Lev. 18:5; Luke 10:28), although this is an over-simplification.

(c) The books of the New Testament relate to the new covenant promised in the Old Testament (Jer. 31:31-34), achieved and fulfilled through the atoning death of the Lord Jesus Christ (Matt. 26:28; Heb.13:20).

(d) The essential message of the New Testament is 'Believe in the Lord Jesus, and you will be saved' (Acts 16:31).

3.   The books of the Old and New Testaments share a common inspiration - the inspiration of the Holy Spirit.

(a) The New Testament speaks often of the Scriptures as a product of the creative activity of God's Spirit. He is their primary author (2 Tim. 3:16; 2 Pet. 1:21).

(b) More than 500 times in the Pentateuch (the first five books of the Bible) is divine authority claimed (e.g. statements such as those found in Deut. 4:5 and Ex. 20:1).

(c) The Lord Jesus Christ promised the Holy Spirit's inspiration to His apostles (John 14:26; 15:26, 27; 16:13).

(d) The apostles claimed to possess His inspiration (Acts 2:33; 15:28; 1 Cor. 4:1; 1 Thess. 1:5; 4:8).

(e) The apostolic writings were put on the same level as other inspired writings, i.e. the Old Testament Scriptures (1 Thess. 5:27; 2 Pet. 3:15).

4. The inspiration of the Bible by the Holy Spirit accounts for the authority it is recognized to have.

(a) It does not look to the Christian Church for its authority, for it possesses its own (1 Thess. 1:5).

(b) The Bible is consequently worthy of our closest attention (Josh. 1:7, 8; 2 Pet. 1:19-21).

5. Everything God requires us to believe is found in the Bible (Acts 8:26-38, see especially verse 35; 1 Cor. 15:3, 4; John 5:39). Its words are neither to be added to nor subtracted from (Deut. 4:2; Rev. 22:18, 19).

6. Every principle that is to govern our life and conduct is to be found in the Bible (i.e. The Beatitudes, Matt. 5:2-12; Paul's practical instructions to the Thessalonians, 1 Thess. 4:1-12; 5:11-22).

7. The Bible contains the good news of the Lord Jesus Christ by which our souls may be saved (John 5:39; 2 Tim. 3:15; John 20:31).

8. By means of the Bible's instruction we may be thoroughly equipped for God's service (Ps. 19:7-11; 2 Tim. 3:16, 17).

---

4. THE INSPIRATION OF THE BIBLE

Question: How do we know that the Bible is the Word of God?

Answer: **The Holy Spirit endorses it as the Word of God, causing us to accept its message and to prove its power in our lives. (To this 'internal' evidence we may add many 'external' evidences that give supporting testimony to the Holy Spirit's endorsement.)**

1. **The Holy Spirit is intimately connected with the Bible.**

(a) All the books of the Bible owe their origin to Him (Matt. 22:43; Acts 28:25; Heb. 3:7).

(b) The writers were 'carried along' by the Holy Spirit's influence (2 Pet. 1:21). The exercise of their natural faculties was not interfered with, yet spontaneously they produced what God planned - so perfectly that what they said, God said (Dan. 9:10).

2. **As the Bible is either read or preached it is the Holy Spirit's particular right to endorse and make certain its truth in the hearts and minds of individual readers, according to His will.**

(a) When the Holy Spirit chooses so to act, the message of the Bible comes home to individuals with great power behind it – the Holy Spirit's power - which results in deep conviction (1 Thess. 1:5).

(b) The message of the Bible is recognized to be then what it is – the Word of God and not human opinion (1 Thess. 2:13).

(c) When such power is known, the call of God to the individual through the Bible, by the working of the Holy Spirit, is answered – that is to say, the message is received, and acted upon. The way in which the promises of the gospel then become real in a person's life confirms the truth of the Bible (Ps. 34:4, 6, 8; 1 Thess. 1:6-8).

(d) The Bible finds a primary place in a person's life as a consequence, transforming it (1 Thess. 1:9, 10; 2:14; Ps. 119: 9-11).

3. **Our conviction that the Bible is the Word of God grows as our Christian experience of God increases.**

(a) Every promise we rightfully claim is fulfilled (2 Cor. 1:20).

(b) The more we know the Scriptures the more we find them relevant and suitable to our need (Ps. 119:49-56).

(c) We find that the Holy Spirit speaks to us through the Bible, whether we read in the Old or the New Testament (Psa. 95:7-11; compare Heb. 3:7-11, noticing verse 7 – 'as the Holy Spirit says, "Today, if you hear his voice"').

(d) The Bible becomes an increasing influence and power in our life (1 Thess. 2:13; Heb. 5:14).

4. **As we consider the 'external' evidences that the Bible is the Word of God our conviction concerning its inspiration is strengthened.**

    There are many such evidences and each is worthy of thought.

(a) The Bible's age.

(b) Its preservation in spite of many attacks.

(c) Its amazing unity, although made up of sixty-six different books, written by over forty authors, over a great period of time.

(d) The prophecies made in the Bible that have been fulfilled (Deut. 28:64; cf. Jer. 30:11; Micah 5:2; Zech. 9:9; 11:12,13).

(e) Its knowledge of human nature.

(f) Its frankness and honesty when dealing with its heroes.

(g) Its superb moral teaching: it never falls short of the highest even in the darkest hours of human history.

(h) Its power to change people's lives.

(i) The testimony of much of contemporary science. The evidence that science gives concerning the creation of the universe, the evidence of geology, archaeology and geography all add confirmation to the fact that the Bible is the Word of God.

(j) Most important of all the 'external' evidences is the Lord Jesus Christ's repeated testimony to the Old Testament as the Word of God (e.g. Matt. 5:18; Mark 12:36).

5. **The essential conviction that the Bible is the Word of God comes not from these 'external' evidences, however, but from the Holy Spirit.**

(a) Spiritual insight is given to Christian believers (1 John 2:20, 27).

(b) The Holy Spirit guides Christians into everything that is true (John 16:13, 14).

(c) Christians are given an understanding that is not natural to fallen human beings (1 Cor. 2:10-12): this explains their growing conviction that the Bible is the Word of God.

5. THE EXISTENCE OF GOD

Question: What proof is there of the existence of God?

Answer: Since God is not visible to the human eye, there can be no 'direct' proof of Him. However He has provided clues to His existence and nature both in creation and in the human beings He has made. Above all, He has given a perfect revelation of Himself in the Person of His Son, Jesus Christ. Added to these evidences, there is the witness of the Bible, and the testimony of those who have come to know God, as they have believed in His Son.

1. **That we should ask this question is evidence of our human sinfulness and corruption.**
   (a) The question itself demonstrates human folly and corruption through sin (Ps. 14:1; 92:6).
   (b) It arises from our sinful pride and rebellion (Ps. 10:4).
   (c) When people do not want to be convinced of God's existence, He may choose to abandon them to their depraved reason (Rom. 1:28).
   (d) Their thinking becomes futile and their wisdom foolishness (Rom. 1:21, 22).

2. **The Bible does not endeavour to answer this question - i.e. to prove God's existence - but it always assumes God's existence.**
   (a) All the wonders of creation are recognized to be expressions of His power (Ps. 19:1).
   (b) All that is good is identified and recognized as coming from Him (Jas. 1:17).

3. **The Bible makes plain that no one has ever seen God the Father: thus visible proof of His existence is not provided for His creatures.**
   (a) No one has ever seen God (John 1:18).

(b)   God is invisible and no one can see Him (1 Tim. 1:17; 6:16).

4.   Although we may gain a real knowledge of God, that knowledge remains incomplete in this life.

(a)   We can never fully comprehend God (Isa. 55:8, 9).

(b)   Our knowledge of God in this present life can be only imperfect and partial (1 Cor. 13:9, 10, 12).

5.   Nevertheless God has provided many impressive indirect proofs of His existence: He has not left Himself without testimony in the world (Acts 14:17).

6.   First, there is the witness of creation.

(a)   Reason points to the need of a first cause, i.e. the world could not make itself: the Bible names that First Cause – God (Gen. 1:1; Ps. 100:3; John 1:1, 3; Acts 17:24).

(b)   For example, in creation we see thought (Ps. 139:14), forethought and planning (Gen. 2:6), laws (Ps. 19:4-6), and life (Gen. 7:15; 26:12-14). Behind such there must be a Thinker (Gen. 1:3, 31; Isa. 55:8, 9), an overruling Providence (Eph. 1:11), a Law-Giver (Isa. 33:22; Jas. 4:12), and a Life-Giver (Acts 17:25).

(c)   God has disclosed from the beginning His everlasting power and divine nature in His creation: the eye of reason may clearly discern truths about God's character from the things He has made (Rom. 1:18-20).

(d)   The heavens declare the glory of God, and the skies proclaim the work of His hands (Ps. 8:1, 3; 19:1; Isa. 40:25, 26; Jer. 10:10-13).

(e)   In creation, God gives clues to His nature, as in the kindness He shows to His creatures (Acts 14:17; Matt. 5:45).

7.   Secondly, there is the witness of human beings themselves.

(a)   The wonder of our bodies points to a Creator (Ps. 139:14).

(b)   The idea of God is written on our hearts since we were made in His image (Gen. 1:26, 27).

(c)   We possess a natural intuition that there is a God: this is seen in human religiousness, mistaken and polluted as it may become (Acts 17:22, 23).

(d)   Our consciences witness to a law within us by nature – and where there is law there is a Lawgiver (Rom. 2:14, 15).

(e)   It is the fool who says, 'There is no God' (Ps. 14:1).

8.   **The witness of creation forms and makes up what we may describe as 'general revelation', that is to say, facts and understanding given to people to observe everywhere in the world, and from which they may draw logical conclusions as to God's existence. We now come to what we may describe as 'special revelation', that is to say, revelation that could not have come to human beings by their study of nature or by their reason.**

9.   **Thirdly, and most important of all the witnesses we shall mention, there is the witness of Jesus Christ.**

(a)   God has revealed Himself to us in Jesus Christ His Son (2 Cor. 4:6).

(b)   The Lord Jesus Christ has made the Father known (John 1:18).

(c)   He is the visible image of the invisible God (Col.1:15-17).

(d)   As God's Son became human and lived here on earth, people saw His glory, the glory that belongs to God alone (John 1:14).

(e)   The human Jesus who could be seen, looked upon and felt, was seen to be the Son of God (1 John 1:1-3). The apostles and disciples needed no more proof of God's existence: through the Son they knew the Father (John 14:7)

(f)   His miracles bore similar witness to His deity (John 20:30, 31).

(g)   To have seen Jesus was to have seen the Father (John 14:9).

10.   **Fourthly, there is the witness of the Bible.**

(a)   The Bible claims to be a revelation from the invisible God (2 Tim. 3:16).

(b)   The predictions it makes, claiming to come from God, are proved true. The good He promises and the evil He threatens (Rom. 1:18), are found to be true in human experience (Isa. 41:23, 24). God challenges the so-called gods of the heathen to do likewise (Isa. 41:22, 23).

11. **The general revelation provided by creation and our human nature, together with the special revelation provided by the Incarnation of Jesus Christ and the Bible, are further confirmed by the witness of the Church of Jesus Christ and the personal experience of its members.**

(a) The confirming witness of the Church of Jesus Christ:

　(i) The early Church had its testimony confirmed by God by means of signs, miracles and many different works of power (Heb. 2:4).

　(ii) The amazing growth of the Church is accounted for satisfactorily only by God's power (Matt. 13:31, 32; Acts 16:5).

　(iii) Its amazing life and continuance are explained by the fact that it is the Church of the living God (1 Tim. 3:15).

　(iv) Its preservation finds a satisfactory explanation in the promise of Jesus Christ (Matt. 16:18; Acts 5:38, 39).

(b) The confirming witness of individual members.

　(i) They have found their search for God rewarded (Heb. 11:6).

　(ii) In knowing Jesus Christ they know God (1 John 1:1-3).

　(iii) They know that the Son of God has come and given them an understanding to know God in personal experience (1 John 5:20).

　(iv) They are sure of God's presence with them (Matt. 28:20; Acts 23:11; Heb. 13:5).

　(v) Their lives and characters are transformed into Jesus Christ's likeness (2 Cor. 3:18; 5:17).

　(vi) They have an irrepressible testimony (Acts 4:20).

12. **Conclusion.**

(a) If people's asking of this question – 'What proof is there of the existence of God?' – is sincere, God will provide the answer in a manner that will leave them in no doubt (Isa. 55:6; Jer. 29:13; Matt. 7:8).

(b) What uniquely convinces us of God's existence is our personal experience of God through Jesus Christ by His Spirit (John 20:28; 2 Tim. 1:12).

---
6. THE BEING OF GOD

Question: What is God in Himself?

Answer: God is Spirit: invisible, without body, personal, great beyond human estimation, life-giving, and supremely powerful.

1. God is Spirit.

(a) John 4:24 – 'God is spirit, and his worshippers must worship in spirit and in truth' – is the nearest approach we get to a definition of the Being of God.

(b) Being spirit, God has no body; a spirit does not have flesh and bones (Luke 24:39).

2. He is invisible.

(a) Being spirit, God is invisible: no one has ever seen Him or can see Him (1 Tim. 6:15, 16).

(b) God is not discernible by our physical senses (John 1:18).

(c) It was because the Jewish people saw no form of God on the day that He spoke to them at Horeb that He instructed them not to make any image of Him of any shape or form (Deut. 4:15).

3. He is personal.

(a) He is a Personal Spirit, revealing Himself to Moses, for example, as 'I AM WHO I AM' (Ex. 3:14).

(b) Personal fellowship may be enjoyed with Him:
   (i) He spoke to Adam (Gen. 2:16, 17; 3:9-19);
   (ii) He revealed Himself to Noah (Gen. 6:13-21);
   (iii) He entered into covenant with Abraham (Gen. 12:1-3);
   (iv) He spoke to Moses, as a friend with friend (Ex. 33:11);
   (v) He makes His home with believing men and women (John 14:23);
   (vi) Christians enjoy fellowship with Him (1 John 1:3).

4. He is very great.

(a) He is the LORD, and there is no other (Isa. 45:6).

(b)   He speaks with supreme authority (Heb. 1:2).

(c)   He alone has immortality inherent in Himself (1 Tim. 6:16) – see 6 (a) below.

(d)   He is infinite: heaven and the highest heaven cannot contain Him (1 Kings 8:27).

(e)   There is no one to whom He is similar or with whom He may be compared (Isa. 40:18).

(f)   There are no limits or bounds to be fixed to any of His characteristics, for example:

  (i)   So far as space is concerned, He is everywhere (Ps. 139:7-10; Jer. 23:24);

  (ii)   So far as time is concerned, He is eternal (Ps. 90:2, 4; Isa. 40:28; Hab. 1:12);

  (iii)   So far as knowledge is concerned, He knows everything (Ps. 139:2-5; 147:5; 1 John 3:20).

(g)   In the light of His greatness, we can see the relevance of the second commandment: 'You shall not make for yourself an idol in the form of anything in heaven above or on the earth beneath or in the waters below' (Ex. 20:4).

5.   God is clearly beyond our complete understanding.

(a)   He lives in a high and holy place (Isa. 57:15).

(b)   His judgments are unsearchable, His ways are untraceable, and His knowledge is beyond our estimation (Rom. 11:33-34; 1 Cor. 2:16).

(c)   He lives in unapproachable light (1 Tim. 6:16).

(d)   We do not now know God perfectly as He is; we are like people seeing a poor reflection as in a mirror (1 Cor. 13:12).

6.   He has life-giving power in Himself.

(a)   Being the source of all being and life, all things trace their beginning from Him (Gen. 1:1).

(b)   God's existence depends upon no one beside Himself; He said to Moses, 'I AM WHO I AM' (Ex. 3:14).

(c)   He has life-giving power in Himself (John 5:26).

(d)   He gives life and breath to everything (Acts 17:25).

7.   He does what He pleases.

(a)   He does whatever He pleases everywhere (Ps. 115:3; 135:6; Dan. 4:35).

(b)   His will always prevails; His purposes are always fulfilled (Isa. 46:10).

(c)   None can resist His will, or say to Him, 'What have you done?' (Rom. 9:20; Dan. 4:35).

(d)   He does with His creatures whatever He pleases: the nations are as nothing before His power (Isa. 40:15, 17).

(e)   His dominion is an everlasting dominion, and His kingdom endures from generation to generation (Dan. 4:34).

---

7. THE ATTRIBUTES OF GOD

Question: What is God like?

Answer: He is holy, righteous, loving, good, wise, all-knowing, eternal, and independent of all His creation.

1.   God is holy.

(a)   The holiness of God is His most outstanding characteristic because it marks Him as quite different and separate from all His creatures (Ps. 99:3; Isa. 40:25; Hos. 11:9).

(b)   Each Person of the Godhead is said to be holy (John 14:26; 17:11; Acts 4:30).

(c)   Holiness is the initial feature of God's character with which men and women are confronted (Ps. 24:3; Isa. 6:3).

(d)   He is majestic in holiness (Ex. 15:11); there is no one holy like Him (1 Sam. 2:2).

(e)   His holiness is such that He cannot overlook wickedness and dishonesty (Micah 6:10-13); His eyes are too pure to look on evil, and He cannot tolerate wrong (Hab. 1:13).

(f)   He wants His spiritual children to share in His holiness (Heb. 12:10; 1 Pet. 1:15, 16).

2.   God is righteous.

(a)   He is righteous, and He does no wrong (Zeph. 3:5; John 17:25).

(b)   He is the God of justice, righteous in all He does (Isa. 30:18–
      even in the bringing of disaster upon His people (Dan. 9:14).

(c)   Righteousness and justice are the foundation of His throne
      (Ps. 97:2).

(d)   He is the righteous Judge (Ps. 7:11), who always does right
      (Gen. 18:25), and who will judge the world with righteousness
      (Ps. 96:13).

(e)   He is proved right when He speaks and justified when He judges
      (Ps. 51:4).

(f)   He does not forget anything His children do for Him and the
      love they show to Him (Heb. 6:10).

3.   God is loving.

(a)   Everything about God displays His love (Ps. 25:10): indeed He
      is love (1 John 4:8, 16).

(b)   He has revealed Himself as the compassionate and gracious
      God, slow to anger, and abounding in unfailing love and
      faithfulness (Ex. 34:6; Ps. 51:1; Joel 2:13; Jonah 4:2; Micah
      7:18).

(c)   His love is so great that it is said to reach to the heavens
      (Ps. 36:5).

(d)   His love for His people cannot be brought to an end; where
      human love would end, His continues (Hos. 11:8-9).

(e)   His love is the basis of the redemption He provides (Hos. 3:1,
      2).

(f)   His love is seen supremely in His sending of His Son into the
      world to be the propitiation - the atoning sacrifice - for our sins
      (1 John 4:8-10).

**4.   God is good - by that we mean that He is in every way all
      that He as God should be, He is perfect.**

(a)   He is good (2 Chron. 30:18; Ps. 86:5; 106:1; 107:1; 118:1), and
      alone so (Mark 10:18).

(b)   His goodness is visible in His creation (Gen. 1:4, 10, 12, 18, 21,
      25, 31; 1 Tim. 4:4).

(c)   His goodness is made plain in what He does (Ps. 119:68;
      104:24-30).

(d)   His goodness is witnessed in His gifts (Ps. 85:12; 145:9;
      Neh. 9:20; Acts 14:17; Jas. 1:17).

(e)   The commandments and the directions He gives are good (Ps. 119:39; Rom. 7:12; Heb. 6:5).

(f)   The promises He makes are good (1 Kings 8:56).

(g)   The will and purpose He provides for our life are good (Rom. 12:2), and no good thing does He withhold from those whose walk is blameless (Ps. 84:11).

(h)   The work that He begins in Christians' lives at their spiritual new birth is a good work (Phil. 1:6).

(i)   Even when God needs to discipline Christians it is always for their good (Ps. 119:67, 71; Heb. 12:10).

(j)   There is no limit to the good He gives to His children in Christ (Rom. 8:32; Eph. 1:3).

5.   God is wise.

(a)   He is the source of wisdom (Dan. 2:22, 23; Isa. 31:2); it belongs to Him (Job 12:13; Dan. 2:20).

(b)   His wisdom is displayed in creation (Ps. 104:24; Prov. 3:19, 20; Jer. 10:12).

(c)   His wisdom is visible in the natural processes of the earth (Isa. 28:23-26).

(d)   His wisdom is demonstrated in the out-working of human history (Isa. 28:29; 31:2).

(e)   He gives wisdom to the wise and knowledge to the discerning (Dan. 2:21).

(f)   His wisdom and understanding have no limit, and are beyond human power to investigate and comprehend (Job 28:12-21; Ps. 147:5; Rom 11:33).

6.   God knows all things.

(a)   Knowing everything, none can instruct Him (1 Cor. 2:16).

(b)   Nothing is hidden from Him (Prov. 15:3; Hos. 5:3).

(c)   He is acquainted with all our ways (Ps. 139:3; Prov. 5:21).

(d)   Everything is uncovered and laid bare before Him (Heb. 4:13).

(e)   If hell and destruction are before Him, how much more then are our hearts (Prov. 15:11)!

7.   God is eternal.

(a)   His years will never end (Heb. 1:11, 12); He is the living God (Rev. 7:2).

(b)   He is the eternal 'I AM' (Ex. 3:14), the first and the last (Isa. 44:6).

(c)   From everlasting to everlasting He is God (Ps. 90:2), who inhabits eternity (Isa. 57:15).

(d)   With Him a day is like a thousand years, and a thousand years are like a day (Ps. 90:4; 2 Pet. 3:8).

(e)   When the everlasting hills and eternal mountains disappear He remains (Hab. 3:6).

8.   God is unchanging.

(a)   He does not change (Mal. 3:6).

(b)   In the midst of change, He remains the same (Heb. 1:12).

(c)   With Him there is no variation or shadow of inconsistency (Jas. 1:17).

(d)   He is unchanging in His purposes and promises (Heb. 6:17); once He has spoken, He does what He has said (Num. 23:19).

(e)   His plans stand forever, and His purposes through all generations (Ps. 33:11).

9.   God is independent of all His creation.

(a)   He made Himself known to Moses as 'I AM WHO I AM' (Ex. 3:14).

(b)   He makes His decisions independently of anyone (Dan. 4:35; Rom. 9:19, 20; 11:33-35; Ps. 115:3).

(c)   He is independent in all His qualities and abilities (Isa. 40:18-24).

---

8. THE TRINITY

Question: **What is meant by saying that God is a Trinity?**

Answer: **The one true God is one in every way, in nature, will and being; but one in three distinct Persons - Father, Son and Holy Spirit.**

(The word 'Trinity' is not found in the Bible. Nevertheless it sums up what the Bible teaches throughout concerning the mystery of God's

Being. The term was first used to preserve truths concerning God's Being from error and false teaching.)

1.   There is one God.

(a)   There is only one living and true God, or divine Being (Deut. 6:4; Mark 12:29; Rom. 3:30; 1 Tim. 2:5; Jas. 2:19).

(b)   Before Him no god was formed; nor will there be one after Him (Isa. 43:10). He is the first and the last (Isa. 44:6).

(c)   Besides Him there is no other (Deut. 4:35).

2.   God exists in three Persons: the Father, the Son and the Holy Spirit.

(a)   Since the beginnings of human history God has revealed Himself as a Trinity: indications of the truth of the Trinity are found in the Old Testament, and in the earliest books of the Bible.

(b)   On occasions God speaks using the first person plural (Gen. 1:26; 11:7; Isa. 6:8).

(c)   The form of God's blessing is threefold (Num. 6:24-26).

(d)   A distinction is made between the Lord and the angel of the Lord, who Himself is God, to whom all divine titles are given and divine worship offered (Gen. 16:10-13; 18:13-14, 19, 25, 33; 22:11-18; 48:15,16; Ex. 3:2,6, 14; 13:21; 14:19; 23:20,21; Josh. 5:13-15; Judg. 6:11-24; 13:3-23).

(e)   As the revelation of the Old Testament is continued, the distinction between the Lord and the angel of the Lord becomes clearer. This messenger of the Lord (Mal. 3:1) is called the Son of God (Dan. 3:25). His personality and divinity are clearly revealed (Zech. 3:1). His origins are from of old, from ancient times (Micah 5:2), the Mighty God (Isa. 9:6), the Lord of David (Ps. 110:1), who was to be born of a virgin (Isa. 7:14), and bear the sins of many (Isa. 53:4-6,10).

(f)   With regard to the Holy Spirit, He is represented in the first chapter of Genesis as the source of order and life in the created universe (Gen. 1:2). In the books that follow in the Old Testament, He is represented as inspiring the prophets (Micah 3:8; cf. 2 Pet. 1:21), giving skill, wisdom, strength and goodness to political leaders and warriors, and to the people of God (Ex. 31:3; Num. 11:17, 25; Deut. 34:9; Judg. 3:10; 11:29; 1 Sam. 10:6; 16:13).

(g) The New Testament provides ample confirmation of the truth of the Trinity. There is the specific evidence of the baptismal formula (Matt. 28:19) and the apostolic benediction (2 Cor. 13:14).

3. The Father, the Son and the Holy Spirit are three distinct Persons: that is to say, these Persons are not simply different modes of appearance God uses in His revelation to us.

(a) The Father says 'I' (John 12:28); the Son says 'I' (John 17:4); the Spirit says 'I' (Acts 13:2).

(b) The Father says 'You' to the Son (Mark 1:11); the Son says 'You' to the Father (John 17:2); the Father and the Son use the words 'He' and 'Him' in reference to the Spirit (John 14:26; 15:26).

(c) Although the work of the Father and the Son is one, Jesus said, 'My Father is always at his work to this very day, and I, too, am working' (John 5:17), implying that their being – in some mysterious way beyond our understanding - is distinct.

(d) The Father loves the Son (John 3:35); the Son loves the Father (John 14:31); the Spirit testifies about the Son (John 15:26).

(e) Some acts are referred to the Father, Son and Spirit: for example, creation and preservation. The Father created the world (Isa. 40:28); the Son created the world (John 1:3); the Spirit created the world (Gen. 1:2; Job 33:4). The Father preserves all things (Neh. 9:6); the Son sustains all things (Heb. 1:3); the Spirit is the source of all life (Ps. 104:30).

(f) Other acts are mainly referred to the Father, others to the Son, and others to the Spirit: for example, in the work and plan of redemption. The Father chooses and calls, the Son redeems by His blood, and the Spirit sanctifies (1 Pet. 1:2).

4. There is a particular order of relationships between the Persons of the Trinity.

(a) The Father is first (John 5:26, 27; Eph. 1:3).

(b) The Son is second: He is the only begotten of the Father and is sent by Him (Ps. 2:7; John 3:16; Heb. 1:5; 1 John 4:14).

(c) The Spirit is third: He is given us by the Father and the Son (John 14:16; 15:26; 20:22).

5.   **The order of relationship does not imply that the Father, the Son and the Holy Spirit do not possess true and equal divinity: their true and equal divinity is insisted upon.**

(a)   The Father is God (1 Cor. 8:6; Eph. 4:6).

(b)   The Son is God (John 1:14, 18; 20:28, 31; Phil. 2:6; Tit. 2:13).

(c)   The Holy Spirit is God (Acts 5:3, 4; 2 Cor. 3:18).

(d)   In the Bible all the divine characteristics are considered as belonging to the Father, Son and Holy Spirit: for example, holiness (Ex. 15:11; Acts 2:27; 1:5); love (John 3:16; Gal. 5:22; Eph. 3:18); omnipotence (Job 42:2; Isa. 9:6; Rom. 1:4 and 1 Cor. 2:4); omniscience (John 21:17; 1 Cor. 2:10; Heb. 4:13); omnipresence (Ps. 139:7-10; Jer. 23:23, 24; Matt. 28:20).

6.   **The Trinity is a mystery beyond our comprehension – to be accepted and believed.**

(a)   We cannot delve into God's secrets that He has not chosen to reveal (Rom. 11:33-36; 1 Tim. 6:16).

(b)   Nor can the angels of heaven fathom the mystery of His being (Isa. 6:2, 3).

(c)   By means of the Scriptures we are given sufficient understanding of the work of the Trinity, in creation, redemption, and sanctification, to be saved and to be brought to eternal glory (Col. 1:11-14; 2 Tim. 3:15-17).

---

9. THE CREATION

Question: What is the Christian explanation of creation?

Answer: The God and Father of our Lord Jesus Christ is the Creator of all things. God the Son and God the Holy Spirit were active in the creation; and God has determined that all creation will belong to the Son.   In the end, acceptance of the truth of the absolute creation of all things by God is a matter for faith rather than scientific proof.

1. Genesis 1 is the foundation of any Christian explanation of creation.

(a) Many of the problems people have about creation are resolved when it is realised that Genesis 1 is an account of God's creation in poetic rather than scientific terms. It is concerned with the fact of creation rather than with providing scientific explanation.

(b) The emphasis is upon what God accomplished in a period of six days by successive creative acts:
Day One: Light (Gen. 1:3-5);
Day Two: The separation of the sky above from the oceans below (Gen. 1:6-8);
Day Three: Dry ground and vegetation (Gen. 1:9-13);
Day Four: The light-giving bodies (Gen. 1:14-19);
Day Five: Birds and fishes (Gen. 1:20-23);
Day Six: Animals and human beings (Gen. 1:24-31).

(c) We cannot state dogmatically what is meant by the word 'day' as used in Genesis 1. It is sometimes used of an indefinite period (Ps. 90:4) or of a very long period of time (2 Pet. 3:8).

(d) The Genesis account of creation is clearly designed to be simple, and intelligible for men and women at all stages in human history, describing the truth of God's complex creation in but few words.

2. God is the Creator.

(a) The Lord created everything (Ps. 33:6; 102:25; Isa. 40:26; 44:24; 45:12; Acts 17:24; Rev. 4:11; 10:6).

(b) He created the heavens (Neh. 9:6; Isa. 42:5; 45:18).

(c) He created the earth and all that is on it (Neh. 9:6; Ps. 90:2; Isa. 42:5; 45:18).

(d) All being comes from God (1 Cor. 8:6): He gives life and breath to all things (Isa. 42:5; Acts 17:25).

(e) From one man He made every nation of people, that they should inhabit the whole earth (Acts 17:26).

(f) He sustains all that He has made (Neh. 9:6; Isa. 40:26,28), for the entire creation is dependent upon His power for its existence (Acts 17:28; Col. 1:17).

3. **The work of creation is said to have belonged both to the Son and the Holy Spirit.**

(a) During the creative period, it was the Holy Spirit who moved upon the face of the waters, bringing forth the order God purposed (Gen. 1:2; Job 26:13).

(b) It was, however, through the Lord Jesus Christ that everything was made, whether spiritual or material, seen or unseen (John 1:3; 10; Col. 1:16; Heb. 1:2).

(c) The Lord Jesus Christ is both the First Principle and the Upholding Principle of the whole scheme of creation (Col. 1:17; Heb. 1:3).

(d) God the Father has ordained that the whole of creation will belong finally to the Son (Heb. 1:2).

4. **Essential facts about God's creation.**

(a) The implication throughout is that God's creation was from nothing by the power of His Word (Gen. 1:1; Ps. 33:6,9; Heb. 11:3).

(b) God performed His work of creation independently of any creature (Job 38:4-11; Isa. 44:24), and He remains independent of His creation (Rom. 9:5).

(c) God did not need to create the world or human beings; it was an act of His free and sovereign will (Prov. 16:4; Acts 17:25; Rev. 4:11).

(d) God created the world for the display of His own glory (Col. 1:16; Rev. 4:11); and thus His eternal power and divinity have been clearly seen through the things that He has made from the very beginning (Rom. 1:20).

(e) The Bible makes no attempt to reveal or to explain how God performed the work of creation. The absolute creation of all things by God is, ultimately, something that we believe because we accept the revelation of God (Heb. 11:3).

(f) The God of creation is the God of redemption (2 Cor. 4:6).

---

10. THE PROVIDENCE OF GOD

Question: Is God in control of everything?

Answer: **God controls all things, working out everything in conformity with the plan and purpose of His own will.**

1.   God's control extends to the whole universe.

(a)   He is the only Ruler, the King of kings, and Lord of lords (1 Tim. 6:15): His throne is in the heavens, and His kingdom rules over all (Ps. 103:19).

(b)   He sustains the whole universe by His powerful word (Neh. 9:6; Heb. 1:3).

(c)   The government of the entire universe is His (Deut. 10:14; Ps. 135:6; Dan. 4:35).

2.   God's control of nature follows.

(a)   All natural forces are in His control (Ps. 29:3-10).

(b)   The elements are at His command (Ps. 68:9; Jonah 1:4).

(c)   All the processes of nature are at His direction (Gen. 8:22; Ps. 107:33,34,38; Jer. 31:35).

3.   God's control of His creatures follows.

(a)   His care, for example, extends to the smallest of His creatures: He gives the beasts their food (Ps. 147:9).

(b)   Not a single sparrow falls to the ground apart from His will (Matt. 10:29).

(c)   He can appoint all His creatures to perform His will (Jonah 1:17; 2:10): even for ravens to convey bread and meat to His servants (1 Kings 17:6).

4.   God's control of human beings - and of evil individuals - follows.

(a)   There are occasions when God, desiring to show His wrath and to make known His power, has put up with evil individuals due for destruction.   His purpose has been to make known the

39

riches of His glory to those whom He has purposed to save (Rom. 9:22, 23).

(b) Sometimes God sees to it that the worst of people are allowed to be exalted so that they may fulfil His purposes without their knowing it (Isa. 10:5, 7).

(c) He uses even the enemies of His people to discipline them in their disobedience (Judg. 2:14, 15, 21-23; 3:12).

(d) On the other hand, He can harden the hearts of His people's enemies so that they fall into His people's hands or even destroy themselves (Josh. 11:20; Judg. 7:22).

5. God's control of nations follows.

(a) God fixed the boundaries for the peoples of the world (Deut. 32:8).

(b) He can make a nation large or small (Obad. 2).

(c) In the affairs of the world, and its rulers, the Lord puts down one leader and lifts up another (1 Sam. 16:1; Ps. 75:7).

(d) He uses heathen nations to accomplish the disciplining of His disobedient people (Isa. 5:26; Amos 3:9-11; 6:14; Hab. 1:12).

(e) So far as it has suited His purposes, He has allowed nations to go their own way (Acts 14:16).

(f) Behind the strange, and sometimes unexpectedly generous actions of unbelieving rulers towards God's people at various times is the working of God in their hearts without their knowledge (Ezra 1:1). Examples are Tiglath-pileser (Isa. 10:6, 7), Cyrus (Isa. 41:2-4), and Artaxerxes (Ezra 7:21)– they pursued their own chosen path, and served the furtherance of God's will, though in their personal lives they were disobedient, self-willed and sinful.

6. God's control of history follows.

(a) His dominion is everlasting and His kingdom endures from generation to generation (Dan. 4:34): thus all the events of human history are under His direct control (Rev. 9:15).

(b) He fixes the epochs of human history and the limits of human territory (Acts 17:26).

(c) God is at work in unrecognized events and processes to achieve His purposes of blessing. It was the Lord who sent Joseph ahead of his brothers to Egypt (Ps. 105:16-22); it was the Lord

who turned the hearts of the Egyptians to hate God's people
(Ps. 105:25); it was the Lord who called Cyrus, a heathen ruler,
'His anointed' because He was going to use him to accomplish
His will for His people (Isa. 44:28-45:4).

(d) The outstanding example of God at work in an event to achieve
His will - unrecognized at first – was the Cross (Acts 4:28;
cf. 2:23).

(e) In all the events of history God is working out His purpose of
calling into one body, the Church, men and women of every
nation and people, saved through His Son Jesus Christ
(Eph. 3:2-11).

7. God's control of all circumstances follows.

a) God, not chance, decides what happens in human affairs
(Prov. 16:33; cf. Jonah 1:7).

(b) Behind every circumstance is the Lord (Amos 3:6).

(c) He can shorten life or lengthen it (Job 1:21; Ps. 102:23).

(d) The Lord brings both prosperity and disaster (Isa. 45:7); success
and victory in battle (1 Sam. 11:13) and the ability to get wealth
are from Him (Deut. 8:18), as too is the power to bring illness
or to remove it (Deut. 7:15).

(e) Ordinary daily needs are within His concern and control
(Matt. 6:30, 33).

(f) The will of God may be worked out in what appears to be a
complete accident (1 Kings 22:28, 34).

**8. God's special control of affairs on behalf of His people
follows.**

(a) God's care extends to all individuals, and especially to His people
(1 Pet. 5:7).

(b) He delivers His people from trouble (Ps. 23:5; 34:7; 107:2).

(c) He can hand His people over to their enemies for a period to
discipline them if need be (Judg. 3:8; 4:2; 6:1).

(d) God is in complete control when His people are persecuted
(Acts 8:1, 4; Phil. 1:28, 29).

(e) He gives a sure footing in life to the righteous (Ps. 33:18, 19).

(f) He supplies every need of His children according to His riches
in glory by Christ Jesus (Phil. 4:19), guaranteeing that everything

in life will be worked out for the spiritual and eternal good that God has in view for them (Rom 8:28).

9. **God's control of Satan is clearly involved, and is taught.**

(a) The Lord can put a restraint upon Satan as He chooses (Job 1:12).

(b) He gives Satan, at times, power to do his wicked worst, but God is always in control (Rev. 9:1; 20:7).

---

11. WAR AND SUFFERING

Question: If God controls everything, why are there wars and suffering?

Answer: Wars, suffering, and other disturbing events, are permitted by God insofar as they may serve to fulfil His purposes; His final and certain purpose is that they will cease.

1. **God's control does not conflict with human responsibility.**

a) God's control of everything does not involve Him in human sin: human beings remain free agents, morally responsible for their decisions (Deut. 30:15-20).

(b) God is unchanging in His holiness, justice and goodness. It is inconceivable that in anything that He does He could do anything other than what is right (Gen. 18:25) - He is eternally self-consistent (Mal. 3:6).

(c) The blame for evil belongs to the sinner (Luke 22:22; Acts 2:23).

2. **God's control in relation to war.**

(a) War is assumed to be a necessary human experience in this world (Judg. 3:1, 2; Matt. 24:6; Luke 21:9).

(b) Wars are the consequence of people forsaking God and pursuing false gods (Judg. 5: 8).

(c) The Lord allows nations to exhaust themselves for nothing, making their schemes profitless, as it suits His purposes (Hab. 2:13).

(d) He permits wars in order to call people to repentance, for wars can be a punishment and a warning to unbelievers (Rev. 9:13-21), although men and women in general refuse to learn the lessons of war, and repent (Rev. 9:18-21).

(e) Wars will cease after the coming of the Day of the Lord and the ushering in of His kingdom (Isa. 2:4; Micah 4:1-8).

3. God's control in relation to suffering.

(a) In the sufferings of the righteous, who have no immunity from suffering (Eccl. 9:2), God's mysterious purposes are worked out (e.g. Job).

(b) Tragedy, accident and suffering are not automatically to be assumed to be the consequences of an individual sufferer's sin (Luke 13:1-5; John 9:1-3).

(c) Suffering of some sort is an indispensable feature of Christian discipleship (Acts 9:16; 2 Tim. 4:5; Heb. 11:32-38; Rev. 1:9).

(d) Suffering has a place in God's loving discipline of His children (Prov. 3:11, 12; Heb. 12:5-11).

(e) While impenitent individuals are not sanctified through suffering (Rev. 16:8,9), believers are restored to God by means of it often after straying from Him (Ps. 119:67).

(f) Suffering is to be patiently endured by Christians for very good reasons (2 Cor. 1:6):

   (i) Suffering accepted submissively, though not understood, honours God and brings blessing in the end (Job 1:21,22; 2:10; 42:1-6,10);

   (ii) Our Lord Jesus Christ is able to help us in our suffering (Heb. 2:18);

   (iii) Suffering is temporary, and is made easier to bear through the knowledge of God's compassion (Lam. 3:31-33);

   (iv) God sets a limit on the suffering, knowing how much we can endure (1 Cor. 10:13);

   (v) No kind of suffering or difficulty can separate Christian believers from Christ (Rom. 8:35-39).

(g) Christians may even rejoice in their sufferings because of their confidence about the benefits that will result (Rom. 5:3-5):

   (i) Proof of the genuineness of their faith (1 Pet. 1:7);

   (ii) Improvement in Christian character (Jas. 1:2-4);

(iii)   Knowledge that fellowship with God is their greatest possession (Ps. 73:13, 14, 21-26; Hab. 3:17-19);

(iv)   The discovery of God's comfort (2 Cor. 1:3-7);

(v)   The encouragement of others through their personal experience of God's comfort (2 Cor. 1:4);

(vi)   A deeper understanding of life and its meaning (Eccl. 7:3);

(vii)   Preparation for the glory to come (1 Pet. 4:13);

(viii)   The spiritual good of others (Gal. 4:13; Phil. 1:12-14).

(h)   God can use suffering so much to people's good that they come to look back upon it with tremendous thanksgiving (Ps. 119:71).

4.   Thus the completeness of God's control is plain.

(a)   God works out everything in conformity with the purpose of His will (Eph. 1:11).

(b)   God's control of everything is really beyond our minds to comprehend (Ps. 92:5-10).

(c)   It is so complete that He can laugh at all His enemies may try to do (Ps. 2:4; Mal. 1:4, 5).

(d)   He does as He pleases, and He does not have to answer to His creatures for what He does (Ps. 115:3; Dan. 4:35; Rom. 9:20).

5.   The completeness of God's control will be demonstrated at the Day of Judgment.

(a)   The judgment of the wicked is certain: the Lord is exalted forever (Ps. 92:7-9).

(b)   God will adequately punish evildoers and vindicate the righteous on the day of judgment (Rom. 2:4-11; 12:19; cf. Ps. 37:14, 15; Mal. 3:13-4:1).

(c)   Evil is not punished as quickly as we anticipate, only because God is patient and gives many opportunities to individuals for repentance (Rom. 2:4; 2 Pet. 3:8, 9; Rev. 2:21).

(d)   The seeming prosperity of the wicked, therefore, is temporary; they are not to be envied (Ps. 37:1, 2, 9, 10).

6.   Christians' proper reaction to God's control of all things.

(a)   Our response should be to declare, 'Great is the Lord' (Mal. 1:5).

(b)   No matter how desperate the circumstances, we should consider God's love and say, 'If God be for us, who can be against us?' (Ps. 107:43; Rom. 8:31).

(c)   Basic sources of fear are removed (Isa. 10:24-27; Matt. 10:31).

(d)   We may look to God for vindication in His perfect timing (Ps. 40:13-15; cf. 1 Pet. 2:23).

(e)   We should be submissive to God in all circumstances, ready to learn what He is going to teach us through them (Ps. 39:9), learning at least contentment in them (Phil. 4:11) since we always have Him with us as our perfect Helper (Heb. 13:6).

(f)   We should pray for those in authority, subjecting ourselves to them, recognizing their establishment by God (Rom. 13:1; 1 Tim. 2:1-4).

(g)   When we do not understand God's seeming delays to remedy wrong, we should say, 'I will wait patiently' (Hab. 3:16; Jas. 5:7-8).

---

12. SIN

Question: **What is sin?**

Answer: **Sin is essentially rebellion against God. Arising from the corruption of the human heart, it is the cause of our separation from God, and the reason for our deserving God's wrath. Sin is our greatest problem.**

1.   Sin is essentially rebellion against God.

(a)   Sin is doing wrong (Dan. 9:5).

(b)   Sin is acting wickedly (Dan. 9:5); it is doing evil in God's sight (Ps. 51:4).

(c)   Sin is turning away from God's commands and laws (Dan. 9:5) - what the Bible calls - 'transgression' (Ps. 51:1).

(d)   Sin is falling short of the glory of God (Rom. 3:23).

(e)   Sin is ignoring God's Word as it comes to us through the messengers He provides (Dan. 9:6; Heb. 3:13).

(f)   Sin is going beyond what is properly allowed; it is lawlessness (Hos. 4:2; 1 John 3:4).

(g)   Sin is rebellion (Dan. 9:5) - the result of hostility to God (Rom. 8:7).

(h)   The essence of sin is to be against God (Ps. 51:4).

(i)   Sin entered the world by Adam and Eve wanting things that belong to God alone (Gen. 3:5).

(j)   Sin ignores God's authority (Gen. 2:16, 17; 3:6).

(k)   Sin casts doubts upon God's character (Gen. 3:4).

(l)   Sin does not accept God's wisdom (Gen. 3:4 6).

2.   Sin is the result of the corruption of the human heart.

(a)   The heart is the wellspring of life (Prov. 4:23).

(b)   Sin begins in the heart (Matt. 5:28).

(c)   All the evil things in people's lives come from within them (Mark 7:21-23).

(d)   God, who searches the heart and examines the mind, declares that the human heart is deceitful above all things, and beyond all cure (Jer. 17:9, 10).

3.   Sin is the cause of our separation from God.

(a)   Our sin is known to God when it is hidden perhaps from everyone else (Ps. 51:4).

(b)   Sin covers us with shame before God (Dan. 9:7).

(c)   Sin separates us from God (Deut. 31:17, 18; Ps. 78:59-62; Isa. 59:1-2; Amos 3:2, 3; Micah 3:4).

(d)   Sin makes impossible therefore, the enjoyment of fellowship with God (Gen. 3:8; 1 John 1:6), for it puts us at a distance from Him (Ps. 51:11).

4.   Sin brings God's wrath upon us.

(a)   We gain an understanding of sin when we appreciate God's holiness (Isa. 6:3, 5).

(b)   God knows the precise extent of our sin (Amos 5:12).

(c)   Gratifying the cravings of our sinful nature, and following its desires and thoughts, we are by nature the objects of God's wrath (Eph. 2:3).

(d)   Sin draws forth God's wrath (Rom. 1:18; 3:5); His wrath remains on sinners on account of their sin (John 3:36).

(e)   God's wrath against sin will be revealed on the Day of Judgment - the Day of His wrath (Rom. 2:5, 6).

(f)   Sin leads to destruction (Matt. 7:13).

5.   Sin is our greatest problem.

(a)   Sin's pathway is all too easy to tread (Matt. 7:13).

(b)   Sin can so deceive us that we flatter ourselves that it will never be found out (Ps. 36:2); but God assures us that our sin will find us out (Ex. 2:11-14).

(c)   Sin is like yeast: it spreads its corruption (1 Cor. 5:6).

(d)   All the time sin is persisted in, there can be no return to God (Hos. 5:4).

(e)   We need to be delivered from God's coming wrath (Rom. 5:9; 1 Thess. 1:10).

(f)   Sin must be atoned for if we are to have fellowship with God (Heb. 2:17; 1 Pet. 3:18).

---

13. THE FALL

Question: What is meant by the fall of man?

Answer: By the fall of man we mean that event in history by which sin came into the world through one man and death through sin.

1.   The fall was preceded by temptation.

(a)   Yielding to deception our first parents, Adam and Eve, fell into sin (1 Tim. 2:14).

(b)   By the devil's cunning, their thoughts were corrupted and they lost their sincere and pure devotion to God (2 Cor. 11:3).

(c)   Our first parents were tempted to doubt God's Word (Gen. 3:2-6).

(d)   They became proud and independent, ready and willing to yield to the temptation expressed in the words 'You will be like God' (Gen. 3:5).

2.   Disobedience was the cause of the fall.

(a)   Having doubted God's Word, our first parents disbelieved it (Gen. 3:4).

(b)   Having disbelieved God's Word, they disobeyed it (Gen. 3:6).

(c)   They disobeyed God's clear command by eating the fruit of the tree of the knowledge of good and evil (Gen. 2:16, 17; 3:6).

(d)   This act constituted rebellion against God's authority (Gen. 2:17).

3. The immediate consequence of the fall.

(a)   Their attitude to God immediately changed: Adam and Eve hid from the Lord God (Gen. 3:8) – an awareness of guilt and separation from God had come.

(b)   They ceased to be spiritual beings in the way in which they had been before their disobedience.   Now men and women are unspiritual (Jude 19); they cannot understand spiritual things (1 Cor. 2:14); they are naturally earthly and unspiritual (Jas. 3:15); they are without God in the world (Eph. 2:12).

(c)   The first man and woman's sin brought the penalty of death upon all (Gen. 2:17; 3:19).

(d)   The first man and woman's experience of the wonder of God's creation was immediately spoiled: childbearing became associated with pain (Gen. 3:16); daily work became a matter of toil (Gen. 3:17-19).

(e)   Their sin had immediate effect on all the creation over which they had been given charge (Gen. 1:28; 3:17-19).

(f)   Continuing trouble was the experience of all who came after our first parents:
    (i)   Murder (Gen. 4:8, 23);
    (ii)   Polygamy (Gen. 4:19);
    (iii)   Revenge (Gen. 4:24);
    (iv)   Immorality (Gen. 6:2);
    (v)   Increasing wickedness (Gen. 6:5).

4.   The continuing consequences of the fall.

(a)   All the immediate consequences of the fall listed above continue.

(b)   As a result of the fall, men and women are astray from God (Isa. 53:6).

(c)   They love darkness rather than light, because their deeds are evil (John 3:19, 20).

(d)   They no longer live to do God's will, although they were made for this purpose (Rom. 3:23).

(e)   They lose the dignity that was theirs by their original creation the more they move away from God (Rom. 1:22, 23).

(f) Instead of being glad at what truth they still know about God, men and women suppress it because it makes them uncomfortable (Rom. 1:18-23).

---

14. ORIGINAL SIN

Question: **What is original sin?**

Answer: **Adam was the responsible head of the human race, and as a consequence his sin is imputed to all. We are born fallen creatures, and we go astray from God from birth.**

1. Adam represented all men and women and so his sin is imputed to us all.

(a) Adam represented all humanity (Rom. 5:12-19; 1 Cor.15:22, 45-49).

(b) It was through Adam that sin entered the world (Rom. 5:12).

(c) The wrongdoing of Adam brought death upon all human beings (Rom. 5:15).

(d) The wrongdoing of Adam established the reign of death (Rom. 5:17).

(e) The result of Adam's sin was condemnation for everyone (Rom. 5:18).

(f) By the disobedience of Adam - one man - the many were made sinners (Rom. 5:19): his sin is reckoned to us all.

(g) The basis on which God deals with us with regard to Adam is the basis on which He deals with us with regard to Christ. As through Adam we were made sinners, so through Christ we may be made righteous (1 Cor. 15:22, 45-49).

2. Being born fallen creatures, we go astray from birth.

(a) We are made in the image of Adam rather than in the image of God (Gen. 5:3; cf. 1 Cor. 15:48, 49).

(b) We are sinful at birth, sinful from the time our mother conceived us (Ps. 51:5).

(c) We go astray and become corrupt from birth (Ps. 14:3; 58:3; Isa. 48:8; Rom. 3:12).

(d)   There is not a righteous person on earth who does what is right and never sins (Eccl. 7:20; 1 Kings 8:46).

(e)   Purity and righteousness are impossible to those who know only human birth (Job 15:14; 25:4).

(f)   The Scriptures represent us all as prisoners of sin (Gal. 3:22).

(g)   Our will is stubborn and evil (Jer. 16:12).

(h)   Our minds are impure: they are corrupted alike in reason and conscience (Eph. 4:18; Tit. 1:15).

(i)   By nature, spiritual things are foolishness to us (1 Cor. 2:14).

(j)   Our hearts are evil from birth (Gen. 8:21; 6:5; Jer. 17:9, 10; Matt. 15:19).

(k)   We are corrupt (Gen. 6:12), not always able to understand our actions (Rom. 7:15).

(l)   Knowing life only according to our sinful nature - that is to say, life lived without the knowledge of God - we set our minds on what that nature desires (Rom. 8:5; John 3:6; Rom. 7:18; 8:7; Eph. 2:3).

(m)   If people do not do right habitually, they are identifiable as children of the devil (John 8:44; 1 John 3:8, 10). (The Bible does not teach the universal fatherhood of God, except in the general physical sense that God is the Creator of all.)

(n)   We are, by nature, the objects of wrath, deserving God's dreadful judgment (Eph. 2:3; John 3:36).

(o)   By reason of our situation described above, it is impossible for us to please God while we remain in this position (Rom. 8:8).

---

15. HUMAN EXISTENCE

Question: **Why do I exist?**

Answer: **The original purpose of the first man's creation ceased to be fulfilled when he rebelled against God. Unreconciled, men and women cannot adequately answer this question. Reconciled, men and women discover themselves to exist in order to know God, to do His will, to glorify Him, and to enjoy Him forever.**

1. **Why do I exist?**

(a) This is one of those fundamental questions to which we see the answer but dimly; the full answer will be revealed and appreciated in the life to come (1 Cor. 13:12).

(b) The question can be answered adequately by God alone: we are assured that everything He made, including the first man, was made for a particular end (Prov. 16:4).

(c) The question is extremely relevant in view of the futility of human life from so many points of view (Ps. 103:15-16; Jas. 4:14).

2. **God's purposes for Adam in his creation provide the first clues to the correct answer to the question, 'Why do I exist?'**

(a) We are here because God created the world, and He created men and women to inhabit it (Gen. 1:26-28; 2:7).

(b) They were created to possess the earth (Gen. 1:28):
   (i)   They were to make the earth serve them (Gen. 1:28);
   (ii) They were to rule all other creatures (Gen. 1:28);
   (iii) They were to work, take care of, and cultivate God's creation (Gen. 2:15; Ps. 104:14);
   (iv) They were intended to enjoy God's creation (Ps. 104:14, 15).

(c) Adam was created to know God:
   (i)   He was made in God's image, and in this he and Eve were unique amongst all of God's creatures (Gen. 1:27; Ps. 8:5-8);
   (ii) He was made to have fellowship with God (Gen. 3:9,10; Amos 4:13);
   (iii) It was intended that he should find his highest satisfaction in having God Himself as his friend (Ps. 27:1, 4);
   (iv) He was created to live in devoted dependence upon God (Matt. 4:4; Luke 10:27).

(d) Adam was created to do God's will:
   (i)   He was to obey God (Gen. 2:16, 17; 3:13; Eccl. 12:13);
   (ii) He was to live by faith and obedience (Gen. 2:15-17);
   (iii) He was made for God's pleasure, as was all of God's creation (Gen. 1:31; Heb. 2:10; Rev. 4:11).

(e)   Adam was created with a capacity to enjoy God forever:
     (i)   Men and women are not merely physical creatures (Matt. 4:4);
     (ii)   They have eternal souls (Mark 8:36).

(f)   In view of God's creation of Adam the answer to the question 'Why do I exist?' is 'I am here to enjoy the earth, to know God, to do His will, and to enjoy Him for ever.'

(g)   But when Adam rebelled against God he lost his way and ceased to know the wonder of God's purposes for human life.
     (i)   Men and women are like sheep gone astray (Ps. 119:176; Isa. 53:6).
     (ii)   Instead of worshipping the Creator, they worship more readily created things (Rom. 1:25).
     (iii)   Yet there remains within them that which makes them feel after God; but they cannot find Him without His help (Job 11:7).
     (iv)   Men and women's greatest need is to be reconciled to God (2 Cor. 5:20).
     (v)   As a result of the saving work of the Lord Jesus Christ in dying for sinners, men and women may be reconciled to God and discover the full wonder of God's purpose for life, that was lost in the beginning (2 Cor. 5:17-19).

3.   The question, 'Why do I exist?' is relevant to men and women who are not reconciled to God through Christ.

(a)   God is patient with us, not wishing that any should perish. We are here to be given an opportunity of coming to repentance (2 Pet. 3:9) before His final judgment descends upon a world that ignores God and is unconcerned to know the answer to this question (2 Pet. 3:10).

(b)   We are here to sow, by means of our lives, so that we may reap an everlasting harvest – for good or ill (Gal. 6:7).

4.   The question has positive answers when we are reconciled to God - for then we are in a position to enter into God's purposes for our life.

(a)   We are here to know God (John 17:3).

(b)   We are here to know and fulfil God's perfect will for our life (Rom. 12:2).

(c)   We are here to be agents for extending Jesus Christ's Kingdom (Mark 16:15; 2 Cor. 5:20).

(d)   We are here to be transformed into Jesus Christ's likeness with ever-increasing glory (2 Cor. 3:18).

(e)   We are here to please God (2 Cor. 5:9).

(f)   We are here to reflect God's glory (Matt. 5:48; 1 Pet. 1:16).

(g)   Our chief purpose in life is to glorify God (1 Cor. 10:31).

    (i)   To glorify God is to appreciate Him (Ps. 92:8), worship Him (Ps. 29:2), love Him (Deut. 6:5), and submit ourselves to Him (Jas. 4:7).

    (ii)   Our desire is that God should be praised in everything (1 Pet. 4:11).

    (iii)   We are here to glorify God in our bodies (1 Cor. 6:20): whatever we do - eating or drinking or anything else– should be done to bring glory to God (1 Cor. 10:31).

(h)   Our glorious anticipation is of enjoying God forever (Ps. 73:25; 1 Thess. 4:17): in the life to come we will be satisfied with seeing God's likeness (Ps. 17:15; 1 Pet. 1:8).

---

16. THE LAW OF GOD

Question: **Why has God given us His law - as, for example, in the Ten Commandments - if it is impossible for us to keep it?**

Answer: **While it is impossible for us to keep God's Law perfectly, God has given it to us as a revelation of His righteousness, of His demands of His creatures, and as a restraint upon human rebellion. By revealing and making us aware of our inability to please God, and the condemnation we deserve, God's Law enables us to see our need of the Lord Jesus Christ, and of the justification made possible by His atoning death.**

1.   The Law and the Ten Commandments.

(a)   The word 'law' is used in many senses.   It may refer to the Old Testament as a whole (Rom. 3:19), or just part of the Old

Testament (Matt. 5:17; 7:12), or even the first five books of the Bible - the Pentateuch (Luke 24:44). Sometimes it is used of those commandments given by God through Moses (Rom. 5:13, 20; Gal. 3:17, 19, 21). Often the term is used to describe the law of God as the expression of God's will (Rom. 3:20; Gal. 3:13).

(b) From the beginning it was recognized that it is God's right to command (Gen. 2:16).

(c) Men and women have a law written within themselves insofar as their hearts and consciences endorse the existence of God's law, even though they may be ignorant of the law of God as it is set forth in the Bible (Rom. 2:14, 15).

(d) The law of God was given to Adam and to Noah (Gen. 2:16,17; 9:6; Rom. 5:12-14), and the law of God, as we know it, came 430 years after the promises of God to Abraham (Gal. 3:17).

(e) The law was given to the Israelites (Ex. 20:1-17; Ps. 78:5) through the ministry of angels (Acts 7:38; Gal. 3:19; Heb. 2:2) and a human intermediary, Moses (Ex. 31:18; Josh. 1:7; John 7:19).

(f) The Ten Commandments are a comprehensive summary of the law of God: the first table of the law expresses our duty toward God (Ex. 20:3-11), and the second our duty toward our fellow human beings (Ex. 20:12-17).

(g) The law is found for us, therefore, in the Scriptures (Jas. 2:8).

(h) The law is a unity, expressing the undivided will of the supreme Lawgiver (Jas. 2:11).

(i) The law makes demands upon us – it calls for action, for obedience (Gal. 2:15, 16).

(j) The law is holy, righteous, good (Rom. 7:12), spiritual (Rom. 7:14), and royal - royal because it belongs to God's kingdom, and is given by the King of kings and the Lord of lords (Jas. 2:8).

(k) Love is the fulfilment of the law (Rom. 13:8, 10). The commandments of God relating to our fellow human beings are summed up in the commandment, 'Love your neighbour as yourself' (Rom. 13:9; Gal. 5:14; Jas. 2:8). Love for God Himself is seen in our love for others (1 John 4:20-21).

2.   The law is meant to be kept.

(a)   God requires that we should keep the whole of His law (Jas. 2:10, 11).

(b)   Thus the prophets conscientiously set the law of God before the people of God (Dan. 9:10).   The Lord Jesus Christ made plain that He had not come to abolish the law but to complete it (Matt. 5:17-19).

(c)   The law of God is to be regarded as the voice of God speaking to us, and to transgress that law is to disobey His voice (Dan. 9:9-11).

(d)   It is our duty to keep God's law (Eccl. 12:13), and the right attitude to it is one of submission (Rom. 8:7).

3.   We cannot of ourselves keep God's law.

(a)   The law requires perfect obedience (Deut. 27:26; Gal. 3:10; Jas. 2:10).

(b)   It requires the obedience of the heart (Ps. 51:6; Matt. 5:28; 22:37).

(c)   While God's image in Adam and Eve was unmarred by sin, they were able to keep God's law (Gen. 1:26), and were sensitive to it, but now men and women have lost all sensitivity (Eph. 4:19).

(d)   Fallen men and women find it impossible to submit themselves as they ought to God's law (Rom. 8:7); their nature finds it uncongenial (Rom. 7:14).

(e)   We cannot render perfect obedience to the law of God (1 Kings 8:46; Eccl. 7:20; Rom 3:10).

(f)   Because the law is a unity, whoever otherwise keeps all of the laws except one is as guilty as the person who has broken all of them (Jas. 2:10).

(g)   We sin against the law (Gal. 2:17, 18) - and all have transgressed it (Rom. 3:9, 23).

(h)   The law silences every mouth, and holds the whole world accountable to God (Rom. 3:19).

4.   The law is not - and never has been – the basis upon which men and women have been justified.

(a)   The law is not to be relied upon for justification because it brings a curse if full obedience is not given to it (Gal. 3:10).

(b)   We cannot, therefore, be justified by the law (Acts 13:39; Rom. 3:20, 28; Gal. 2:16; 3:11). (It needs to be said, however, that justification is in complete harmony with the law - Rom. 3:31.)

(c)   The law can produce no promise, only a threat of wrath to come (Rom. 4:15): it has no power to bestow life (Gal. 3:21).

(d)   The law was only a shadow of the good things that were coming through our Lord Jesus Christ, and not the realities themselves (Heb. 10:1): for example, by observing or keeping the law no one receives the Spirit of God (Gal. 3:2, 5).

(e)   Thus the law has never been the basis upon which people have been justified or credited righteousness as, for example, in the case of Abraham (Gal. 3:6, 7).

(f)   The splendour of the law is completely outshone by the splendour of the gospel (2 Cor. 3:10).

5.   The penalty for disobedience to God's law is death.

(a)   It is a dreadful thing to reject the law of the Lord Almighty (Isa. 5:24).

(b)   If we do not keep the whole law of God, we are guilty of breaking it all (Jas. 2:10).

(c)   To reject God's law and not to keep God's statutes is to merit God's judgment (Amos 2:4) and wrath (Rom. 4:15).

(d)   God's law that was intended to bring life actually brings death (Rom. 7:10; 2 Cor. 3:6).

6.   God's law is a schoolmaster to bring us to Christ.

(a)   The law provided a preparatory discipline until Christ appeared to make possible the fulfilment of God's promise of the gospel.

(b)   An obvious purpose of the law is the restraint of lawbreakers and rebels (Gal. 3:23; 1 Tim. 1:9).

(c)   The real function of the law is to make us recognize and be conscious of sin (Rom. 3:20): it is the straight-edge of the law that shows us how crooked we are (Rom. 7:7).

(d)   For example, we would never have felt guilty of the sin of coveting if we had not heard the law saying, 'Do not covet' (Rom. 7:7).

(e)   The law was like a strict schoolmaster or supervisor in charge of us until we could go to the school of Christ and learn to be justified by faith in Him (Gal. 3:24, 25).

(f)   Once we have such faith in Christ, we are free from the law's supervision (Gal. 3:25), although not from its authority and influence.

7.   Christ redeems men and women from the necessity of keeping the law as the condition of justification and acceptance with God.

(a)   Our complete failure to obey God's law in its entirety makes it necessary for our salvation to depend, not on our righteousness, but upon the righteousness of another – Jesus Christ (Isa. 64:6; Phil. 3:9).

(b)   Jesus Christ became man to take away the sins of many people - that is to say, the consequences of their breaking God's law (Heb. 9:28; 1 John 3:5).

(c)   Jesus Christ redeemed us from the curse of the law's condemnation by becoming a curse in our place when He was crucified (Gal. 3:13).

(d)   Jesus Christ means the end of the struggle for righteousness by the law for everyone who believes in Him (Rom. 10:4).

8.   The law of God and the Christian life.

(a)   Christians are to recognize that the law is good in itself and has a legitimate and important function in their lives, as it is directed against any and every action that contradicts the sound teaching of the gospel (1 Tim. 1:8-11).

(b)   God's Law is of continuing significance for Christians: His laws are written on our hearts, and set in our understandings - even as the Old Testament anticipated (Heb. 8:10; Jer. 31:31-34).

(c)   The commandments of God are not burdensome (1 John 5:3).

(d)   Christians recognize that their first obligation is to love the Lord their God with all their heart and soul and mind, and their neighbours as themselves (Matt. 22:37-40; Rom. 13:10). Such love demands obedience to God's commandments (1 John 5:2, 3).

---

17. THE FIRST COMING OF CHRIST

Question: **Why did Christ come?**

Answer: **As promised in the Old Testament Scriptures, Christ came into the world to save sinners by His death upon the Cross, according to the set purpose and plan of God, that the way should be open for sinners to obtain a right relationship with God and the gift of eternal life.**

1. **The Lord Jesus Christ emphasized the purposes for which He did not come.**
(a) He did not come to call the righteous (Matt. 9:13; Mark 2:17; Luke 5:32).
(b) He did not come to condemn or judge the world (John 3:17; 12:47).
(c) He did not come to abolish the law or the prophets (Matt. 5:17).
(d) He did not come to be served and waited upon (Mark 10:45).

2. **Christ came because it was the Father's will.**
(a) He came down from heaven (John 6:38).
(b) He did not come of His own accord or His own initiative (John 7:28).
(c) He was sent into the world (John 4:34; cf. 3:16).
(d) He did not come to do His own will (John 6:38).
(e) He came from the Father (John 8:42; 16:28; 17:8).
(f) He came to do the Father's will (John 4:34; 6:38; 8:29; Luke 2:49).
(g) His aim throughout His earthly ministry was to please the Father (John 5:30).

3. **Christ came to fulfil the Scriptures.**
(a) He came as the One promised in the Old Testament as the Messiah and Saviour (Luke 7:20; John 6:14; 11:27).
(b) He came to fulfil all the promises God had made about the coming One (Matt. 11:3,4,5,6): to preach good news to the poor,

to proclaim freedom for the prisoners and recovery of sight for the blind, to release the oppressed, and to proclaim the year of the Lord's favour (Luke 4:18,19).

(c) Thus He came first to His own people – the Jewish people – to whom He had been promised (John 1:11).

(d) Most of all He came to fulfil the Scriptures that show that the Messiah had to suffer for others and then rise from the dead (Mark 14:49; Isa. 53; Acts 8:30-35; 17:3).

4. Christ came to reveal the Father to us.

(a) He came to make the Father known - His grace and truth - for no one has ever seen God, but the only begotten Son, who is at the Father's side, has made Him known (John 1:17, 18).

(b) He came to testify to the truth about God (John 18:37).

(c) He came to complete the law, or, expressing it in another way, to reveal more completely what God requires of us (Matt. 5:17).

(d) He came to give to us the words of the Father (John 3:34; 7:16; 8:26; 14:24).

(e) He came to speak what the Father had commanded Him to say – and His words are the words of eternal life (John 12:49, 50).

(f) One of the reasons why Christ is called 'the Light' is that He revealed the Father (John 3:19).

5. Christ came to save sinners - this is the stress of the Bible.

(a) He came into the world to save sinners (1 Tim. 1:15).

(b) Acting on the principle that it is the sick who need a doctor and not the well, He came to call sinners to repentance (Matt. 9:12, 13; Mark 2:17; Luke 5:32).

(c) Because of His purpose to save sinners, He spent His time with them, much to the disgust of the self-righteous (Matt. 11:19).

(d) He came to seek and to save the lost (Matt. 18:11; Luke 15:1-32; 19:10; John 10:16).

(e) He came to be the Saviour of the world (John 12:47; 1 John 4:14)– to make it possible for God to save those in danger of perishing (John 3:16).

(f) He came that we might believe on Him and be saved (John 3:16, 17; 6:29).

6. Christ came, therefore, to die.

(a) He made it plain to His disciples that He had to go to Jerusalem, there to suffer much from the elders, chief priests and scribes, to be put to death, and to be raised again on the third day (Matt. 16:21; Mark 8:31; Luke 9:22) - all in accord with what was written of Him in the law of Moses, in the prophets and the Psalms (Isa.53:12; Luke 22:37; 24:44-47).

(b) He came into the world with the deliberate intention of dying upon the Cross (John 12:27; Acts 2:23).

(c) He came to give His life a ransom for many (Mark 10:45).

(d) He came to be lifted up on the Cross just as the snake was lifted up by Moses in the desert (John 3:14; 12:34).

(e) He came to give His own flesh for the life of the world (John 6:51).

(f) He was constantly aware of the terrible suffering that was ahead of Him in His crucifixion (Luke 12:50).

(g) The whole programme of His earthly life moved towards the Cross as its climax (John 7:6, 8, 30; 8:20; 12:23, 27; 13:1; 17:1; Luke 24:6, 7).

(h) He came to be the propitiation – the atoning sacrifice - for our sins (1 John 4:10).

7. Christ came that through His death for sinners, we might have a right relationship with God, and eternal life.

(a) He came that those who accept Him may receive a right relationship with the Father (Matt. 10:40; Luke 10:16; John 13:20).

(b) He came that, by means of the Cross, He might be the way to God for us (John 14:6).

(c) He came to proclaim the good news of peace through the reconciliation made possible by the Cross (Eph. 2:16, 17).

(d) He came to bring us spiritual life (John 5:40; 6:51, 58; 10:10; 20:31; 1 John 4:9).

(e) He came so that everyone who has faith in Him as the crucified and risen Messiah should possess eternal life (John 3:14, 15; 6:40, 51, 58; 17:3).

---

18. THE DEITY OF CHRIST

Question: **How do we know that Christ is God?**

Answer: **The deity of Christ, confirmed by His perfect life, unique ministry and triumphant Resurrection is vigorously affirmed by the prophets, the apostles and the cumulative testimony of the Bible.**

1.   We have Christ's own claims to deity.

(a)   There were occasions when He openly claimed to be the Messiah (Mark 14:61-64; Luke 22:66-71; John 4:25, 26).

(b)   To claim Messiahship was to claim deity (Ps. 2:6-12; Isa. 9:6; Zech. 13:7).

(c)   The Jews recognized this implication of Jesus' claim to Messiahship (John 10:33).

(d)   He made unique claims for Himself (John 6:35; 8:12; 10:7, 9; 10:11; 11:25; 14:6; 15:1).

(e)   He declared Himself to be one with the Father (John 10:30; cf. 5:18).

(f)   He accepted the declaration of Thomas, 'My Lord and my God!' (John 20:28, 29).

2.   Everything about His life serves to substantiate His claims to deity.

(a)   There is the evidence of His supernatural conception and birth (Matt. 1:18-25; Luke 1:26-56; 2:1-40).

(b)   There is the evidence of His sinless life:

   (i)   He committed no sin and no deceit was found on His lips (1 Pet. 2:22).

   (ii)   He could ask a question that only a perfect human being would rightly dare to ask, 'Can any of you prove me guilty of sin?' (John 8:46).

   (iii)   Pilate's wife called Him 'That innocent man' (Matt. 27:19).

   (iv)   Judas said, 'I have betrayed innocent blood' (Matt. 27:4).

   (v)   The dying thief declared, 'This man has done nothing wrong' (Luke 23:41).

(vi)   The Roman soldier in charge of the crucifixion declared, 'Surely this was a righteous man' (Luke 23:47).

(vii)   No amount of provocation caused Him to act wrongly (1 Pet. 2:23).

(c)   There is the evidence of His remarkable insight and knowledge:

   (i)   He needed no evidence from others about individuals, for He could tell what people were really like (John 2:24, 25);

   (ii)   He knew His betrayer from the beginning (John 6:70, 71; 13:10, 11);

   (iii)   He anticipated Peter's denial and restoration (Luke 22:31-34).

(d)   There is the evidence of His unique teaching: the authority of His teaching astonished all who heard Him (Matt. 7:28, 29; John 7:45, 46). The prophets, for example, said, 'This is what the Lord says' (Ezek. 21:9), whereas Jesus said, 'I tell you the truth' (Matt. 5:18).

(e)   There is the evidence of His miracles:

   (i)   These were never selfish or merely spectacular (Matt. 4:5-7).

   (ii)   Those who witnessed the miracles sensed themselves to be in the presence of God (Mark 1:27; Luke 5:26; 7:16; 9:43).

   (iii)   The miracles were 'signs' of Christ's deity (John 20:30-31). The Jewish exorcists invoked the name of the Lord, but Jesus commanded, and evil spirits, the wind and the waves obeyed Him (Mark 1:27; 4:41).

(f)   There is the overwhelming evidence of Christ's resurrection:

   (i)   All the gospel writers record it in detail (Matt. 28:1-20; Mark 16:1-20; Luke 24:1-53; John 20:1- 21).

   (ii)   Both Peter and Paul make mention of it in their letters (1 Pet. 1:3, 21; 1 Cor. 15).

   (iii)   The apostolic preaching emphasised the Resurrection as the chief witness to Christ's deity (Acts 2:32; 3:15, 26; 4:33).

   (iv)   God the Father declared Christ to be His Son by the resurrection, thus endorsing every claim Christ had made (Rom. 1:4).

3.   **To the evidence of Christ's claims and unique life to His deity, there must be added the witness of the prophets, including John the Baptist.**

(a)   Some of the prophetic psalms spoke of a divine Messiah (Ps. 2:6-12; cf. Heb. 1:5; Ps. 45:6, 7; cf. Heb. 1:8, 9; Ps. 110:1; cf. Heb. 1:13).

(b)   Isaiah spoke of the Messiah whose name would be called Wonderful Counsellor, Mighty God, Everlasting Father, and Prince of Peace (Isa. 9:6).

(c)   Jeremiah declared that the Messiah would be called 'The LORD Our Righteousness' (Jer.23:5, 6; cf. 1 Cor. 1:30).

(d)   Micah speaks of the Messiah as One whose origins have been of old, from ancient times, from everlasting (Micah 5:2).

(e)   Zechariah records God speaking of the Messiah as His fellow, the One close to Him (Zech. 13:7).

(f)   John the Baptist not only described his ministry as making straight the way of the Lord (John 1:23; cf. Isa. 40:3) but he testified that Jesus is the Son of God (John 1:34).

4.   **We have also the witness of the apostles to the deity of Christ.**

(a)   Peter's confession, 'You are the Christ, the Son of the living God' (Matt. 16:16), marked a vital stage in the spiritual understanding of the apostles.

(b)   The apostles saw Christ's glory as He lived among them, such glory as befits the Father's only Son (John 1:14; 1 John 1:1).

(c)   John bears witness:

    (i)   'The Word became flesh and made his dwelling among us' (John 1:14; cf. 1:1-4);

    (ii)   John identifies the glory of the Lord that Isaiah witnessed as the glory of Christ (Isaiah 6:1-3; John 12:41);

    (iii)   The truth of Christ's deity was the great fundamental for John (John 20:31; 1 John 5:20).

(d)   Peter bears witness:

    (i)   He heard the testimony of God the Father concerning Jesus Christ His Son (2 Pet. 1:16-18);

    (ii)   He speaks in Trinitarian terms of the Father, the Son and the Holy Spirit (1 Pet. 1:2).

(e)   Paul bears witness:

    (i)   The first truth he proclaimed after his conversion was that Jesus 'is the Son of God' (Acts 9:20).

    (ii)   The Church, he declares, God 'bought with his own blood (Acts 20:28).

    (iii)   In Christ all the fulness of the Deity lives in bodily form (Col. 2:9).

5.   Finally, we have the witness of the Bible itself.

(a)   References to God in the Old Testament are in the New Testament applied to Christ.
Examples:

    (i)   Christ is the Lord (Isa. 40:3; cf. Matt. 3:3);

    (ii)   Christ is the First and the Last (Isa. 44:6; Rev. 1:17);

    (iii)   Christ is the Judge (Eccl. 12:14; cf. 1 Cor. 4:5).

(b)   The works of God are ascribed to Him:

    (i)   The work of creation was His (John 1:3; 1 Cor. 8:6; Col. 1:16; Heb. 1:2);

    (ii)   The work of preservation in providence is His also (Heb. 1:3).

(c)   Characteristics that belong only to God are ascribed to Christ:

    (i)   He is everywhere present (Matt. 28:20);

    (ii)   He is all-powerful (Phil. 3:21; Rev. 1:8);

    (iii)   He knows everything (John 16:30; 21:17; Rev. 2:23);

    (iv)   He is unchanging (Heb. 13:8);

    (v)   He forgives sins (Mark 2:7, 10; Col. 3:13).

Conclusions.

1.   The deity of Christ throws amazing light upon the love of God: God Himself came to redeem men and women (2 Cor. 5:19).

2.   Christ is worthy of our worship: all God's angels worship Him (Heb. 1:6), as does the whole of heaven (Rev. 5:11, 12).

3.   His deity gives unique value to His death: by His death we may be redeemed for God and set free from all wickedness (Tit. 2:14; Rev. 5:9).

4.   Christ is the object of Christians' faith: men and women are to be urged to believe on the Lord Jesus Christ and be saved (Acts 16:31).

5.   The Church is built upon the truth of Christ's deity (Matt. 16:18).

6.   Christians' relationship to Christ is the most important reality of their life (Phil. 3:7-11).

---

19. THE INCARNATION

Question: How do we know that Christ is both God and man?

Answer: In both the Old and the New Testaments Christ is declared to be both God and man, united in one person.   Many infallible proofs of the truth of this mystery are provided.

1.   **The Old Testament prophecies spoke of the coming Messiah, or Christ, as both God and man.**
(a)   The Psalms provide many examples of such prophecies (Ps. 2; 22; 45; 72; 110).
(b)   Christ's human and divine nature was portrayed by Isaiah (Isa. 9:6, 7).
(c)   The prophecies concerning the Messiah, that took for granted His deity, spoke also of His body, or His humanity (Isa. 50:6).
(d)   Micah prophesied that the Christ to be born was One whose 'origins are from of old, from ancient times' (Micah 5:2).

2.   **The New Testament speaks of Christ as both God and man.**
(a)   Christ, who is God, was made man, without ceasing to be God (John 1:1-3, 14) – He was made in human likeness, He was revealed in human form (Phil. 2:7, 8).
(b)   As the apostle John expresses it, 'The Word became flesh and made his dwelling among us. We have seen his glory, the glory of the One and Only, who came from the Father, full of grace and truth' (John 1:14).
(c)   The testimony of the apostles was that the man Christ Jesus was the Word, the Son of God (1 John 1:1-3).
(d)   That Christ became flesh did not mean that His deity was any the less: in Him 'all the fulness of the Deity lives in bodily form' (Col. 2:9).

3. **Christ's virgin conception points to His perfect deity and perfect humanity.**

(a) He was born of a human mother, without a human father (Luke 2:6, 7; Gal. 4:4).

(b) He became flesh through being conceived by the power of the Holy Spirit in the womb of Mary (Matt. 1:20); the Holy Spirit came upon her, and the power of the Most High overshadowed her; these facts explain the holiness of the child, and His identity as the Son of God (Luke 1:35).

(c) The virgin conception had been promised by God through the prophet Isaiah (Isa. 7:14; 8:8; Matt. 1:23). Through this event God began to fulfil His promises made throughout the centuries that He would Himself visit and redeem His people (Matt. 1:21ff; Luke 1:31ff, 68-75; 2:10ff, 29-32).

4. **We are given ample proof of Christ's deity.**

(a) Passages of Scripture in the Old Testament speaking of the Lord Jehovah are applied to Christ in the New Testament (Num. 21:5,6, cf. 1 Cor. 10:9; Ps. 102:25-27, cf. Heb. 1:10; Isa. 6:1-10, cf. John 12:40,41; Isa. 8:13,14, cf. Luke 2:34; Rom. 9:33; Isa. 40:3,4, cf. John 1:23; Isa. 45:22, 23, cf.Rom. 14:11, Phil. 2:10,11; Mal. 3:1, cf. Matt. 11:10).

(b) Works and activity that particularly belong to God are said to belong to Christ: for example, creation (John 1:3; 1 Cor. 8:6; Heb. 1:2); the sustaining of the universe (Heb. 1:3; John 5:17); and miracles (John 20:30; cf. John 2:11).

(c) Characteristics that belong to God alone are said to belong to Christ: for example, He is everywhere (Matt. 28:20; John 14:23; Eph. 3:17); He is eternal (John 1:1; Rev. 1:11; Micah 5:2); He is unchanging (Heb. 1:11, 12; 13:8); He knows all things (John 21:17; Rev. 2:23); He has majesty and glory equal to His Father (John 5:23; Phil. 1:2; 2:6, 9, 10; Rev. 5:13).

(d) The names given to Him bear witness to His deity: for example, He is clearly called God (John 1:1; 20. 28; Acts 20:28; Rom. 9:5; Phil. 2:6; 1 Tim. 3:16; Heb. 1:8); He is called the Son of God (John 1:18; Rom. 8:3); He is called Lord (1 Cor. 8:5, 6) – 'Lord' being the word used in the Greek translation of the Old Testament for the name of God, 'Jehovah' or' Yahweh'.

5. We are given ample proof of His humanity.

(a) God sent His own Son in the likeness of sinful flesh – the word 'likeness' implies that Jesus was similar to sinful human beings in His earthly life, yet not absolutely like them (Rom. 8:3; Phil. 2:7), because He was without sin (Heb. 4:15).

(b) He shared our humanity (Heb. 2:14).

(c) He had all that is essential in a human being: a body (Luke 24:39; Heb. 2:17; 10:5; 1 John 1:1); a soul (Matt. 26:38; Mark 14:34); a will (Matt. 26:39), affections (Mark 3:5; Luke 10:21; John 11:5), and particular abilities (Luke 2:52).

(d) He knew tiredness (John 4:6), thirst (John 4:7; 19:28), tears (John 11:35; Heb. 5:7), and all human weakness, with one exception (Heb. 4:15).

(e) He shared fully in all our experiences, especially in the realm of temptation, except that He never sinned (2 Cor. 5:21; Heb. 4:15; 1 Pet. 2:22).

(f) Possessing a human body Christ endured physical suffering (1 Pet. 4:1); He was put to death in the body (1 Pet. 3:18).

6. It was only by Christ being both God and man that salvation could be obtained for sinful men and women.

(a) Christ's body was a fundamental part of God's plan of salvation (Heb. 10:5).

(b) God the Father caused Christ to be made flesh of a pure virgin, to live among men and women, that He might be obedient to death, even death on a cross (Isa. 50:6; John 1:14; Luke 1:35; Phil. 2:8; 1 Tim. 3:16).

(c) The reconciliation, that God purposed, was accomplished by Christ's death in His physical body (Eph. 2:15,16; Col. 1:22).

(d) The new and living way for sinners into God's presence by the blood of Christ was possible solely by means of Christ's taking human flesh upon Himself (Heb. 10:19, 20).

(e) It was by becoming a human being, that, going through death as a man, He destroyed him who had the power of death, that is, the devil, and set free those who lived their whole lives in slavery to their fear of death (Heb. 2:14, 15).

(f) Through taking human nature upon Him, He has made it possible for sinners to escape from the corruption that is in the world, and participate in the divine nature (2 Pet. 1:4).

67

(g) It was necessary that Christ should become man that the human nature that had offended should suffer. By His substitutionary death, He satisfied God's just wrath against our sins and made atonement for them (Heb. 2:10-18). There is only one God and one Mediator who can reconcile God and people, the man Christ Jesus (1 Tim. 2:5).

7. **Christ's perfect deity and perfect humanity are essentials of the Christian faith.**
(a) Fundamental to the Christian faith is that Christ, the Son of God, came 'in the flesh' (1 John 4:2; 2 John 7).
(b) Any denial of the reality of Christ's 'flesh', that is to say, that He was not truly a man, is heresy (1 John 2:22-25; 4:1-3; 5:5-12; 2 John 7, 9-11).

8. **The fact of Christ being the Word made flesh - what we call 'The Incarnation' - is beyond the understanding of the human mind.**
That Christ is truly God and perfect man is a mystery, revealed to us in the Scriptures, yet beyond our complete understanding, being something that causes even the angels to admire the wisdom and goodness of God (1 Tim. 3:16; 1 Pet. 1:12).

---

20. THE CROSS

Question: **What happened when Christ died upon the Cross?**

Answer: **He offered up Himself as a sacrifice, bearing the punishment due to sinners, fulfilling God's plan whereby men and women might be reconciled to Him through Christ.**

1. **The Cross cannot be understood unless the plight of men and women in their sin is understood and appreciated.**
(a) We are in danger of perishing (John 3:16).
(b) We have all sinned against God (Rom. 3:23).
(c) Our sins have separated us from God (Isa. 59:2).
(d) Sin has brought death upon us as its wages (Rom. 5:12; 6:23).

(e) We are by nature the objects of God's wrath (John 3:36; Eph. 2:3).

2. The Cross was no accident but the set purpose and plan of God (Acts 2:23).

(a) Before the world was founded God the Father determined that His Son should fulfil the function of a Saviour for sinners (1 Pet. 1:20).

(b) The Father and the Son entered into a compact and a covenant. The Son was to accomplish the work assigned to Him (John 12:27; 17:2, 4), and the Father promised that as a result a great number of men and women from all nations would be given to Him as His inheritance (Ps. 2:7-8) and He should be supreme Head to the Church (Eph. 1:22; Phil. 2:7-11; Heb. 12:2).

(c) The world was prepared for the great event of the Cross by many symbols and illustrations:

   (i) The Old Testament sacrifices all looked forward to the coming of Jesus and His death upon the Cross for sinners (John 1:29, 36; Heb. 9:24; 10:3-14).

   (ii) The Passover Lamb was a picture of Jesus (Ex. 12:21-23; 1 Cor. 5:7) and Jesus used the feast of the Passover to establish the Lord's Supper as a reminder of the meaning of His death (Luke 22:7-22).

3. The initiative in the Cross was God's.

(a) Loving the world so much God gave His Son (John 3:16).

(b) It was God's will to crush Him and cause Him to suffer (Isa. 53:10).

(c) The bitter experience of the Cross was accepted by the Son as the Father's will (Matt. 26:39, 42).

(d) The design of the whole plan of Christ's atoning death for our sins and His satisfying God's anger against us was the Father's (Rom. 3:25).

4. Christ willingly died upon the Cross.

(a) Before the creation of the world Christ had committed Himself willingly to the Cross (Isa. 50:4-7; Heb. 10:5-10; 1 Pet. 1:20).

(b) He laid down His life (John 10:11, 18).

(c) He poured out His life to death (Isa. 53:12).

(d) He gave Himself up as an offering and a sacrifice to God (Eph. 5:2).

5. Christ bore the punishment due to sinners.

(a) He bore the sin of many (Isa. 53:12; 1 Pet. 2:24).

(b) He bore the wrath of God against sin that sinners deserve (John 3:36; Rom. 1:18; 1 John 2:2; 4:10).

(c) He bore the curse of the law that sinners through their disobedience deserve to experience – death and separation from God (Gal. 3:10, 13; Isa. 59:2; Rom. 5:12; Mark 15:34).

(d) He bore the pains of death and the grave that sinners deserve (Ps. 18:5; Mark 15:33, 34).

6. We cannot overemphasize either the worth or the eternal character of Christ's sacrifice.

(a) The punishment He suffered was sufficient to satisfy for the transgressions of all because He who suffered was not only a man, but God also. He was of infinitely more value than all those who had offended (Rom. 5:9; Heb. 9:13, 14).

(b) His sacrifice was final – once and for all – and utterly sufficient for all time (1 Pet. 3:18; Heb. 9:26; 10:11-14).

7. The benefits achieved by Christ's death.

(a) The justice of God was satisfied (Isa. 53:11).

   (i) The punishment sin deserves has been allotted and carried out (Isa. 53:4-6; 2 Cor. 5:21).

   (ii) God has shown Himself just and may justify all those who have faith in Jesus (Rom. 3:26; 2 Cor. 5:21).

(b) Redemption from the power of sin, death and hell was made possible for sinners:

   (i) The price of redemption has been paid in full by Christ (Matt. 20:28; Mark 10:45; 1 Tim. 2:6) – the price being His own precious blood (Acts 20:28; 1 John 1:7).

   (ii) Christ has utterly overcome and defeated Satan, death and the powers of hell, that hold us captive. The devil's power is broken (Heb. 2:14). As a consequence the power of death is broken too (John 5:24; Heb. 2:14; 1 Cor. 15:55-57). Furthermore, through Christ we may escape the coming wrath of God (1 Thess. 1:10).

(c)   The new covenant that God had promised was confirmed:
    (i)   It was promised when Adam sinned (Gen. 3:15).
    (ii)   Both Christ and the covenant were promised to Abraham (Gen. 12:3; Gal. 3:8, 16).
    (iii)   Yet more details were promised through the prophets (Jer. 31:31-34; 32:40).
    (iv)   This new covenant could come into operation only by the work of Jesus as Mediator (Heb. 8:6, 10-13).
    (v)   A testament or a covenant demands a death – a testament is operative only after a death – and Christ made valid the new covenant by the shedding of His blood, the blood of the eternal covenant (Heb. 9:14-26; 13:20).

(d)   Grace and glory are assured for all who enter into this new covenant:
    (i)   Having given His Son to die such a death, there is nothing good and beneficial that God will fail to lavish upon those who are saved by it (Rom. 8:32; Heb. 4:16).
    (ii)   Every spiritual benefit in this life and in that to come is assured (Eph. 1:3-14).
    (iii)   Eternal life is the gift of Christ to those who are saved by His death (John 14:1-6; 17: 2-3).

(e)   These benefits may be summed up in the word 'reconciliation'. Through God's work in Christ of reconciling the world to Himself, our sins and misdeeds need no longer be counted against us (2 Cor. 5:18, 19).   United to Christ we may receive a new life altogether (2 Cor. 5:17) and be declared righteous by God (2 Cor. 5:21).

8.   Only by Christ's death may we be reconciled to God.
The message of the gospel is plain: be reconciled to God through Christ (2 Cor. 5:18-20).

21. THE RESURRECTION

Question: **What is the significance of the Resurrection of Christ?**

Answer: **God the Father raised Christ from the dead, in fulfilment of the Scriptures and of Christ's own promises, declaring Christ to be His Son, and His acceptance of Christ's redemptive work, guaranteeing the justification, spiritual life and final resurrection of all believers.**

1.   The fact of the Resurrection is at the core of the gospel.

(a)   The Resurrection was the work of the Father (Acts 2:24; 3:15; 10:40; Eph. 1:20; Col. 2:12) by the power of the Spirit (Rom. 8:11; 1 Pet. 3:18).

(b)   The centrality of the Resurrection is seen in the trouble to which the New Testament goes, and the Gospels especially, to give the facts concerning our Lord's appearances.   Jesus appeared to Mary Magdalene (Mark 16:9; John 20:18), the women (Matt. 28:8, 9), Simon Peter (Luke 24:34), two disciples (Luke 24:13-35), all the apostles, except Thomas (John 20:19, 24), Thomas himself (John 20:26-28), the apostles at the Sea of Tiberias (John 21:1), the apostles in Galilee (Matt. 28:16, 17), about 500 disciples (1 Cor. 15:6), James (1 Cor. 15:7), all the apostles (Luke 24:51; Acts 1:9; 1 Cor. 15:7), and Paul (1 Cor. 15:8).

2.   The Resurrection was central in the witness of the apostles.

(a)   'We are witnesses' was their theme (Acts 3:15; 1 Cor. 15:14, 15).

(b)   Every apostle had to be a personal witness of Christ's Resurrection (Acts 1:22).

(c)   The distinctive characteristic of their preaching was the power with which they bore witness to the Resurrection of Christ (Acts 4:33).

(d)   They knew and preached a living Christ (Acts 25:19; 2 Tim. 2:8).

3. **The Old Testament Scriptures demanded that the Resurrection should take place.**

(a) The Messiah was not to be allowed to experience decay (Ps. 16:10; Acts 13:34, 35).

(b) Everything written about Christ in the law of Moses, the prophets and the Psalms demanded fulfilment (Luke 24:44; John 20:9; Acts 26:22, 23).

4. **Christ foretold His Resurrection.**

(a) At the beginning of His ministry He had hinted at it (John 2:19-22).

(b) When Peter confessed Jesus as the Messiah, the first clear revelation about the Resurrection was given to the disciples (Matt. 16:21).

(c) The experience of the Transfiguration was not to be reported until after the Resurrection (Mark 9:9).

(d) Jesus clearly foretold His Resurrection to the disciples (Matt. 20:19; Mark 14:28).

5. **The Resurrection was necessary to demonstrate irrefutably the truth of all Christ's claims.**

(a) By His life, words and miracles Jesus had made many claims (Luke 11:20; John 10:18; 11:25; 14:6).

(b) From the lips of a mere human being such claims would have been blasphemous (Matt. 26:63-66). If such a one died and remained dead as other people then the charge of imposter would be true but if He rose again from the dead the truth of His claim – that He was from God and was the Son of God– would be vindicated (Matt. 27:63-66; cf. Acts 5:38, 39, applying the latter words for the moment to the Resurrection.)

6. **The Resurrection was necessary to give final proof of Christ's deity.**

(a) The Resurrection was a declaration of the Father, as promised in the Old Testament, that Jesus is His Son (Ps. 2:7; Acts 13:33).

(b) By raising Christ to life again by the power of the Holy Spirit, God the Father clearly and obviously marked Christ out as His Son - the Son of God, the Second Person of the Trinity (Rom. 1:4).

(c)   It was impossible for death to keep Christ in its grip (Acts 2:24) – of God alone can such a claim be justly made.

7.   Without the Resurrection we would not know that Christ's death achieved its objects so far as sin is concerned.

(a)   Without it the gospel would be null and void (1 Cor. 15:14).

(b)   Without it there would be no hope of forgiveness (1 Cor. 15:17).

(c)   Without it we would be utterly lost with no possibility of salvation (1 Cor. 15:19).

(d)   Jesus' Resurrection declares the acquittal of believers from every charge that was against them on account of their sins (Rom. 4:25; 8:34).

8.   The Resurrection was necessary to provide a solid basis for faith.

(a)   Christ showed Himself alive by many convincing proofs (Acts 1:3).

(b)   God's acceptance of Christ's work is demonstrated by the Resurrection (see 7, above): through Christ men and women may approach God with confidence (1 Pet. 1:21).

(c)   The Resurrection gives our faith substance (Rom 10:9,,10; 1 Cor. 15:17).

9.   The Resurrection was necessary to give a living hope.

(a)   Christians' hope or assurance arises from Christ's Resurrection: through His Resurrection we receive new life (Rom. 6:4; Col. 2:12; 1 Pet. 1:3).

(b)   Believers have a living hope regarding the resurrection of the dead, for God who raised up Christ will raise up them also (1 Cor. 15:20, 23; Acts 26:23; 1 Cor. 6:14; 2 Cor. 4:14).

(c)   Believers have a living hope regarding the resurrection of the body, for Christ's Resurrection is the pattern of theirs (Luke 24:35, 39, 42, 43; John 20:20, 27; Rom. 6:5; 1 Cor. 15:49; Phil. 3:21).

10.   The Resurrection was necessary to demonstrate that Christ may be known today.

(a)   Paul proved the truth of this experience, at first to his great amazement (Acts 9:1-9).

(b)   Paul then made the knowing of Christ, and the experiencing of the power of His Resurrection, an objective of his life (Phil. 3:10).

11.   The Resurrection was necessary to give assurance of the final just judgment of the world.

(a)   People wrongly condemned Christ; God the Father vindicated Him by the Resurrection, thereby judging those who dealt with Christ so falsely (Acts 2:22-24).

(b)   God will have the world judged and justly judged by Christ - He has given proof of this by His Son's Resurrection (Acts 17:31).

12.   The Resurrection was necessary to illustrate that the last word is always with God.
People called Christ a 'deceiver'; God the Father - by the Resurrection—- declared Him 'My Son' (Matt. 27:63-66; Ps. 2:7; Rom. 1:4).

---

22. THE ASCENSION

Question: **What happened when our Lord Jesus Christ ascended to heaven?**

Answer: **At the Ascension our Lord Jesus Christ returned to the Father and was glorified - the final proof of His completed sacrificial work.   He entered then upon His work as priest and king upon the throne– no longer needing to offer atoning sacrifice to God– giving gifts to His Church, and guaranteeing her security and final presence with Him in heaven. He waits now for the time of His final victory.**

1.   The Ascension.

(a)   The Ascension was a vital link in a chain of fulfilled prophecy, promised both in the Old Testament (Ps. 110:1; Acts 2:32-36) and by our Lord Jesus Christ Himself (Matt. 26:64; John 6:62; 7:33; 14:28; 16:5; 20:17).

(b) It took place forty days after the Resurrection (Acts 1:3).

(c) It took place at the Mount of Olives (Luke 24:50; cf. Mark 11:1; Acts 1:12).

(d) It was witnessed by the apostles, after He had talked with them (Mark 16:19) and then lifted up His hands to bless them (Luke 24:50, 51).

(e) He was lifted up, and a cloud took Him out of their sight (Acts 1:9).

(f) The return of the Lord Jesus Christ will be after the pattern of the Ascension (Acts 1:11).

2. What the Ascension was.

(a) It was an act of God's power (Eph. 1:19-22).

(b) It was the necessary completion of our Lord Jesus Christ's death and Resurrection: it proved the full acceptance by God of His single sacrifice for sins for all time (Heb. 10:12); it marked Him out as Lord, even as the Resurrection marked Him out as the Son of God (Phil. 2:9-11; Acts 2:34-36; cf. Rom. 1:4).

(c) It was the visible ascent of our Lord Jesus Christ, according to His human nature, from earth to heaven (Mark 16:19; 1 Peter 3:22): He was exalted to the place in the universe He had laid aside when He humbled Himself to assume our humanity (Eph. 4:9,10).

(d) It marked the Lord Jesus Christ's return to the Father: He went to Him who had sent Him into the world (John 6:62; 7:33; 14:28; 16:5; 20:17).

(e) It included a further glorification of the human nature of our Lord Jesus Christ: He carried His humanity with Him back to heaven (Hebrews 2:14-18; 4:14-16), and He was highly exalted and glorified in doing so (Acts 2:33; John 7:39; 1 Tim. 3:16), the Father honouring Him with the highest possible honour (Eph. 1:20-22).

3. The significance of the Ascension.

(a) God the Father's acceptance of His Son into glory declared decisively and finally His acceptance of Jesus' sacrifice for our sins (Heb. 1:3; 9:12; 10:11-14).

(b)   The Lord Christ entered upon His work as a royal priest upon the throne, no longer needing to offer atoning sacrifice to God (Heb. 7:26, 27; 8:1; 10:21); He entered into heaven to appear now before God on our behalf, representing our cause before the Father (Heb. 9:24).

(c)   The Lord Jesus Christ, demonstrated by the Ascension to be Lord (Matt. 28:18; Acts 2:36), entered upon His work as King; He is seated at the right hand of God (Matt. 26:64; Acts 2:33; Rom. 8:34; Col. 3:1; Heb. 1:3; 10:12; 12:2; 1 Pet. 3:22), a picture of the unique position the Father has given Him of kingly power and authority over angels, authorities and powers in heaven and on earth (Daniel 7:13,14; Matt. 26:64; Eph. 1:21,22; 4:10; Col. 1:16-18; Heb. 1:13; 1 Pet. 3:22).

(d)   The Lord Jesus Christ ascended to receive, as Conqueror, the gifts promised Him for His Church (Eph. 4:8; Ps. 68:18): He ascended to send forth the Holy Spirit (John 7:39; 16:7; Acts 2:33).

(e)   The Ascension of Christ and the consequent outpouring of the Spirit made possible the numerous gifts of the Spirit that the Church enjoys (Eph. 4:8,11-13).

(f)   The Lord Jesus Christ ascended to prepare a place for Christians (John 14:2): He is their forerunner, preparing the way for them (Heb. 6:20; cf. Acts 7:56).

(g)   Christians are already set with the Lord Jesus Christ in heavenly places, for they are made to share by grace, through faith, the Resurrection and Ascension of Christ (Eph. 2:6): their citizenship is now in heaven and their thoughts and affections should be set there (Phil. 3:20; Col. 3:1,2).

(h)   In Christ's Ascension Christians have the assurance of a place in heaven (2 Corinthians 4:14; John 14:19) and of their own glorification (Phil. 3:21): God's purpose in giving Christians a share in the Resurrection and Ascension of their Lord is that in the coming ages He might show the immeasurable riches of His grace in kindness toward them in Christ Jesus (John 17:24; Eph. 2:7).

4.   **What the Lord Jesus Christ does at God's right hand.**

(a)   He lives forever, holding a permanent priesthood (Rev. 1:18; Heb. 7:24).

(b)   He rules and protects His Church as its Head (Eph. 1:22-23), helping the members in need (Heb. 2:18; 4:15), and giving them power to do great works (John 14:12).

(c)   He governs the universe, and to the end that God's purposes for the Church may be fulfilled (Heb. 1:3; Eph. 1:5-14).

(d)   He intercedes for His people on the basis of His completed sacrifice (Rom. 8:34): He is our Advocate with the Father (1 John 2:1).

(e)   He waits for the time of His final victory: all His enemies shall be subdued (Ps. 110:1; Acts 2:35; 1 Cor.s 15:24-26; Heb. 10:13).

(f)   His Ascension in power is the prelude to His coming in power as the divine Judge (Daniel 7:13,14; Matt. 26:64; John 14:28; Acts 10:42; 2 Thess. 1:6-10).

---

23. THE HOLY SPIRIT

Question: Who is the Holy Spirit?

Answer: He is the Lord and Giver of Life, the third Person of the Trinity, to be worshipped and glorified with the Father and the Son.   He is most commonly presented to us as the Executor of God's purposes, whether in creation, revelation or redemption.

1.   **He is unique.**
There is but one Spirit (1 Cor. 12:13; Eph. 4:4).

2.   **He is a Person - not simply an influence or a power.**

(a)   He is spoken of as 'He' and not as 'It' (John 16:13).

(b)   He is spoken of as a Person – the Counsellor or Advocate (John 14:16, 26; 15:26; 16:7).

(c)   He may be grieved (Isa. 63:10; Eph. 4:30).

(d)   He is insulted by those who arrogantly reject His testimony to the Lord Jesus Christ and despise His saving work (Heb. 10:29).

3.   He is God.

(a)   He is the Spirit of the living God (2 Cor. 3:3; 1 Pet. 4:14).

(b)   Sovereignty is ascribed to Him (1 Cor. 12:11).

(c)   Old Testament references to God are revealed in the New Testament to have been references to the Holy Spirit (Ex. 17:7; cf. Heb. 3:7-9; Isa. 6:3, 8-10; cf. Acts 28:25-27; Ps. 78:17, 21; cf. Acts 7:51).

(d)   The qualities ascribed to the Holy Spirit are the qualities ascribed everywhere to God alone: He is everywhere present (Ps. 139:7-13; 1 Cor. 12:13); He knows everything (1 Cor. 2:10); He has all power (Luke 1:35; Rom. 8:11; 15:19).

(e)   To lie to the Spirit is to lie to God (Acts 5:3-5).

(f)   He is to be obeyed (Gal. 5:16-25).

(g)   Blasphemy against Him is the worst of all sins (Matt. 12:31, 32; Mark 3:28, 29; Luke 12:10).

(h)   His intercession for God's people is in accordance with God's will (Rom. 8:27).

(i)   To cause offence to the Spirit is to deserve the severest judgment (Heb. 10:29).

4.   He is the Third Person of the Trinity.

(a)   He is one with the Father and the Son (Matt. 28:19; 2 Cor. 13:14; 1 Cor. 12:4-6; Eph. 4:4-6).

(b)   He is sent by both the Father and the Son and He acts for them both (John 15:26).

5.   He was the Agent of God's first creation.

(a)   He was active in creation, bringing order out of chaos (Gen. 1:2).

(b)   By God's Spirit the heavens were made beautiful (Job 26:13).

(c)   The Spirit of God was responsible for the creation of men and women (Job 33:4; cf. Gen. 2:7; Ps. 104:29, 30).

6.   He is the Author of the Scriptures.

(a)   He inspired the Scriptures (2 Tim. 3:16): individuals, carried along by the Holy Spirit, spoke and wrote from God (Acts 1:16; 2 Pet. 1:21).

(b)   The Scriptures are His testimony (Heb. 10:15).

(c)   He compelled the prophets to speak (Ezek. 11:5; Zech. 7:12; Micah 3:8).

(d)   He inspired individuals to prophesy (Luke 1:67; 2:26, 27, 29-32).

(e)   He revealed to the apostles and prophets the truth concerning Christ and the gospel, at the time determined by God (Eph. 3:4-6).

(f)   He speaks today through the Scriptures (Heb. 3:7).

7.   He was active with regard to the Incarnation.

(a)   By His power the virgin conception was accomplished (Luke 1:35).

(b)   Mary was found to be with child through the Holy Spirit (Matt. 1:18, 20).

(c)   The Spirit descended upon Jesus like a dove at His baptism (Mark 1:10ff).

(d)   The Spirit led and directed Christ during His ministry (Matt. 4:1; Mark 1:12).

(e)   The Spirit equipped Christ for His ministry (Luke 4:1-18; Acts 10:38).

(f)   Christ possessed the Spirit without limit (John 3:34).

(g)   Christ's works of power were by the power of the Spirit of God that was His (Luke 11:20; cf. Matt. 12:28; Acts 10:38).

(h)   The Spirit filled Christ with joy during His earthly life and ministry (Luke 10:21).

(i)   The Spirit raised Christ from the dead (Acts 2:24; cf. Rom. 1:4; Heb. 13:20; 1 Pet. 3:18.).

8.   He is the Agent of God's new creation in Christ – the Church.

(a)   The Holy Spirit's activity in God's new creation is all-important:

    (i)   He puts the redeemed in possession of the results of the Father's love and the mediation of Christ (John 7:37-39; 2 Cor. 3:7-11);

(ii)   Justification takes place in the name of the Lord Jesus and by the Spirit of God (1 Cor. 6:11);

(iii)   Through the Spirit the redeemed are brought into the one body, the Church, this act being described as a baptism (1 Cor. 12:13);

(iv)   The Spirit is the Author of the new birth (John 3:5, 6; 2 Cor. 5:17). Whereas the written law condemns us to death, the Spirit gives life (2 Cor. 3:6; Gal. 5:25). Where the Spirit is, there is life (Ezek. 37:1-14; Rom.8:1, 2, 11; John 6:63).

(b)   The Holy Spirit is directly associated with the extension of God's new creation - the Church (Matt. 28:19, 20; cf. Acts 1:4, 8):

(i)   He ensures that messengers are raised up and people sent forth to proclaim the gospel (Matt. 9:38; cf. Acts 13:2, 4; 16:6, 7, 10; 20:28);

(ii)   He accompanies the preaching of the gospel with His power (1 Pet. 1:12);

(iii)   He shows people their need of salvation by convicting them of sin (John 16:8-11);

(iv)   He testifies about Christ (John 15:26), and by His influence men and women are enabled to say 'Jesus is Lord' (1 Cor. 12:3);

(v)   Given to every believer as a result of Christ's work (John 7:39), He binds believers together in one body in spiritual unity (Eph. 4:3, 4);

(vi)   For the care of the Church the Spirit raises up guardians or pastors (Acts 20:28);

(vii) In each Christian the Spirit desires to manifest Himself in a particular way, for some useful purpose (1 Cor. 12:4-11);

(viii) He allots varying gifts to Christians (Rom. 12:6~8);

(ix)   The Spirit's purpose in all this is to prepare God's people for works of service, so that the body of Christ may be built up (Eph. 4:11-13).

24. THE HOLY SPIRIT AND THE CHRISTIAN

Question: **What is the relationship of the Holy Spirit to the Christian?**

Answer: **The Holy Spirit is the gift of the Father and the Son to believers to live within them. He gives them spiritual life, assures them of their relationship to God as His children, and communicates to them the benefits of the gospel.**

1. **The Holy Spirit is Christ's promised gift to believers.**
(a) Christ asked the Father that the Spirit might be believers' possession forever (John 14:16).
(b) The Spirit is sent by Christ from the Father (John 15:26; 16:7).
(c) He is called 'the Spirit of Jesus' (Acts 16:7) and 'the Spirit of Christ' (Rom. 8:9; 1 Pet. 1:11).
(d) He is received not by observing the law but by believing the good news made known through Jesus Christ (Gal. 3:2, 3, 14).

2. **The Holy Spirit works in believers the miracle of the new birth.**

(a) Unless we are born again by the Holy Spirit we cannot see the kingdom of God (John 3:3, 5).
(b) We start our Christian lives in the first place as the Spirit gives us spiritual life (Gal. 3:3).
(c) If we do not have the Spirit of Christ we do not belong to Christ (Rom. 8:9).

3. **The Holy Spirit is, therefore, the source of believers' spiritual life (Gal. 5:25).**
(a) By nature men and women are spiritually dead (Eph. 2:1).
(b) The Spirit gives spiritual life to spiritually dead people (Eph. 2:1-7; cf. Ezek. 37:14; Rom. 8:2, 11; John 6:63).

4. **The Holy Spirit testifies with Christians' spirits that they are God's children (Rom. 8:16).**

(a) He makes believers sure of their union with Christ (1 John 3:24; 4:13).

(b) As the Spirit of God's Son, He calls out to God in our hearts, 'Abba! Father!' (Gal. 4:6).

5. The Holy Spirit dwells within Christian believers.

(a) The possession of the Spirit is a distinguishing mark of Christians (Rom. 8:9).

(b) The bodies of Christians are the temples of the indwelling Holy Spirit (1 Cor. 3:16, 17; 6:19; cf. Isa. 57:15; 2 Tim. 1:14).

(c) By reason of the Spirit living with them, and in them, Christians know Him (John 14:17).

(d) The Spirit dwells with Christians forever (John 14:16, 17).

6. The Holy Spirit sanctifies Christians.

(a) The Holy Spirit makes Christians holy – He sets them apart for God (2 Thess. 2:13; 1 Pet. 1:2).

(b) The Holy Spirit is completely contrary in His desires to the desires of our sinful nature (Gal. 5:16), and He helps us to fight against it so that we do not gratify its demands (Gal. 5:17).

(c) The Holy Spirit enables us to put to death the misdeeds of the body – those activities of our lower nature that displease God (Rom. 8:13).

(d) By the power of the Spirit our characters are transformed (Gal. 5:22-24).

7. The Holy Spirit produces the character of Christ in Christians.

(a) The Holy Spirit purposes to transform us into the Lord's likeness, with ever-increasing glory (2 Cor. 3:18).

(b) Love, joy, peace, patience, kindness, goodness, faithfulness, gentleness, and self-control are His fruit (Gal. 5:22, 23).

(c) We would expect the Holy Spirit to produce these characteristics for He is the Spirit of Jesus Christ (Acts 16:7; Rom. 8:9; Gal. 4:6; Phil. 1:19; 1 Pet. 1:11).

8. The Holy Spirit strengthens Christians.

(a) His help and resources are available to us (Phil. 1:19).

(b) He strengthens and encourages us (Acts 9:31).

(c)   He gives special help in times of difficulty and opposition (1 Pet. 4:14).

9.   The Holy Spirit helps Christians to pray.

(a)   He helps us to keep on in prayer (Eph. 6:18).

(b)   He inspires prayer by the love He places in our hearts for our fellow-believers (Rom. 15:30).

(c)   He prompts our 'groanings' – those inner feelings that words cannot express – for He is in them, and He conveys their meaning to the Father (Rom. 8:26).

10.   The Holy Spirit instructs Christians, interpreting to them the Scriptures.

(a)   The Holy Spirit explores everything, even the deep things of God and His thoughts (1 Cor. 2:10, 11).

(b)   The Spirit reveals spiritual truths that would otherwise be hidden from us (1 Cor. 2:10).

(c)   The Spirit communicates all that God has freely given us in His Son (1 Cor. 2:12).

(d)   The Spirit testifies pre-eminently about Christ (John 15:26).

(e)   The Spirit gives us discernment (1 Cor. 2:14).

(f)   The Spirit guides us into all the truth (John 16:13).

(g)   The Spirit speaks to us today in the Scriptures (Heb. 3:7).

11.   The Holy Spirit gives power to Christians' endeavours in witness.

(a)   He gives power to witness and to fulfil the Lord's command to evangelize (Matt. 28:19; cf. Acts 1:4, 8).

(b)   He makes preaching to carry His power so that those who hear know that it is God's message (1 Cor. 2:4,5).

12.   The Holy Spirit guides Christians.

(a)   He guides us into the way of victory over sin (Gal. 5:16).

(b)   He leads and directs us in our service for God (Acts 16:6, 7; Rom. 8:14).

(c)   He prompts right action at particular times (Luke 2:27).

(d)   He guides to the right solution of difficult problems (Acts 15:28).

13. **The Holy Spirit imparts gifts to Christians for the service of God (Rom. 12:6-8).**

(a) He equips us to help in the task of building up Christ's Church (Eph. 4:11-13).

(b) He gives the right gift or gifts for all the varieties of service and the many forms of work there are (1 Cor. 12:4-6).

(c) He enables us to fulfil useful purposes within the Church for the common good (1 Cor. 12:7).

14. **The Holy Spirit communicates the spiritual benefits of the gospel to Christians.**

(a) He makes God's love to flood our hearts (Rom. 5:5).

(b) He communicates joy (Rom. 14:17; 1 Thess. 1:6).

(c) He makes us overflow with the joy of Christian hope (Rom. 15:13; Gal. 5:5).

15. **The Holy Spirit is God's seal of ownership on us and His guarantee of what is to come to us in the future (2 Cor. 1:22).**

(a) God has shaped us for a wonderful future in glory (2 Cor. 4:16-5:5).

(b) We are reborn by the Spirit to a great and wonderful inheritance that nothing can destroy or spoil or wither (1 Pet. 1:3, 4; Eph. 1:14).

(c) The Spirit is God's guarantee that we will enter upon this inheritance (Eph. 1:14).

16. **Christians' appropriation of the help of the Holy Spirit.**

(a) The Holy Spirit's illumination is given in answer to prayer (Eph. 1:16,17).

(b) Our heavenly Father delights to give the Holy Spirit to those who ask Him (Luke 11:13).

(c) As we live in obedience to God, so we know more and more of the Spirit (Acts 5:32).

(d) We are to let the Spirit direct the course of our life, as we endeavour to keep in step with Him (Gal. 5:25).

25. DEFINING A CHRISTIAN

Question: What is a Christian?

Answer: A Christian is someone who, having understood the ABC of the gospel of Christ, has received Christ, has taken his or her stand upon Him, and experiences salvation through Him.

1. The gospel that has to be understood.

(a) The appointed time, concerning which the prophets in the Old Testament had spoken and to which the people of God had looked forward, has come.   Through Christ, God has visited and redeemed His people (Acts 2:14-21).

(b) This act of God, intervening in human history, is to be seen in the life of Jesus Christ, the Messiah, sent by God, rejected, and put to death by men, and raised to life by God (Acts 2:32-36).

(c) By His death and resurrection Jesus Christ has conquered sin and death and opened the kingdom of heaven to all believers. In no one else is salvation to be found (Acts 4:12).

(d) The proofs of God's present power in the world are to be found in Jesus' resurrection and the evidences of the Holy Spirit's working in the Church (Acts 4:33; Rom. 1:4; Eph. 1:19, 20).

(e) This is but the beginning of God's kingdom.   Christ will come again as Judge, and God's kingdom will be finally established (Acts 3:19-21; 17:30, 31; 2 Thess. 1:7-10).

(f) Therefore all people everywhere should repent and be baptised in the name of Jesus the Messiah for the forgiveness of their sins, and thus receive the gift of the Holy Spirit (Acts 2:38).

2. Fundamental to people's understanding of the gospel is their appreciation, therefore, of at least the following truths:

(a) Jesus is the Christ, the Son of God (John 11:27; 20:31; 1 John 4:15).

(b) Christ's purpose in coming into the world and in dying upon the cross was to save sinners (1 Tim. 1:15).

(c) Christ's resurrection was God the Father's declaration of Christ as His Son and His satisfaction with His saving work (Rom. 1:4).

(d) To enter into the benefits of Christ's work – to know forgiveness, the gift of God's Spirit and a place in His kingdom - repentance and public acknowledgement of Christ are required (Acts 2:38).

(e) Christians recognize their personal sinfulness (Rom. 7:24; cf. Luke 18:13).

(f) Christians know their personal indebtedness to Christ in that He gave His life a ransom for them (Mark 10:45; Gal. 2:20; 1 Pet. 2:24).

3. The benefits the gospel promises.

(a) Deliverance from condemnation (John 3:18; Rom. 8:1).

(b) Justification (1 Cor. 6:11).

(c) The gift of the Holy Spirit (1 Cor. 2:12).

(d) Eternal life (John 3:16, 36).

(e) Reconciliation with God (2 Cor. 5:18-21).

(f) Membership of the people of God (1 Pet. 2:9, 10).

(g) Membership of the kingdom of God's Son, the Lord Jesus Christ (Col. 1:13).

(h) The resurrection of the body (1 Cor. 6:14).

(i) Endless fellowship with Christ (John 14:1-3; 1 Thess. 4:17).

4. A Christian is someone who, having understood the ABC of the gospel, has received Christ.

(a) The words 'believe' and 'receive' are more or less identical (John 1:12; 1 Cor. 15:1, 2).

(b) The call to believe on the Lord Jesus Christ for salvation comes home to the individual with deep conviction by the power of the Holy Spirit (1 Cor. 2:1-5; 1 Thess. 1:5).

(c) The call of God to believe on the Lord Jesus Christ is responded to (Acts 16:31-34; 1 Cor. 1:9, 23, 24; Rom. 10:9).

(d) Jesus Christ is received into the individual's life, and spiritual birth takes place by the Holy Spirit (John 1:12, 13; 3:3-7).

5. A Christian is someone who, having understood the ABC of the gospel, has received Christ, and takes his or her stand upon Christ (1 Cor. 15:1).

(a) They recognize that being bought with a price, they do not belong to themselves any more (1 Cor. 6:20; 7:23).

(b) The word 'stand' speaks of assurance: they know that they have eternal life (1 John 5:13; cf. 1 John 2:3, 5; 3:14; 4:13).

(c) The expression 'taking a stand' implies action: their stand is seen first by baptism (Acts 2:38, 41; 1 Cor. 1:13), and the confession of their lips that Jesus is Lord (Rom 10:9).

(d) They take their stand by identifying themselves with all who have similarly received the gospel (Acts 2:41-47; 1 Cor. 1:2; 6:1, 2).

(e) They recognize themselves to be members of the body of Christ, the Church (1 Cor. 12:13, 27).

(f) They recognize themselves to be God's Church – those whom He has made holy through Jesus Christ (1 Cor. 1:2; 6:11).

(g) They love the Lord Jesus Christ and show that love by obedience to Him (1 Cor. 16:22; John 14:21).

(h) They wait expectantly for Christ (1 Cor. 1:7; 11:26; 1 Thess.1: 10).

6. A Christian is someone who, having understood the ABC of the gospel, has received Christ, and, having taken his or her stand upon Christ, experiences salvation through Christ.

(a) When Christians first believed, they experienced salvation, e.g. they were washed, sanctified and justified (1 Cor. 6:11), they were enriched by Christ (1 Cor. 1:5); they found the cross the power of God (1 Cor. 1:18), and Christ became to them all they needed (1 Cor. 1:30).

(b) But salvation is also the present experience of Christians: they continue to call on the name of the Lord Jesus Christ (1 Cor. 1:2); they continue to receive God's grace and to be enriched by Christ (1 Cor. 1:4, 5; 15:10; 16:23).

(c) Their sins have been forgiven (1 Cor. 15:17) and they are freed from the power of sin (Rom. 8:2; 1 Cor. 6:12; 8:9).

(d) They know the power of the Spirit in their life (1 Cor. 6:19, 20; 12:7).

(e) They are kept by God's power (1 Cor. 1:8; 1 Pet. 1:5).

7.   **Being a Christian.**

(a)   Just to believe that there is one God does not make a person a Christian (Jas. 2:19).

(b)   Being a Christian is not a matter of being born in the right country or belonging to the right race (John 1:13).

(c)   Being a Christian is not just being zealously religious, for one can be such without being a Christian (Rom. 10:2, 3).

(d)   Being a Christian is not simply trying one's best to please God by good works (Eph. 2:8, 9).

(e)   A Christian knows that what matters is not self-achieved righteousness gained by obedience to the law, but rather that genuine righteousness that God gives as we put our faith in Jesus Christ (Phil. 3:8, 9).

(f)   The word 'Christian' began as a description of the disciples of Christ (Acts 11:26; 9:1).

(g)   A Christian is not self-made, but Christ-made (2 Cor. 5:17; cf. John 3:3, 7).

(h)   All Bible definitions or descriptions of a Christian have one thing in common: they all imply a personal relationship to God through Jesus Christ (1 Cor. 1:9; 1 John 1:3; Col. 3:1).

(i)   The name 'Christian' is something that the Christian is to live up to (1 Pet. 4:16).

(j)   The desire of a Christian is that others might come to faith in the Lord Jesus and be saved (Acts 26:29; Rom. 10:1).

---

26.   REGENERATION

Question: What is regeneration?

Answer: It is the supernatural work of the Holy Spirit by which those who are dead in trespasses and sins are made spiritually alive.

1.   **Regeneration deals with our dead spiritual state.**

(a)   We are by nature dead in our transgressions and sins (Eph. 2:1).

(b)   Human nature is sinful (Rom. 8:3).

(c)   Human life is governed very much by our sinful nature and its desires (Rom. 8:4, 5).

(d)   While our lives are governed by their lower nature, besides being in a state of hostility to God, we cannot please God (Rom. 8:7, 8).

(e)   Spiritual things are foolishness and beyond the grasp of us while we are unregenerate (1 Cor. 2:14).

(f)   Regeneration deals with our dead condition (Eph. 2:1, 4, 5– we are made spiritually alive.

2.   Our dead spiritual state is beyond our power to deal with.

(a)   With lives governed by our lower nature we cannot please God (John 3:6; Rom. 8:7, 8).

(b)   Righteous things we have done are not sufficient to achieve the attainment of spiritual life (Tit. 3:5).

(c)   We can do no more about it than we can change the colour of our skin or animals their fur (Jer. 13:23).

3.   Regeneration is the supernatural work of the Holy Spirit.

(a)   It is supernatural because it is due to the immediate power of Almighty God – witnessed, for example, in Paul's regeneration (Acts 9:1-9; 1 Cor. 15:8; Gal. 1:15, 16).

(b)   The Holy Spirit makes us spiritually alive (Eph. 2:1, 4, 5).

(c)   He acts according to the will of God the Father (John 1:13; 2 Cor. 5:18; Gal. 4:6; Tit. 3:5; Jas. 1:18).

(d)   He acts on the grounds of Christ's saving work by His death and resurrection (Tit. 3:5, 6; 1 Pet. 1:2, 3).

(e)   The Spirit's work of regeneration is a work of tremendous power – creative power (2 Cor.4:6; 5:17).

(f)   His work is as sovereign, mysterious and irresistible as that of the wind (John 3:8).

(g)   It is as dramatic as birth (John 3:3) and resurrection (Eph. 2:4, 5; Col. 2:13).

(h)   The unenlightened human mind finds the new birth impossible to understand because of its supernatural character (John 3:4).

4.   Various descriptions are given of this work of the Spirit.

(a)   It is spoken of as a birth (John 3:3-8; Jas. 1:18; 1 Pet. 1:23).

(b)   It is spoken of in terms of adoption: by it we become the children of God (John 1:12, 13; Rom. 8:15, 16).

(c)   It is spoken of as a new creation (2 Cor. 5:17).

(d)   It is spoken of as renewal (Tit. 3:5).

(e)   It is spoken of as passing from death to life (Rom. 6:13; 1 John 3:14).

5.   Regeneration is a necessity if we are to enter heaven.

(a)   Unless we are born again, we cannot see the kingdom of God (John 3:3).

(b)   Only through being born again can we have 'a living hope' (1 Pet. 1:3).

6.   The Holy Spirit uses various means to bring about His work of regeneration in people's lives.

(a)   The word of truth - i.e. the inspired Scriptures – is His main instrument (Jas. 1:18).

(b)   The living and enduring Word of God is imperishable seed that brings forth spiritual life under the power of the Spirit (1 Pet. 1:23).

(c)   The preaching of the gospel is the most frequent means, therefore, He uses to bring His work to light (1 Pet. 1:25).

(d)   The Holy Spirit accompanies true gospel preaching with life–giving power (1 Cor. 2:2-5; 1 Thess. 1:5, 6).

(e)   He uses those, therefore, who preach the gospel (1 Cor. 4:15; 2 Cor. 5:20).

7.   There may be visible evidences that the Holy Spirit's work of regeneration is taking place but these evidences are for the most part beyond observation (John 3:8).

(a)   Conviction of sin is frequently seen to be present (John 16:8-11; Acts 2:37).

(b)   It is as those who have been regenerated look back after their new spiritual birth that they realise that God was at work in their lives before ever they realised it (Gal. 1:11-17).

8.   The work of regeneration may be said to have taken place when we have saving faith in Christ (John 1:12, 13; 2 Thess. 2:13).

(a)   Faith is more the effect of regeneration than the cause of it, insofar as it is the Holy Spirit who brings us to faith in Christ: He opens our hearts to give heed to the message of the gospel (Acts 16:14).

(b)   Faith and regeneration, however, may take place at more or less the same time (Acts 2:37-41; 8:26-38).

9.   The effects of the work of regeneration in a person's life.

(a)   The most important truth is that we have a new life implanted in us by the Holy Spirit: the Holy Spirit enters our soul and remains there as a principle of a new life (Rom. 7:6; 8:9).

(b)   We are made clean, or sanctified, by the Spirit (Tit. 3:5).

(c)   We are renewed spiritually (Tit. 3:5), and we may live a new life (Rom. 6:4).

(d)   We have a new heart - a heart that wants to obey God (Ezek. 11:19, 20).

(e)   We are a new creation - the old has passed away, the new has come (2 Cor. 5:17; Gal. 6:15).

(f)   This new creation is seen in good works produced in our life, that God prepared in advance for us to do (Eph. 2:10).

(g)   God is at work in us (Phil. 2:13; Heb. 13:20, 21).

(h)   We are no longer slaves to sin (Rom. 6:6).

(i)   We receive a new nature - a participation in the divine nature (2 Pet. 1:4) - created after the likeness of God in true righteousness and holiness (Rom. 8:29; Eph. 4:24; Col. 3:10).

(j)   This inner nature is renewed day by day (2 Cor. 4:16).

(k)   As a result of this new life and nature, we can appreciate spiritual things because we are given spiritual discernment (1 Cor. 2:14; 2 Cor. 4:6).

(l)   We possess a new appetite for spiritual things (1 Pet. 2:1, 2).

(m)   We delight in the law of God in our inner being (Rom. 7:22).

(n)   We may be said to know God (Jer. 24:7; Col. 3:10).

(o)   We hate sin because our new nature cannot sin and is opposed to it (1 John 3:9; 5:18 – notice that the verb 'to sin' here is in the present tense, and speaks of continual and habitual action. John is not saying that as regenerate men and women we cannot sin but rather that we cannot consistently and deliberately do so).

(p)   We are protected from the evil one (1 John 5:18) and will be presented without fault before God (Phil. 1:6; Jude 24).

(q)   We become, together with all the regenerate, the first fruits of a new creation (Jas. 1:18) - the kingdom of God (John 3:3).

(r)   We possess this as a living hope through the resurrection of Jesus Christ from the dead – life after death, eternal life and an inheritance in heaven (1 Pet. 1:3-5).

(s)   Three outstanding proofs of regeneration are given by John in his first New Testament letter: those who are regenerate believe that Jesus is the Christ (1 John 5:1), practise righteousness, i.e. do right things as their habit (1 John 2:29; 3:9; 5:18), and love their fellow-Christians (1 John 4:7).

---

27. CONVERSION

Question: What is conversion?

Answer: Conversion is turning from sin, to be the servants of the living and true God, through repentance and personal faith in Jesus Christ. It is a work in which God takes the initiative, and in which He requires our response, as the gospel is understood.

1.   Conversion is turning with sincerity to God.

(a)   It is turning to the living God, our Creator (Acts 14:15).

(b)   It is the acknowledgement of God in a manner not practised previously (Gal. 4:8, 9).

(c)   Conversion conveys literally the idea of a turning from and a turning to: repentance and faith correspond to these two ideas (1 Thess. 1:9).

(d)   Conversion must be of the heart to receive the benefits that God promises (Deut. 4:29; Acts 15:8).

2.   Conversion is a possibility for men and women on the grounds of the Lord Jesus Christ's work on behalf of sinners.

(a)   Conversion is for sinners (Ps. 51:13).

(b)   God sent His Son into the world so that it might be possible for sinners to be turned from their wicked ways through the gift of repentance and forgiveness of sins (Luke 24:46, 47; Acts 3:26; 5:31).

3.   Conversion's negative aspect is repentance.

(a)   Conversion comes about as transgressors are taught God's ways (Ps. 51:13).

(b)   It is accompanied by an understanding of who God is and what He requires of us (Jer. 24:7).

(c)   It comes about when we realise the contrast between our ways and God's (Ps. 119:59).

(d)   It means turning from what we know to be wrong (Acts 3:26).

(e)   It means turning from idols (1 Thess. 1:9), from empty worship and confused conceptions of God (Acts 14:15).

(f)   It means turning from spiritual darkness and the power of Satan (Acts 26:18).

(g)   It means ceasing to stray from God (1 Pet. 2:25).

(h)   Repentance is an essential part of conversion (Acts 3:19; 26:20).

4.   Conversion's positive aspect is faith in Christ.

(a)   Conversion takes place when Christ is revealed to a person (Gal. 1:15, 16).

(b)   It is the result of being confronted with the Person and claims of Christ (Acts 9:5, 6).

(c)   It is the expression of faith in Christ (Acts 11:21).

(d)   It means recognising Christ as the Shepherd and Overseer of our souls and returning to Him (1 Pet. 2:25).

5.   Conversion is a necessity for entry into the kingdom of heaven.

(a)   Unless we change direction and become as little children, we cannot enter the kingdom of heaven (Matt. 18:3).

(b)   Essential blessings, necessary for entry into the kingdom of heaven, come by conversion alone:

   (i)   Forgiveness (Acts 3:19);

   (ii)   The purifying of the heart (Acts 15:9);

   (iii) Rescue from the coming wrath (1 Thess. 1:10);

(iv)   A place amongst those who are sanctified by faith in Christ (Acts 26:18).

6.   Conversion marks the beginning of the Christian life in a person's experience.

(a)   The converted person is a new creation (2 Cor. 5:17).

(b)   At conversion we receive the gospel, take our stand upon it, are saved by it, and hold firmly to it (1 Cor. 15:1, 2).

(c)   We receive the forgiveness of sins (Acts 26:18).

(d)   We receive the gift of the Holy Spirit (Acts 15:8).

(e)   We begin to serve the living and true God (1 Thess. 1:9).

(f)   We are committed to obedience to God (Deut. 30:2).

(g)   We discover that God has purposes for our life (Gal. 1:15, 16).

(h)   We witness by means of baptism to what has happened in our life (Acts 2:38; 8:36-38; 9:18; 16:15, 33).

7.   The initiative in conversion is God's.

(a)   Conversion is God's work (John 6:44; Acts 11:18; 21:19; 2 Tim. 2:25).

(b)   It is God's work in us (Jer. 24:7; Acts 16:14; Phil. 1:6).

(c)   God sometimes uses unpleasant circumstances to bring conversion about in the lives of men and women (Ps. 78:34).

(d)   It is the result of God's grace to us (Acts 11:21, 23; Gal. 1:15).

(e)   It takes place at God's will and choice (Acts 9:1-8; 15:7; Gal. 1:15).

(f)   It is the consequence of the work of God the Holy Spirit (Acts 10:44-48).

(g)   It is a blessing from God (Acts 3:26).

(h)   The praise is God's (Gal. 1:24).

8.   Conversion reveals the response God requires from us as we hear the gospel.

(a)   Conversion is the step God requires of us if He is to restore us to Himself (Hos. 6:1; Acts 3:19).

(b)   In conversion, we respond to God's command to repent (Acts 17:30).

(c)   Conversion means becoming like children before God – completely submissive to what He commands we must do if we would enter His kingdom (Matt. 18:3).

9. **Conversion is the great work that God uses His servants to help bring about in the world in people's lives.**

(a) Conversion follows upon hearing the word of the gospel and believing (Acts 15:7).

(b) God uses His messengers to bring conversion about in the lives of people (Acts 26:17, 18).

(c) Preaching has a vital place in conversion: God uses it to bring people back to Himself (Luke 1:16; Acts 26:17, 18).

(d) Conversion takes place as the messengers of the gospel are welcomed and their message obeyed (1 Thess. 1:9).

(e) Conversion may come about through the testimony of converted people to God's mercy and salvation (Ps. 51:12, 13).

(f) Conversion is the work of Christ that He is pleased to accomplish through His servants in the lives of those to whom they proclaim the message of repentance and faith (Acts 11:21; Rom. 15:18; 1 Thess. 1:9).

10. **Conversion is commanded by God.**

(a) Men and women are exhorted to repent, and to turn to God, so that their sins may be wiped out (Acts 3:19).

(b) The delay in God's judgment of the world springs from His desire that people may heed His warnings and obey His command to be converted (2 Pet. 3:8, 9).

---

28. REPENTANCE

Question: What is repentance?

Answer: Repentance is turning from sin to God, as a result of a change of mind and heart about sin.

1. **The necessity of repentance.**

(a) God commands it of all people everywhere (Acts 17:30).

(b) Unless we repent, we will perish (Luke 13:3, 5).

(c) Repentance is the first response demanded of us if we are to respond to the gospel of Jesus Christ (Acts 2:38).

(d) Repentance is the first condition God imposes if we are to find Him (Zech. 1:3, 4; Acts 20:21).

(e)   Repentance is a condition of cleansing (Isa. 6:5-7).

(f)   Repentance is a condition of forgiveness (Luke 24:47; Acts 3:19).

(g)   Repentance is a condition of entry into the kingdom of heaven (Matt. 4:17).

(h)   Repentance is a condition of eternal life (Acts 11:18).

(i)   Repentance is a condition of escaping the judgment of God upon sin (Acts 17:30, 31).

2.   Repentance is turning from sin to God.

(a)   Repentance is the result of the eyes of the mind being opened to understand our need as sinners before God (Acts 26:17, 18).

(b)   Repentance is associated with the idea of turning (Acts 3:19; 26:20).

(c)   Repentance is turning away from acts that lead to death (Heb. 6:1); it is turning from wicked ways (2 Chron. 7:14); it is turning from our sins and giving attention to God's truth (Dan. 9:13); it is turning away from our evil ways to God (Ezek. 33:11).

(d)   Repentance involves the recognition of sin as failure to keep God's decrees or laws (Mal. 3:7).

(e)   Repentance means seeing how awful sin is in God's sight (Ps. 51:4), and recognising the afflictions of our own heart (1 Kings 8:38).

(f)   Conviction of sin is necessary for repentance to take place (Acts 2:37, 38).

(g)   Repentance involves a real sorrow and grief because of sin (Luke 22:62; 2 Cor. 7:8-10).

(h)   Repentance brings such a sense of shame (Ezra 9:6-15; Jer. 31:19) that we despise ourselves for our sin (Job 42:6).

(i)   Repentance is the wicked forsaking their evil ways and thoughts and returning to the Lord, that He may have mercy on them and freely pardon them (Isa. 55:7).

(j)   Repentance means inevitably a fundamental break with the past (Luke 9:23, 24; 14:26, 27, 33).

3.   Characteristics of true repentance.

(a)   Unfortunately false repentance is a possibility: Saul (1 Sam. 15:24-30) and Ahab (1 Kings 21:27-29) provide examples of false repentance.

(b)   True repentance springs from a recognition of God as the Lord (Jer. 3:22).

(c)   It is seen in sorrow for sin (Joel 2:12; 2 Cor. 7:9).

(d)   It is rational and openly declared (Hos. 14:2).

(e)   It is accompanied by confession, renunciation and dedication (Hos. 14:1-3).

(f)   It is wholehearted (Joel 2:12, 13).

(g)   It is humble (Jonah 3:6; 2 Chron. 7:14; Jas. 4:9, 10).

(h)   It is a work and a gift of God (Acts 11:18).

4.   Motives for repentance.

(a)   God's character is a tremendous encouragement to repentance. He is gracious and compassionate, slow to anger and abounding in love (Joel 2:13).

(b)   God's patience with us should lead us towards repentance (2 Pet. 3:9).

(c)   God's kindness is meant to lead us to a change of heart about sin (Rom. 2:4).

(d)   God pleads with us to repent (Isa. 30:15).

(e)   God never despises repentance (Jonah 3:9; Luke 15:7, 10).

(f)   Christ came to call sinners to repentance (Luke 5:32).

(g)   Repentance is called for in the light of what God has accomplished for sinners through Christ's saving work (Acts 3:18, 19; 5:31).

(h)   Repentance is the first part of conversion, and faith in the Lord Jesus Christ is the second (Acts 20:21; Mark 1:15).

5.   Evidences of repentance.

(a)   True repentance brings no regret but leads to salvation (2 Cor. 7:10).

(b)   Practical reformation is to be expected (Judg. 6:25-27; Luke 19:8).

(c)   Actions follow that give proof of a change of mind about sin (Joel 2:12; Acts 26:20), especially restitution where necessary (Ezek. 33:14-16).

(d)   Repentance produces appropriate fruit (Matt. 3:8; Luke 13:6-9).

---

29. FAITH

Question: What is faith?

Answer: Faith is both a decisive act and a sustained attitude. It begins as an act, by which we abandon reliance on ourselves to merit salvation, have a firm conviction as to the truth of God's promises of mercy in Jesus Christ, and depend sincerely upon them. After this, faith becomes a habit of our life.

1. Faith rests on certain facts that the apostles were careful to preach (1 Cor. 11:23; 15:1-8; 1 Thess. 2:13; 4:1, 2).

2. These facts are easy to determine.
(a) Jesus is the Christ, the Son of God (John 20:31; Acts 9:20).
(b) He died for our sins so that we might die to sins and live for righteousness (1 Pet. 2:24).
(c) He was buried and was raised to life again on the third day (Rom. 4:25; 1 Pet. 1:3).
(d) His death and resurrection took place according to the manner in which God had promised beforehand in the Old Testament Scriptures (1 Cor. 15:3, 4).
(e) On the grounds of what Jesus Christ accomplished we may receive forgiveness and the gift of the Holy Spirit (Acts 2:38, 39).

3. These facts have to be received (1 Cor. 15:1).
(a) The facts themselves have to be understood (Acts 17:2, 3; 18:4, 19).
(b) Intellectual assent has to be given to them (Luke 24:45; Acts 28:27).

4. A stand has to be taken then upon these facts (1 Cor. 15:1).
(a) This stand involves a personal confession of Christ as the Son of God (Matt. 16:16; Rom. 10:10).

(b)   A personal belief that Christ died for our sins (Gal. 2:20; 1 Tim. 1:15).

(c)   A personal belief that God raised Christ from the dead (Rom. 10:9).

(d)   Thus faith moves beyond the facts to trusting a Person – the Lord Jesus Christ (Acts 16:31; John 1:12; 3:16).

5.   The stand that is taken upon these facts – significantly known as 'the faith' (Jude 3) - involves the abandonment of all confidence in human merit and works for the obtaining of salvation.

(a)   No confidence in externals, whether of race, social status, religious zeal, or legal rectitude is allowed (Phil. 3:3-9).

(b)   No confidence in righteous things we may have done is permissible (Tit. 3:5).

6.   When we come to true faith in Christ, faith becomes then a sustained attitude of our life.

(a)   Faith makes us sure of what we hope for (Heb. 11:1).

(b)   Faith makes us certain of what we do not see (Heb. 11:1).

(c)   Faith becomes the principle by which we live (2 Cor. 5:7).

(d)   We are defended in the battles of the Christian life by the shield of faith (Eph. 6:16).

(e)   We fight the good fight of faith (1 Tim. 6:12).

7.   Such a habit of faith in our life makes a tremendous difference to our life.   The men and women of faith, described in Hebrews 11, who did not fully know 'the faith' of the gospel, provide helpful illustrations.

(a)   Faith makes us offer only our best to God – Abel (Heb. 11:4).

(b)   Faith makes us reckon walking with God the most important thing in life - Enoch (Heb. 11:5).

(c)   Faith makes us concerned for the saving of our family - Noah (Heb. 11:7).

(d)   Faith makes us obey God, even blindly sometimes – Abraham leaving Haran (Heb. 11:8).

(e)   Faith makes us live after the manner of refugees in the world, holding lightly to its possessions – Abraham and his immediate descendants (Heb. 11:9, 10, 13-16).

(f)   Faith makes us change our mind about things thought impossible – Abraham and Sarah (Heb. 11:11, 12).

(g)   Faith makes us render complete obedience to God no matter what He demands - Abraham and Isaac (Heb. 11:17-19).

(h)   Faith makes us concerned for the spiritual well being of the generations to follow - Isaac blessing Jacob and Esau (Heb. 11:20).

(i)   Faith gives us confidence in the face of death – Jacob and Joseph (Heb. 11:21, 22).

(j)   Faith makes us co-operate actively with God's purposes as we know them - Moses' parents (Heb. 11:23).

(k)   Faith makes us live a life that is different and separate from the standard set by the world - Moses (Heb. 11:24-26).

(l)   Faith takes away our fear of people - Moses as to Pharaoh (Heb. 11:27).

(m)   Faith leads to the activity that comes from obedience – the Passover and the crossing of the Red Sea (Heb. 11:28, 29).

(n)   Faith brings victory and success – the fall of Jericho (Heb. 11:30).

---

30. THE AWAKENING OF FAITH

Question: How do we come to saving Christian faith?

Answer: **By the effective working of the Holy Spirit in our hearts, as the gospel is made known to us, calling us, without reference to our merits, from the dominion of darkness and transferring us into the kingdom of God's dear Son.**

1.   **As the facts of the faith (see Question 29:1) are presented to us, the Holy Spirit convinces us of their truth.**

(a)   He is the Spirit of truth (John 16:13).

(b)   God's message is received, not as a word of human origin, but as it actually is, the word of God (1 Thess. 2:13).

2. **As we recognize the truth of the facts of the faith, the Holy Spirit enables us to apply them to ourselves.**

(a) He uses the law of God to reveal to us our sin (Gal. 3:21-24; Rom. 7:7).

(b) And thus He brings us to conviction of sin and repentance (John 16:8-11; Acts 2:37, 38).

3. **Having convinced us of our sin, the Holy Spirit makes plain the remedy for our sin.**

(a) The good news of Jesus and the benefits of His death and resurrection come to us not simply with words, but also with the Holy Spirit and with deep conviction (1 Thess. 1:5).

(b) He brings glory to the Lord Jesus Christ by taking from what is His and making it known to us (John 16:14).

4. **The result is faith built not upon human wisdom but on God's power (1 Cor. 2:5).**

(a) Faith has come about not through the force of subtle human arguments, but through a demonstration of the Holy Spirit's power (1 Cor. 2:4).

(b) The Lord has added to the number of those whom He is saving (Acts 2:40, 41; cf. 2:47).

(c) No longer does the individual belong to the dominion of darkness but to the kingdom of God's dear Son (Col. 1:13).

5. **This effective working of the Holy Spirit in our hearts to bring us to faith in Christ is without reference at all to our merits (Tit. 3:5; Rom. 4:5; Eph. 2:4-10; 2 Thess. 1:11).**

---

31. JUSTIFICATION

Question: What is justification?

Answer: Justification is the free and undeserved act of God, by which He reckons to a sinner, through faith, the righteousness of Christ, declaring the sinner just and right before Him.

1. **Justification has to do with the justice and righteousness of God.**
(a) He is the just God and everything He does demonstrates His justice (Rom. 3:25, 26).
(b) He is the Lord and Judge of all the earth, who always does right (Gen. 18:25).
(c) His righteousness is seen in His judgment and condemnation of those who disobey His laws (Ps. 7:11; Isa. 5:16; Acts 17:31; Rom. 2:5).

2. **Men and women are unrighteous before God.**
(a) No-one living is righteous before God (Ps. 143:2).
(b) All have sinned and fall short of the glory of God (Rom. 3:23).

3. **Theoretically, the law of God is a means of justification.**
(a) By perfect obedience to the law of God an individual could be justified before God (Lev. 18:5; Rom. 2:13; 10:5).
(b) However, all people everywhere have broken God's law (Rom. 10:5; cf. 9:31) – it has served to bring an awareness of sin (Rom. 3:20).
(c) The endeavour to keep the law of God, therefore, can bring about neither righteousness nor justification before God (Rom. 3:21; Gal. 2:16, 21; 3:11).
(d) Works or acts of obedience can neither satisfy God's justice, fulfil His law nor stand up to His standard (Ps. 130:3, 4; 143:2; Isa. 64:6; Luke 17:10).
(e) The thought of God bringing us into judgment is, therefore, terrifying (Ps. 143:2).

4. **God alone could deliver us from the condemnation that rightly awaits us; and the situation required an amazing solution.**
(a) Clearly, the wrong that is in men and women's lives could not be put right by their obedience to the law of God (Job 9:2, 3, 20; 25:4; Rom. 3:21; 9:30-32).
(b) Whatever way God determined for righting the wrong that was in us, it had to be adequate for all, without distinction, and consistent with His own justice (Rom. 3:21-26).

103

(c)   The answer was the gospel: it is the revelation of God's plan for making us right in His sight (Rom. 1:16, 17).

(d)   The wonder of God's new covenant is that we may be reconciled to God (2 Cor. 5:20), all the demands of God's law having been satisfied (2 Cor. 3:9).

(e)   The law and the prophets testified beforehand of this way of justification that God purposed (Rom. 3:21).

(f)   Abraham is an example of God's justifying grace: he believed God, and it was credited to him as righteousness (Gen. 15:6; Rom. 4:3).

5.   Justification, therefore, is necessarily an act of God, something beyond our power to accomplish.

(a)   It is a legal term, meaning to acquit (Rom. 8:33; cf. Deut. 25:1; Prov. 17:15).

(b)   While God is the Judge, He is also the justifier (Rom. 3:26, 30; 4:5; 8:33; Gal. 3:8).

(c)   The amazing thing is that He justifies the wicked (Rom. 4:5): for His own sake, He blots out their transgressions and will not remember their sins (Isa. 43:25).

6.   Justification depends upon what Christ has done for sinners.

(a)   The grounds of it are what Christ accomplished for sinners (Acts 13:39).

(b)   God could justify the ungodly only through Christ's dying, at the right time, for them (Rom. 5:6).

(c)   God presents Christ to us as the One whose sacrificial death has atoned for our guilt and removed the judgment soon to happen that our rebellion against Him has brought upon us (Rom. 3:24-26).

(d)   Christ redeemed us from the curse of the law by becoming a curse for us (Gal. 3:13).

(e)   God made Christ, who had no sin to be sin for us, so that in Him we might become the righteousness of God (2 Cor. 5:21; cf. Isa. 53:5).

(f)   Thus Jesus Christ, acting on behalf of sinners, has satisfied the claims of God's law and justice (Gal. 4:4, 5), and has put away their sins by His blood (Rom. 3:25; 5:9).

(g) By justifying men and women on the basis of Christ's sacrificial death God demonstrates both His justice and His love (Rom. 3:25, 26; 1 John 4:10).

7. On the basis of Christ's sacrificial death, God reckons to believers the righteousness of Christ.

(a) Of Christ's righteousness there was no doubt (Matt. 3:15, 17; 1 Pet. 3:18): justification is by the imputing of His righteousness to the sinner (Rom. 3:22; 5:18; 1 Cor. 1:30; 2 Cor. 5:21).

(b) To be justified is to receive the righteousness of Christ, for which alone the Lord accepts us as holy and righteous (Isa. 43:25; Rom. 3:21-26; 4:5; Phil. 3:9).

(c) God pronounces us to be free from all guilt and declares us to be right with Him because His Son has taken the punishment for our sins and has satisfied His anger against us (Rom. 3:24-26).

(d) Christians are described as 'the righteous' as a consequence (1 Pet. 4:18).

8. Justification is a free gift from God.

(a) Men and women are justified freely by God's grace alone (Rom. 3:24).

(b) The righteousness God bestows through Christ is a gift (Rom. 5:17; Phil. 3:9).

(c) Consequently, all room for human boasting is removed (Rom. 3:27).

9. The means of our entering into justification is by faith.

(a) The righteousness God offers is to be apprehended through faith in Jesus Christ and the merits of His blood (Rom. 1:17; 3:22, 26; 4:3-5, 13; 9:30; 10:4, 6, 10).

(b) Justification depends upon faith to be effective (Acts 13:39; Rom. 3:25, 28; 4:5).

(c) It is by believing in our heart that we are made right with God (Rom. 10:10).

(d) Faith, therefore, is credited to us as righteousness (Gen. 15:6; Ps. 106:31; Rom. 4:3-11, 23, 24; Gal. 3:6).

10.   The benefits justification brings.

(a)   The first benefit of justification is peace with God (Rom. 5:1).

(b)   It is to be justified from everything from which we could not be justified by the law of Moses; it means the forgiveness of sins (Acts 13:38, 39).

(c)   It frees us from condemnation (Isa. 50:8, 9; 54:17; Rom. 8:33, 34).

(d)   No one can bring any charge against those whom God justifies (Rom. 8:33).

(e)   Being justified, believers can rejoice in deliverance from God's wrath (Rom. 5:9).

(f)   God has so justified believers that they have nothing to fear at God's judgment seat (Rom. 8:1).

(g)   The peace justification brings carries with it access to God (Rom. 5:2).

(h)   Justification brings us into union with God and makes us children and heirs of God (Rom. 8:14-17; Gal. 3:26; 4:4-7).

(i)   It is on the basis of their justification that believers are in Christ, and know Christ, together with all the benefits Christ has gained for them (Rom. 8:32; Phil. 3:9-11).

(j)   Justification brings tremendous joy: the joy of the hope of sharing the glory of God (Rom. 5:2); joy in sufferings because we know God's good purposes for His children are fulfilled through them (Rom. 5:3); and, supremely, joy in God Himself (Rom. 5:11).

(k)   Justification assures believers that they possess eternal life (Rom. 8:10, 11; Tit. 3:7).

(l)   Justification means that absolutely nothing can separate us from the love of God in Christ Jesus our Lord (Rom. 8:31-39).

(m)   It is the basis of true happiness (Rom. 4:6-8; Ps. 32:1, 2).

(n)   No wonder it is the believer's most precious possession - nothing else can compare with its value (Phil. 3:7-9).

---
32. BEING A CHRISTIAN

Question: **What are the benefits and privileges of being a Christian?**

Answer: **The benefits and privileges of being a Christian are, principally, union with Christ, adoption by God into His family, Christian liberty, a spiritual right to the sacraments of the new covenant, the fellowship of all Christians, and the resurrection of the body.**

1.   Union with Christ.
(a)   The purpose of all that Christ did was that Christians might be united with Him and live together with Him (1 Thess. 5:10):
   (i)   They were crucified with Him (Rom. 6:6);
   (ii)   They were buried with Him (Rom. 6:4; Col. 2:12);
   (iii)   They died with Him (Rom. 6:8; 2 Tim. 2:11);
   (iv)   They were made alive with Him (Col. 2:13);
   (v)   They were raised with Him (Col. 2:12; 3:1);
   (vi)   They are made co-heirs with Him (Rom. 8:17);
   (vii)   They are to suffer with Christ (Rom. 8:17);
   (viii) They are to share in His glory (Rom. 8:17);
   (ix)   They will reign with Him (2 Tim. 2:12; Rev. 20:4).
(b)   The union is like that of a Head and a Body:
   (i)   Christ is the Head of the Body, the Church (Col. 1:18), and Christians, like the many limbs and organs in a single body, constitute the one body of Christ (1 Cor. 12:12);
   (ii)   Christians are meant to grow up in all things into Christ, who is the Head (Eph. 4:15).
(c)   The union is like that of a husband and wife:
   (i)   Christ is the Head of the Church, as the husband is the head of the wife (Eph. 5:23);
   (ii)   Christians are promised to Christ, as a pure bride to her bridegroom (2 Cor. 11:2; Eph. 5:25-27; Rev. 21:9).
(d)   The union is like that of a foundation to a building:
   (i)   Christ is the rock upon which we are built (Matt. 16:18);

(ii)   We become part of God's spiritual building or house, as we are joined to Christ, the chief cornerstone, through faith (Eph. 2:19-22; 1 Pet. 2:4-7).

(e)   The Holy Spirit brings Christians into their living relationship and union with Christ, and there can be no such experience without the Holy Spirit (Rom. 8: 9, 11).

(f)   It is through being in Christ that God gives us every possible spiritual benefit (Eph. 1:3).

2.   Adoption by God into His family.

(a)   Before the creation of the world God chose Christians in Christ to become His holy and blameless children, to live within His constant care (Eph. 1:4, 5).

(b)   God's love has caused Him to bestow upon those who receive His Son the right to become His children (John 1:12, 13; 1 John 3:1).

(c)   Christians receive the Spirit of adoption, so that they are rightly able to cry, 'Abba, Father!' (Rom. 8:15-17).

(d)   As God's children, Christians share His treasures, and all that God gives to His Son belongs to them as well (Rom. 8:17).

(e)   Christians wait for the redemption of their bodies that will mean that at last they have entered into their full rights as God's children in Christ (Rom. 8:23).

(f)   The whole creation may be described as waiting in eager expectation to see the wonderful sight of the children of God coming into their own (Rom. 8:19).

3.   Christian Liberty.

(a)   Christ came to proclaim freedom for captives, and release from darkness for prisoners (Isa. 61:1, 2; Luke 4:18, 19). When Christ sets us free, we are free indeed (John 8:32, 34, 36; Gal. 5:1).

(b)   Christ sets us free from the fear of death (1 Cor. 15:55-57; Heb. 2:14, 15).

(c)   Christ delivers us from that slavish attitude of fear that so easily can characterize life without God (Rom. 8:15).

(d)   Christ has redeemed believers from the curse of the law's condemnation, by Himself becoming a curse for them when He was crucified (Gal. 3:13): no condemnation now hangs over the head of those who are in Christ Jesus (Rom. 8:1).

(e) The burden of all the Jewish ceremonial is removed through Christ (Acts 15:10, 11; Gal. 5:1).

(f) Christ makes us free from slavery to sin (John 8:32, 34, 36). Though Christians once used to be slaves to sin, having now wholeheartedly obeyed the form of teaching to which they were entrusted, they have been set free from the service of sin, and have become the servants of righteousness (Rom. 6:17, 18).

(g) Christians' freedom, however, is not a freedom to do evil, but a freedom to serve God (1 Pet. 2:16).

(h) Christians are freed from the bondage of the law, but it remains a rule for them of life and holiness: God puts His law within Christians and writes it upon their hearts (Jer. 31:31-34).

(i) Christians are not under law, but under grace (Rom. 6:14).

(j) The law is not nullified or undermined by the insistence on faith; rather it is given its proper place (Rom. 3:31).

4.   A spiritual right to the sacraments of the New Covenant.

(a) The first sacrament of the New Covenant is baptism:

  (i)   It was appointed by Christ Himself for all disciples (Matt. 28:19, 20; Mark 16:15, 16);

  (ii) It is administered in the name of the Trinity (Matt. 28:19);

  (iii) It is a symbol of an individual's reception of the gospel (Acts 2:37, 38, 41; 8:12; 16:14, 15);

  (iv) It symbolizes repentance and faith in the Lord Jesus (Acts 2:38);

  (v)   It symbolizes confession of Christ's Lordship (Acts 19:5);

  (vi) It symbolizes admittance into God's family (Acts 2:38, 41, 47; 8:12; 9:18; 1 Cor. 12:13);

  (vii) It symbolizes entry into all the benefits of Christ's death and resurrection (Rom. 6:3, 4).

(b) The second sacrament of the New Covenant is the Lord's Supper:

  (i)   The Lord's Supper is a proclamation of the Lord's death by words and symbols (1 Cor. 11:26);

  (ii) It was established and commanded by Christ (Matt. 26:26-29; 1 Cor. 11:23);

  (iii) It continually reminds Christians of Christ's sacrifice for them (Luke 22:19, 20; 1 Cor. 11:23-26);

(iv)   By means of it Christians acknowledge their sharing in the benefits of Christ's death (1 Cor. 10:16, 17; 11:23-26);

(v)   In it Christians have fellowship with Christ and with one another (1 Cor. 10:16, 17, 21);

(vi)   In it Christians make their thanksgiving to God (1 Cor. 10:16; Rom. 12:1);

(vii) The Lord's Supper is to be continued until Christ returns (1 Cor. 11:26).

5.   The Fellowship of all Christians.

(a)   God gives His people singleness of heart and action (Jer. 32:39).

(b)   The people of God are one as the Father and the Son are one (John 17:22) - and Jesus' prayer to His Father had this unity as a main petition (John 17:11, 21).

(c)   Jesus, the Great and Chief Shepherd, has one flock to which all Christians belong (John 10:16).

(d)   The fellowship of believers – sometimes called 'the communion of saints' – arises from Christians belonging to one Body, of which there is one Spirit (Eph. 4:4).

(e)   All Christians are baptized by the Spirit into one Body, whether Jews, Gentiles, slaves or free, and they all have experience of the same Spirit (1 Cor. 12:13).

(f)   Though many, Christians form one body in Christ, and each member belongs to all the others (Rom. 12:5; 1 Cor. 12:12).

(g)   The fellowship or communion of believers, therefore, is the sense of identity and belonging we have with all Christians through our common allegiance to the Lord Jesus, the truth (Eph. 4:13; 2 John 1).

(h)   The fellowship Christians have together arises from their fellowship with the Father and the Son (1 John 1:3).

(i)   Christians should seek to express their fellowship and union outwardly by avoiding all dissensions among themselves, being perfectly united in mind and thought (1 Cor. 1:10, 11; Phil. 2:1, 2; 1 Pet. 3:8).

(j)   This fellowship of all Christians is given practical expression in the fellowship of the local church according to the pattern revealed in the New Testament (Acts 11:26; 14:23; 20:17, 28; 1 Cor. 4:17; Heb. 10:25; 13:17).

6.   The Resurrection of the Body.

(a)   God does not abandon believers to the grave, but He has made known to them the path of life, which leads to joy in His presence, and eternal pleasures at His right hand (Ps. 16:9-11).

(b)   Believers have the assurance of the resurrection of the body through their risen Redeemer (Job 19:25-27; 1 Thess. 4:14).

(c)   The resurrection of the dead will be the first consequence of Christ's second coming (1 Thess. 4:16).

(d)   Believers will be made alive through Christ (1 Cor. 15:22).

(e)   Harvest provides a good illustration of the kind of thing that will happen.   What we sow is not the body that is to be but only a seed (1 Cor. 15:37); just as to every kind of creature and thing God has given a particular body, so He has determined the particular nature of the resurrection body (1 Cor. 15:38-44).

(f)   The body characterized by decay, dishonour, weakness, and suited only for this present life, will be raised an imperishable, glorious body, full of power, and perfectly fitted for life in the world to come (1 Cor. 15:42-44).

(g)   The transformation will take place in a flash, in the twinkling of an eye (1 Cor. 15:51, 52).

(h)   The assurance of the resurrection of the body is a tremendous comfort and encouragement to the Christian (1 Cor. 15:58; 1 Thess. 4:18).

(i)   And after the glorious event, Christians will be with Christ forever (1 Thess. 4:17).

---

33. ASSURANCE

Question: **How can we be sure that we are Christians?**

Answer: **By the conviction we have from the Holy Spirit, through our obedience to the gospel, that we are children of God and heirs of eternal life. The genuineness of this conviction is demonstrated by right belief in Christ, righteous conduct and love for other Christians.**

1. **First, we need to be clear as to what being sure includes.**

(a) The spiritual benefits concerning which Christians are encouraged to be sure are many and include:

   (i) Election (Ps. 4:3; 1 Thess. 1:4; 2 Pet. 1:10);

   (ii) Salvation and redemption (Isa. 12:2; Job 19:25; Rom. 5:9; 1 Cor. 1:30; 1 Thess. 5:9);

   (iii) Peace with God through our Lord Jesus Christ (Rom. 5:1);

   (iv) Adoption into God's family (Rom. 8:16; 1 John 3:1, 2, 9, 10; 4:4; 5:2, 18, 19);

   (v) Knowing God (1 John 2:3; 5:20);

   (vi) Union with God and Christ (1 Cor. 6:15; 2 Cor. 13:5; Eph. 5:30; 1 John 2:5; 3:24; 4:13);

   (vii) Membership of God's kingdom (Col. 1:13; Heb. 12:28);

   (viii) Inseparability from the love of God (Rom. 8:38, 39);

   (ix) Deliverance from all evil (Ps. 3:6, 8; 27:3-5; 46:1-3; 2 Tim. 4:18);

   (x) God's continuing and perfecting work in us (Phil. 1:6);

   (xi) The right to pray and the assurance of God's answer (1 John 3:21, 22; 5:14, 15);

   (xii) God's help in affliction (Ps. 73:26; 2 Cor. 4:8-10, 16-18);

   (xiii) God's sure help in death (Ps. 23:4; Acts 7:59; Phil. 1:23);

   (xiv) A glorious resurrection (Job 19:26; Ps. 17:15; Phil. 3:21; 1 John 3:2);

   (xv) Eternal life (1 John 5:13).

2. **The grounds of our being sure that we are Christians, and all that this includes, as seen above.**

(a) Firstly, God wants us to be sure (2 Cor. 13:5): His will is that those who believe in the name of the Son of God may know that they have eternal life (1 John 5:13).

(b) Secondly, the basis of any assurance we have concerning being Christians is that God has spoken to us through His Son Jesus Christ (Heb. 1:1, 2), and all that He wants us to know is contained in the Scriptures, the Word of God (2 Tim. 3:14-17; 1 John 1:1-3).

(c) The Scriptures give us God's promises in Christ through which assurance comes (2 Cor. 1:20, 21).

(d) Understanding of God's truth brings a wealth of assurance through knowing Christ with real certainty (Col. 2:2).

(e) Thirdly, assurance springs from an understanding of God's character: for example, His holiness (1 John 1:5), His faithfulness and justice (1 John 1:9), and His love (1 John 4:8-10, 16, 19).

(f) Our Christian assurance is not in ourselves, and not in the truth of God's Word alone, but in God Himself – 'I know whom I have believed' (2 Tim. 1:12).

(g) Fourthly, assurance is particularly related to a full understanding of the gospel as being not the word of human beings, but the Word of God (1 Thess. 2:13; 1 John 2:20, 21).

(h) In particular, our understanding concerns the deity of our Lord Jesus Christ and His finished work upon the Cross (1 John 1:1-3, 7; 2:1, 22, 23; 4:2, 3, 15; 5:5, 10, 13, 20): Christ fully satisfied the law's demands for us; He is freely offered to all who hear the gospel; all who receive Him and depend upon Him will be saved (1 John 2:1, 2, 12; 3:5, 8, 16; 4:10; compare John 1:12; 3:16).

(i) Fifthly, a further ground of assurance is the awareness that we do believe in the manner God commands (1 John 3:23; 5:13).

(j) Assurance is the result of faith in Christ (Eph. 3:12).

(k) It is important to realize that the work of assurance is the Holy Spirit's: He witnesses to us, in the first place, that the gospel message is true (1 John 2:20, 27; 3:24; 4:13); He gives an inward assurance to us that our response to the gospel is genuine (1 Thess. 1:5).

(l) His presence in our life is the proof that our response to the gospel has been authentic (Acts 2:38, 39; 5:32; 15:8; Rom. 8:15,16; Gal. 3:2; 4:6; Eph. 1:13, 14; 4:30).

(m) Assurance springs from the witness of the Holy Spirit within us (1 John 3:24; 5:6, 8, 9, 10): we may know that we dwell in God and He in us because of the presence of His own Spirit in our life (1 John 4:13).

3. The tests to be applied to our conviction that we are Christians to prove its genuineness.

(a) It is necessary to apply these tests because a false assurance is possible; therefore, tests, such as an examination of the quality of our daily life (Tit. 1:16), are to be applied.

(b) The first test is whether we possess right belief concerning the Lord Jesus Christ (1 John 3:23; 5:13).

(c) Those who have right belief confess that Jesus is the Christ (1 John 2:22; 5:1); that He is the Son of God (1 John 3:23; 5:5, 10), and that He came in the flesh (1 John 4:2; 2 John 7).

(d) The second test is whether we are marked by righteous conduct: those who are born of God do what is right (1 John 2:29; 3:10).

(e) Righteous conduct is described in different ways:

(i) Walking in the light (1 John 1:7);

(ii) Obedience to God's commandments (1 John 2:3-6; 3:24);

(iii) The desire to live as Jesus lived (1 John 2:6);

(iv) Deliverance from the spirit, attitudes and goals of the world (1 John 2:15-17; 3:14-18; 5:5, 19);

(v) Self-purification (1 John 3:3);

(vi) Ceasing to sin habitually (1 John 3:5, 6, 9; 5:18).

(f) The third test is whether we love other Christians (1 John 3:10-22; 4:8-12, 16, 20, 21): we know that we have passed from death to life because we love other Christians (1 John 3:14).

(g) By loving one another we show that we know God and are living in Him, and that He lives in us (1 John 3:23, 24; 4:7).

(h) When our life stands up to these tests we may assure our hearts before God that we are Christians and children of God, even when we are conscious of our natural sinfulness (1 John 3:19-21).

(i) When, however, the application of these tests does not produce a satisfactory proof of genuineness any assurance people may seem to have is unjustified (1 John 1:6; 2:4, 9-11, 23; 3:6-10; 4:8, 20; 2 John 9; 3 John 11).

4.   The results of being sure that we are Christians.

(a)   Joy (1 Pet. 1:8; 1 John 1:4).

(b)   The banishment of any unworthy fear of God (1 John 4:17-19).

(c)   The avoidance of sin (1 John 2:1).

(d)   Confidence in God and boldness before Him (1 John 3:19-22; 5:14, 15; compare Heb. 10:19-22).

---

34. PERSEVERANCE

Question: Can true Christians go so far from God as to become lost?

Answer: True Christians cannot go so far from God that they become lost, although they may backslide. They stand firm to the end because they are held fast by God. Apostasy indicates people were never true Christians.

1.   Christians must stand firm to the end – this is commanded (Matt. 10:22; 24:13; Mark 13:13).

(a)   It is by standing firm that Christians gain the well being of their souls (Luke 21:19; cf. Heb. 10:39).

(b)   Maintained obedience to the teaching of the Lord Jesus Christ is the proof of discipleship (John 8:31).

(c)   To those who, by persistence in doing good, seek glory, honour and immortality, the Lord will give eternal life (Rom. 2:7).

(d)   To those who are overcomers Christ gives the right to eat of the tree of life (Rev. 2:7).

(e)   Christians share in all that Christ promises so long as they steadily maintain until the end the confidence and trust with which they began (Heb. 6:11, cf. 3:6, 14).

(f)   The perseverance – endurance - of Christians is a condition of their reigning with Christ (2 Tim. 2:12).

(g)   We are not left in any doubt as to the nature of this perseverance; it is perseverance in:

(i)   Holiness or likeness to Jesus Christ (Rom. 8:29; 2 Thess. 2:13; 1 Pet. 1:2);

(ii)   The knowledge of God (Col. 1:10);

(iii)   The faith – i.e. being firm on the Christian foundations, not moved from the hope held out in the gospel (Col. 1:23);

(iv)   Christian behaviour and fruitfulness (Col. 1:10);

(v)   Faithfulness to Christ (Rev. 14:12);

(vi)   Obedience (John 14:15, 23; 15:10);

(vii)   Running the race of the Christian life marked out for us (Heb. 12:1, 2);

(viii) Good works (Gal. 6:9; Eph. 2:10; 1 Thess. 1:3);

(ix)   Fruitfulness (Matt. 7:17; John 15:4, 5, 8, 16; Col. 1:10);

(x)   Standing firm in the Lord (Phil. 4:1).

2.   True Christians will hold fast to the end.

(a)   Having begun a good work in the lives of Christians, God continues it to completion, right up to the day of Jesus Christ (Phil. 1:6; cf. 1 Cor. 1:8).

(b)   Stirred by the exhortations of the Bible, true Christians will make every effort to enter into God's promises, thus confirming their calling and election, increasing their assurance that there will be a rich welcome for them into the eternal kingdom of our Lord and Saviour Jesus Christ (2 Pet. 1:11).

(c)   The warnings God has given against drifting away from our faith in the Lord Jesus are used by the Holy Spirit to keep true Christians from that peril (Heb. 2:1; 6:9; 10:39).

(d)   The testing of genuine faith brings perseverance (Jas. 1:3)– the reaction of true Christians to testing gives proof of their membership of God's family (Rom. 5:3-5; 2 Thess. 1:4; Heb. 10:36; Rev. 13:10).

(e)   A fight there will be, but perseverance also (Eph. 6:13).

(f)   It is the Father's will that the Son should lose none of those whom He has given to Him (John 6:39; 10:27-29).

(g)   God's gifts and His call to us are irrevocable (Rom. 11:29).

(h)   Nothing is able to separate God's elect in Christ from His love (Rom. 8:29-39).

3. **True Christians are not immune from backsliding although they cannot commit apostasy.**

(a) Perseverance does not rule out backsliding, but it does rule out apostasy (Rev. 2:2; with 4-7; 2:9, with 20-29).

(b) Christians may backslide (as some of the Hebrew Christians did) but they can never apostatize (Heb. 5:11-6:12, especially 6:9).

(c) Though Christians fall, they are restored through God's help (Ps. 37:23, 24).

4. **True Christians hold fast to the end because they are held fast by the Lord.**

(a) Christians do not keep themselves; they are shielded by God's power, through faith until the coming of the salvation that is ready to be revealed in the last time (1 Pet. 1:5; Rom. 14:4).

(b) God will never forsake His people: His justice and His faithfulness forbid that He should (Ps. 37:28; 2 Thess. 3:3).

(c) He will fulfil His purposes for His people, and nothing can hinder them (Ps. 138:8; John 10:27-29; Rom. 8:28-30; 1 Thess. 5:24).

(d) Even in the times of His people's ignorance and stupidity the Lord keeps His hand upon them (Ps. 73:21-24; cf. Luke 22:31, 32).

(e) He keeps His people strong to the end, in keeping with His faithfulness and calling (1 Cor. 1:8, 9).

(f) Perseverance is the consequence of being strengthened with the Lord's glorious power so that we have all the patience and endurance we need (Col. 1:11; Eph. 6:13).

(g) Satan's desires to shake Christians from their faith are not permitted by the Lord - Peter's case, for example (Luke 22:31, 32).

(h) The glory or praise for the perseverance of Christians is entirely God's (2 Tim. 4:18).

(i) Christians, therefore, may be sure of their security (Ps. 37:28; 73:24; 2 Tim. 4:18).

(j) This assurance should not lead to slackness but to all the greater diligence in the Christian life (Phil. 2:12, 13; 2 Pet. 1:10).

5. **Apostasy indicates that people were never true Christians.**

(a) Straightforward apostasy is the proof that people were never, in fact, Christians, although they appeared to be such (1 John 2:19).

(b) The parable of the sower indicates that perseverance is the test of reality (Mark 4:3-8, 13-20).

(c) Cases of falling away, or apostasy, are recorded (1 Tim. 1:19; 2 Tim. 2:17, 18), but in no case is there proof that the persons concerned were true believers (1 John 2:19).

(d) We are reminded, therefore, that not all who call themselves God's children are necessarily such (Matt.7:21-23; Rom. 9:6-8).

6. **Fundamental doctrines of the Christian faith underline the truth of what we call final perseverance.**

(a) It follows on from election (Jer. 31:3; Matt. 24:22-24; 1 Thess. 1:2-4).

(b) It follows from the covenant by which God the Father gave to His Son His people, as the reward of His obedience and suffering (Ps. 2:8; Jer. 32:40; John 17:2-6; Heb. 13:20, 21).

(c) It springs from the once-for-all nature of Christ's atoning death (Heb. 10:14).

(d) It follows from the union of Christians with Christ (John 17:24; Rom. 8:1; Gal. 2:20).

(e) It follows from the presence of the Holy Spirit in Christians forever (John 14:16; 2 Cor. 1:21, 22; 5:5; Eph. 1:13, 14).

(f) It follows from the effectiveness of Christ's intercession for His people (John 17:11, 15, 20; Rom. 8:34; Heb. 7:25; cf. Luke 22:31, 32).

---

35. SANCTIFICATION

Question: **What does God require of us most of all when we have become Christians?**

Answer: **The comprehensive words that sum up what God requires of us are sanctification and holiness. Sanctification is the process of which holiness is the completed state. In sanctification, God's will is that our sinful attitudes and actions should be put to death, our nature and character renewed after the image of God in Christ, our obedience to God increased, so that we live to please God. All these things take place through the power and help of the Holy Spirit.**

1. Sanctification and holiness.

(a) God's will for us is our sanctification (1 Thess. 4:3; 1 Pet. 1:16).

(b) God's call to Christians is to live a holy life (1 Thess. 4:7).

(c) The necessity for holiness springs from the fact that the Lord our God is holy (Lev. 11:44; 1 Pet. 1:15, 16).

(d) The Lord Jesus Christ gave Himself for us to redeem us from all wickedness and to purify for Himself a people that are His very own, eager to do what is good (Tit. 2:14).

(e) Our supreme aim as Christians is to be the achieving of holiness (Heb. 12:14).

2. Sanctification - of which holiness is the completed state – is a continuous process.

(a) It is the continual endeavour to bring holiness to completeness (2 Cor. 7:1).

(b) It is a progressive work, and involves the complete personality: the spirit, the soul and the body (1 Thess. 5:23).

(c) Entire sanctification will not be realized until our weak mortal bodies are transformed to be like Christ's glorious body (Phil. 3:21; 1 John 3:2).

3. **Sinful attitudes and actions are to be put to death in our lives** (Rom. 8:13; Col. 3:5).

(a) Belonging to the Lord brings the immediate obligation to depart from iniquity (2 Tim. 2:19).

(b) God's judgment and condemnation no longer rest upon Christians because of their sin (Rom. 8:1), but this does not mean that we may ever regard sin lightly (Rom. 6:1, 2; 1 John 2:1).

(c) We are to put off the sinful ways of our former way of life (Eph. 4:22).

(d) While there is necessarily a battle with indwelling sin (Rom. 7:14-25; 1 John 1:8; 2:1), sin is not to have the mastery over us (Rom. 6:12, 13).

(e) Sexual immorality and uncleanness are not to be given any place in our life (1 Thess. 4:3, 7).

(f) The more our sanctification proceeds the more we hate our sin (Job 42:5, 6; Isa. 6:5; Rom. 7:24).

4. **Our nature and character are to be renewed after the image of God in Christ.**

(a) Sanctification is a call to share God's moral perfection (1 Pet. 1:16).

(b) The goal of sanctification is always presented as likeness to Christ: God has chosen Christians to bear the family likeness of His Son (Rom. 8:29; Phil. 1:9-11; 2 Pet. 1:5-8).

(c) God's purpose is that we should copy Christ and be like Him (1 Cor. 11:1; Phil. 2:5).

(d) As we are made new in the attitudes of our minds by the Holy Spirit, so we are able to put on our new self, created to be like God in true righteousness and holiness (Eph. 4:22-24).

5. **Obedience to God is to grow and increase.**

(a) Nothing we do outwardly has value to God without the willing obedience of the heart (1 Sam. 15:22).

(b) He requires that His commandments shall be upon our heart (Deut. 6:5, 6).

(c) Practical righteousness is observing all the Lord's commandments and regulations blamelessly (Luke 1:6).

(d) We please God as we keep His commandments (1 John 3:22).

(e)   We are to keep in step with the Holy Spirit as He reveals to us what God requires (Gal. 5:25).

(f)   While our obedience is always imperfect (Ps. 130:3), God will always receive the offering of our obedience and of ourselves to Him as holy and acceptable, when we are His children in Christ (Rom. 12:1; Phil. 4:18; Heb. 13:16).

6.   All these things take place by the power and help of the Holy Spirit.

(a)   Our confidence as we seek to work out the salvation God has given us is that He Himself is at work in us, giving us the will and power to achieve His purpose (Phil. 2:13).

(b)   The Holy Spirit is the agent of our sanctification, even as of our regeneration (1 Cor. 6:11; 1 Thess. 4:7, 8).

(c)   Strength for the Christian life comes by the personal indwelling of the Holy Spirit (Eph. 3:16; 2 Cor. 4:16).

(d)   The Holy Spirit assists us in putting to death the misdeeds of the body (Rom. 8:13).

(e)   The Holy Spirit assists in the gradual transformation of our character to that of Christ (2 Cor. 3:18; cf. Rom. 8:29): He takes from what is Christ's and makes it known to us (John 16:14).

(f)   The Holy Spirit assists believers in actual obedience: He implants a supernatural habit and principle in us enabling us to obey God's will (Rom. 8:2).

(g)   The Holy Spirit strengthens our will to obey our Lord Jesus Christ and His commandments (1 Pet. 1:2; 1 John 3:24).

7.   The instrument the Holy Spirit uses principally for our sanctification is the Word of God.

(a)   It is declared to be God's chosen instrument (John 17:17).

(b)   Our way of life can be kept pure by guarding it according to God's Word (Ps. 119:9).

(c)   Holiness comes from instruction in God's ways, and walking in His paths (Isa. 2:2-5).

(d)   It is for this reason that Christ gives, by His Spirit, gifts to enable the people of God to be instructed in the Word of God (Eph. 4:11-16; 1 Tim. 5:17).

(e) Our sharing in God's holiness involves chastisement on occasions and some of the experiences that lead to greater sanctification are not always pleasant at the time (Heb. 12:10, 11).

8. Many incentives and motives for holiness and sanctification are set before the Christian.

(a) Reverence and respect for God (2 Cor. 7:1; 1 Pet. 1:17).

(b) The mercy of God to us in Christ (Rom. 12:1, 2).

(c) The promises of God (2 Cor. 7:1).

(d) The freedom to which we have been called in Christ, enabling us to please God (Gal. 5:1, 13-16).

(e) The prospect of Christ's return (Tit. 2:12, 13; 1 John 3:2, 3).

(f) God's gift of the Holy Spirit and the implications of that gift (Gal. 5:16-26; 1 Thess. 4:7, 8).

---

36. BAPTISM

Question: What is baptism?

Answer: It is an act of obedient discipleship, appointed by Christ, and administered in the name of the Trinity. It symbolises repentance, faith in the Lord Jesus Christ, and confession of His Lordship, admittance into the family of God, entry into all the benefits of His death and resurrection, and the desire to live a new life through the power of the Holy Spirit.

1. Baptism was appointed by Christ Himself for all disciples.

(a) Christ Himself was baptized, setting an example to all who would follow Him (Mark 1:9-11; Matt. 3:13-17; Luke 3:21, 22).

(b) Speaking of His own baptism, He declared it an act of obedience in order to fulfil all righteousness, that is to say, in order to do all that God requires (Matt. 3:15).

(c) Baptism was Christ's practice with regard to those who became His disciples during His ministry (John 3:22, 26; 4:1) although Christ did not Himself baptise, leaving it to His disciples (John 4:2).

(d)   Baptism was part of the great commission, given to the apostles, after the Resurrection, to be the first thing in which believers were to be instructed of all that Christ commanded (Matt. 28:19, 20; Mark 16:15, 16).

2.   **It is administered in the name of the Trinity.**

(a)   It is to be administered always in the name of the Father, the Son and the Holy Spirit (Matt. 28:19).

(b)   The identity of the baptizer is unimportant (John 4:2; 1 Cor. 1:14-17) - this fact may explain why our Lord refrained from baptizing disciples (John 4:2), and why Paul and Peter appear to have done the same (1 Cor. 1:14-16; Acts 10:48).

3.   **It is a symbol of the individual's reception of the gospel.**

(a)   It is the consequence of the Lord having opened an individual's heart to give heed to the gospel (Acts 16:14, 15).

(b)   It is a mark of a person's reception of the gospel – of the Word of the Lord (Acts 2:37, 38, 41; 8:12).

(c)   It should follow immediately upon confession of faith in Christ (Acts 2:38).

(d)   It is the first act of obedient discipleship (Acts 9:18; 16:14, 15, 33; 22:16).

(e)   It is a badge of discipleship (Matt. 28:19; John 3:22).

(f)   It is an experience that every Christian is to share (Eph. 4:5).

(g)   It is taken for granted in the New Testament that all believers will be baptized (Matt. 28:19; Acts 2:38, 41; 8:12; 10:47; Rom. 6:3; 1 Cor. 1:13; Gal. 3:27).

4.   **It symbolizes repentance and faith in the Lord Jesus Christ.**

(a)   Baptism is an outward sign of repentance – of turning in repentance from sin to God (Acts 2:38).

(b)   It is the personal expression of faith in the Lord Jesus Christ and His gospel (Mark 16:15, 16; Acts 8:12, 13, 36-38; 16:31–33).

5.   **Participation in baptism is the confession of Christ's Lordship.**

(a) Baptism is always associated with Christ's name, in that the individual makes a public confession concerning Him (Acts 2:38; 8:16; 22:16).

(b) It is the acknowledgment of Jesus as Lord (Acts 2:38; Rom. 10:9, 10; 1 Cor. 12:3).

(c) It implies the beginning of committed fellowship with, and allegiance to, the Lord Jesus Christ (Acts 2:38-42; 10:47, 48; Gal. 3:26, 27).

(d) It is the public testimony of the individual that he or she has become Christ's property (Acts 16:15; 19:5) – the expression 'in the name' of someone being used commercially for the transfer of property.

(e) As Lord, Christ's command is to be obeyed (Mark 16:16); to Him the believer must be faithful (Acts 16:14, 15).

6.   It symbolizes admittance into God's family.

(a) It marks the believer's admittance into God's family, the Church of Christ (Acts 2:38-47; 9:17, 18).

(b) It is the outward sign of a believer's new birth into God's family (John 3:5).

(c) It is a mark of his or her entry into the membership of Christ's body (1 Cor. 12:13).

7.   It symbolises entry into all the benefits of Christ's death and resurrection.

(a) Baptism is a visual aid of the gospel, in that it portrays Christ's death and resurrection and the salvation that comes to men and women as they turn in repentance and faith to Christ (Rom. 6:3, 4).

(b) It is a picture of an individual entering into the benefits of the new covenant, sealed with Christ's blood, even as Noah, believing God's promise to him, entered the ark (1 Pet. 3:18-22).

(c) It is, therefore, a picture of a Christian's cleansing from sin through Christ's death (Acts 2:38) - it is the outward and visible sign of inward and spiritual cleansing (Acts 22:16; Heb. 10:22).

(d) It speaks symbolically of the gift and blessing of new life by the gift and indwelling of the Holy Spirit (Acts 2:38). To experience the reality of what baptism signifies, the individual must be born again of God's Spirit (John 3:5; 1 Cor. 12:13).

8. **Participation in baptism expresses the desire individuals have to live a new life through the power of the Holy Spirit.**

(a) It is a symbolical burial of believers' old life (Rom. 6:3, 4; Col. 2:12), and renunciation of their old relationship to sin, because Christ's death has become their death by faith (Rom. 6:11, 12).

(b) It is a symbol of the beginning of the new life in Christ, of participation in the resurrection life of the Lord Jesus Christ, that is possible by the help and power of the Holy Spirit (Rom. 6:4, 5; Col. 2:11, 12).

(c) It is a symbol of believers' willingness to present their bodies to God, as instruments for the doing of God's will (Rom. 6:13).

(d) It symbolises the end of our service of sin, and the beginning of our committed service to God (Rom. 6:16, 17).

---

37. THE LORD'S SUPPER

Question: What is the Lord's Supper?

Answer: **The Lord's Supper is the symbolic meal that Christ established and commanded; in which Christians remember Christ's sacrifice continually; in which they acknowledge their sharing in the benefits of His death; at which they have fellowship with Christ and with other Christians; and make their thanksgiving to God.**

1. **The Lord's Supper is a symbolic meal.**

(a) The Lord's Supper is a proclamation of the Lord's death by words and symbols (1 Cor. 11:26).

(b) Christ's body is represented by the bread (1 Cor. 11:24).

(c) Christ's blood is represented by the wine (1 Cor. 11:25).

(d) The bread is broken and the wine is poured out as symbols of Christ's death upon the Cross (Matt. 26:26; Mark 14:22; Luke 22:19, 20; 1 Cor. 11:24, 25).

(e)   Both the bread and the wine are to be distributed to Christians as they sit at the Lord's Table (Matt. 26:26, 27; Mark 14:22-28; Luke 22:19, 20; 1 Cor. 11:23, 24, 26).

(f)   The Lord's Supper was prepared for, in symbol, by the Jewish Passover (1 Cor. 5:7, 8; Ex. 12:21-28): even as the Passover proclaimed the mercy of God in redeeming His people under the old covenant, so the Lord's Supper proclaims God's redeeming mercy under the new covenant (1 Cor. 1 1:26).

(g)   The Lord's Supper took place at the Passover feast and was established according to the pattern of the Passover (Matt. 26:17-19; Mark 14:1, 2, 12-16; Luke 22:14-20; John 13:21-30; compare Ex. 12).

(h)   The bread that was eaten with the lamb in the Passover feast was put to a new use (Matt. 26:26).

(i)   The third cup of the Passover, 'the cup of blessing' (compare 1 Cor. 10:16) was also put to a new use (Matt. 26:27, 28).

(j)   By reason of its significance, the Lord's Supper must be regarded as quite distinct from all other meals (1 Cor. 11:29).

2.   The Lord's Supper was established and commanded by Christ.

(a)   The Lord Jesus Christ established it at the Passover meal with His disciples on the night of His betrayal (Matt. 26:26-28; 1 Cor. 11:23).

(b)   Christ gave certain actions to be imitated every time the symbolic meal is repeated (1 Cor. 11:23ff).

(c)   The Lord's Supper, in its institution, was a meal that Christ earnestly desired to share with His disciples (Luke 22:15).

(d)   In establishing the symbolic meal Christ commanded that it should be regularly repeated (Luke 22:19; 1 Cor. 11:25).

(e)   Because Christ established the meal it is called the Lord's Supper (1 Cor. 11:20), and the table of the Lord (1 Cor. 10:21). It is described as the breaking of bread (Acts 2:42; 20:7) because Christ broke the bread (Luke 22:19; 24:30, 35). It is also called the 'eucharist' or 'thanksgiving' (1 Cor. 10:16) because Christ gave thanks when He took the cup (Matt. 26:27).

(f)   The apostle Paul received a direct revelation from the Lord Jesus Christ regarding the institution of the Lord's Supper and the importance of its continuance and repetition (1 Cor. 11:23; cf. Gal. 1:12; 2:2).

(g) We are not surprised, therefore, that the Lord's Supper was a regular act of the early Church (Acts 2:42); they used to assemble on the first day of the week for the breaking of bread (Acts 20:7).

3. By means of the Lord's Supper Christians remember Christ's sacrifice continually.

(a) The Lord's Supper sets forth Christ's death for us (1 Cor. 11:26).

(b) The purpose is that we should recall to mind Christ's sufferings on our behalf (Luke 22:19; 1 Cor. 11:24, 25).

(c) It is a remembrance, or a memorial, meal (1 Cor. 11:23-25).

4. By means of the Lord's Supper Christians acknowledge their sharing in the benefits of Christ's death.

(a) The Lord's Supper declares that the new covenant that God promised has been established through the saving work of His Son (1 Cor. 11:25).

(b) It reminds us of our sharing by faith in the benefits of His death (John 6:53, 63; 1 Cor. 10:16).

(c) The Lord's Supper is a symbol of our sharing or partaking of Christ (1 Cor. 10:17).

5. In the Lord's Supper Christians have fellowship with Christ and with other Christians.

(a) The Lord's Supper is an act of communion with Christ (1 Cor. 10:16).

(b) Christians, therefore, who take part in the Lord's Supper should be in uncompromised fellowship with the Lord Jesus Christ (1 Cor. 10:21).

(c) The Lord's Supper is an act of fellowship with other Christians: it is the time when Christians 'come together' (1 Cor. 11:17, 18, 20, 33, 34; 1 Cor. 10:17; Acts 20:7).

(d) The Lord's Supper expresses the union of Christians with one another (1 Cor. 10:17; 12:13).

(e) The fellowship which believers have with the Lord Jesus Christ in the Lord's Supper is a pledge of the fulfilled fellowship they will have in the kingdom of God (Mark 14:25; Luke 22:16).

6.   In the Lord's Supper Christians make their thanksgiving to God.

(a)   The Lord's Supper is a reminder of the death of Christ to bring forth our thanksgiving (1 Cor. 11:24, 25).

(b)   We are to give thanks for the bread and wine as Christ did, remembering that they are symbols of His broken body and His outpoured blood (1 Cor. 11:23, 24).

(c)   Thus the Lord's Supper is the particular time when we offer our thanksgiving to God for Christ and His redeeming work (1 Cor. 10:16).

(d)   Being more aware of God's mercies towards us at the Lord's Supper than at any other time, the sacrifice of thanksgiving should include the offering of ourselves to God (Rom. 12:1).

(e)   Christians who take part in the Lord's Supper should be willing to dedicate themselves completely to Christ (1 Cor. 10:21).

(f)   To take part properly in the Lord's Supper we need to have done with our old kind of life and to be living to the full our new life in Christ (1 Cor. 5:7, 8): renewed dedication of ourselves to this end is part of our thanksgiving.

7.   The Lord's Supper is a tremendous help to the spiritual life of Christians.

(a)   The Lord's Supper strengthens our faith and refreshes our souls – this fact is true every time we consider the love of God to us (Rom. 8:35-39; 1 John 3:1-3).

(b)   At the Lord's Supper we may feed spiritually upon Christ (John 6:32, 33, 35, 50, 51): those who rightly receive the bread and the wine, by living faith, receive Christ and the benefits of His death (1 Cor. 10:16).

8.   Unfortunately, it is possible for Christians to take part in the Lord's Supper unworthily.

(a)   The Lord's Supper needs to be entered upon with care (1 Cor. 11:27).

(b)   Christians should examine their lives before they eat their share of the bread and drink of the cup (1 Cor. 11:28).

9.   The Lord's Supper is to be continued until Christ returns.
(a)   The Lord's Supper looks forward to our Lord Jesus Christ's return (1 Cor. 11:26).
(b)   The Lord's Supper will no longer be necessary when He returns (1 Cor. 11:26).

---

38. THE CHURCH

Question: **What is the Church of Christ?**

Answer: **The Church consists of those of every race, every land and every age who have been chosen by God the Father, purchased by Christ's blood and sanctified by the Holy Spirit.**

1.   The descriptions the Bible gives of the Church.
(a)   God's very own people (2 Cor. 6:14-18; Eph. 2:19; 4:12; Rev. 21:2, 3).
(b)   The new and true Israel, established in Christ (Gal. 3:29; 6:16; 1 Pet. 2: 9, 10).
(c)   The company of those whom the Lord has called to Himself (Acts 2:39).
(d)   Those who are 'in Christ' (Rom. 8:1; 16:7; Phil. 1:1).
(e)   The company of those everywhere who call upon the name of our Lord Jesus Christ (1 Cor. 1:2).
(f)   The company of those who believe (Acts 4:32).
(g)   God's household, and the family of believers (Gal. 6:10; 1 Tim. 3:15; Heb. 10:21).
(h)   God's building (1 Cor. 3:10).
(i)   God's temple (1 Cor. 3:16, 17), the dwelling in which God lives by His Spirit (Eph. 2:22).
(j)   Christ's flock (John 10:11, 16; Acts 20:28; Heb. 13:20).
(k)   The body of Christ (1 Cor. 12:14-27; Eph. 1:22, 23; 5:29, 30; Col. 1:24).
(l)   The bride of Christ (Eph. 5:21-33; Rev. 21:2, 9; 22:17).

2. **The members of the Church are chosen by God the Father.**

(a) They were chosen in Christ before the creation of the world (Eph. 1:4).

(b) In love God predestined them to be adopted into His own family through Jesus Christ (Eph. 1:5).

(c) As God's elect, they become members of that people for whom the Lord Jesus gave Himself that they might be His very own (Tit. 1:1; 2:13,14).

(d) The Church is made up of those who have been called by God out of darkness into His marvellous light (Rom. 1:5, 6; 2 Tim. 1:9; 1 Pet. 2:9, 10).

3. **The members of the Church are cleansed from sin through Christ's blood.**

(a) The Church was bought by the blood of Christ (Acts 20:28; Eph.5:25; Heb. 9:12).

(b) Christ loved the Church and gave Himself up for her, that she might be cleansed and sanctified (1 Cor. 6:11; Eph. 5:25-27).

(c) Christ gave Himself to redeem her members from all wickedness (Tit. 2:14).

(d) Thus the Church is made up of those who were once alienated from God by sin but have been brought near to Him through the blood of Christ (Eph. 2:11-13).

(e) They are members of the Church through the blood of the new and eternal covenant (Heb. 13:20).

4. **The members of the Church are sanctified by the Holy Spirit who lives within them to this end.**

(a) Members of Christ's Church were chosen that they should be holy and blameless in God's sight (Eph. 1:4), conformed to the likeness of God's Son (Rom. 8:29), and purified (Tit. 2:14).

(b) This work of sanctification is the Holy Spirit's, that He unceasingly performs throughout the Christian's life (Phil. 1:6; 1 Thess. 4:7, 8; 1 Pet. 1:2).

(c) Thus the Church is the company of those who have received the Holy Spirit through faith in the Lord Jesus Christ (Acts 11:17; Rom. 8:9), and have been born again of God's Spirit (John 3:5-8).

5. **Some of the conclusions the Bible draws for us.**

(a) The Church belongs to God - it is His household (Gal. 1:13; 1 Tim. 3:15).

(b) God alone knows exactly who are the true members of the Church (2 Tim. 2:19).

(c) The sole right of adding new members to the Church is the Lord's (Acts 2:47).

(d) The Church is made up of those of every race who have been brought together in Christ, to become a dwelling in which God lives by His Spirit (Eph. 2:11-22; Rev. 5:9, 10).

(e) Thus the Church of Christ ignores all divisions of race or social distinctions, making all its members one (1 Cor. 12:13).

---

39. BECOMING A MEMBER OF THE CHURCH

Question: How do we become members of the Church?

Answer: **Through the new birth by living faith in Jesus Christ.**

1. **Jesus Christ is the foundation of the Church.**

(a) No one can lay any other foundation than the one already laid, which is Jesus Christ (1 Cor. 3:11).

(b) The Church is built upon Him, even though He is the stone the builders rejected (Acts 4:11, 12; Eph. 2:20; 1 Pet. 2:6-8).

2. **Living faith in Christ, therefore, is essential.**

(a) It is by coming to Him, the living foundation stone of the Church, that we become part of God's spiritual building - the Church (1 Pet. 2:4, 5).

(b) As we believe that Jesus is the Son of God and confess Him as Lord, through the help of the Holy Spirit, we become members of the Church of Christ (Matt. 16:16-18; John 20:31; 1 Cor. 12:3).

(c) Those who thus hear God's call to become members of Christ's Church do so by means of the Word of God and the work of the Holy Spirit (John 3:8; Acts 16:14; 1 Cor. 4:15; 1 Pet. 1:23).

3.   Such living faith means that the new birth has taken place.

(a)   We become members of the Church by new birth (John 3:5-8).

(b)   We belong to Christ and His Church through our possession of the Holy Spirit (Rom. 8:9).

(c)   All believers are brought into the one Body of Christ – the Church – by the same Holy Spirit (1 Cor. 12:13).

4.   The Church of Christ is made up, therefore, of those who have a personal relationship to Christ.

(a)   They know Him (Phil. 3:10; 2 Pet. 3:18).

(b)   He is their Shepherd (John 10:14; 1 Pet. 2:25; 5:4).

(c)   As members of His Body, they have a living relationship to Him, the Head (John 15:5; Eph. 4:11-16).

---

40. BELONGING TO THE CHURCH

Question: What does belonging to the Church of Christ involve?

Answer: It involves, first and foremost, obedience to Christ's control, and the recognition in practice of the implications of the relationship we have towards all other members of the Church fellowship. Those implications include caring for one another, submitting to necessary discipline, maintaining spiritual unity, and offering together spiritual sacrifices acceptable to God through Jesus Christ.

1.   Membership of the Church of Christ involves, first and foremost, obedience to Christ's control.

(a)   The Church is His Body (Eph. 1:23).

(b)   The Church, therefore, is to be subject to Christ in everything (Eph. 4:15, 16; 5:24).

(c)   Christ is to be set apart in the heart as Lord (1 Pet. 3:15).

(d)   The love of the members of the Church for Christ, the Head, is seen in their obedience to His commandments (John 14:15); for example, in their zeal for good works (Matt. 5:16, compared with Tit. 2:14).

2. **Membership of the Church of Christ involves recognizing the relationship we have to all other Christians.**

(a) We are members of the same Body (1 Cor. 12:4-27; Eph. 1:22, 23; 5:30; Col. 1:24); and, therefore, individually members one of another (Rom. 12:4, 5).

(b) We constitute together God's people (1 Pet. 2:9, 10).

(c) We belong to the same family or household (Gal. 6:10; Heb. 10:21).

(d) We are sheep of the same flock (Acts 20:28, 29; Heb. 13:20).

(e) We are citizens of the same heavenly kingdom (Phil. 3:20; Heb. 11:16; 12:28; Rev. 21:2, 3).

(f) We are together a chosen people, a royal priesthood and a holy nation (1 Pet. 2:9, 10).

3. **Membership of the Church of Christ involves fulfilling the implications of this relationship that we have with all other Christians.**

(a) By living in fellowship (Acts 2:42-47; Heb. 10:24, 25; 1 John 1:3, 7; 2:19).

(b) By caring for one another (1 Cor. 12:7; Gal. 6:10; 1 Pet. 5:2; 1 John 3:16-18).

(c) By accepting the family discipline (1 Cor. 5:12, 13; 6:4; Eph. 5:4; Tit. 3:10; Heb. 13:17).

(d) By maintaining spiritual unity (Eph. 4:2, 3; Phil. 2:1, 2).

(e) By offering together the spiritual sacrifices of our spiritual priesthood which are acceptable to God through Jesus Christ (1 Pet. 2:5): for example, praise (Heb. 13:15), thanksgiving (Ps. 50:14; 107:22), prayer (Ps. 141:2), the offering of our bodies to Him (Rom. 12:1), doing good and sharing what we have with others (Heb. 13:16).

41. THE WORK AND DESTINY OF THE CHURCH

Question: **What is the work of the Church? And what is going to happen to the Church?**

Answer: **The work of the Church –in brief – is to proclaim the gospel of Christ, making disciples of all who believe, until, as the bride of Christ, she is presented to Christ at His return.**

1. **The work of the Church is to proclaim the gospel of Christ (Matthew 28:18-20; Acts 1:8).**

(a) Christians are to declare the praises of Him who has called them out of darkness into His wonderful light – principally by the change that the gospel has brought into their lives (1 Pet. 2:9; 3:15).

(b) The main function of the Church is testimony to Jesus Christ (John 15:27; Acts 4:33; 10:42; Rev. 11:7; 12:11, 17).

(c) The purpose the Lord Jesus Christ had for the Church from the beginning was the preaching of repentance and forgiveness of sins in His name to all nations (Luke 24:47; Mark 16:15; Acts 1:8).

2. **The work of the Church is to make disciples of all who believe the gospel.**

(a) Believers are to be baptized in the name of the Father, and of the Son, and of the Holy Spirit (Matt. 28:19).

(b) They are to be taught to obey all that the Lord Jesus Christ has commanded (Matt. 28:20).

(c) They are to be taught all that God has revealed to us in His Son, and brought to full maturity as members of Christ's Body, the Church (Col. 1:28).

3. **The end always in view is the return of Christ and the presentation of the Church to Him as His bride.**

(a) No matter how dark the days may be, and how apparently hopeless the Church's situation may appear, she will triumph (Matt. 16:18).

(b)   Christ loves the Church, and He will demonstrate that love before the enemies of the Church (Rev. 3:9; compare 2 Thess. 1:5-10).

(c)   The Church will be gathered from every part of the earth, with no member missed at Christ's return (Matt. 24:31; Mark 13:27; Luke 21:27, 28).

(d)   Her final destiny is to be presented to Christ as a radiant Church, without any blemish (Eph. 5:27), His glorious bride (2 Cor. 11: 2; Rev. 21:2).

---

42.   MEMBERSHIP OF A LOCAL CHURCH

Question: Why belong to a church?

Answer: The New Testament takes it for granted that every Christian will join together with other Christians in the membership of a local congregation for only then can the implications of common membership of the Church of Christ find expression - that is to say, in fellowship, mutual care, submission to necessary discipline, the maintenance of spiritual unity, and the offering together of spiritual sacrifices acceptable to God - and the work of the Church be effectively carried out - that is to say, in the proclamation of the gospel and the making of disciples in a particular area.

1.   The New Testament gives an essential place to the local church in the life of the Christian.

(a)   The local church is not to be despised by the Christian (1 Cor. 11:22).

(b)   The New Testament refers to patterns of behaviour in the church, meaning the local church (1 Cor. 14:19, 28, 35); and the directions given by the apostles were given in the first place to churches (1 Cor. 16:1).

c)   As the work of evangelism progressed in the first century Christians were gathered together as soon as possible into churches (Acts 13:1; 14:23; 15:41; 20:17; Rev. 1:11).

(d) Usually, wherever Christians were to be found, elders were ordained (Acts 14:21-23), and a local church situation was incomplete where elders had not been appointed (Tit. 1:5).

(e) Christians were assumed to be in such a close relationship together that they acknowledged certain individuals as leaders (Heb. 13:7), and the latter knew themselves to be under-shepherds of the local company of Christians (Acts 20:28; 1 Pet. 5:2).

(f) The New Testament takes it for granted that Christians living in the same locality will have regular fellowship, assembling together as a company of believers (1 Cor. 1:2; 14:23; 2 Cor. 1:1; 1 Tim. 3:15).

(g) Christians are instructed not to neglect meeting together (Heb. 10:25).

(h) The early Christians were in such an established relationship with one another that they could speak of some who 'went out from us' who 'did not really belong to us' (1 John 2:19).

(i) Christians are to strive to excel in building up the local church (1 Cor. 14:12).

(j) The instinctive act of Paul after his conversion was to identify himself with the Christians in Damascus, and then with those at Jerusalem on his arrival there (Acts 9:19, 26).

2. The descriptions the Bible gives of the Church as a whole demand that Christians meet together as ordered congregations in their localities.

(a) The flock of God gathers together under the leadership of the under-shepherds whom the Chief Shepherd, Christ, has appointed (Heb. 13:20; 1 Pet. 2:25; 5:2-4).

(b) The members of the body of Christ are members of one another and are intended, therefore, to be in the closest possible association together (1 Cor. 12:24-27).

(c) The picture of the church as the family of believers implies a close relationship (Gal. 6:10).

(d) A brick is only a building as it is together with other bricks, properly joined to them: so too with the Christian (1 Pet. 2:4, 5).

3.   **To belong to a church is a practical demonstration of the recognition of our relationship in Christ to our fellow-believers.**

4.   **It enables us to live in fellowship.**

(a)   The logical consequence of receiving the Holy Spirit is to want to live in fellowship with other Christians (Rom. 8:9; Phil. 2:1, 2).

(b)   Constant fellowship is possible through the local church as in no other way (Acts 2:42).

(c)   The fellowship is to be so close that mutual encouragement can be given both to love and to do good works (Heb. 3:13; 10:24).

5.   **It enables us to fulfil Christ's command to remember His death and its significance by means of the Lord's Supper.**

(a)   To do this together is a vital part of Christian fellowship (Acts 2:42; 1 Cor. 10:16, 17).

(b)   The early Christians gathered together on the Lord's Day to break bread in remembrance of Christ's death (Acts 20:7).

(c)   Christians need to come together regularly in the local church for the Lord's Supper (1 Cor. 11:23-34).

6.   **It enables us to get to know our fellow-believers and thus to care for one another.**

(a)   We may do good effectively to the family of believers only as we know who they are by coming together in the fellowship of the local church (Gal. 6:10).

(b)   By close association with one another Christian love is able to find the positive and practical expression it needs (John 13:35).

(c)   Through church membership we are able to strengthen one another (Luke 22:32), restore one another when fallen (Gal. 6:1), and carry each other's burdens (Gal. 6:2).

(d)   By means of the local church the exercise of spiritual gifts for the benefit of one another is made possible (1 Cor. 12:14-28).

7. **It shows our acceptance of the family discipline of the Church, expressed, as it can only be, through the local church.**

(a) The Lord Jesus Christ taught that the local church is essential for maintaining the right kind of discipline amongst God's people (Matt. 18:15-20).

(b) It is taken for granted in the New Testament that all Christians will be so committed to a local church that they will be within the discipline of that church (1 Thess. 5:12; 1 Tim. 5:17; Heb. 13:17; 1 Pet. 5:1-5).

(c) Christians are to be in such an association of membership together that they can discipline members who bring dishonour to Christ (1 Cor. 5:1-13).

8. **It is a practical expression of spiritual unity.**

(a) Christians feel within themselves the desire to express the oneness they know and experience in Jesus Christ (Gal. 3:28).

(b) No effort of love or of tolerance is to be spared to preserve the unity that the Spirit gives (Eph. 4:2, 3).

(c) The common life Christians have in Christ brings a common care for unity (Phil. 2:1, 2).

9. **It enables us to offer regularly the corporate spiritual sacrifices that honour God.**

(a) By means of the local church, Christians make their praise and prayers corporate (Acts 2:42, 47; 12:5, 12; Heb. 13:15).

(b) Through the knowledge Christians have of one another's needs, associated as they are in the local church, they are able to do good to one another and to share what they have with others (Heb. 13:16).

(c) They are able to fulfil their financial obligations too to the work of Christ's Church (1 Cor. 16:2; Phil. 4:14-19).

10. **It is the instrument God uses to proclaim the gospel of Christ in an area.**

(a) The testimony of the corporate life of a local church should be such a powerful influence for evangelism that the Lord adds continually to the number of His people (Acts 2:42-47).

(b)   The local church is the key instrument for the Word of the Lord to ring out to people everywhere (1 Thess. 1:1, 8).

11.   It is the provision God has made for the instruction of believers that they should become mature disciples.

(a)   Christians are to be taught all that the Lord Jesus Christ requires of His disciples (Matt. 28:19): to this end God gives to local churches pastors and teachers, so that Christians may be fed and built up by the Word of God (Acts 20:28; Eph. 4:11-16; 1 Pet. 2:2; 5:2).

(b)   The most important part of the elders' work is the preaching and teaching of the Word of God (1 Tim. 5:17).

(c)   Christians are expected to be in a situation where they will be contributing to the financial support of those who give themselves to preaching and teaching (Gal. 6:6; 1 Tim. 5:17, 18).

(d)   The local church, faithfully taught, is one means God uses to preserve the pure teaching and preaching of the gospel (2 Tim. 2:2).

---

43. THE DEVIL

Question: What do we know about the devil?

Answer: The devil is the great enemy of God and men and women, the opposer of all that is good and the promoter of all that is evil. He has been defeated already by Christ's death and resurrection, and this defeat will be complete and clear to all at the end of this present age.

1.   The devil's history.

(a)   He is one of the fallen angels exalted in rank and power above all the rest (Jude 6; 2 Pet. 2:4).

(b)   He fell from the truth in which he once stood (John 8:44).

(c)   He is represented as a star fallen from the sky to the earth (Rev. 9:1).

(d)   He sinned, probably by reason of pride (1 Tim. 3:6).

(e)   From the time of his first rebellion against God, the devil has sinned continuously (2 Pet. 2:4; 1 John 3:8).

2.   He is called by many names.

(a)   He is called Satan (Matt. 16:23; Luke 22:31; Rev. 12:9; 20:2).

(b)   He is the evil one (1 John 2:13, 14; 3:12; 5:18).

(c)   He is the ruler of the kingdom of the air, the spirit who is now at work in those who are disobedient to God (Eph. 2:2).

(d)   He is the prince of the demons (Matt. 9:34; 12:24).

(e)   He is the god of this age (2 Cor. 4:4).

(f)   He is called Beelzebub (Matt. 12:24, 27; Luke 11:15, 18, 19).

(g)   He is the tempter (Matt. 4:3; 1 Thess. 3:5).

(h)   He is called the ancient serpent (Rev. 12:9).

(i)   He is called the dragon (Rev. 12:3, 4, 7, 9, 13, 16, 17; 20:2).

3.   The devil's power.

(a)   He has great power: he showed Christ all the kingdoms of the world in a moment of time (Matt. 4:8; Luke 4:5).

(b)   All who are without Christ and the new birth are under the control of the devil and his agents (Eph. 6:12; 1 John 5:19)— to be outside of the Church of Christ is to belong to Satan (John 8:44; 1 Cor. 5:5; 1 Tim. 1:20),

(c)   The whole world is under his control (1 John 5:19), for he is its prince or ruler (John 12:31; 14:30; 16:11; 2 Cor. 4:4; Eph. 2:2; 6:12).

(d)   Men and women have the devil as their father, and they are his children (John 8:44; 1 John 3:10).

(e)   To be in his power is to be spiritually blind, and in spiritual darkness (Acts 26:18).

(f)   He is pictured as a strong man, whose house contains men and women as his possessions.   He must be overpowered and bound before his house can be broken into (Matt. 12:29; Mark 3:27; Luke 11:21, 22).

(g)   His power is such that Christ prayed against him on behalf of His disciples (John 17:15).

4. **Some of the devil's characteristics.**

(a) He is the enemy of everything that is right, full of all kinds of deceit and trickery, and his principal activity is perverting the right ways of the Lord (Acts 13:10).

(b) He is evil (Matt. 6:13; John 17:15; 1 John 2:13, 14; 3:12; 5:18, 19).

(c) He is a liar, the father of lies, and there is no truth in him (John 8:44).

(d) He is crafty, cunning and deceitful (Gen. 3:1; 2 Cor. 11:3, 4; Eph. 6:11).

(e) He is presumptuous and conceited (Matt. 4:5, 6; 1 Tim. 3:6).

(f) He is malicious: he makes false accusations and charges against God's people (Job 1:6-12; 2:4; Zech. 3:1; Rev. 12:9-11).

(g) He is fierce and cruel (Luke 8:29; 9:39, 42): he prowls around like a roaring lion (1 Pet. 5:8).

(h) He is a murderer (John 8:44; 1 John 3:12).

(i) His activity is continuous (Rev. 12:10).

5. **His activity in general.**

(a) Sin is his characteristic activity (1 John 3:8): he was the originator of the fall (Gen. 3:1, 6, 13-15).

(b) He is active everywhere (Job 1:7; 2:2).

(c) He masquerades as an angel of light (2 Cor. 11:14), and so too do his agents (2 Cor. 11:15).

(d) He causes false beliefs and practices to arise (1 Tim. 5:15): every anti-Christian movement and spirit is a result of his activity (2 Thess. 2:9).

(e) He encourages men and women in every sort of evil and deceit (2 Thess. 2:10; Rev. 3:9).

(f) He engineers counterfeit miracles, signs and wonders, and every sort of evil that deceives those who are perishing (2 Thess. 2:9, 10; Rev. 16:14).

(g) He misapplies the Scriptures to achieve his own wicked ends (Matt. 4:6).

(h) Through depending upon human wisdom rather than divine, men and women can become his agents without being aware of the fact (Matt. 16:23; Mark 8:33): the devil prompted Judas Iscariot to betray Jesus (John 13:2).

(i)   He opposes God's work (Zech. 3:1; Matt. 13:38, 39; 1 Thess. 2:18), especially the preaching of the gospel (Matt. 13:19; Mark 4:15; Luke 8:12; 2 Cor. 4:4).

6.   His attacks upon Christians.

(a)   He does battle against all who obey God's commandments and confess that they belong to Jesus (Luke 22:31; 1 Pet. 5:8, 9; Rev. 12:17).

(b)   He is always looking for opportunities to cause trouble to Christians (Eph. 6:11; 1 Tim. 3:7; Jas. 4:7; Rev. 12:10).

(c)   He tries to gain the upper hand over believers (2 Cor. 2:11): he tells of the pleasures of sin but not of its consequences (Gen. 3:4, 5); he tells half-truths for the truth (Gen. 3:5).

(d)   He tries to tempt by any means possible, trying one temptation after another (Matt. 4:1-10; Mark 1:13; Luke 4:2, 13).

(e)   He frequently tempts through our human appetites (Gen. 3:1-6; Matt. 4:2, 3; Luke 4:2, 3; 1 Cor. 7:5).

(f)   He tempts us to use spiritual powers selfishly (Matt. 4:3; Luke 4:3), and to presume upon God's care (Matt. 4:5,6; Luke 4:9-11).

(g)   He encourages doubts and questionings, together with compromise (Gen. 3:1, 4; Matt. 4: 8, 9; Luke 4:5-7).

(h)   He tempts us through our lack of self-control (1 Cor. 7:5).

(i)   He seeks to bewitch us so that we take our eyes off our Lord Jesus Christ and His Cross (2 Cor. 11:14; Gal. 3:1).

(j)   He would encourage us in evil – even to lie to the Holy Spirit (Acts 5:3).

(k)   He inspires the persecution of Christians (Rev. 2:10, 13).

7.   Christ's conquest of the devil at the Cross.

(a)   The devil had no hold on Christ (John 14:30); his power and authority are inferior to those of Christ (Luke 11:17-22).

(b)   Christ shared in our humanity so that by death He might destroy him who had the power of death, that is, the devil (Heb. 2:14; 1 John 3:8).

(c)   Christ's conflict with the devil came to a head at the Cross: He disarmed the devil and all his powers, and made a public spectacle of them at His resurrection, triumphing over them by the Cross (John 12:31; 16:11; Col. 2:15; Heb. 2:14; 1 John 3:8).

(d) So far as Christ is concerned, the devil is a conquered enemy (Luke 10:18).

(e) The Lord Jesus' people enter into His victory over the devil (Rom. 16:20).

8. The devil's limits.

(a) The devil's power has been given to him, and can, therefore, be taken away from him by God (Luke 4:6): he knows his time is short (Rev. 12:12).

(b) He is allowed liberty, within bounds, to test and tempt Christians (Job 1:1-12; 2:1-6; Luke 22:31, 32; 2 Cor. 10:13).

(c) The Father is able to protect from the evil one those whom He has given to His Son out of the world (John 17:15).

(d) His activity can even be used by God to accomplish some good purpose (1 Cor. 5:5; 2 Cor. 12:7).

9. The devil's end.

(a) His final defeat will take place at the last day, and his ultimate condemnation and punishment are sure at the judgment of that day (Jude 6; Rev. 20:10).

(b) He is to be crushed by God under our feet (Rom. 16:20).

(c) Eternal fire is prepared for the devil and his angels at the final judgment (Matt. 25:41).

10. Meanwhile, the devil is to be overcome by Christians.

(a) Christians are not to be ignorant of his schemes (2 Cor. 2:11).

(b) They are dependent upon Christ's protection and activity on their behalf for deliverance from the devil (Luke 22:31, 32; Rom. 8:34; Heb. 7:25).

(c) The devil is overcome by the blood of the Lamb and by the testimony of Christians to Jesus (Rev. 12:11).

(d) As Christians resist the devil he will flee from them (Jas. 4:7).

(e) The spiritual armour God provides for Christians is sufficient to enable them to stand against the devil's wiles (Eph. 6:11). Dressed in this complete armour, Christians can withstand successfully all his attacks (Eph. 6:13).

44. THE RETURN OF CHRIST

Question: Will Christ come again?

Answer: Christ will come again, as promised, at a time not told us, in the same way as He was seen to return to heaven.

1.   Christ's second coming is clearly promised in the Bible.

(a)   The Lord Jesus Christ Himself promised, 'I will come back' (Matt. 25:31; John 14:3).

(b)   His second coming is promised by the Old Testament prophets (Dan. 7:13, 14; Zech. 14:5).

(c)   The apostles bore witness to Christ's second coming (Acts 3:20).

(d)   Peter declares that Christ will be revealed (1 Pet. 1:13).

(e)   John declares that Christ will appear and Christians will see Him as He is (1 John 3:2).

(f)   Paul preached with urgency in view of the appearing of our Lord Jesus Christ yet to come (1 Tim. 6:14).

(g)   The Lord's Supper is intended to be a perpetual reminder of the Lord's second coming for it is an 'interim' measure 'until he comes' (1 Cor. 11:26).

(h)   A common greeting amongst the early Christians seems to have been 'Maranatha' - 'Come, O Lord!' (1 Cor. 16:22).

2.   Signs of Christ's coming again are indicated in the Bible.

(a)   The second coming of Christ will be preceded by anguish and perplexity among the nations (Luke 21:25).

(b)   There will be signs in sun and moon and stars (Matt. 24:29; Luke 21:25).

(c)   The second coming will be preceded by concern and fear over coming events: people will faint from terror, apprehensive of what is coming on the world (Luke 21:26).

(d)   The second coming will be preceded by the appearance of many antichrists (1 John 2:18).

(e)   Many will abandon the faith and false teaching will be on the increase (1 Tim. 4:1-3).

3.   **The precise time of Christ's second coming is not stated.**

(a)   It is natural for us to want to know the timing of everything (Mark 13:4).

(b)   But no one knows the day or the hour of Christ's second coming, except the Father (Matt. 24:36; Mark 13:32).

(c)   We are not intended to know the exact time (Acts 1:6, 7).

(d)   Christ will be sent by the Father at the appointed time (Acts 3:20, 21).

(e)   Christ's coming will be at the unexpected moment (Matt. 24:44; Luke 12:40) - in the twinkling of an eye (1 Cor. 15:51-52).

(f)   His coming will be sudden (Mark 13:36) - like lightning (Matt. 24:27) or a thief in the night (1 Thess. 5:2; 2 Pet. 3:10; Rev. 16:15).

(g)   The world will be totally unprepared for the second coming of Christ even as it was unprepared for the coming of the flood in the time of Noah (Matt. 24:38).

(h)   There is no delay regarding the Lord's coming (Heb. 10:37): the only reason for any appearance of delay in the Lord's return is God's patience, in that He does not want anyone to perish, but everyone to come to repentance (2 Pet. 3:9).

(i)   The coming of the Lord Jesus approaches with the passing of each day (Heb. 10:25).

(j)   His coming will be soon (Rev. 22:7, 12, 20).

(k)   His coming is always to be considered as being at hand (Rom. 13:12; 1 Pet. 4:7).

4.   **We are told something of the manner in which Christ will come.**

(a)   He will come in the same way as He was seen to go into heaven (Acts 1:9-11).

(b)   He will come from heaven (Acts 3:21; Phil. 3:20; 1 Thess. 1:10; 4:16).

(c)   He will come visibly (Matt. 24:30; Mark 13:26; 14:62; 1 John 3:2; Rev. 1:7).

(d)   He will come openly (Matt. 24:27), and personally (Acts 1:11) - His coming will mean His presence after His absence (John 14:2, 3).

(e) He will come on the clouds of heaven with power and great glory (Matt. 24:30; 26:64; Rev. 1:7) – the glory of His Father (Matt. 16:27).

(f) He will come with His angels (Matt. 16:27; 25:31; Mark 8:38; 2 Thess. 1:7), and with all those who belong to Him, in blazing fire (1 Thess. 3:13; 2 Thess. 1:7).

5. Christ's second coming should continually influence Christians in their character and conduct.

(a) We are to set our hopes fully on the grace that will be given us when the Lord Jesus Christ returns (1 Pet. 1:13).

(b) We are to anticipate the sight of the Lord Jesus Christ (1 Pet. 1:8).

(c) We are to long for His appearing (2 Tim. 4:8), eagerly awaiting it (1 Cor. 1:7; Phil. 3:20; 1 Thess. 1:10; Tit. 2:13) and praying for it (Rev. 22:20).

(d) Having this hope before us, we will find ourselves stimulated to pursue purity and holiness (1 Thess. 3:13; 2 Pet. 3:11, 12; 1 John 3:3).

(e) Our conduct will be influenced and regulated by this truth as it is ever before us (1 Pet. 4:7-11).

(f) We will use the apparent 'delay' in the Lord's return to bring about people's salvation by the preaching of the gospel (2 Pet. 3:15), at the same time speeding His coming by this activity (2 Pet. 3:12).

(g) We will aim at being alert and ready for the Lord Jesus when He comes (Matt. 24:42; 25:5, 6; Mark 13:33, 35-37; Luke 12:40; 21:36).

(h) We will live remembering that time is short (1 Cor. 7:29).

(i) We need constant reminding of Christ's coming (Rev. 22:7, 12, 20).

6. Unbelievers find the Second Coming a cause for scoffing.

(a) Unbelievers often scoff at Christ's coming (2 Pet. 3:3, 4).

(b) People, who prefer to follow their own evil desires, scoff at the promise of Christ's coming, deliberately ignoring the Word of God (2 Pet. 3:3-7).

(c)   Unbelievers will, nevertheless, be overtaken and surprised by the reality of the Lord's second coming (Matt. 24:37-39; 1 Thess. 5:1, 2; 2 Pet. 3:10).

---

45. THE CONSEQUENCES OF CHRIST'S RETURN

Question: What will happen when Christ returns?

Answer: Our Lord Jesus Christ's glory will be seen, and the resurrection of the dead and the transformation of all believers will take place.   The judgment will follow, with the division of all men and women, either to be with Christ forever or to suffer the punishment of eternal destruction and exclusion from the presence of the Lord.   The end of all things as we know them will come, and the Father will be glorified in it all.

1.   Christ's glory will be seen.
(a)   The second coming will be an occasion of glory for Christ (Matt. 25:31).
(b)   Everyone will see Him (Mark 13:26; Rev. 1:7).
(c)   He will be seen sitting at the right hand of the Mighty One, and coming on the clouds of heaven (Mark 14:62).
(d)   His glory will be revealed (1 Pet. 4:13).
(e)   He will be glorified in His own people and marvelled at among all believers (2 Thess. 1:10).

2.   The resurrection of the dead will take place, and the transformation of all believers.
(a)   Christ's grace will be revealed to believers in a manner unknown before (1 Pet. 1:13).
(b)   The completeness of the Christian's salvation will be revealed (Heb. 9:28; 1 Pet. 1:5).
(c)   A most important aspect of this completeness will be the resurrection of the dead (1 Cor. 15:23, 51-54).
(d)   Christians will be made like Christ (1 John 3:2): at His coming the Lord Jesus Christ will change our lowly bodies to be like

His glorious body, by the power that enables Him to bring everything under His control (Phil. 3:21).

3.   Following the resurrection of the dead, believers will be gathered together.

(a)   At His coming Christ will gather together all believers (Matt. 24:31; 1 Thess. 2:19; 3:13; 4:15-17; 5:23; 1 John 2:28).

(b)   Christ will send out the angels and gather His elect from the ends of the earth to the ends of the heavens (Mark 13:27).

(c)   Christ will gather His people to Himself (2 Thess. 2:1) - both those who had died before His coming and those alive on earth at the time (John 14:2, 3; 1 Thess. 4:16, 17).

(d)   The gathering together of all His people is likened to the gathering in of the harvest (Rev. 14:14-16).

4.   Then the judgment will be held.

(a)   Every man and woman will acknowledge Christ as Lord (Phil. 2:9-11) and therefore as the supreme judge (Acts 17:31).

(b)   The second coming will be a time of reckoning (Luke 12:40-48).

(c)   Christ will be ashamed of those who have been ashamed of Him and of His words (Mark 8:38).

(d)   He will bring to light, at His coming, the things now hidden in darkness and will expose the motives of people's hearts (1 Cor. 4:5).

(e)   His coming will bring distress to some, because of the judgment He will bring (Rev. 1:7).

(f)   The Lord's coming will mean Christians having to stand before Christ the judge (2 Cor. 5:10; 1 Thess. 2:19): this giving of account to Him will not be with regard to the condemnation they deserve because of sin (Rom. 5:1; 8:1) but as to the rewards they may receive on account of faithfulness to Him (1 Cor. 3:8, 14).

5.   The final division of men and women will come after the judgment.

(a)   Men and women without the knowledge of God, and who have refused to obey the gospel of our Lord Jesus Christ, will suffer the punishment of everlasting destruction and exclusion from the presence of the Lord and from the majesty of His power (2 Thess. 1:8, 9).

(b)   The judgment of God will be executed by God's angels on unbelievers (Rev. 14:17-20).

(c)   Believers will enter into the full wonder of everlasting life and the enjoyment of God's presence forever (1 Thess. 4:17; 2 Thess. 1:10).

(d)   Christ will take believers to Himself that where He is they may be also (John 14:2, 3).

6.   **The end of all things as we now know them will take place.**

(a)   The coming of the Lord will announce the end of things as we know them on this earth (2 Pet. 3:7, 10-13).

(b)   The heavens will disappear with a loud roar, and the elements will be destroyed by fire, and the earth and everything in it will be laid bare (2 Pet 3:10).

(c)   After the dissolution of this world, a new heaven and a new earth, the home of righteousness, will be revealed (2 Pet. 3:13).

7.   **The Father will be glorified in all that happens.**

(a)   All that He ever promised long ago through His holy prophets will take place (Acts 3:21).

(b)   As all men and women are compelled to confess that Jesus Christ is Lord, that confession will have one great end - the glory of God the Father (Phil. 2:11).

(c)   After destroying all dominion, authority and power, there will come the end of all the events connected with Christ's coming, when He will hand over the kingdom to God the Father (1 Cor. 15:24).

(d)   When everything is subjected to Christ, then He Himself will be made subject to the Father who put everything under His Son (1 Cor. 15:28).

46. THE JUDGMENT

Question: **What will happen at the judgment?**

Answer: **Christ will be the Judge and all will appear before Him. The perfect justice of God and the undeniable guilt of all men and women will be plain and beyond dispute. Those justified through faith in Christ will be acquitted from the guilt of sin and will receive rewards according to their faithfulness; the unbelieving will receive their final condemnation.**

1.   The timing of the judgment.

(a)   Our Lord Jesus Christ spoke of a judgment that was still future (Matt. 12:41).

(b)   Judgment is the certainty that follows everyone after death (Heb. 9:27).

(c)   God has set a day when He will judge the world with justice by the man He has appointed, and He has given proof of this to all by raising Him from the dead (Acts 17:31; Rom. 2:16).

(d)   The judgment will take place at the coming of the Lord Jesus Christ (Matt. 25:31-46; 2 Tim. 4:1; 2 Pet. 3:7).

(e)   The judgment will be preceded by the resurrection of the dead (John 5:28, 29).

(f)   The day of judgment will be followed by the dissolution, by means of fire, of the heavens and earth that now exist, according to God's promise (2 Pet. 3:7).

2.   Christ will be the Judge.

(a)   God the Father judges no one, but has committed to the Son the task of judging all men and women (John 5:22, 27).

(b)   The Lord Jesus Christ is the One appointed by God as the Judge of the living and the dead (Acts 10:42; 2 Tim. 4:1).

(c)   The separation of the wheat from the chaff (Matt. 3:12; Luke 3:17), and the sheep from the goats (Matt. 25:32, 33) will be His responsibility.

(d)   Christ will come the second time, therefore, as Judge (Matt. 25:31-46).

3.   All will appear before God's judgment seat.

(a)   The Old Testament declares that God will bring to judgment both the righteous and the wicked (Eccl. 3:17).

(b)   Judgment will be held on all nations (Matt. 25:32; cf. Joel 3:12).

(c)   All will have to give an account to the Judge (Heb. 9:27), the great and the small (Rev. 20:12), the living and the dead (2 Tim. 4:1; 1 Pet. 4:5).

(d)   We must all stand before God's judgment seat, and give account of ourselves, so that we may each receive what is due to us for the things done while in the body, whether good or bad (Rom. 14:10, 12; 2 Cor. 5:10).

(e)   The fallen angels will also be finally judged at the judgment (2 Pet. 2:4; Jude 6).

4.   God's perfect justice will be seen.

(a)   The judgment is pictured as a harvest - there will be no doubt which is wheat and which is chaff (Joel 3:13; Matt. 3:12; Luke 3:17).

(b)   God's righteous judgment will be revealed (Rom. 2:5; 3:4-6) – the judgment will demonstrate His righteousness and justice (Ps. 98:9; Acts 17:31).

(c)   God's judgment will be a precise and just retribution (Obad. 15), perfectly related to people's ways and deeds (Hos. 12:2), and according to God's perfect records (Dan. 7:10; Rev. 20:12).

(d)   The judgment will be in proportion to the opportunities and privileges of men and women: every one to whom much has been entrusted will find much more will be asked (Luke 12:48).

(e)   The judgment will be individual and personal (Matt. 25:42-45).

(f)   God will give to each person according to what he or she has done (Rom. 2:6).

(g)   Those who have had no opportunity of knowing the law given to Moses, or the gospel, will be judged according to the law written on their hearts to which conscience bears witness (Rom. 2:12, 14, 15).

(h)   All who have had the law of Moses will be judged by it (Rom. 2:12).

(i)   Neglected opportunities of repentance and faith increase the condemnation men and women will experience at the judgment (Matt. 11:20-24; Luke 11:31, 32).

(j)   If men and women have deliberately kept on sinning after they have received the knowledge of the truth, their condemnation will be all the greater (Heb. 10:26, 27).

(k)   Although all our questions about the judgment cannot be answered now, we know that the Judge of all the earth will do right (Gen. 18:25).

5.   The guilt of all will be plain.

(a)   Account will have to be given for the words we have spoken (Matt. 12:36).

(b)   Every hidden thing, including the motives of the heart, will be exposed to God's judgment (Eccl. 12:14; 1 Cor. 4:5).

(c)   Actions will be judged (Eccl. 11:9; 12:14; Rev. 20:13) and the deeds of men and women will return upon their own heads (Obad. 15).

(d)   Unpardoned sinners cannot stand before such a judgment and deserve to live (Ps. 130:3); no one living is righteous before God (Ps. 143:2).

(e)   All will be found guilty: those without the law have perverted the light that comes from nature (Rom. 1:21-23), and those with the law have failed to keep it (Gal. 3:10-12).

(f)   No one will have anything to say in self-defence – every mouth will be silenced (Rom. 3:19).

(g)   The words of Christ will be a witness against those who have rejected Him and His teaching (John 12:48).

(h)   The judgment is a fearful prospect (Heb. 10:27).

(i)   The first part of the judgment will be the separation of those who have accepted God's way of salvation from those who have thought they could gain salvation by their own works (Matt. 25:31-33).

(j)   Those whose names are in the Lamb's book of life will escape the judgment of condemnation on account of sin (Luke 10:20; Phil. 4:3; Rev. 20:12; 21:27) because, having seen the folly of trusting in their own righteousness (Isa. 64:6), through faith in Christ, they have been made right with God (2 Cor. 5:21).

6.   Acquittal from the guilt of sin will be granted to those who have been justified by faith.

(a)   There is no condemnation for those who are justified through faith in the Lord Jesus Christ (Rom. 5:1; 8:1).

(b)   Christians have complete confidence for the day when Christ will judge all men and women (1 John 4:17); they will be unashamed before Him at His coming (1 John 2:28).

(c)   Christ will acknowledge Christians openly in the presence of the Father (Matt. 25:34-40; Rev. 3:5), presenting them blameless and holy (1 Cor. 1:8; 1 Thess. 3:13), having delivered them from the condemnation their sins deserve (Rom. 8:1, 33, 34).

(d)   The key to deliverance from this judgment, therefore, is a personal relationship to the Lord Jesus Christ (Matt. 10:32, 33; Mark 8:38; Heb. 10:29).

(e)   Salvation from the judgment that sin deserves is possible through the Lord Jesus Christ alone (1 Thess. 5:9, 10).

(f)   Having been acquitted from all guilt, Christians will join with Christ in judging the world (1 Cor. 6:2; compare Matt. 19:28; Luke 22:28-30; Rev. 20:4).

7.   Those who have refused to acknowledge God and to obey the gospel of our Lord Jesus Christ will be condemned.

(a)   Eternal judgment is a first principle, an elementary teaching, of the gospel (Acts 24:25; Heb. 6:1, 2).

(b)   The children of the evil one will be revealed and their destiny made known (Matt. 13:24-30, 36-43, 47-50).

(c)   The judgment will be a time of misery for those who have rejected the Lord Jesus Christ (2 Thess. 1:8, 9; Rev. 1:7).

(d)   Those who have rejected the truth and followed evil will experience God's wrath and eternal punishment (Rom. 2:8; Jude 15; Rev. 20:15).

(e)   The punishment of evildoers will be final and complete (Matt. 13:40-42; 25:46).

(f)   No one will be able to resist the judgment (Matt. 3:12; Luke 3:17; cf. Amos 9:1-4).

8.   Christians will he rewarded by Christ.

(a)   To those who by persistence in doing good seek glory, honour and immortality, Christ will give eternal life (Rom. 2:7; Jude 24; Rev. 20:12, 15).

(b)   He will come as the righteous Judge, judging His people by the gospel - the law that gives freedom (Jas. 2:12) - that He may reward them for their faithfulness (Luke 19:17; 2 Tim. 4:8; Jas. 1:12).

(c)   Every Christian's service will be subject to scrutiny and examination (1 Cor. 3:9-14): there will be rewards for faithful service (1 Cor. 3:9-15; 2 Tim. 4:8; Rev. 11:18).

(d)   Christians will discover the value of the work they have done for Christ (2 Cor. 1:14; Phil. 2:16).

9.   The effect the knowledge of the coming judgment should have upon Christians.

(a)   The certainty of judgment is a great incentive to urgent preaching (2 Cor. 5:11; 2 Tim. 4:1, 2).

(b)   Unbelievers are to be warned of the future judgment (Acts 24:25): this warning provides an incentive to repentance (Acts 17:30, 31) and to faith in Christ (Isa. 28:16, 17; John 3:17, 18).

(c)   The certainty of the judgment is an incentive to holiness (2 Pet. 3:11, 14): the fact that Christians too must stand before the judgment seat of Christ is not to promote fear but the desire to please Him now, so that they may be pleasing to Him then (2 Cor. 5:9, 10).

---

47. THE RESURRECTION OF THE BODY

Question: Will our bodies be raised to life again?

Answer: All will rise from the dead, believers to the resurrection of life, and unbelievers to the resurrection of judgment.   Christ's resurrection will be the pattern of the believer's.

1.   There will be a resurrection both of the righteous and the wicked.

(a)   The resurrection of the dead will take place at the second coming of the Lord Jesus Christ (1 Cor. 15:23; 1 Thess. 4:14).

(b)   The resurrection of the dead is a fundamental part of the Christian gospel (1 Cor. 15:12, 13; Heb. 6:1, 2).

(c) Many of the details of the resurrection of the dead are not revealed to us (1 Cor. 15:51) but it will take place according to the Scriptures and by the power of God (Matt. 22:29), who gives life to the dead and brings into existence what did not exist before (Rom. 4:17).

(d) The resurrection of the dead will take place in a flash, in the twinkling of an eye (1 Cor. 15:52).

(e) All who are in their graves will hear Christ's voice and will come out of them – those who have done good will rise to live, and those who have done evil to be condemned (John 5:28, 29).

(f) For some the resurrection of the dead will mean awaking to everlasting life and for others to shame and everlasting contempt (Dan. 12:2).

(g) There will be a resurrection of both the righteous and the wicked (Acts 24:15), of those whose names are in the book of life and those whose names are not (Rev. 20:11-15).

(h) The Scriptures assure us of the resurrection of the dead (Matt. 22:29).

(i) The resurrection of the dead was anticipated and promised in the Old Testament:

    (i) It was hinted at in God's words to Moses, 'I am … the God of Abraham, the God of Isaac, and the God of Jacob' (Ex. 3:6; cf. Matt. 22:32).

    (ii) It was promised that the dead will live, and that their bodies will rise (Isa. 26:19).

    (iii) It was promised that multitudes of those who sleep in the dust of the earth will awake - some to everlasting life, and others to shame and everlasting contempt (Dan. 12:2).

(j) The Lord Jesus Christ spoke of raising up believers at the last day (John 6:39, 40,44).

(k) By His own resurrection Christ has destroyed death and has brought life and immortality to light through the gospel (2 Tim. 1:10) - the Christian confidence concerning the resurrection of the dead springs from Christ's resurrection (1 Cor. 15:12-20).

(1) The apostles proclaimed in Jesus the resurrection of the dead (Acts 4:2).

2. **Addressed as it is to Christian believers, the New Testament concentrates on the resurrection of believers.**

(a) Christ will raise up at the last day all who have believed in Him and inherited eternal life, according to the Father's will (John 6:40).

(b) By God's great mercy Christians have been born again to a living hope through the resurrection of Jesus Christ from the dead (1 Pet. 1:3) - Christians are children of the resurrection (Luke 20:36).

(c) Christ's resurrection is the pledge of believers' resurrection (2 Cor. 4:14).

(d) That there should be no resurrection of the dead is inconceivable in the light of Christ's resurrection (1 Cor. 15:12).

(e) Even as Christ was raised from the dead, so will believers be raised (1 Cor. 15:20). Just as death came into the world through a man, Adam, so now the resurrection of the dead comes through another man, our Lord Jesus Christ (1 Cor. 15:21).

(f) The precise details of the resurrection of the dead will cause some to question, almost inevitably - 'How are the dead raised? With what kind of body will they come?' (1 Cor. 15:35).

(g) The resurrection body will be something quite beyond our present experience (1 Cor. 15:35-49).

(h) Harvest provides an illustration of the kind of thing that will happen at the resurrection: the body that is sown is not the body that will be, but the two are directly related (1 Cor. 15:36-38).

(i) The resurrection body will be a real body: even as to every kind of creature and thing God gives its own body, so He has determined the particular nature of the resurrection body (1 Cor. 15:38-42).

(j) The perishable body sown in death will be raised imperishable (1 Cor. 15:42); the body sown in dishonour at death will be raised in glory (1 Cor. 15:43); the body sown in weakness will be raised in power (1 Cor. 15:43): the natural body sown in death will be raised a spiritual body (1 Cor. 15:44).

(k) Even as the physical body has borne the likeness of the earthly man - of Adam - so the spiritual body will bear the likeness of the man of heaven – our Lord Jesus Christ (1 Cor. 15:49).

(l)   Believers will all be changed at the resurrection of the dead (1 Cor. 15:51): the imperishable will replace the perishable; the immortal will replace the mortal (1 Cor. 15:53).

(m)   The dead in Christ will rise first, being given their resurrection bodies (1 Thess. 4:16); and then all living believers will be caught up together to meet the Lord in the air; and so we will be with the Lord for ever (1 Thess. 4:17).

(n)   Those still alive at Christ's coming will experience the transformation of body necessary for their entry into heaven (Phil. 3:21) - that is to say, they will be given a body identical with those raised from the dead.

(o)   The resurrection of the dead will be followed by entry into God's presence (2 Cor. 4:14): from the resurrection of the dead onwards we will be with the Lord forever (1 Thess. 4:17).

3.   The resurrection of Christ tells us something of the nature of the resurrection body of the believer.

(a)   Christians will be like Christ (1 John 3:2): Christ will change their lowly bodies so that they are made like His glorious body by the power that enables Him to bring everything under His control (Phil. 3:21).

(b)   From what we are told, we know that the resurrection body will be like Christ's resurrection body (Phil. 3:21; 1 John 3:2).

(c)   Our Lord's resurrection body seems to have been similar to His body as it was before:
  (i)   The disciples were able to clasp the Lord Jesus by the feet as they worshipped Him (Matt. 28:9).
  (ii)   He could be touched (Luke 24:39; John 20:27).

(d)   But Christ's body was clearly different in some ways:
  (i)   His body appears to have passed through the grave clothes (John 20:6-8).
  (ii)   When He walked on the road to Emmaus with the two disciples they did not immediately recognize Him (Luke 24:13-35).
  (iii)   He was able to eat food, if He wanted (Luke 24:41-43).
  (iv)   He was able to pass through shut doors (John 20:19, 26).

(e)   Uncertain of so many aspects not yet revealed to us about the resurrection of the body, of its reality we are certain, for Christ was the first-fruits, by His own resurrection, of the resurrection of the dead to come (1 Cor. 15:20, 23).

4.   The encouragement that the assurance of the resurrection brings to believers.

(a)   The resurrection of the dead is a tremendous encouragement to Christians (1 Thess. 4:18) – those who have fallen asleep in Christ are not lost (1 Cor. 15:18).

(b)   The resurrection of the dead is a great encouragement to our commitment and persistence in God's service (1 Cor. 15:58).

(c)   The assurance of life after death means that Christians are not afraid of putting their lives in danger for the sake of the gospel – the reward of this life can be reaped in the life to come (1 Cor. 15:32).

(d)   The assurance of the resurrection of the dead takes away fear of death - it gives confidence in the face of death and the terrors that can be associated with it (1 Cor. 15:31; Heb. 11:35).

(e)   Christians are to be envied for the glorious assurance they have of resurrection on the grounds of Christ's (1 Cor. 15:19, 20).

---

48. LIFE AFTER DEATH

Question: What happens when we die?

Answer: The body returns, as dust, to the earth as it was, and the spirit returns to God.   The body may be described as asleep, and for the Christian the return of the spirit to God means to be consciously with Christ.

1.   The body sleeps.

(a)   The picture of sleep is frequently used of the dead (Matt. 9:24; John 11:11; 1 Cor. 11:30; 1 Thess. 4:13).

(b)   The description of the dead as asleep would seem to have particular reference to the body rather than the spirit: at death the body returns to dust, and the spirit to God who gave it (Eccl. 12:6, 7); while the body may sleep (Acts 7:60), the spirit may be with God (Acts 7:59).

(c)   To die before the coming again of the Lord Jesus is to leave the body (Phil. 1:24).

(d)   The human body is but a temporary home for the human spirit, to be replaced by something better (2 Cor. 5:1-5).

2.   The spirit lives.

(a)   It is important to remember that, for Christians, eternal life has already begun: those who have heard Christ's word, and believed God who sent Him, possess eternal life; they will not be condemned because they have crossed over from death to life (John 5:24).

(b)   The soul – the 'soul' and 'spirit' are often used as meaning the same – is not affected by the death of the body (Matt. 10:28).

(c)   That the dead lived in spirit was implied in the Old Testament (Ex. 3:6; Matt. 22:31, 32).

(d)   Death is gain for the Christian (Phil. 1:21).

(e)   When Christians die, they live; they cannot really die (John 11:25, 26).

3.   The Christian's spirit is immediately with Christ from the moment of death.

(a)   Jesus told the penitent thief, 'Today you will be with me in paradise' (Luke 23:43).

(b)   Statements made by the apostle Paul have no meaning unless they speak of conscious existence immediately following death:

    (i)   To be away from the body is to be at home with the Lord (2 Cor. 5:8);

    (ii)   To die and to be with Christ is better by far than to continue ordinary human existence (Phil. 1:23);

    (iii)   The spirit is with Christ, and is made perfect (Heb. 12:23).

(c)   In the light of what we have seen from the Scriptures we may say that Christians who have died before the coming of the Lord Jesus are without their bodies, but have conscious enjoyment of the Lord's presence. Their quickened spirits wait for the day of resurrection when they will be united with their resurrection bodies.

4.   Death holds no fear for the Christian.

(a)   Every Christian is to have the assurance that our Lord Jesus Christ destroyed death and the devil who held the power of death (2 Tim. 1:10; Heb. 2:14).

(b)   The Christian will never really die (John 8:51; 11:26).

(c)   Death cannot separate the Christian from God (Rom. 8:38, 39).

(d)   Death has lost both its victory and its sting (1 Cor. 15:55).

(e)   Victory over death is so complete that it can be described as belonging to the Christian (1 Cor. 3:22).

(f)   The Christian's attitude to death is the very opposite of despair (Phil. 1:21-23).

(g)   The Christian, seeing things properly, would prefer to be away from the body and at home with the Lord (2 Cor. 5:8).

---

49. HEAVEN

Question: What do we know about heaven?

Answer: Heaven is the eternal dwelling place of God and of His angels, the place from which Christ came at His Incarnation and to which He returned at His Ascension.   All the language the Bible uses to describe heaven expresses the perfection of the eternal life that Christians will experience there. With such assurance may Christians regard it as their eternal home that they are described as citizens of heaven while here on earth.

1.   Heaven is the eternal dwelling place of God (Matt. 5:16; 12:50; Rev. 3:12; 11:13) and of His angels (Matt. 18:10; 22:30; Rev. 3:5).

(a)   The Father is said to be 'in heaven' (Matt. 5:45; 6:1, 9; 7:11, 21; 10:33; 12:50; 16:17; 18:10, 14, 19; Mark 11:25).

(b)   He is the architect and builder of heaven (Heb. 11:10) - He is the Lord of heaven (Dan. 5:23; Matt. 11:25).

(c)   He reigns in heaven (Ps. 11:4): He does as He pleases with the powers of heaven and the people of the earth (Dan. 4:35; Ps. 135:6).

(d)   He fills heaven (1 Kings 8:27; Jer. 23:24); His glory (Acts 7:55) and majesty (Heb. 8:1) are visible there.

(e)   Heaven is the place from which God speaks to men and women today (Heb. 12:25); He answers His people from heaven as they call on Him in prayer (1 Chron. 21:26; 2 Chron. 7:14; Neh. 9:27; Psa. 20:6).

(f)   God sends His judgments from heaven (1 Sam. 2:10; Dan. 4:13-17; Luke 17:29; Rom. 1:18).

2.   Christ came from heaven and returned to heaven.

(a)   From heaven Christ came to become Incarnate (John 3:13, 31, 32; 6:38, 42, 50; 1 Cor. 15:47).

(b)   At His Ascension He returned to heaven (Mark 16:19; 1 Pet. 3:22).

(c)   Heaven, since the Ascension, is the scene of His present life and activity (Acts 7:55; Eph. 6:9; Heb. 8:1).

(d)   At God's right hand, He intercedes for His people, caring for their interests (Rom. 8:34; Heb. 7:25; 9:24).

(e)   He prepares a place in the Father's house for His people (John 14:2, 3).

(f)   All authority in heaven and on earth has been given Him (Matt. 28:18), with angels, authorities, and powers in submission to Him (1 Pet. 3:22).

(g)   He is the King of heaven (Matt. 25:34, 40; Luke 19:15; John 18:36).

(h)   He will come from heaven at His second coming (Matt. 24:30; Phil. 3:20; 1 Thess. 4:16; 2 Thess. 1:7).

3.   Heaven is not part of this creation and is quite different from it (Heb. 9:11).   We must distinguish 'heaven' from 'the heavens' where birds, clouds, sun and stars, etc., are to be found.

(a)   Heaven is the place of the 'real' (Heb. 8:5).

(b)   Heaven is a place of peace because all the ills and evils of this world are gone forever (Luke 19:38; Rev. 21:4).

(c)   Heaven is holy (Deut. 26:15; Ps. 20:6; Isa. 57:15).

(d)   Heaven is everlasting (Ps. 45:6; 89:29).

(e)   Heaven is indescribable in its happiness and satisfaction (Rev. 7:17).

4.   Descriptions of heaven aid our understanding.

(a)   It is described as paradise (Luke 23:43; 2 Cor. 12:2, 4).

(b)   It is likened to a granary – Christians being the wheat (Matt. 3:12).

(c)   It is called the Father's house (John 14:2).

(d)   It is described as a city, prepared by God for His people (Heb. 11:16) - Mount Zion, the heavenly Jerusalem, the city of the living God (Heb. 12:22).

(e)   It is described as a heavenly country – better than anything known on earth (Heb. 11:16).

(f)   It is described as a rest (Heb. 4:9, 10).

(g)   It is described as the Christian's inheritance (Matt. 25:34; 1 Pet. 1:4).

5.   The grounds of entry into heaven.

(a)   The inheritance of heaven is not by legal right but through a promise (Gal. 3:18).

(b)   Those who inherit it will recognize that they do not deserve to do so by reason of their own merits (Matt. 25:37-39).

(c)   All who gain entry into heaven do so through Jesus the Mediator of a new covenant and the merits of His atoning sacrifice (Heb. 12:24).

(d)   Heaven will be made up of those of every nation and language who have been redeemed by Jesus Christ (Matt. 25:32; Rev. 5:9, 10).

6.   Entry into heaven is impossible for some.

(a)   Entry is impossible for those who are not 'born again' (John 3:3).

(b)   Those whose lives are characterized by the acts of the sinful nature have no place there (Gal. 5:19-21; Eph. 5:5).

(c)   The devil and his angels can have no place in heaven (Matt. 25:41).

7.   What heaven will mean to Christians.

(a)   To enter heaven will be to be blessed by the Father (Matt. 25:34).

(b)   There they will have the things they have hoped for and heard about in the word of truth, the gospel (Col. 1:5).

(c) In heaven they will be holy, and able to see the Lord (Heb. 12:14).

(d) In heaven they will have their new and glorified bodies (2 Cor. 5:1).

(e) They will be able to see Christ's glory (John 17:24).

(f) They will receive their reward (Matt. 5:12; 25:34-40; Heb. 10:34-36).

(g) They will enjoy never-failing treasures that they have stored up for themselves (Matt. 6:20; Luke 12:33).

(h) The imperfect will have vanished and perfection will have come (1 Cor. 13:10).

(i) Their knowledge will be whole, like God's knowledge of them now (1 Cor. 13:9, 10).

(j) All the puzzles of this human life will be resolved (1 Cor. 13:12).

8. The relationship of Christians to heaven now.

(a) They are heirs of heaven: since the creation of the world God has been preparing it for all the redeemed (Matt. 25:34).

(b) Their names are written in heaven (Luke 10:20; Heb. 12:23)– a ground for true rejoicing.

(c) Their citizenship is in heaven (Phil. 3:20).

(d) They know heaven to be their true city or home (Heb. 13:14).

9. The effect the fact of heaven should have upon Christians.

(a) There should be a great longing for heaven in their hearts (Heb. 11:16; cf. 11:10).

(b) They should set their standards by those of heaven – as they know them from the Bible – rather than by those of this world for now their true citizenship is in heaven (Phil. 3:17-20).

(c) They should hold loosely to their earthly property and possessions, never allowing them to be all-important (Heb. 10:34).

(d) They should set their minds on things above, where Christ is, rather than on earthly things (Col. 3:2).

50. HELL

Question: **What do we know about hell?**

Answer: **Hell is the place of everlasting punishment and banishment from God's presence, the future dwelling-place of all who have neglected God and disobeyed the gospel of Christ.**

1. Hell is the place of banishment and punishment.

(a) Hell is the place of banishment from God's presence (Matt. 7:23; 25:41).

(b) It is the sphere of the manifestation of the wrath to come, from which Christ delivers believers (1 Thess. 1:10); there God's wrath against all godlessness and wickedness will be revealed (Rom. 1:18).

(c) To be cast into hell is to be separated from Christ, to be cursed, to be cast into the eternal fire prepared for the devil and his angels and to be eternally punished (Matt. 25:41, 46).

(d) Hell means eternal exclusion from the presence of the Lord and from the majesty of His power (2 Thess. 1:9).

(e) People's presence in hell is the direct result of their choices made during their earthly life (Luke 16:19-31).

(f) It is the dwelling place of all the wicked, those who have lived their lives without God (1 Sam. 2:9; Ps. 1:5, 6; 9:17).

(g) The cowardly, the unbelieving, the vile, the murderers, the sexually immoral, those who practise magic arts, the idolaters and all liars will be cast into hell (Rev. 21:8), that is to say, those who do not know God and do not obey the gospel of our Lord Jesus Christ (2 Thess. 1:8, 9).

(h) The body suffers in hell (Matt. 5:29).

(i) The soul suffers also in hell (Matt. 10:28).

(j) The punishment of hell is eternal (Isa. 33:14; Rev. 20:10).

(k) There is no transfer from hell to heaven (Luke 16:26).

(l) We are born on the road to hell, and the majority remain upon it (Matt. 7:13, 14).

2.   The descriptions the Bible gives of hell.

(a)   Hell is described as a dark imprisonment (2 Pet. 2:4) and darkness (Matt. 22:13).

(b)   It is like a bottomless pit, an abyss (Rev. 9:1).

(c)   It is a place of bondage, darkness and weeping (Matt. 22:13).

(d)   It is like everlasting burning (Isa. 33:14), unquenchable fire (Matt. 3:12; Mark 9:44), a fiery furnace (Matt. 13:42), consuming fire (Isa. 33:14), eternal fire (Matt. 18:8; 25:41), and a lake of fire (Rev. 20:14).

(e)   It is a place of torment (Luke 16:23) - there is no rest day or night (Rev. 14:10, 11).

3.   The right attitude to hell.

(a)   God has no desire that men and women should remain on the road to hell but that they should reach repentance (2 Pet. 3:9); our desire for them should be the same.

(b)   Christ came to deliver men and women from perishing – that is to say, from death and hell (John 3:16).

(c)   Christians should seek to save men and women from the road to hell (Jude 23).

---

51. LOYALTY TO GOD

Exodus 20:3: 'You shall have no other gods before me.'

Question: What does the first commandment teach?

Answer: The first commandment teaches that our first loyalty is to God Himself and idolatry of any sort is forbidden. The loyalty that is acceptable to God is sincere, unreserved, and carefully maintained.

1.   Loyalty to God is His proper due for two principal reasons: God's uniqueness, and the redemption He has provided.

God's uniqueness

(a)   There is only one God (2 Sam. 22:32; 1 Cor. 8:4): He is God in heaven above and on the earth below (Deut. 4:39).

(b)   God made us (Ps. 100:3): He is the almighty Creator who spreads the sky over empty space and suspends the earth on nothing (Job 26:7); He alone has power over creation (Jer. 14:22).

(c)   None can be compared with God: He is altogether different and unique in His majesty and glory (Ps. 98:4-9; Isa. 44:6).

(d)   While to some people, there are many so-called gods, whether in heaven and on earth (1 Cor. 8:5, 6), these have no existence in the real world (1 Cor. 8:4), and are worthless and impotent (Jer 14:22).

(e)   When other so-called gods are confronted with the Lord, men and women are compelled to acknowledge that 'the Lord– He is God' (1 Kings 18:39); He has every right to our exclusive loyalty and the false gods of human creation are not worthy to be mentioned in the same breath (Isa. 45:5, 21, 22; Jer. 10:1-10).

(f)   We are to acknowledge the Lord's uniqueness and take it to heart (Deut. 4:39), the only proper conclusion being that we should keep His decrees and commands (Deut. 4:40).

God's provision of redemption

(g)   The Lord liberated His people from their slavery in Egypt (Ex. 20:2), and Christians know a similar and even greater deliverance and redemption (1 Pet. 1:18, 19).

(h)   The supreme loyalty of Christians is to the Lord Jesus Christ (Eph. 5:21), who loved them and gave Himself for them (Gal. 2:20).

(i)   Even as the Passover feast served to keep fresh in the Israelites' memory the deliverance God gave them (Ex. 12:14), so the Lord's Supper keeps fresh in Christians' memories the redemption God achieved for them through the death of His Son, our Lord Jesus Christ (1 Cor. 11:23-26).

2.   Loyalty to God forbids idolatry in any form.

(a)   Many who are without a true knowledge of God worship idols of gold, silver, bronze, iron, wood and stone, made by their own hands (Ps. 135:15-17; Dan. 5:4, 23).

(b) By such idolatry people exchange the glory of the immortal God for images made to look like mere people or birds and animals and reptiles (Rom. 1:23), and then trust in them (Hab. 2:18).

(c) The error of idolatry is that it worships and serves created things rather than the Creator (Judg. 8:24-27; Rom. 1:25).

(d) But idolatry is not limited to the worship of material idols of human manufacture, for anything or any person claiming our primary loyalty becomes 'another god' (Col. 3:5).

(e) Idolatry begins in the heart (Deut. 11:16), and whatever has most of our heart and thoughts is our god (Luke 12:34).

(f) Whatever people boast of tends to be a god to them: for example, wisdom (Jer 9:23, 24), human strength or resourcefulness (Jer.17:5), righteous actions (Isa. 64:6), respectability and reputation (Luke 18:11).

(g) Wealth is a most common idol (Job 31:24-28; Matt. 13:22; Mark 10:22), and covetousness is identified as idolatry (Eph. 5:5; Col. 3:5).

(h) People make a god of pleasure (2 Tim. 3:4), especially of their physical appetites, insofar as they are proud of what they should be ashamed of, and life on this earth and its desires are the limit of their horizons (Phil. 3:19).

(i) Having the heart set on the things of this world and its desires is a form of idolatry (2 Tim. 4:10; 1 John 2:15-17).

(j) Even Christian leaders can become idols, having the place in people's affections and loyalty that belongs to God (1 Cor 1:11, 12).

(k) Idolatry dishonours God (Dan. 5:23): it represents people's rejection of God (Rom. 1:18-23), their forsaking of Him (Jer 1:16), their refusal to listen to what He says to them (Jer 13:10, 11) and their turning away from Him (Judg. 2:17).

(1) Idolatry is spiritual prostitution or adultery (Judg. 2:17; cf. Jas. 4:4).

(m) Idolatry calls forth God's judgment (Hos. 8:4; Amos 5:25-27; Micah 1:7): those who run after other gods will be filled with sorrow, in marked contrast to those who serve Him (Ps. 16:4, 8-11).

(n)   Idolatry must be uprooted (Micah 5:14), utterly destroyed and the Lord's rightful place re-established (Judg. 6:25-27), for He can be served only as other gods are put away (Josh. 24:14).

3.   Loyalty to God must be sincere, unreserved and carefully maintained.

Sincere loyalty

(a)   The Lord is to be served with all faithfulness (Josh. 24:14).

(b)   Professions of loyalty that are insincere only serve to increase sin (Hos. 8:11); our motives must be right as well as our actions (Amos 5:18-27).

(c)   Loyalty to God is a spiritual matter, and includes, in the light of God's uniqueness and redemption, the presenting of our bodies to Him as living and holy sacrifices - the kind He can accept (Rom. 12:1).

(d)   God looks for loyalty that springs from willing minds (1 Chron. 28:9).

Unreserved loyalty

(e)   God demands our first loyalty (Josh. 24:14); He will countenance no rival for He is a jealous God (Ex. 20:5; 34:14), in that He will not give His glory - which includes our praise and loyalty – to anyone or anything else (Isa. 42:8).

(f)   We have to choose whom we will worship: the one true God, the Lord, or the so-called gods that abound around us (Josh. 24:14, 15; 1 Thess. 1:9).

(g)   Love for God must be total and unqualified: He is to be loved with all our heart, soul, and mind (Matt. 22:37).

(h)   'I belong to the LORD' should be our glad testimony (Isa. 44:5).

Carefully maintained loyalty

(i)   We are to hold fast to the Lord our God (Josh. 23:8), which means being careful to keep on loving Him (Josh. 23:11).

(j)   To avoid idolatry we need to guard our hearts (Deut. 11:16), deliberately fleeing from idolatry of any sort (1 Cor. 10:14), and keeping ourselves away from anything that might take God's place in our hearts (1 John 5:21).

(k) This carefully maintained watchfulness is necessary because behind idolatry of every kind there is the activity of Satan (1 Cor. 8:5; 10:19, 20; cf. Acts 5:3), and he is unceasing in his evil attacks (1 Pet: 5:8).

(l) We are to be always thinking of the Lord (Ps. 16:8), having our eyes ever on Him (Ps. 25:15).

4. Loyalty to God is rewarded.

(a) There is no limit to the benefits that come when we are faithful in our loyalty to the Lord (Deut. 28:1-14).

(b) Loyalty to the Lord - the supreme wisdom - brings a long, good life, riches, honour, pleasures and peace (Prov. 3:13-18).

(c) Those committed to the Lord discover the secret of joy (Isa. 56:7).

(d) When the Lord is our God, we may be sure of His blessing (Ps. 67:5, 6), knowing that the whole of our life is under His control, with everything fitting into His good purposes (Rom. 8:28).

(e) The rewards of loyalty extend beyond this life with the promise of the gift of the kingdom of God (Luke 12:32), and a never-ending share in our Saviour's glory and honour (1 Pet. 5:4).

---

52. WORSHIP OF GOD

Exodus 20:4-6: 'You shall not make for yourself an idol in the form of anything in heaven above or on the earth beneath or in the waters below. You shall not bow down to them or worship them; for I, the LORD your God, am a jealous God, punishing the children for the sin of the fathers to the third and fourth generation of those who hate me, but showing love to a thousand generations who love me and keep my commandments.'

Question: What does the second commandment teach?

Answer: **The second commandment teaches that God alone is to be worshipped, without any visual symbols of Him, and in strict accordance with the manner in which He has revealed Himself to us.**

1.   God is to be worshipped.

(a)   Worship is God's due as our Creator (Ps. 100; Rom. 1:25): it is the natural expression of our obedience to the first commandment (Ex. 20:3).

(b)   Worship is the giving of glory, honour, and thanks to God (Rev. 4:9); and in our worship of Him we acknowledge that He alone is worthy to receive such (Rev. 4:11).

2.   God alone is to be worshipped.

(a)   The Lord Himself is the proper object of all worship (Ex. 20:2, 3).

(b)   He is jealous of His honour as the one Lord (Ex. 20:5); He will not give His glory to anyone else (Isa. 42:8).

(c)   He will share neither our affection nor our obedience with any other (Ex. 20:5, 6).

3.   God is to be worshipped without any visual symbols of Him.

(a)   We are forbidden by this commandment both to worship images of other so-called gods and to use images of the one true God (Ex. 20:4).

(b)   God is against any representation of Himself (Lev. 26:1): we are not to make for ourselves 'an idol in the form of anything in heaven above or on the earth beneath or in the waters below' (Ex. 20:4).

(c)   People act corruptly when they make an image of God, in the form of any figure whatsoever (Deut. 4:15-19), so that we may conclude that idolatry is not only the worship of false gods, but even the worship of the one true God by images.

(d)   This demand that the Lord should be worshipped without visual images is reinforced in the Old Testament by the reminder that the Israelites saw no form of God on the day that the Lord spoke to them at Horeb. Since the Lord did not give a visible form of Himself, but instead spoke to them, so now we are not to use visual symbols of Him but simply to obey His Word (Deut. 4:15-19).

Reasons for the prohibition of visual symbols of God

(e)   God's glory is jeopardised when images are used in worship

(Isa. 40:18-31): wherever we go in creation, all things were created by God, and are subject to Him, thus making it foolish and inappropriate to seek a likeness of Him in the created order (Ex. 20:4, Deut. 5:8).

(f)   When people picture their god in human form they soon reckon to it their own human weaknesses (1 Kings 18:26-29).

(g)   Furthermore, it is impossible to make an image of the one true God because God is spirit (John 4:24): He cannot be made static or controlled, as manufactured images would suggest.

(h)   God requires us to guard against unworthy conceptions of Him, and of creating false images of Him in our hearts (Ex. 20:4, 5).

4.   God is to be worshipped in the manner He has laid down.

(a)   The second commandment insists that worship must be in accord with divine revelation; we are warned against ways of worship that lead us to dishonour God and to put aside His truth (Ex. 20:4, 5).

(b)   We are to receive nothing, practise nothing, and own nothing in the worship of God except what is of His appointment (Rev. 22:8, 9).

(c)   We are called upon to recognise that God is so great that we may worship Him acceptably only when we do so in the manner He chooses to lay down (Isa. 55:8, 9; Rom. 11:33, 34).

(d)   There is a wrong as well as a right way to worship God: God is spirit and those who worship Him must worship in spirit and in truth – i.e. spiritually and in reality (John 4:23, 24).

(e)   The New Testament reveals that there is only one image of God that is wholly true and worthy, and that is the Lord Jesus Christ Himself who is the image of the invisible God (Col.. 1:15-17): thus all Christian worship centres around God's Son because in His face we see the glory of God as nowhere else (2 Cor. 4:6; cf. John 1:14, 18).

5.   God desires worship springing from love, and expressed in obedience (Ex. 20:6).

(a)   Worship is in vain if the feelings of the heart do not correspond with the expression of the lips (Isa. 1:11-17; Amos 4:4; 5:18-27; Matt. 15:8, 9).

(b) Acceptable worship is a response to God's mercy (Rom. 12:1, 2): we love Him because He first loved us (1 John 4:19).

(c) Our worship is expressed in obedience to His Word rather than any respect for visual images of God (Deut. 4:15-19).

(d) True worship presupposes the willingness to obey God (Josh. 5:14, 15; Isa. 6:1-8).

(e) At conversion we turn from idols to worship and serve the living and true God with joy (1 Thess. 1:6-9).

---

53. REVERENCE

Exodus 20:7: 'You shall not misuse the name of the LORD your God, for the LORD will not hold anyone guiltless who misuses his name.'

Question: **What does the third commandment teach?**

Answer: **The third commandment teaches us to avoid all wrong use of God's Name, to treat His Name with the greatest respect, and to make it our deliberate purpose to honour and reverence Him.**

1. **The special use of the word 'Name' in the Bible.**

(a) Names have meanings, and this particularly applies to the Name of God (Ex. 3:13-15).

(b) God's Name proclaims and reveals His character (Ex. 33:19), all that He is and all that He does (Ex. 34:5-7).

(c) God's Name is linked, therefore, with His attributes and characteristics, and the Book of Psalms provides many illustrations: righteousness (Ps. 89:15, 16); saving power (Ps. 96:2); holiness (Ps. 99:3, 4); goodness (Ps. 100:4, 5); mercy (Ps. 119:132); love (Ps. 138:2); faithfulness (Ps. 138:2); splendour (Ps. 148:13).

(d) The adjective most commonly associated with God's Name is 'holy' (Ps. 33:21; 103:1; 106:47; 145:21).

(e) So close is the identification of the Lord with His Name that He may be spoken of as The Name (Isa. 30:27; cf. Prov. 18:10).

2. **Ways in which God's Name is used wrongly.**

(a) **Perjury.** Perjury is the sin of taking an oath in the Name of God and then uttering falsehood (Lev. 19:12; Num. 30:2; Deut. 6:13; Ps. 15:4; Zech. 5:4).

(b) God's Name is treated with irreverence when people shrug aside promises and oaths made in His Name, holding them of little account (Jer. 34:16), and when they make a vow they never intend to keep (Deut. 5:11)

(c) Solemn and legal oaths are not prohibited; it is the abuse of them that is wrong (Lev. 19:12; cf. Rom. 9:1; 2 Cor. 1:23).

(d) **Rash and unnecessary swearing.** When people introduce God's Name into their conversation by an oath simply to strengthen what they are saying, they use His Name wrongly (2 Kings 5:20).

(e) Even swearing by heaven is swearing by God's throne, and swearing by the earth swearing by His footstool (Matt. 5:33-35; cf. Matt. 23:21, 22).

(f) Jephthah, for example, rashly swore an oath in God's Name that was entirely out of keeping with God's character (Judg. 11:30, 31).

(g) **Blasphemy.** Blasphemy is to treat irreverently the Majesty of God (Ps. 74:18), to utter His Name, and then to curse Him (cf. Lev. 24:11).

(h) Blasphemy occurs when people deliberately defy God by mentioning His Name and casting doubt upon His character (2 Kings 19:4,10,22).

(i) **Unnecessary and irreverent use of God's Name in ordinary conversation** (Matt. 7:21-23).

(j) Sarah, for example, wrongly put the whole weight of blame upon Abraham for their shared mistake concerning Hagar, and unnecessarily brought God's Name into her conversation for emphasis (Gen. 16:5).

(k) **Offering worship, supposedly to God, while living a godless life** (Mal. 2:13-16).

(l) To say we are the Lord's by offering Him worship but without wanting to obey Him, so that our worship becomes mere words, spoken thoughtlessly, is to use His Name wrongly (Isa. 29:13).

(m) God's Name is brought into disrepute by bad conduct on the part of those who profess loyalty to Him (Prov. 30:9).

(n)   Absalom, for example, expressed the desire to worship the Lord, and gave the appearance of doing so, only to further a political conspiracy (2 Sam. 15:7, 8, 12); he used God's Name for a completely unworthy purpose.

3.   Ways by which we honour and reverence God's Name.

(a)   **Praise and Thanksgiving.** We honour God's Name by praising Him for the wonders of His grace towards us (Joel 2:26), and for the glorious truth that everything about Him is good (Ps. 54:6).

(b)   **Meditation and study.** We reverence the Lord by thinking about His Name, and pondering all He has revealed to us of Himself (Mal. 3:16).

(c)   **Love.** We show our reverence for God by loving His Name (Ps. 5:11), and being jealous for His interests (Ps. 69:9; John 2:17).

(d)   **Carefulness.** We reverence God's Name by keeping before us His holiness, and speaking about Him with care, encouraging one another to serve and worship Him with holy reverence and awe (Ps. 89:7; Heb. 12:28, 29).

(e)   **Obedience.** We show our respect for God's Name by living in conformity to the will and character His Name reveals (Micah 4:5; 6:8).

(f)   **Prayer.** We honour God by calling upon Him in prayer for help because it is His Name, His unchanging character, that gives us the assurance that He hears and answers prayer (Ps. 99:6).

(g)   **Confidence.** We reverence God by showing publicly that our confidence is in Him, and that, having committed ourselves to Him, we can wait with assurance and without impatience for His answer (Ps. 52:9).

(h)   **Evangelism.** We reverence God's Name by taking seriously the knowledge that He alone is the supreme Lord, whose saving deeds need to be made known in all the world around (Isa. 12:4).

(i)   **Truthfulness.** We honour and reverence God's Name by being committed to complete truthfulness in every sphere for one of the main purposes of the third commandment is to prevent us ever calling upon God to confirm a lie (Ex. 20:7). God is truth (John 1:14, 14:6) and He calls us to commitment to truth (Eph. 4:25; 5:9; 6:14).

---

54. REST

Exodus 20:8-11: 'Remember the Sabbath day by keeping it holy. Six days you shall labour and do all your work, but the seventh day is a Sabbath to the LORD your God.   On it you shall not do any work, neither you, nor your son or daughter, nor your manservant or maidservant, nor your animals, nor the alien within your gates.   For in six days the LORD made the heavens and the earth, the sea, and all that is in them, but he rested on the seventh day. Therefore the LORD blessed the Sabbath day and made it holy.'

Question: What does the fourth commandment teach?

Answer: The fourth commandment teaches that the keeping of one day in seven as a Sabbath (a rest) is a special means of honouring God our Creator and Redeemer, and of renewing our minds, bodies, and souls in the manner their constitution and well-being require.

It encourages us to put aside, on a weekly basis, material considerations, so that the worth of God, the well-being of our soul, and spiritual issues and concerns, may properly occupy our thoughts and more effectively influence our living.

1.   **The change from Saturday, i.e. the original Sabbath, to Sunday.**

(a)   The vital element in the commandment is that there should be six days of work followed by one day of rest, the particular day set apart is not the essence of the commandment (Ex. 20:9-11).

(b)   The first Christians soon recognised that Old Testament regulations for the Sabbath are part of the ceremonial law that has been fulfilled in our Lord Jesus Christ, so that they are no longer binding on God's people (Rom. 14:5-6; Col. 2:16, 17).

(c)   In principle, every day is the Lord's Day, and is equally suitable for worship (Acts 2:46).

(d)   Yet it was also appreciated that if the purposes of the day are to be fulfilled it should be the same day for all, as far as possible (Acts 20:7; notice in 1 Cor. 11:17-20 the emphasis on 'coming together as a church').

(e)   It soon became the practice to meet on Sunday in honour of our Lord's resurrection from the dead 'on the first day of the week' (John 20:1).

(f)   The Lord Jesus appeared to His disciples on the first Easter Sunday, and again on the following Sunday (Matt. 28:9,10; Luke 24:13-49; John 20:10-23).

(g)   There are references to Christians meeting on 'the first day of the week' (Acts 20:7; 1 Cor 16:2), and it would seem to have been the recognised day for them to gather together.

(h)   The change not only bore witness to the Resurrection, but it emphasised the difference between the Christian Sunday and the Jewish Sabbath. The Jewish Sabbath came at the end of six days and spoke of a rest to come, the Christian Sunday comes at the beginning of the week symbolising 'the rest' that Jesus Christ has won for those who trust in Him.

2.   The reasons for the appointment of the Sabbath.
First, God's own glory.

(a)   It is His Sabbath (Ezek. 20:16, 21, 24).

(b)   God's glory is His own Person: when we observe the Sabbath we display the likeness of God in a pattern of work and rest since He made us in His own image (Gen. 1:26,27).

(c)   The Sabbath provides us with a special opportunity for remembering and meditating upon His work of creation and redemption. We cannot do this without finding ourselves wanting to praise Him, and thus to honour Him (Ps. 50:23).

(d)   By our proper use of the Sabbath we honour God by acknowledging His claim upon both our time and service (Ex. 23:12, 13, 25).

Secondly, our own good.

(e)   God blessed the seventh day, i.e. He made it for our benefit and blessing (Gen. 2:3).

(f)   The Sabbath was made to benefit people, not people to benefit the Sabbath (Mark 2:27) - that is to say, it was made for our own true well-being in body, mind and soul. The need for one day's rest in seven is built into our physical and mental constitution. It is not something that was peculiar to the Jews as part of their religious heritage, but something that is a necessity for all. As we need daily rest, so we need a weekly rest.

Thirdly, a covenant sign.

(g)   It is a reminder of the covenant between God and His people forever (Ex. 31:13, 17; Ezek. 20:12).

(h)   It helps God's people to remember that they have a special and unique relationship to the Lord who sets them apart for Himself, for His own possession (Ex. 31:13).

3.   Our duties regarding the Sabbath or Sunday.

(a)   **To remember it.**

    (i)   The word 'remember' (Ex. 20:8) bears the meaning of imprint or mark so as to be recognised. We are to imprint its importance upon our minds, and by our speech and actions mark it out as recognisably different from other days.

    (ii)   To remember it is to regard it as a delight (Isa. 58:13).

    (iii)   To remember it is to count the keeping of it an honour and privilege (Isa. 58:13).

(b)   **To keep it holy** (Ex. 20:8).

    (i)   The idea behind the word 'holy' is that of being cut off, separated, or set apart.

    (ii)   God calls upon us to set one day in seven apart, and to view and use it differently from the rest.

    (iii)   We keep it holy by using it in such a way that we show that the Lord has our first loyalty.

(c)   **To lay aside our daily work** (Ex. 20:9, 10).

    (i)   Work is an essential element in God's plan for human life (Gen. 2:15) but human beings and animals also need rest from work (Ex. 23:12).

(ii)   We are, therefore, commanded to rest (Ex. 31:15): 'On it you shall not do any work' (Ex. 20:10).

(iii)   We are to put aside our ordinary callings and activities on this one day in seven (Neh. 13:15-18).

(iv)   The Hebrew word 'shabbâth' translated 'Sabbath' means cessation, intermission or rest.

(d)   **To allow others the same opportunity of rest** (Ex. 20:10).

(i)   We are to do our utmost to ensure that, so far as our own conduct is concerned, others may enjoy rest too.

(ii)   We have a measure of responsibility to see that others have the opportunity of rest: 'You shall not do any work, neither you, nor your son, or daughter, nor your manservant or maid servant, nor your animals, nor the alien within your gates.'

(e)   **To remember God's powerful acts of creation and redemption.**

(i)   We are to remember God's rest from His great work of creation (Ex. 20:11): God Himself 'worked' for the first six days and 'rested' on the seventh day (Gen. 1:31; 2:1-3).

(ii)   We are to remember God's redemption: the Jews were instructed to remember on the Sabbath how they had been slaves in the land of Egypt, and how the Lord their God brought them out of Egypt with a mighty hand and an outstretched arm (Deut. 5:15).

(iii)   Christians remember on the Lord's Day a far greater deliverance in which they were redeemed from their empty way of life, lived without God, with the precious blood of Jesus Christ, in whom they have come to trust knowing that He was raised from the dead on the first day of the week for their justification (Rom. 4:25; 1 Pet. 1:18, 19).

(iv)   The particular focus of Christian worship, therefore, is upon the glory of the Risen Lord Jesus (Rev. 1:10-18).

(v)   We delight ourselves in the Lord, calling the Sabbath a delight for it provides an opportunity of finding our joy in Him (Isa. 58:13, 14).

(f) **To engage in humanitarian action.**
  (i)   It is lawful to do good on the Sabbath (Matt. 12:12).
  (ii) It is imperative to do good on the Sabbath (Luke 13:10-17 – notice the word 'should' or 'ought' in verse 16).
  (iii) We are to seize the special opportunities it affords of doing good to others (e.g. Mark 2:1-5; Luke 13:10-17; 14:1-6; John 9), and that clearly includes activities such as visiting someone in hospital, opening our homes to the lonely, and calling in to see the elderly and house-bound.
  (iv) The Lord's Day is never to be an excuse for avoiding rightful duties to our fellow men and women (Mark 3:1-6).

(g) **To remember that it is God's institution.**
  (i)   The choice of one day in seven was not a human choice, but God's: God made it holy (Gen. 2:3).
  (ii) 'In six days the LORD made the heavens and the earth, the sea, and all that is in them, but he rested on the seventh day. Therefore the LORD blessed the Sabbath day and made it holy' (Ex. 20:11).

4.   Benefits of observing the Sabbath principle.
  (The reason for using the term 'the Sabbath principle' is that contemporary life with its complex machinery and shift systems frequently involves some people working on the recognised 'Sabbath,' i.e. Sunday. Where this is the case, both employers and employees should be strongly encouraged to observe the principle by giving and recognising another day that week in its place, and insisting that it should be taken as a day of rest and not an opportunity for overtime.)

(a) **Blessing from God.**
  (i)   We will find our joy in God and know God-given success in our endeavours (Isa. 58:14).
  (ii) We will obtain our full share of the blessings God promises (Isa. 58:14).

(b) **Rest and renewal.**
  (i)   By rest both we and all associated with us, including animals, are refreshed (Ex. 23:12).

(ii)   We will renew our strength, according to His promise to those who put their hope in Him (Isa. 40:31).

(c)   **A necessary corrective is imposed upon our proneness to self-seeking** (Amos 8:5, 6).

    (i)   We deliberately turn aside from our own business, from seeking our own interests or attending to our own affairs in order to honour the Lord (Isa. 58:13).

    (ii)   By putting aside 'getting' for a day at least, we symbolically reject covetousness as a motive for living (Col. 3:5-7).

    (iii)   We remember on the 'Sabbath' that this world is not all-important and that there is another world and kingdom to be put first (Matt. 6:33; Col. 3:1-4).

    (iv)   We deliberately turn aside for a brief while from the natural preoccupations of our daily work so that the well-being of our soul, and spiritual issues and concerns occupy our thoughts and more effectively influence our living (Ps. 73:16, 17; 77:12, 13; 2 Cor. 4:18; Heb.10:10, 13-18).

(d)   **The proper exercise of our soul in the worship of God.**

    (i)   We delight ourselves in the Lord (Isa. 58:13, 14), making the Sabbath a day of joy as we do so.

    (ii)   We esteem a day in His courts better than a thousand elsewhere (Ps. 84:10).

    (iii)   We are provided with the opportunity to cultivate our spiritual life, a priority we are encouraged to pursue (Ps. 27:4, 8; 2 Pet. 3:18).

(e)   **The strengthening of family life and unity.**

    (i)   All the members of a family are instructed and encouraged to rest together (Ex. 20:10).

    (ii)   It is a day for being at home, in our own place (Ex. 16:29).

(f)   **The encouragement and profit of Christian fellowship.**

    (i)   We are able to enter into the worship and fellowship of God's people (Ps. 55:14; 122:1; 132:7).

(ii)   We are able to benefit from the teaching of God's Word (Luke 4:31; 6:6; Acts 13:14, 15, 44; Acts 17:2; 18:4).

(iii)   Assembling ourselves together, we may spur one another on to love and good deeds (Heb. 10:24).

(g)   **A helpful anticipation and reminder of the everlasting rest God prepares for His believing people.**

(i)   God's rest on the seventh day is a type of the Sabbath-rest that God will yet give to His people (Heb. 4:4, 9).

(ii)   Our Lord Jesus Christ, having completed His work for us by His death and resurrection, has entered into His rest, and one day we are going to share in that eternal rest in heaven (John 14:2, 3).

---

55. RESPECT FOR, AND SUBMISSION TO, PROPER AUTHORITY

Exodus 20:12: 'Honour your father and your mother, so that you may live long in the land the Lord your God is giving you. '

Question: What does the fifth commandment teach?

Answer: The fifth commandment teaches the general principle of paying respect to whom respect is due, and honour to whom honour is due by underlining the fundamental and specific responsibility children have to honour their parents, a responsibility that is at the very heart of a nation's well-being.

1.   The meaning of the word 'honour.'

(a)   The Hebrew word for 'honour' is 'kabed' with the basic meaning of 'to be heavy' from which comes the sense of making weighty, and of placing great value upon a person. Thus to honour our parents is to regard them as eminently worthy of respect - to recognise that they deserve a 'weight' of respect.

(b)   The Greek equivalent of the Hebrew word, used in the New Testament, 'timao', conveys the thought of fixing a valuation, and, by implication, to revere.

(c)   To honour our parents, therefore, is to fix a right valuation upon their worth, causing us to respect them.

(d)   The honour we give to our parents is to be a reflection of the honour we know we ought to give to God our heavenly Father (Mal. 1:6).

(e)   The honouring of parents is part of practical holiness (Lev. 19:2, 3).

2.   The duties of children to their parents.
Reverence and respect

(a)   Children are to respect their parents (Lev. 19:3).

(b)   Negatively, this means never to mock or scorn them (Prov. 30:17), curse them or speak evil of them (Ex. 21:17; Prov. 20:20; Matt. 15:4), or attack them (Ex. 21:15).

(c)   Positively, it means to honour them deliberately by speaking well of them, respecting them, providing for them and showing them courtesy (cf. Gen. 47:7, 11, 12; 1 Kings 2:19, 20).

Demonstrated and genuine love

(d)   The love of children for their parents is always assumed in the Bible: such love is a first, and entirely natural, love (Matt. 10:37).

(e)   Love, to be acceptable to God, must be genuine and without hypocrisy (Rom. 12:9).

(f)   Children should be unashamed of showing their affection for their parents (Gen. 46:29).

Obedience to their commands

(g)   Both parents are to be obeyed (Deut. 21:18), and in everything, where possible and right (Eph. 6:1; Col. 3:20).

(h)   To honour parents, therefore, is the opposite of stubbornness and rebelliousness towards them (Deut. 21:18).

(i)   We honour our parents by giving deference or regard to their requests (1 Kings 2:20), neither despising their instruction nor their direction (Prov. 1:8; 15:5).

Submission to their discipline

(j)   The rightful submission of children to parents is to respect them for the discipline they exercise (Prov. 15:5; Heb. 12:9).

(k) Proper discipline, rightly appreciated, is not a disadvantage to a son or daughter but rather a benefit and privilege (Prov. 3:11-12; Heb. 12:5-8).

Faithfulness to their interests

(l) Children can fall into the peril of regarding lightly their parents' property: someone who, in effect, robs father or mother and says, 'It's not wrong' is no better than a murderer (Prov. 28:24).

(m) To honour our parents is to give them joy by living wisely, and we do the right thing when we aim at giving them this joy (Prov. 23:24, 25).

Repaying the love, care and trouble they have given

(n) To honour our parents is to care for them, and to provide for them when they are in need – in other words, to make some return to them, not least financially, if that is the help required (1 Tim. 5:4).

(o) Children are not to conceive excuses - least of all religious excuses - for not fulfilling their obligations to their parents (see the 'Corban' argument in Mark 7:9-13).

3.   The limitations of the rightful submission of children to parents.

(a) The obedience and subjection God commands are neither absolute nor universal – they are 'in the Lord' (Eph. 6:1), i.e. in such things as parents require us to do with the Lord's authority.

(b) If anyone, including parents, demands what is contrary to the law and will of God, then we ought to obey God first (Acts 5:29).

(c) Furthermore, the time must come when children recognise their independence of their parents, and this comes naturally at the time of marriage (Matt. 19:5, 6; Mark 10:6-8).

(d) Prior to marriage men and women usually have their closest bond with their parents, and owe them the greatest obligation; the new bond and obligation that marriage brings transcends the old (Eph. 5:31).

(e) A man's duty to his wife, and a woman's duty to her husband, and their united duty to their children, clearly bring a change of priorities so far as their relationship and duties to their parents are concerned, although no lessening of respect and proper responsibility for them (Eph. 5:21-33).

(f)   If at any stage parents try to make loyalty to themselves a priority over their children's loyalty to God, they demand what is unlawful: love for God ought to be so great that the best of human loves is 'hatred' by comparison (Luke 14:26).

(g)   Nevertheless, all commands about loyalty to Jesus Christ must be seen in the context of genuine respect for parents as a Christian duty (Mark 7:9-13).

(h)   We may be sure that the priority of loyalty to God will never be detrimental to the well-being of those we love most, much as we may not see how it can be so at the time (see Abraham and Isaac in Genesis 22:1-8).

4.   The responsibilities that the rightful submission of children to their parents places upon the parents.

(a)   Parents must recognise their unique responsibilities for their children for they are their first and foremost educators (Prov. 4:1-4).

(b)   Parents must manage their own households well, ensuring that their children obey them with proper respect (1 Tim. 3:4).

(c)   Parents should be clear as to the kind of qualities and goals they should encourage in their children, so that they do not place false objectives before them (Prov. 23:22-25).

(d)   Children are gifts from the Lord (Gen. 4:1; 25:21; Ruth 4:12, 13; 1 Sam. 1:5, 6, 11). Parents do well to give their children back to the Lord, as it were, lending them to Him for as long as they live (1 Sam. 1:11, 27, 28).

(e)   Children are given to parents to rear and to train up in the way they should go (Prov. 22:6): they are to be nurtured like tender plants with a view to their future fruitfulness in character (Ps. 128:3).

(f)   God desires godly offspring from the marriage union (Mal. 2:15).

(g)   Parents' actions and words in relation to their children are all to be with their spiritual good in view - what the New Testament calls 'the training and instruction of the Lord' (Eph. 6:4).

(h)   Parents must be careful in their exercise of parental discipline, recognising two fundamentals: first, foolishness is bound up in the heart of a child and it takes more than words to dislodge it

(Prov 22:15), and, secondly, character is a plant that grows more sturdily for some cutting back (Prov. 15:32, 33; 5:11, 12; Heb. 12:11), and from early days (Prov. 13:24; 22:6; 29:15).

(i)   The motive of love is to be behind every exercise of discipline (Prov. 13:24), and love demands that a restraint should be placed upon children by their parents when they do wrong (1 Sam. 3:13).

(j)   Parents are to instruct their children from their earliest days in the law of God (Eph. 6:4; cf. Josh. 8:35) with loving persistence (Prov. 1:8; 4:7-13).

(k)   Parents need to be in a good and loving relationship to their children so that their children expect to receive instruction from them (Prov. 4:1-4).

(l)   Parents are not to make it difficult for their children to obey the commandment, 'Honour your father and your mother,' by making unreasonable demands (Col. 3:21), needlessly provoking them to anger (Eph. 6:4), perhaps by favouritism (Gen. 37:3,4) or by neglect (2 Sam. 14:13, 28; 1 Kings 1:5,6).

(m)   An important factor in a child's upbringing is not the money parents have with which to supply their children's needs but rather the example they set (Prov. 20:7): parents pass on a heritage for good or ill according to their fear of God (Ps. 25:12, 13; Hos. 4:6).

(n)   Parents are to be examples of loyalty to God, never allowing their children to take precedence over their own discipleship of our Lord Jesus Christ (Matt. 19:29; Mark 10:29; Luke 18:29, 30).

(o)   Parents are to be an example too of dutiful children in relation to their own parents (Luke 6:31).

5.   Examples of obedience to this commandment.

(a)   Joseph is an outstanding example of obedience to this commandment in his concern for his father (Gen. 43:7), his provision for him (Gen. 45:9-13), his demonstrated affection (Gen. 46:28-34), his high regard for him (Gen. 47:7, 27-31), and his obedience (Gen. 50:1-14).

(b)   Our Lord Jesus Christ is the supreme example of obedience to this commandment, as to all others, in His earthly submission and obedience (Luke 2:51), and His concern and provision for His widowed mother (John 19:26, 27).

6.   Examples of disobedience to this commandment.

(a)   The two sons of Eli – Hophni and Phinehas– are sad examples of disobedience to this commandment in that they refused to listen to their father's rebuke (1 Sam. 2:25), and had no regard for the Lord or His commandments, with disastrous consequences (1 Sam. 2:12; 4:11, 17).

(b)   A second example of disobedience is the manner in which the Jews evaded obedience to the implications of this commandment to maintain needy parents by instead insincerely vowing their property to the Temple (Mark 7:1-13; cf. Matt. 15:1-6).

7.   The fundamental importance of this principle of respect for, and submission to, parents.

(a)   This commandment is the application of a general Christian principle: we are to pay respect to whom respect is due, and honour to whom honour is due (Rom. 13:7 cf. Mark 12:17).

(b)   Parents are the first authority we learn to respect and the pattern of submission we learn towards them influences our respect for everyone. We are taught to show proper respect to all (1 Pet. 2:17), so that, for example, we rise in the presence of the old, show respect for the elderly (Lev. 19:32), and give proper recognition to widows by caring for them financially and in other ways open to us (1 Tim. 5:3).

(c)   Inevitably the pattern of submission we learn from our earliest years influences our submission in other spheres: those who show proper respect and submission to parents are unlikely to find difficulty in honouring civil authorities (1 Pet. 2:17) or treating employers with due respect (1 Pet. 2:18) - in other words, the well-being of a people or a nation begins in the home.

---

56. RESPECT FOR LIFE

Exodus 20:13: 'You shall not murder.'

Question: What does the sixth commandment teach?

Answer: **The sixth commandment condemns murder, which is the deliberate, malicious and unlawful taking of life, and teaches the sanctity of human life which, as a gift from God, is to be neither violated nor threatened, whether by actions, threats, motives or words.**

1. **Life is a gift from God and is sacred.**
(a) Human breath and life are God's prerogative (Gen. 2:7; Isa. 42:5; Dan. 5:23).
(b) Human life is sacred (Gen. 9:6), so sacred that even the life of a murderer is not to be carelessly taken away (Gen. 4:15).
(c) Human life is sacred because male and female were made in the image of God (Gen. 1:27; 9:6).
(d) A person's life is his or her most important possession (Matt. 16:26; Mark 8:37; John 15:13; cf. Acts 27:18, 19, 22).
(e) Human redemption in and through our Lord Jesus Christ emphasises the sanctity of human life (John 10:10, 28; Rom. 5:21).

2. **Murder violates God's commandment.**
(a) It despises God's sixth commandment and is evil in His sight (2 Sam. 12:9).
(b) It offends, more than any other sin, the commandment 'Love your neighbour as yourself' (Rom. 13:9).
(c) It offends the special value given to human life because of the awareness that every race was created by God from one forefather (Acts 17:26).
(d) God hates murder (Prov. 6:16, 17).
(e) Murder cannot be concealed from God (Isa. 26:21; Jer. 2:34) and it cries out for His vengeance (Gen. 4:10).

3. **Human attitudes and emotions that can give rise to murder are forbidden by this commandment.**

(a) At first sight the sixth commandment appears to be concerned with the murderous act alone (Ex. 20:13), but the Lord Jesus gave the commandment a further and deeper meaning: all sins that lead to murder, and are the causes of it, are forbidden (Matt. 5:21-26). Anger and hatred are two of the most obvious examples.

Anger

(b) Anger, like a fire, can be kindled and do great damage (Ps. 124:3).

(c) Anger is an act of the sinful nature (Gal. 5:20).

(d) Anger can be foolishly harboured and kept alive (Amos 1:11; Eccl. 7:9).

(e) Anger and insult can constitute the spirit of murder (Matt. 5:22), and be the cause of it (Gen. 49:6).

(f) A distinction is recognised between anger and malice, in that the former under control is sometimes allowable (Eph. 4:26, 27), but malice - mental murder - is always evil (1 John 3:15).

Hatred

(g) Hatred is synonymous with darkness, and walking in darkness (1 John 2:9).

(h) Hatred distorts our perspective (1 John 2:11).

(i) Murder is the fruit of hatred (1 John 3:15).

(j) Murder is first committed in the heart and then completed by actions: e.g. Cain and Abel (Gen. 4:5, 8), Saul (later known as Paul) who breathed out murderous threats against the Lord's disciples (Acts 9:1) and was a 'murderer' before his conversion (Acts 9:1, 4, 5; 22:4, 7; 26:10).

4. **There are important exceptions in the taking of human life that are not infringements of this commandment.**
    The civil authority and the exercise of capital punishment.

(a) The just punishment of crime by magistrates is not murder: human governments are God's agents to bring just punishment on wrongdoers (Rom. 13:1-7; 1 Pet. 2:13-17).

(b) The assumption is always present that there are crimes deserving of death (Gen. 9:6; Acts 25:11).

(c) Under the Mosaic law the death penalty was stipulated for certain offences (Lev. 24:17; Num. 35:20, 21; Deut. 19:11-13), and the institution of capital punishment for murder would seem to be of permanent obligation (Gen. 9:5, 6).

War

(d) The lawfulness of defensive war is distinctly recognised in the Bible, and the taking of life in time of war is not murder (Judg. 5:23; 1 Sam. 15:2, 3).

(e) When consulted through the Urim and Thummin, or by the prophets, as to the rightness of military enterprises, God answered (Judg.20:27, 28; 1 Sam. 14:36, 37; 23:1-5).

(f) Since magistrates are given power of life and death over their citizens, they plainly have the right to declare war in self-defence (Rom. 13:1-7; 1 Pet. 2:13-17).

Manslaughter

(g) The life of a person taken away by accident is not murder (Deut. 19:4, 5).

(h) The cities of refuge were intended to provide a place of safety for those guilty of manslaughter so that their case could be properly judged (Num. 35:9-28).

(i) The life of a person taken in self-defence is not murder (Ex. 22:2).

5. The implications of this commandment are many.

(a) Love for our neighbours means the protection and preservation of their life (Luke 10:25-37).

(b) The opposite of murder is self-sacrificing love (1 John 3:11-18), which should be the Christian norm (Phil. 2:5-8; 1 Pet. 2:21-25).

(c) We need to guard our hearts if we would avoid breaking this commandment (Prov. 4:23; Matt. 5:21-26).

(d) We should never let the sun go down while we are angry, or have any other harmful and wrongful attitude of heart (Eph. 4:26).

(e) Human relationships matter to God (1 John 4:21; 5:1).

(f)   Attitudes and works recognised as incitements to murder are to be recognised by Christians as belonging to their old life, and are to be put away, e.g. bitterness, anger, brawling, slander, and malice (Eph. 4:31; Col. 3:8; cf. 1 Pet. 2:1).

---

57. THE SANCTITY OF MARRIAGE

Exodus 20:14: 'You shall not commit adultery.'

Question: What does the seventh commandment teach?

Answer: The seventh commandment teaches the sanctity of marriage and, by implication, forbids all impurity of thought, speech and behaviour.

1.   God's establishment of marriage.
(a)   Marriage is a divine institution (Gen. 2:24).
(b)   It was founded before the existence of civil society, and it is, therefore, not simply a human social convention but a creation ordinance (Gen. 2:18-24).
(c)   It was founded on the nature of humankind as constituted by God: He made male and female and ordained marriage as an indispensable provision and condition for the continuance and well-being of the human race (Gen. 1:27,28; 2:18-24).
(d)   One of God's purposes in marriage, therefore, is human reproduction and fruitfulness (Gen. 1:28; Ps. 127:3-5).
(e)   Children are to be brought up within the marriage relationship (Prov. 5:15-17), and God desires godly offspring from the marriage union (Mal. 2:15).
(f)   The other equally important purpose of marriage is the support and help that marriage partners are able to give one another (Gen. 2:20-24).
(g)   For the welfare of the human race marriage is not to be within certain close family relationships (Lev. 18:6-18, 20:11-21; Deut. 22:30; 27:20, 22, 23).
(h)   Beneficial as marriage is, the marriage relationship is not to be coveted (Ex. 20:17; cf. 1 Cor. 7:1, 8).

(i) Marriage brings its own cares and distractions, and can bring divided loyalties in that God is not served with the same freedom from distraction as before marriage (1 Cor 7:32-34).

(j) Considerations arising from the kingdom of God and its best interests may cause some men and women to forego the privileges and joys of marriage (Matt. 19:11, 12; 1 Cor 7:7).

(k) Marriage is a relationship limited to this life, for at the resurrection men and women do not marry but are like the angels in heaven (Matt. 22:30; Mark 12:25; Luke 20:35).

2.   The proper pattern of behaviour in marriage.

(a) The natural aim of marriage partners is to please one another (1 Cor. 7:32-34).

(b) Passionate lust is not to characterise the sexual relationship within marriage but rather holiness and honour (1Thess.4:4,5), with a proper recognition of the other marriage partner's marital rights (1 Cor. 7:3).

(c) The marriage relationship is to be modelled upon that between the Lord Jesus Christ and His Church: the husband is to love, protect and cherish his wife as himself; and the wife is to love, honour and obey her husband (Eph. 5:21- 30).

(d) The secret of happy marriage is that neither party should demand his or her rights but that each should give to the other love and service – willingly and freely (Eph. 5:21-33).

(e) Marriage partners need to appreciate the real nature of their oneness, and its mystery, which means understanding that to hurt one's partner is to hurt oneself (Eph. 5:28-33).

(f) A married couple are to find joy in one another, and to keep strictly to one another; they are each other's cistern or well from which alone they are to drink (Prov. 5:15-20).

3.   The sanctity of marriage.

(a) At marriage two people become one (Matt. 19:4-6; Mark 10:6-9).

(b) Marriage is for life, and this is the Lord's ruling (Matt. 19:9; Mark 10:11, 12; Luke 16:18; 1 Cor. 7:10, 11, 39).

(c) Marriage is a compact between a man and a woman to live together, as husband and wife, until separated by death (Gen.

2:23, 24; Rom. 7:2, 3), and God is a witness to the marriage covenant (Mal. 2:14).

(d)   It is the most intimate and sacred relationship that can exist between human beings, and all other human relationships, if necessary, must be reckoned as secondary to it (Gen. 2:24; Eph. 5:31).

(e)   It is the point at which adult children rightly recognise their independence of their parents, and enter into a oneness with a marriage partner that is deeper than what they have known with their parents (Matt. 19:5, 6; Mark 10:7-9).

(f)   The marriage compact is permanent, and cannot be dissolved at the will of either of the parties; it is only properly dissolved by the death of one of the marriage partners (Matt. 5:31, 32; 19:3-9; Mark 10:2-12; Luke 16:18).

(g)   Marriage should be honoured by everyone, and the marriage bed kept pure – that is to say, faithfulness in marriage is vital to its well-being (Heb. 13:4).

(h)   The sanctity of marriage is underlined in that it is made the symbol of the relationship between God and His people (Isa. 62:5; cf. Hos. 2:14-23).

(i)   It is used to illustrate the union between the Lord Jesus Christ and His Church (Eph. 5:22-33; Rev. 19:7, 9; 21:9).

(j)   The uncompromising nature of our Lord Jesus Christ's teaching on marriage surprised even His disciples (Matt. 19:8-10).

4.   Adultery.

(a)   To commit adultery is to sin against God as well as against another human being (Gen. 20:6), for it offends God's law (Ex. 20:14).

(b)   We cannot break the seventh commandment without in some way wronging or cheating someone (1 Thess. 4:6).

(c)   Adultery offends the commandment, 'Love your neighbour as yourself' (Rom. 13:9).

(d)   Adultery is the final expression of thoughts given place to in the heart and expressed in the eyes (Matt. 5:28).

(e)   Adultery is the separating of those whom God has joined together (Matt. 19:6; Mark 10:9).

(f)   If a husband divorces his wife, except for marital unfaithfulness, and marries another, he commits adultery (Matt. 19:9; Mark

10:11, 12); similarly, a wife is an adulteress if, apart from the same exception, she marries another man while her husband is still alive (Rom. 7:3).

(g) Marriage can be dissolved through marital unfaithfulness on the part of one partner, the implication being that the mysterious sense in which the Bible declares a husband and wife to be one has been dreadfully abused and marred (Matt. 19:9).

(h) If a husband divorces his wife on the grounds of marital unfaithfulness, however, and marries another, he commits no offence, and likewise with the wife if she is the offended party (Matt. 19:9; Mark 10:11, 12).

(i) Adultery indicates an absence of the fear of God (Mal. 3:5).

(j) To fail to recognise the sanctity of marriage is to bring God's judgment upon the individual (Heb. 13:4), and His judgment is certain (1 Cor. 6:9, 10).

(k) Divorce is contrary to the whole purpose of God in marriage (Mark 10:1-12; cf. Gen. 12:14-20), and its sinfulness should remind men and women of the seriousness of marriage before they embark upon it (Matt. 19:10).

5. The implications of this commandment in regard to personal purity.

(a) The commandment forbids all impurity of thought, speech and behaviour (Matt. 5:27-30; Eph. 5:4).

(b) In other words, it extends to the heart, mind and imagination as well as to the body and external actions (Matt. 5:28).

(c) To look at a married person of the other sex with lustful desire is adultery of the heart (Matt. 5:27-28).

(d) We need to keep a strict watch, therefore, over our heart for what goes on there affects everything we do (Prov. 4:23; Matt. 15:19; Mark 7:21).

(e) God's will is our sanctification which means avoiding all forms of sexual immorality (1 Thess. 4:3).

(f) We are to learn to control our body in a way that is holy and honourable (1 Thess. 4:4, 5).

(g) God calls us not to impurity but to the most thorough purity, and anyone who makes light of the matter is not making light of a human instruction but of God's commandment (1 Thess. 4:8).

(h)   Christian believers in particular must preserve their chastity because their bodies have become the temples of the Holy Spirit (1 Cor. 6:15, 19).

---

58. RESPECT FOR PROPERTY

Exodus 20:15: 'You shall not steal.'

Question: What does the eighth commandment teach?

Answer: The eighth commandment teaches us to have a proper respect for other people's property, and forbids all forms of theft. By implication, it teaches the right of private property, and the legitimacy and honourableness of lawfully acquired wealth.

1.   **The right of private property.**
(a)   The earth is the Lord's (Ps. 24:1; 50:9-12), so that although we have been granted use of the property and wealth of the world our right remains a derived and temporary right (Gen. 1:28-30).
(b)   God has so constituted us that we desire and need this right of exclusive possession, and the foundation of the right of property, therefore, is God's will (Ex. 20:15).
(c)   In the Old Testament all held their piece of land as an inheritance from the Lord, and the removal of a boundary stone, indicating that inheritance, was an offence against God Himself (Deut. 19:14).
(d)   The prophets looked forward to the coming days of universal peace that included private property as one of its great blessings (Micah 4:3, 4).
(e)   Personal property is to be respected (Deut. 23:25), and throughout the Bible the individual's right to personal property is maintained (1 Kings 21:1-27).
(f)   Even the community of goods that the early Church chose to practice for a while did not involve the denial of the rights of property (Acts 5:4).

(g) The eighth commandment, therefore, forbids all violations of the rights of property (Ex. 20:15).

2. Examples of the many different forms of theft.

(a) Borrowing, and then failing to return what has been borrowed (Ps. 37:21).

(b) Failure to clear oneself of debt when able to do so (2 Kings 4:7).

(c) False weights and dishonest scales (Amos 8:5; Micah 6:10, 11).

(d) General dishonesty in buying and selling (Lev. 25:14).

(e) Misuse of one's employer's property or time (Tit. 2:9, 10).

(f) Wasting someone else's possessions (Luke 16:1).

(g) Failure to seek the owner of something we have found (Lev. 6:2-5).

(h) Taking unfair advantage of either the ignorance or the needs of others (Prov. 11:26).

(i) Paying bad wages, or withholding or delaying their payment (Lev. 19:13; Mal. 3:5; Jas. 5:4).

(j) Indifference of children in their use of their parents' property (Prov. 28:24).

(k) Failing as adult sons or daughters to make some return to our parents when they need help (Prov. 28:24; Mark 7:10-13; 1 Tim. 5:4, 8).

3. The importance of honesty and trustworthiness in regard to other people's possessions.

(a) We are to seek the good of our neighbour rather than seeking only our own good (1 Cor. 10:24).

(b) As employees we are to show complete faithfulness to our employer's interests (Tit. 2:9, 10).

(c) Honesty and integrity are to characterise our work (Eph. 4:28).

(d) We are to strive after honesty in little things for that sets the pattern for larger responsibilities (Luke 16:10).

(e) We are not to give any encouragement to others in defrauding those who have committed some trust to them (Ps. 50:18; Prov. 29:24).

(f) In regard to other people's property and possessions, justice and justice alone is what we are to follow (Deut. 16:20).

(g)   Theft offends the commandment, 'Love your neighbour as yourself' (Rom. 13:9).

(h)   At the root of all forms of stealing is selfishness (Eph. 4:28).

(i)   Theft is something that God detests (Jer. 7:9, 10), and it brings His judgment upon those responsible (Zech. 5:3, 4).

4.   Wealth is not in and of itself wrong, but it must be obtained lawfully and honourably.

(a)   The eighth commandment requires that whatever wealth we possess should be lawfully obtained (Ex. 20:15).

(b)   Property is not evil in itself but like all material possessions it can present dangers to our spiritual well-being (Deut. 6:10-12; Luke 12:15).

(c)   To obtain wealth by dishonesty brings the probability of its quick disappearance (Prov. 13:11); whereas the harder it is to earn honestly, the more we are likely to possess in the long-term (Prov. 13:11).

(d)   The most lawful and honourable means of obtaining wealth is to work for it (Eph. 4:28).

(e)   In fulfilling our daily work we are to think not only of ourselves but also of those who are in any kind of material need whom we can help (Isa. 58:9, 10; Eph. 4:28; 1 John 3:17) - the implication being that possessions are a trust from God.

(f)   The clear implication of the eighth commandment, therefore, is that we are to restore anything that we have unjustly obtained or taken from others (Lev. 6:2-5; Luke 19:8; Eph. 4:28).

---

59. TRUTHFULNESS

Exodus 20:16: 'You shall not give false testimony against your neighbour.'

Question: What does the ninth commandment teach?

Answer: The ninth commandment forbids in principle all untruth and falsehood, and in particular perjury, and proclaims the necessity of truthfulness of speech.

1. **Implicit in the ninth commandment is the importance of the tongue.**

(a) Truthfulness has special reference to our speech (Eph. 4:25; Col. 3:9).

(b) The abuse of the gift of speech and the wrong use to which words are put are sins to which the Bible draws considerable attention (e.g. Ps. 120:1-3; cf. Ps. 5:9; 12:2-4; 36:1-4; 52:1-4; 64:1-6.)

(c) We sin most easily in our words (Eccl. 5:1, 2; Isa. 6:5).

(d) We all make mistakes in all kinds of ways, but those who can claim that they never say the wrong thing can consider themselves perfect, for if you can control your tongue you can control every other part of your personality (Jas. 3:2).

(e) The tongue can speak deceit (Micah 6:12), be full of poison (Rom. 3:13), and be capable of great damage (Job 5:21).

(f) The tongue can practise deceit (Rom. 3:13), express malice (Dan. 3:8-12), and bring about mischief (Ps. 36:3,4).

(g) The tongue has a terrifying power, comparable to that of poison and of fire (Jas. 3:1-12).

(h) In the light of the tongue's potential for good or evil, we are instructed to be extremely careful in the manner in which we speak of others (Lev. 19:16).

2. **God's own character is necessarily reflected in this commandment as in all others.**

(a) The Lord is revealed to us as the true God (2 Chron. 15:3; Jer. 10:10; John 17:3; 1 Thess. 1:9, 10, cf. 1 John 5:20).

(b) Our Lord Jesus Christ is the truth (John 14:6): everyone on the side of truth listens to Him (John 18:37).

(c) The Holy Spirit is the Spirit of truth (John 15:26; 1 John 5:6): He guides those whom He indwells into all that is true (John 16:13).

(d) God is the God of truth and all truth derives its importance and worthiness of respect from Him (John 17:3; 1 John 5:20).

(e) God cannot lie (Tit. 1:2; Heb. 6:18; cf. Rom. 3:4); to lie would be to contradict Himself, and God cannot deny Himself (2 Tim. 2:13).

(f) It is God's perfection to be consistent with Himself, and all His ways are truth (Ps. 111:7,8; cf. Deut. 32:4; Isa. 25:1).

(g) God requires truth in the inner parts – true honesty of heart (Ps. 51:6).

(h) The Lord has a controversy with us when we choose to put aside truth (Hos. 4:1, 2).

3. In particular, the ninth commandment forbids perjury.

(a) The ninth commandment exemplifies what is the worst form of lying: taking a solemn oath in court and then by failure to tell the truth, or by deliberately misrepresenting it, to put someone's reputation or life in danger (Ex. 20:16).

(b) The commandment forbids the spreading of a false report, or conspiring with others to misrepresent the truth (Ex. 23:1).

(c) False witness takes place when an individual states what is untrue in order to safeguard the interests of someone else, perhaps for personal gain (Isa. 5:22, 23).

(d) The commandment, therefore, forbids us to have anything to do with a false charge, and to have no involvement in the harming of the innocent and the righteous (Ex. 23:7).

(e) The commandment forbids the taking of a bribe, for a bribe blinds people's eyes to justice, and injures the cause of those who are in the right (Ex. 23:6-8),

(f) Those who bear false witness against their neighbours always do them serious harm (Prov. 25:18).

(g) By bearing false witness we may even put a person's life in jeopardy (1 Kings 21:13; Ps. 35:11, 12).

(h) The false witness is a traitor (Prov. 14:25).

(i) False witness, like other sins, arises from the evil corruption of the heart (Matt. 15:19).

(j) The bearing of false witness indicates an absence of the fear of God (Mal. 3:5).

(k) God hates false oaths (Zech. 8:17), and He sees to it that a false witness will not go unpunished (Prov. 19:5).

4. In principle, the commandment forbids all untruth and falsehood.

(a) Slander, for example, consists of making false statements about people in order to defame or injure them, and is, in effect, fighting and injuring people with the tongue (Jer. 18:18).

(b) We are not to injure others by initiating or accepting lies or false reports that are harmful to people's good names (Col. 3:8, 9).

(c) Hatred is frequently behind slander (Ps. 41:7-9; 109:2, 3).

(d) Slander comes from an evil heart (Luke 6:44, 45), and is detestable to the Lord (Prov. 6:16-19).

(e) Deceit (Ps. 120:2; Rom. 3:13), falsehood (Eph. 4:25), and flattery (Ps. 5:8, 9; 78:36) are likewise forbidden.

(f) False judgments and wrong forms of criticism are also snares into which we may fall, and they constitute sin in the light of this commandment. The command forbids all rash and unwarrantable judging of other people's hearts and destinies that is usually accompanied by ignorance of our own (Matt. 7:1-5); we are all in danger of criticising others too quickly (Mark 9:38-41; Luke 9:49, 50).

(g) Tale-bearing and gossip are both aspects of slander (Lev. 19:16; Prov. 17:9; Rom. 1:30, 2 Cor. 12:20; 1 Tim. 5:13).

(h) All these and similar departures from truth bring conflict (Prov. 26:20), separate close friends (Prov. 16:28; 17:9), and are utterly destructive (Prov. 11:9).

(i) All who love and practise falsehood are excluded from the kingdom of God (1 Cor. 6:9, 10; Rev. 22:14, 15).

(j) Untruth and falsehood are Satan's habitat (John 8:44), and both lying (Acts 5:3) and slander (Rev. 12:10) are identified with him.

(k) We will be judged for every careless word we utter (Matt. 12:36, 37).

(l) Christians, therefore, are to rid themselves of every form of deceit and falsehood (Eph. 4:25, 31; 1 Pet. 2:1; 3:10; cf. Ps. 34:13).

5. The ninth commandment proclaims the necessity of truthfulness of speech.

(a) The commandment aims at the preservation and promotion of truthfulness: people should speak only the truth and what is helpful (Zech. 8:16; Eph. 4:29).

(b) The Lord Jesus Christ, our example in everything, demonstrated this necessity: no deceit was found in His mouth (1 Pet. 2:22).

(c) Truth is to be spoken from the heart (Ps. 15:2).

(d)   We should mean what we say, ensuring that our speech is both direct and clear (Matt. 5:37; Jas. 5:12).

(e)   We may expect truthful speech to be accompanied by the power of God (2 Cor. 6:7).

(f)   The necessity of truthfulness in us rests upon God's truthfulness (1 Pet. 1:15, 16; cf. John 18:37); upon our exercise of truthfulness depends our experience of fellowship with God (1 John 1:5-10).

---

60. CONTENTMENT

Exodus 20:17: 'You shall not covet your neighbour's house.   You shall not covet your neighbour's wife, or his manservant or maidservant, his ox or donkey, or anything that belongs to your neighbour.'

Question: What does the tenth commandment teach?

Answer: The tenth commandment forbids wrong attitudes to the possessions and position of others, especially attitudes of uncontrolled desire, envy and jealousy.   It teaches rather that we should be content with what God has given to us, and covet those things He wants us to have and that will never harm anyone.

1.   **Defining covetousness.**

(a)   Covetousness, like all other sins, comes from within, out of our hearts (Mark 7:21-23).

(b)   It relates particularly to our desires, and our desires find their source in our hearts (Ps. 37:4; Rom. 1:24).

(c)   Desires characterise both the body and mind, and prior to the experience of new birth they dominate our lives (Rom. 6:12; Eph. 2:3): we are tempted when we are lured and enticed by our desires (Jas. 1:14, 15).

(d)   Covetousness is essentially selfish desire (Prov. 21:26; Luke 12:15), indicating a basic discontent with what we already possess (Heb. 13:5).

(e) The desires of our hearts and minds are prompted usually by what our eyes see and upon which they choose to focus (Gen. 3:6; Josh. 7:21; Prov. 27:20).

(f) Covetousness, then, establishes a place in our thoughts (Luke 12:17), usually in the form of secret thoughts about the possessions of others (Micah 2:1, 2).

(g) Covetousness is an aspect of loving the world, and the things in the world, with the sad consequence that love for God is absent (1 John 2:15, 16).

(h) It is God's law that brings home to us a real awareness of what covetousness is (Rom. 7:7).

2. Some of the objects of covetousness.

(a) Objects of covetousness are mentioned in the commandment itself - for example, our neighbour's home, spouse, employees and possessions (Ex. 20:17)– and there are many forms of covetousness (Luke 12:15; Rom. 7:8).

(b) Covetousness finds its preoccupation with all that is in the world (1 John 2:16).

(c) Covetousness may have material possessions as its principal object, such as clothes (Josh. 7:20, 21; Acts 20:33) or property (1 Kings 21:2).

(d) Covetousness may have its focus upon money (Acts 20:33; 1 Tim. 3:3; 6:9) – see, for example, Gehazi (2 Kings 5:20-24); Judas (Matt. 26:14, 15; John 12:6); and Ananias and Sapphira (Acts 5:1-10).

(e) Covetousness may have as its wrongful object a physical or sexual relationship (Eph. 4:19; 5:3-6) – covetousness can lead a person into adultery (Matt. 5:28).

(f) Covetousness may have as its object position and prestige (1 John 2:16) or an ability (Acts 8:18, 19).

3. Some of the snares of covetousness.

(a) It leads to deceit in that our lips will try to cover up often the desires that are in our heart (Ezek. 33:31; 1 Thess. 2:5).

(b) It makes us slaves to our inward passions and desires (Tit. 3:3; 2 Pet. 2:19).

(c) It makes us blind to the fact that life is more than food, and the body more than clothes (Luke 12:23).

(d) It makes us essentially selfish in that we think principally of ourselves (Luke 12:19, 21).

(e) It leads us to store and hoard rather than to use our possessions to profit others (Matt. 6:19).

(f) It causes us to store up for a future that may never be, as well as neglecting the final accounting with God we must all make (Luke 12:20, 21).

(g) It shuts our life to the helpful influence and transforming power of God's Word (Mark 4:19).

(h) It encourages us to put aside, and ultimately destroy, all other moral values (2 Tim. 3:2-5).

(i) It brings trouble to those connected with us (Josh. 7:10-26), especially to our own family (Prov. 15:27).

(j) It always brings antagonism and conflicts (Jas. 4:1, 2) because by it malice, envy and hatred enter into our lives (Tit. 3:3).

(k) It provides no true satisfaction (Eccl. 5:10; Hab. 2:5), but misery (1 Tim. 6:10) and ultimate poverty (Prov. 28:22).

4. The sinfulness of covetousness.

(a) It is disobedience to the tenth commandment (Ex. 20:17).

(b) It is idolatry, in that the covetous worship a false god (Eph. 5:5): the original desire may be after something lawful in itself but it grows to such a selfish intensity that it gains the place that God alone should have in our life (Col. 3:5).

(c) It lies behind many disagreements and disputes that spoil human relationships (Luke 12:13, 14; Jas. 4:1, 2).

(d) It breaks one of the great summaries of the commandments, 'Love your neighbour as yourself' (Rom. 13:9).

(e) It is through covetousness that we often break other commandments of God: e.g. covetousness leads to not providing for and honouring our parents (Mark 7:11), murder (Prov. 1:18, 19; Jer 22:17; Ezek. 22:12, 27), adultery (2 Sam. 11:2-5), theft (Josh. 7:21), lying (2 Kings 5:20-27), and false accusation (Acts 16:19-21).

5. The commandment teaches us to be content with what God has given to us - the opposite of covetousness.

(a) The willingness to work honestly for our living is put in opposition to covetousness (Acts 20:33-35).

(b) The awareness that our heavenly Father knows our needs, and supplies what is best for us, leads us to appreciate how inappropriate regrets or complaints are in regard to what we possess (Matt. 6:31-33; Rom. 8:28).

(c) Contentment for Christian believers is based upon the certainty of our Lord Jesus Christ's promises, His presence with us (Heb. 13:5), and the glorious assurance that He gives us all we need (Ps. 16:5, 6).

(d) Our contentment needs to be not in what we expect others to give, or what we may strive after, but in what God unfailingly provides for us by one means or another (Phil. 4:10-13).

(e) Contentment does not come easily to the majority of us, but it is a virtue that can be learned (Phil. 4:11), as the Lord Jesus becomes the strength of our life (Phil. 4:13).

(f) Those who follow the example of the Lord Jesus Christ remember and act upon His words, 'It is more blessed to give than to receive' (Acts 20:35).

6. There is a right kind of coveting.

(a) We usually associate coveting with unlawful desires but it can be used in a good sense as, for example, of the men and women of faith throughout the centuries who have coveted a better country, that is, a heavenly one, so that God is not ashamed to be called their God, for He has prepared a city for them (Heb. 11:16).

(b) There is a place for coveting spiritual leadership if God has given the necessary potential, and our honest motive is the well-being of God's people and the glory of our Lord Jesus Christ (1 Tim. 3:1; 1 Pet. 5:2-4).

(c) It is right to covet the best for others (2 Cor 11:2; cf. Rom. 10:1).

(d) Christians are to covet earnestly the best spiritual gifts, and most of all love (1 Cor. 12:31; 13:1) - coveting like this does harm to no one but only good!

---

61. TEMPTATION

Question: **What is temptation and how is it to be viewed and overcome?**

Answer: **Temptation is seduction into disobedience to God. It is to be viewed as a constant peril, and is overcome only by daily watchfulness and dependence upon God.**

1. **Defining and describing temptation.**

(a) To be tempted is to be faced with the seeming attractiveness of sin so as to be in danger of being drawn into it – an experience common to all (1 Cor. 10:12).

(b) Temptation forces us to decide for or against God, and Satan tries by means of it to separate us from God (Gen. 3:1-19).

(c) God is never the author of temptation, so that He can never be charged with being responsible for our sins (Jas. 1:13).

(d) Satan, the prince of this world (John 12:31; 14:30; 16:11), is the tempter, who endeavours to take advantage of our desires (1 Cor 7:5; 1 Thess. 3:5; Jas. 1:14).

(e) Some distinction must be made between temptations and trials, especially as the New Testament usually employs the identical Greek word for both, the right translation into English being determined by the context - when God's involvement is clear, testing is in view rather than temptation (Gen. 22:1-19; cf. Heb. 11:17-19; Job 1:6-22; 2:1-7).

(f) Temptation may come in various ways, but most obviously through our eyes (2 Sam. 11:2; Job. 31:1; Matt. 5:27,28), our physical desires (1 Cor. 7:5) and the weakness of our body (Mark 14:38).

(g) Temptation may come through pride of position or status that inflates us and makes us forget our place before God (Acts 12:21-23).

(h) Temptation may come through striving to help someone else, as we find ourselves tempted by the sins into which they have fallen (Gal. 6:1).

(i)   Temptation may come through the most unlikely instrumentality, like a best friend who misinterprets God's will for us, and wants us to choose an easy way rather than God's way (Matt. 16:22, 23).

2.   The encouragement of our Lord's temptation to the Christian.

(a)   The temptations the Lord Jesus Christ experienced immediately after His baptism and again in the Garden of Gethsemane placed Him in a situation of open choice between surrender to God's will or revolt against it (Matt. 4:1-11; 26:36-46; Mark 1:12, 13; 14:32-42; Luke 4:1-13; 22:40-46).

(b)   The three temptations were attempts to reduce the Lord Jesus to disobedience: first, to use His power for purposes out of keeping with His mission (Matt. 4:2, 3; Luke 4:3, 4); second, to invoke God's help on His own behalf (Matt. 4:5-7; Luke 4:9-11); third, to give up His obedience to God, and to follow Satan (Matt. 4:8-10; Luke 4:5-8).

(c)   It is because He Himself has been tempted by such suffering that He is able to help so adequately those who are now tempted in the same way (Heb. 2:18) - although He Himself did not sin (Heb. 4:15).

(d)   His perfect understanding encourages us to approach in His Name the throne of grace with perfect confidence, that we may receive mercy and find grace to help us when we need it (Heb. 4:16).

(e)   When we do fall before temptation, He acts as our High Priest, and we receive forgiveness in Him (Col. 1:13, 14; Heb. 4:14-16), as we honestly and contritely confess our sins (1 John 1:9).

3.   Overcoming temptation.

(a)   As a fruit of self-knowledge we must be aware of our weakness and our particular personal weaknesses (Matt. 26:41; Mark 14:38).

(b)   We must recognise our essential dependence, therefore, upon our Lord Jesus Christ (John 15:5; Phil. 4:13).

(c)   We must practice spiritual watchfulness (Mark 14:38; 1 Cor. 10:12; Gal. 6:1; 1 Pet. 5:8), sometimes taking preventative actions (1 Cor. 7:5).

(d)   We must learn lessons from our past mistakes (Job 31:1) and our previous experience of God's faithfulness (1 Cor. 10:13).

(e)   We must deliberately put on the full armour of God (Eph. 6:10-17), and then use our two principal weapons - the Scriptures (Eph. 6:17; cf. Matt. 4:4, 7, 10; Luke 4:4, 8, 12) and prayer (Eph. 6:18; cf. Mark 14:38).

(f)   We must pray for discernment to know when to run from temptation (2 Tim. 2:22) and when it is God's will to withstand Satan and his enticements (Jas. 4:7; 1 Pet. 5:9), by the exercise of faith in the Lord Jesus (Eph. 6:16).

(g)   We must be in no doubt that God's purpose is that by the power of His Son, we may be able to stand our ground, and after we have done everything, to stand (Eph. 6:10-13).

---

62. WORLDLINESS

Question: What is worldliness and why is it so serious?

Answer: Worldliness is essentially love of the world as it manifests itself in sinful cravings, the lust of the eyes, and boasting of human achievements.   It is so serious because it is in complete opposition to loving God.

1.   **Worldliness needs to be seen against the background of the Christian's position in the world.**

(a)   As God made the world, it was good (Gen. 1:31; 1 Tim. 4:4).

(b)   The course of this world, however, has been tragically affected by men and women, through whose fall, on account of disobedience, death came into the world and spread to everyone (Rom. 5:12-14).

(c)   The whole world is under the control of the prince of this world, the devil (John 12:31; 16:11; Eph. 2:2; 1 John 5:19).

(d)   The whole world has become guilty before God (Rom. 3:19); and even the created world has been subjected to frustration and longs for liberation from its bondage to decay (Rom. 8:20-22).

(e)   But it is into this world as it is, a world that has fallen into the power of sin and destruction, that God has sent His Son in order to reconcile it to Himself (2 Cor. 5:19-21).

(f)   Christians are those who have been delivered from this present evil world (or age) through the death of the Lord Jesus Christ for their sins (Gal. 1:3, 4), so that they now appreciate that they live in a world that is going to pass away (1 Cor. 7:31).

(g)   Because Christians live in the world, they must have dealings with the world (1 Cor. 5:9, 10; Phil. 2:15), but they must resist the world's pressures to squeeze them into its mould (Rom. 12:2), and they must endeavour to live as those who are dead to it (Gal. 6:14).

(h)   Christians are assured that everything belongs to them – including the world - but they themselves do not belong to the world any more (John 15:19; 17:14, 16; Col. 2:20) because they belong to the Lord Jesus Christ (1 Cor. 3:21-23).

(i)   Christians are to see the world as the sphere of their obedience to Christ (Matt. 28:19, 20): it is God's harvest field (Matt. 9:38; Luke 10:2), in which they are harvesters, and also sowers, by functioning as salt and light (Matt. 5:13-16), always holding out the word of life, the gospel (Phil. 2:16).

(j)   Because Christians are not taken out of the world at their new birth, it is important that they do not allow themselves to be conditioned or corrupted any longer by the world (Jas. 1:27).

2.   Defining worldliness.

(a)   Worldliness is the expression of the state of our heart (Mark 7:21-23), by our love of the world as a matter of deliberate choice (Jas. 4:4; cf. 2 Tim. 4:10), by which we live according to worldly wisdom rather than the wisdom God is willing to provide (Jas. 3:13-18; cf. 1:5).

(b)   Worldliness revolves, first, around sinful cravings, uncontrolled evil desires (1 John 2:16).

(c)   Without a right relationship to God, human life is dominated by the lusts and desires of this world, for there is little else for which to live (Tit. 2:12; 1 Pet. 4:1-4; 2 Pet. 1:4), and before their new birth Christians lived their lives obeying the cravings of their sinful nature and following its passions and desires (Eph. 2:3).

(d) Selfish desires are always fighting for satisfaction, wanting us to indulge them, often leading us into personal conflicts and quarrels (Jas. 4:1-4).

(e) The desires of our sinful nature constantly set themselves against the guidance and direction of the Holy Spirit (Gal. 5:16, 17); and Satan aims to fill our lives with evil desires (John 8:44).

(f) This aspect of worldliness, with its emphasis on human desires, constituted the first temptation to which our Lord was subjected in the challenge to command a stone to be made bread (Luke 4:1-4).

(g) Worldliness revolves, secondly, around the lust of the eyes (1 John 2:16), one expression of which is covetousness.

(h) Eyes are the instruments of desire (Josh. 7:21): the eye is the lamp of the body - when our eyes are good, our whole body is full of light, but sadly the converse is also true (Luke 11:34-36).

(i) The desires of our eyes may often act on the false principle or philosophy that stolen water is sweet and food eaten in secret is delicious (Prov. 9:17).

(j) The lust of the eyes often has a sexual connotation (Job 31:1; Matt. 5:28, 29).

(k) Covetousness can lead to other sins, such as dishonesty (2 Kings 5:19-27) and murder (1 Kings 21:1-16; Jas. 4:2).

(l) This aspect of worldliness was the second temptation Satan placed before our Lord Jesus Christ when in a flash he showed Him all the kingdoms of this world, and offered them to Him - at a price (Luke 4:5-7).

(m) Worldliness revolves, thirdly, around foolish and arrogant boasting, the empty pride we so often have in possessions and position (1 John 2:16).

(n) It is lust for advantage (Matt. 20:20, 21).

(o) It is hankering after status and human praise (Acts 12:21-23).

(p) It is desire for self-importance, revealed often in boasting and bragging (Luke 18:11, 12; Jas. 4:16).

(q) It is yearning for possessions (Gen. 13:11; Josh. 7:21; Luke 12:13-21).

(r) Wrongful preoccupation with possessions is the cause of much human anxiety (Matt. 6:34).

(s)   This aspect of worldliness was the third temptation Satan placed before the Lord Jesus as he encouraged Him to claim an open manifestation of God's protecting power, purely for personal prestige and pride of position (Luke 4:9-12).

(t)   Worldliness, in essence, therefore, is love of the world and everything it craves (1 John 2:15).

3.   The seriousness of worldliness.

(a)   It finds its roots in our hearts rather than in the things we do or the places we frequent (1 John 2:15, 16), and God looks on the heart (1 Sam. 16:7).

(b)   In direct opposition to God's will for us (1 John 2:16, 17), it is in total opposition to love for the Father (1 John 2:15), and constitutes unfaithfulness to God or spiritual adultery (Ps. 73:27; Jas. 4:4), a plain opposite of godliness (Tit. 2:13, 14).

(c)   It indicates a failure to appreciate the passing nature of this world (Heb. 12:25-27; 1 John 2:17), and the neglect of the all-important questions: 'What good will it be for a man if he gains the whole world, yet forfeits his soul? Or what can a man give in exchange for his soul?' (Matt. 16:26; Mark 8:36; Luke 9:25).

(d)   It demonstrates where our heart is (Luke 12:33, 34), and where our treasures are to be found (Matt. 6:19-21), for it is impossible to serve God and money (Matt. 6:24; Luke 16:13).

(e)   It boasts of itself rather than of God and treats life as if God does not exist (Jas. 4:13-17).

(f)   Worldliness is serious because it grows: it begins in the mind, shows itself in conduct, and becomes established in attitudes (Ps. 1:1).

(g)   It chokes spiritual growth and fruitfulness (Luke 8:14), and it may indicate that an individual is without the Spirit (Jude 19; cf. Rom. 8:29; 2 Cor. 13:5).

(h)   Christians who are worldly in spirit and attitude grieve the Holy Spirit (Jas. 4:4, 5).

(i)   Worldliness takes away a Christian's appreciation of worship and fellowship (Ps. 84:10; cf. Heb. 10:25).

(j)   Worldliness may make us turn aside from that to which we have set our hand, a task that we know to be God's will (2 Tim. 4:10).

(k)   It may even reach a point at which we are worse off at the end than we were at the beginning through our entanglement again with the world's corruption (2 Pet. 2:20, 21).

4.   The antidote to worldliness is the constant practice and pursuit of a number of objectives.

(a)   We are to understand that the purpose of our redemption by the death of Christ is that, having been redeemed and made His people (Tit. 2:13, 14; cf. Gal. 1:3, 4; 1 Pet. 1:18, 19, 2 Pet. 2:20), we should say 'No' to ungodliness and worldly passions, and, instead, live self-controlled, upright and godly lives, while we await our Saviour's return (Tit. 2:12, 13; cf. 2 Pet. 1:3, 4).

(b)   We need to recognise our true character now in the world as aliens and strangers on the earth (Heb. 11:13; 1 Pet. 1:17; 2:11), because of our heavenly citizenship (Eph. 2:19; Phil. 3:20) and our commitment to make God's kingdom our primary concern, leaving it to Him to add to us what He knows we need of this world's possessions (Matt. 6:33).

(c)   The understanding that we are called upon to enter into the privilege of being friends of God (Isa. 41:8; John 15:14; Jas. 2:23; 4:4; Rev. 3:20), a privilege that demands whole-hearted obedience to Him as a condition of our enjoyment of this unspeakable benefit (John 14:21, 23).

(d)   The daily renewed offering of ourselves to God without reserve, in the light of His mercy towards us, so that instead of being conformed to this world we are instead transformed by the renewal of our mind, so that we prove in daily experience what is good and acceptable and perfect (Rom. 12:1, 2), determining to discover and to do God's will in everything (1 Thess. 4:3; 1 Cor. 10:31).

(e)   Honesty to examine ourselves (1 Cor.10:12; 11:28; 2 Cor. 13:5), and to exercise self-control over our desires where they war against the best interests of our soul (1 Pet. 2:11); and if ever we are uncertain as to the rightness of our desires to present them to God in prayer for His judgment and guidance (Jas. 4:1-3).

(f)   The key antidote to worldliness is the frank recognition of its seriousness and the active pursuit of sanctification, guided by God's Word (John 17:17).

63. SPIRITUAL DECLINE

Question: **What is spiritual decline or backsliding?**

Answer: **Spiritual decline, or backsliding, is turning back from following the Lord. It takes a variety of forms, but it always begins with the thoughts, and eventually it shows itself in a life that is no longer wholehearted in its devotion to the Lord Jesus Christ.**

1. **Spiritual decline describes what is often expressed as backsliding.**
(a) It is our ceasing to make every effort to progress in holiness and obedience (2 Pet. 1:5-11).
(b) It is to turn back from following the Lord, not asking for His guidance and not seeking His blessing as before (Zeph. 1:6).
(c) It is the turning of our heart away from God after other gods or objectives (1 Kings 11:9), so that the heart is not wholly devoted to Him (1 Kings 11:4).
(d) It is to forget God and the indebtedness we should feel to Him (Hos. 2:13).
(e) It is to be unfaithful to God (Hos. 5:7), for inevitably the attempt is made to serve two masters (Matt. 6:24).
(f) It is the abandonment of the love for Christ that we knew at first as Christians (Rev. 2:4).
(g) It is the pushing of the Lord Jesus Christ outside our life, almost unconsciously (Rev. 3:20).
(h) It is spiritual adultery (Hos. 1:2; Jas. 4:4).

2. **The form that spiritual decline or backsliding takes varies a great deal but certain stages, not always in the order outlined, may be discerned.**
(a) It all begins with the thoughts: the mind may somehow be led astray from a sincere and pure devotion to Christ (2 Cor. 11:3).
(b) Little by little the private aspects of the Christian life – such as private prayer – are neglected (Jas. 4:2, 3; Luke 18:1).
(c) Slackness in service soon follows (Heb. 6:10-12).

(d)   Appreciation of opportunities for fellowship, public worship, and the ministry of God's Word lessens, and this declining appreciation leads to neglect of them (Ps. 84:10; Heb. 5:11-14; 10:25).

(e)   In spite of this obvious decline, we may be complacent about it, a form of spiritual short-sightedness (Amos 6:1, 4-7; 2 Pet. 1:9; Rev. 3:17).

(f)   It is more than likely that we will be inclined to criticise more spiritual fellow-Christians (Phil. 1:15-17).

(g)   We begin to forget and lose the wonder of the Cross – the manner in which we were first cleansed from our past sins (2 Pet. 1:9).

(h)   Whereas we ought to be able to teach others the Christian faith, we need, in fact, someone to teach us again the elementary truths of God's Word (Heb. 5:12).

(i)   We lose our appreciation of the deeper truths of the faith and of the Bible (1 Cor. 3:2; Heb. 5:12-14).

(j)   We become unskilled in using the Bible, whereas once we found it easy to apply it to life and conduct (Heb. 5:13).

(k)   We lose our ability to discern good from evil in the everyday situations of life (Heb. 5:14).

(l)   God's promises no longer seem very great and precious, and they cease to influence the course of our life (Heb. 6:12; 2 Pet. 1:4).

(m)   God's guidance in daily living is no longer sought (Jer. 2:13; Zeph. 1:6).

(n)   Compromise, in situation after situation, makes our spiritual life – and life in general – more and more unstable (Jas. 1:5-8), and the process accelerates (Gal. 5:9).

(o)   In the end, if unchecked, we become completely ineffective and unproductive in our knowledge of the Lord Jesus Christ (2 Pet. 1:8).

3.   The causes of spiritual decline or backsliding are many and it may be caused by just one factor or the combination of several.

(a)   The neglect of prayer or, on the other hand, the offering of prayer from the wrong motives, with conduct in opposition to God's revealed will (Jas. 4:2, 3).

(b) Giving in to sin, with the sin unrepented of and unconfessed (Ps. 32:1-5; 51:3, 4; Gal. 6:1).

(c) Disobedience to the obvious and known will of God (Jonah 1:2-3; Jer. 8:5-7; Neh. 9:26; 1 Cor. 10:23).

(d) Life's worries, wealth and pleasures (Luke 8:14; Rom. 12:2; 2 Tim. 4:10; 1 John 2:15-17; Jas. 4:1-4).

(e) A human relationship - especially with someone of the opposite sex - taking the place that God alone should have (1 Kings 11:4; 2 Cor. 6:14).

(f) Discouragement, through the power of unbelief - this seems to have been the situation of the Jewish Christians addressed in the Letter to the Hebrews (Heb. 6:9-20).

(g) Never having been properly established in the Christian life, as was the case with some of the Corinthian believers (1 Cor. 3:1-4).

(h) Self-assurance - instead of self-distrust and trust in Christ - is a cause of spiritual decline (Prov. 16:18; Mark 14:29-31; 1 Cor. 10:12).

(i) The pursuit of false and unworthy ambitions (Jas. 4:3).

(j) A lack of self-examination (1 Cor 11:31).

4. The consequences of spiritual decline or backsliding.

(a) It grieves the Holy Spirit (Eph. 4:30).

(b) It makes us useless in the fulfilling of God's purposes in the world (Matt. 5:13).

(c) The joy of God's salvation is forfeited (Ps. 51:12).

(d) The sense of God's presence is lost (Num. 14:43; Isa. 59:2, 9-11).

(e) The ability to teach others God's ways is lost (Ps. 51:12, 13).

(f) Some form of idolatry is soon practised (Zeph. 1:4-6).

(g) All kinds of sins and sinful ways may follow (Prov. 14:14; Isa. 1:5-6; Hos. 4:1-19), not least those that arise from unlawful associations (Hos. 5:7).

(h) We may find ourselves so carried away that we discover ourselves to be contending for the world against God (Judg. 6:28-32).

(i) Backsliding leads to a complacency that is full of danger (Rev. 3:17; 1 Cor. 10:12).

(j) It makes us nauseating to Christ (Rev. 3:16).

(k)   Unchecked, it is liable to increase (Jer. 8:5; 14:7).

(l)   It brings us under God's displeasure (Ps. 78:57-59).

(m)   It brings the discipline and judgment of God (Hos. 11:5-7); it results in reproof and chastisement from Christ (Rev. 3:19).

---

64. SPIRITUAL RESTORATION

Question: **How may Christians in spiritual decline, i.e. backsliders, be restored?**

Answer: **Christians in spiritual decline, i.e. backsliders, may be restored when they come to themselves, realise the seriousness of their position and carefully fulfil the conditions given in the Scriptures. As the conditions are fulfilled, God's promises come into operation to accomplish full and glorious restoration.**

1.   **The restoration of backsliders or Christians whose spiritual life is in decline is clearly taught in the Bible.**

(a)   Backsliders' state is not hopeless (Ps. 37:23, 24; Prov. 24:16).

(b)   Nothing, however, can be done for us as backsliding Christians until we feel restless and miserable (Mark 14:72) - our consciences need to be probed and stirred (John 21:15-17).

(c)   Restoration is achieved only by God's help (Hos. 12:6).

(d)   Backsliders are exhorted to return to the Lord (2 Chron. 30:6; Isa. 31:6; Jer. 3:12-14, 22; Hos. 14:1-3).

(e)   The Lord uses chastisement to bring backsliders back to Himself (Hos. 2:6; 5:15; 6:1).

(f)   Spiritual Christians may be used by God to restore backsliding Christians (Gal. 6:1; Jas. 5:19) – perhaps by a pointed question (Gal. 4:15) or by direct confrontation and accusation (2 Sam. 12:1-7).

(g)   Restoration can take place only when we have come to themselves (Luke 15:17), perhaps through seeing the chastising hand of God in our circumstances (Jonah 2:2-4).

2. **The Lord promises – on clearly stated conditions - the pardon of backsliders and the reviving of Christians whose spiritual life is in decline (2 Chron. 7:14).**

(a) The recognition that deliverance belongs to the Lord – it is not in the power of believers on their own to achieve (Jonah 2:9).

(b) The remembrance of the rightful jealousy God has for His people (Deut. 32:16, 21; Ex. 20:5; 34:14; Zech. 8:2; Jas. 4:5).

(c) All arrogance must be removed – self-assurance must be put aside (Jas. 4:6).

(d) Submission to God – backsliders' return must be accompanied by the humbling of pride, or else any profession of seeking God is of no value (Jas. 4:6; cf. Hos. 5:5-7).

(e) Resistance to the devil, for he will always contest any move to return to the Lord (Eph. 6:16; Jas. 4:7; 1 Pet. 5:8, 9).

(f) Drawing near to God (2 Chron. 7:14; Jas. 4:8) - prayers for restoration are provided in the Bible for our help and guidance (Ps. 80:3; 85:4; Lam. 5:21).

(g) The sin of backsliding is to be confessed (Jer 3:13, 14; 14:7-9) and the merits of our Lord Jesus Christ's atoning death depended upon, even as when we were first converted (1 John 1:7-9).

(h) The snares and temptations that have turned us aside are to be resolutely abandoned (Isa. 1:15-20; 2 Chron. 7:14; Ps. 24:4; Jas. 4:8) - backsliding is soon renewed if repentance is not real (2 Cor. 7:10); remorse, therefore, is not to be mistaken for repentance (Judg. 2:4, 5, 11-23).

(i) Self-humbling before God (Prov. 3:34; Jas. 4:6; 1 Pet. 5:5).

3. **As the conditions God lays down are fulfilled, so His promises come into operation to accomplish restoration.**

(a) Praying now out of the right motives, we will receive that for which we ask (Jas. 4:2, 3).

(b) The Holy Spirit, who has been grieved, will immediately assist us in our efforts to return to the Lord (Jas. 4:5).

(c) As we seek to humble ourselves before God in submission, we will be given grace from God (Jas. 4:6); this grace will include help in resisting the devil to the end that he may flee from us (Jas. 4:7).

(d) As we draw near to God, so God will come close to us (Jas. 4:8).

(e) As we confess our sins, God is just, and may be trusted to forgive us our sins and to purify us from all unrighteousness (1 John 1:9).

(f) As we continue to humble ourselves before the Lord, so the Lord will lift us up anew into the joys of new life in Christ (Jas. 4:10).

(g) Our desire and ability to teach other sinners God's ways will be regained (Ps. 51:13).

(h) There is no doubt whatsoever about the Lord's healing, love and reviving, if the conditions are fulfilled (Hos. 14:4-7; Jer. 3:22) - the love that first pardoned our sins heals backsliding (Micah 7:18).

4. From what has been deduced from the Bible about spiritual decline or backsliding, certain results clearly follow upon restoration after such an experience.

(a) The regaining of the joy of God's salvation (Ps. 51:12).

(b) A greater appreciation of Jesus Christ - the Saviour and Restorer of the soul.

(c) An increased hatred of sin.

(d) A more sensitive awareness to the first approaches of sin and temptation.

(e) A new appreciation of the provision God has made for spiritual growth through the Lord's Supper, Bible reading, prayer, fellowship, worship and regularly benefiting from teaching and preaching.

(f) A renewed and deepened dedication to the service of our Lord Jesus Christ (Jonah 3:1-3; John 21:15-17).

---

65. CHRISTIAN WORSHIP

Question: **What does the Bible teach about worship?**

Answer: **Worship is our acknowledgement of God in a manner acceptable to Him. Worship therefore requires a wholehearted dependence upon the Lord Jesus Christ and the way He has opened up for us into God's presence; recognition of the inwardness and spiritual nature of true worship; and an obedient awareness that the worship of God cannot be separated from conduct that honours Him.**

1. **Worship is our acknowledgement of God in a manner worthy and pleasing to Him.**

(a) The English word 'worship' means 'worthship' and denotes the worthiness of the person receiving the special honour on account of worth. Worship and service are presented to us as being virtually the same - the identical Hebrew word can be used for either 'worship' or 'service' and the same holds true in the New Testament use of the Greek word for 'worship.'

(b) Worship is rejoicing in all that God is, and giving Him the glory, i.e. ascribing to Him the things that rightly belong to Him, such as glory, honour, power, salvation, and thanksgiving (Rev. 4:9, 11; 19:1, 7).

(c) Worship can be simply that of the individual (Gen. 24:26), but the emphasis is more generally upon corporate worship (Ps. 42:4).

2. **God alone is to be worshipped.**

(a) The primary reference of worship is Godward - it is 'to God' (Col. 3:16).

(b) Worship presupposes that God exists and that He rewards those who earnestly seek Him (Heb. 11:6).

(c) God does not live in temples made by human hands. He is not far from each one of us: 'In him we live and move and have our being' (Acts 17:24-28).

(d)   God wants the people of the nations to seek Him, in the hope that they might reach out for Him and find Him (Acts 17:27).

(e)   God alone is to be worshipped, and the revelation God has given forbids us to worship anyone besides Him (Ex. 20:3; Matt. 4:10; Rev. 19:10).

(f)   We must beware of worshipping either the things that God has made or the messengers He sends (Rom. 1:25; Rev. 19:10; 22:9).

(g)   Worship is God's due as our Creator (Ps. 100:1-3; Rom. 1:25; Rev. 4:11) - He is the Maker of the world and everything in it, the Lord of heaven and earth (Acts 17:24).

(h)   Worship is God's due as our Redeemer (John 3:16); God the Father is the source of all blessing, and is therefore to be praised and thanked (Eph. 1:3).

(i)   God in Christ is the definite, special object of Christian worship (Eph. 5:19, 20): spiritual worship of God is synonymous with joy in Christ, and a renunciation of all human effort to achieve salvation (Phil. 3:3).

(j)   In worshipping Christ we worship the Father (Eph. 5:19, 20; Col. 3:16, 17), for He is the Son of God (Matt. 14:33), the image of the invisible God (Col. 1:15; Heb. 1:3).

(k)   Our praise and thanksgiving go to the Father through the Lord Jesus Christ, and in His Name (Eph. 5:20).

(l)   The Lord Jesus, as the Lamb who was slain, is rightly the centre of our worship (Rev. 5:8-14), to the glory of God the Father (Phil. 2:11).

(m)   Christians are to come together for worship (1 Cor. 14:26; Heb. 10:24, 25), and such worship is appropriate as often as God's people have the opportunity of meeting (Acts 2:46, 47).

(n)   The particular day for worship, however, is the first day of the week, the Lord's Day (Acts 20:7; Rev. 1:10).

3.   The basis of worship.

(a)   Whenever we worship God, we are confronted with the great and glorious, but awesome truth, that God is holy (Ps. 24:3, 4; Isa. 61:4; 1 John 1:5-7).

(b)   Worship rests upon God's revelation as to how acceptable worship is possible for sinners; and Christian worship rests specifically upon God's revelation in Jesus Christ and the way

He has opened up for us into God's presence (Eph. 2:13-18; Rev. 1:12-18).

(c) Worship depends upon God's mercy: He is graciously willing to be approached by us (Ps. 5:7; 138:2).

(d) We can approach God solely on the grounds of what the Lord Jesus Christ has done: by virtue of His blood shed for us in His atoning sacrifice, we may have confidence to come before God (Heb. 10:19).

(e) The Lord Jesus Christ has opened for us a new and living way into God's presence (Heb. 10:20).

(f) We may draw near to God with a sincere heart in full assurance of faith, having our hearts sprinkled to cleanse us from a guilty conscience and having our bodies washed with pure water (Heb. 10:22).

(g) In view of such a provision, worship is part of our thankfulness to God (Heb. 12:28): the soul, the heart, and the flesh of believers long to express worship to God (Ps. 84:2).

(h) Every new experience of God's grace in the Lord Jesus Christ increases our desire to worship God (Ps. 27:5, 6; Luke 5:8; Rev. 1:12-17).

(i) Worship should be our instinctive reaction to the discovery of every evidence of God's working on our behalf (Judg. 7:15).

4. Characteristics of true worship.

(a) The place of worship is not important, but the manner of worship is (John 4:20-24).

(b) Worship of God must be on the basis of a knowledge of God that is true (Acts 17:23) - a fact which underlines the importance of the understanding given to us in the Scriptures (John 4:22); worship must be according to God's Word, and not according to human ideas and precepts (Isa. 29:13; Mark 7:6-8).

(c) Expressed another way, worship requires some glimpse of God's glory (Josh. 5:13-15; Isa. 6:1-5; 2 Cor. 4:6).

(d) Reverence and awe are to characterise our worship of God (Ps. 5:7; Heb. 12:28).

(e) We should never enter into worship carelessly, allowing our lips to be hasty and glib in expressions of worship (Eccl. 5:1, 2).

(f) The worship we offer to God is to be spiritual, that is to say, deeply and genuinely felt and aided by God's Holy Spirit (John

4:23, 24; Phil. 3:3), for God delights not in outward acts but in the spiritual worship of the heart (Ps. 40:6; 50:7-15).

(g) The worship we offer to God is to be sincere (Isa. 1:11-15): it is acceptable to Him only as our motives are right (Amos 5:18-27).

(h) Worship is worthless if the feelings of the heart do not correspond with the expression of the lips (Mark 7:6, 7); God has regard to our worship when it is sincere and the best we can offer; but He has no regard to what is merely formal, mechanical and less than our best (Gen. 4:3-5).

(i) Worship is to combine fervour with the use of the mind (1 Cor. 14:14, 15); the mind and understanding are to be active in our worship of God (1 Cor 14:14),

(j) Worship should always include the spirit of submission to God (Josh. 5:14), for it cannot be separated from obedience (Josh. 5:14, 15; 1 Sam. 15:22; cf. Gen. 22:1-5).

(k) Worship should cost us something (2 Sam. 24:22-24, Mal. 1:6-11; cf. Gen. 4:1-7): it is better not to worship God at all than to offer what is knowingly and deliberately inferior.

(l) Worship is to be conducted in a fitting and orderly way (1 Cor. 14:40), for God is not a God of disorder, but of peace (1 Cor. 14:33).

(m) Worship is also to be edifying, for although its primary reference is Godward, it is also intended to provide spiritual encouragement for believers (Col. 3:16); nothing is to find a place in the worship of God that does not build believers up in the Lord (1 Cor. 14:26).

(n) In our meeting together, we are to think of one another and how we can encourage one another towards love and good deeds (Heb. 10:24, 25). By our worship of God in our hymns, psalms and spiritual songs, we should be speaking to one another (Eph. 5:19).

(o) Even though God's concern is with the inward attitude of the heart rather than outward activity (John 4:24), worship is expressed by posture (Rev. 5:14; 7:11; 19:4; cf. Phil. 2:10); the outward attitude of the body is not a matter of indifference (Gen. 24:26; Ex. 33:10; 1 Chron. 29:20).

5.   Worship and morality.

(a)   It is important to notice that the major definitions of worship in the New Testament are all inward and ethical (Rom. 12:1,2; Heb. 13:15, 16; Jas. 1:27).

(b)   Worship has no value apart from the person who offers it (Gen. 4:4, 5); Abel's faith in God as he worshipped was decisive for his acceptance (Heb. 11:4); Cain's life and conduct made plain the insincerity of the worship he offered to God (1 John 3:12).

(c)   Worship of God must be accompanied by righteousness of life (Ps. 40:6-8; Isa. 1:10-17; Amos 5:21-24; Micah 6:6-8): the worship that the Lord requires is a matter not of sacrifices, but rather of justice, mercy, and a humble walk with Him (Micah 6:6-8).

(d)   God is as concerned with the morality of His people as with their worship (Jer. 7:2-7, Mal. 3:3-5): worship is not acceptable to God if we are knowingly in a wrong relationship to someone, without having sought to rectify the situation (Matt. 5:23, 24).

(e)   Worship is linked with our service of others (Heb. 13:15, 16; Jas. 1:27); worship must never be an excuse for passing over need (Luke 10:25-37; Acts 3:1-10, noting verse 1).

6.   Parts of worship.

(a)   Our worship should always contain praise to God for the understanding we have of His activity on our behalf (Ps. 27:6); through Jesus we continually offer to God a sacrifice of praise, that is, the fruit of lips that confess His name (Heb. 13:15).

(b)   Thanksgiving should have a regular place in all worship (Ps. 136:1-26; Jonah 2:9; Eph. 5:19, 20).

(c)   Prayer is part of worship (Luke 2:37; 1 Cor 14:14-17).

(d)   By reason of particular circumstances, perhaps the need for guidance from God, or the necessity of making a decision, fasting alongside prayer may sometimes be part of worship (Luke 2:37; Acts 13:2).

(e)   Psalms, hymns and spiritual songs have a place in Christian worship (Acts 16:25; 1 Cor. 14:26; Col.. 3:16; Jas. 5:13) for the Holy Spirit inspires a joy that expresses itself in them (Eph. 5:18, 19).

(f)   We may have fragments of early Christian hymns in the New Testament (e.g. Eph. 4:4-6; 5:14; Phil. 2:5-11; 1 Tim. 1:17; 2:5, 6; 6:15, 16, 2 Tim. 2:11-13; Rev. 4:11).

(g)   Singing must be rooted in the Word of Christ, for it has as one of its purposes the living of His words in our hearts (Col. 3:16).

(h)   The Lord's Supper is part of Christian worship (Acts 20:7; 1 Cor. 11:23-34).

(i)   Worship consists of giving money to God for the benefit of others (1 Cor. 16:1, 2): our gifts can represent a fragrant offering, an acceptable and pleasing sacrifice to Him (Phil. 4:18).

(j)   Worship includes the reading of the Scriptures (Col. 3:16; Jas. 1:22), and the preaching of the Word (Acts 20:7; 1 Cor. 14:19); it is to include instruction and encouragement for believers (1 Cor. 14:31).

(k)   Christians are to seek to contribute to worship (1 Cor. 14:26), which means that we should always be participators rather than merely spectators.

7.   The experience of worship.

(a)   As we worship God, by means of all the different parts and aspects of worship, we desire to be in God's presence, to behold His beauty, and to seek Him (Ps. 27:4; 63:2).

(b)   Worship will sometimes be a timely way of escape for us (1 Cor. 10:13): living in the world and making our witness there, we shall often be oppressed by the spirit of the world, and the evil prevalent in it, but our means of relief and temporary escape will be the worship of God (Ps. 73:1-28; 120:1-7).

(c)   Worship should be a humbling experience (Gen. 18:27; Job 42:5, 6; Isa. 6:1-5).

(d)   In worship we should draw near to God to listen (Eccl. 5:1, 2), for it may be a time when His will is made known and His guidance given (Acts 13:1-3).

(e)   As we worship the Lord and regain our spiritual balance and equilibrium, we see things more clearly and in a better light (Ps. 73:16, 17).

(f)   We should not forget that worship is part of our witness to God in the world (1 Pet. 2:9, 10; cf. 1 Cor 11:26).

(g)   There will be occasions when God will use the worship of His people as a powerful instrument of conviction in the lives of unbelievers who may be present (1 Cor. 14:24, 25).

---

66. PRAYER

Question: **What is prayer and how should we use it?**

Answer: **Prayer is the fellowship we know with God as our Father through our Lord Jesus Christ, in which we express our dependence upon Him, and ask Him for the good things He encourages us to seek from Him, both for ourselves and others.**

1.   Defining prayer.

(a)   Prayer is asking God for the good things He wants to give to His children (Matt. 7:7, 11; Luke 11:9, 10; Col. 1:9; Jas. 1:5,6); it is sharing with Him what we or others lack (John 2:3; Jas. 1:5).

(b)   Prayer is the pouring out of our hearts to God (Ps. 62:8).

(c)   If we know that a desire is right, we may ask for its fulfilment with confidence and assurance (Rom. 10:1); if, however, we are not sure, we may bring our desire to God, in the form of a request, to which His answer may be 'No' (Rom. 1:10; 2 Cor. 12:7-9; 1 Thess. 3:10).

(d)   Prayer is the surrendering of our wills to God (Matt. 6:10)– the Lord Jesus Christ is our example here as in the Garden of Gethsemane He three times prayed the same prayer (Matt. 26:39, 42, 44).

(e)   Prayer is being with God, since it is not always asking but sometimes simply an expression of fellowship with Him, with the desire on our part to be in His presence (Ps. 27:4) – we try to be still before Him, recognising that He alone is God (Ps. 46:10,11), and we share our life with Him (Rev. 3:20).

(f)   Prayer is conversation with God (Gen. 18:23-33; Ex. 5:22,23; 6:1, 10-12; Deut. 3:23-26): God says 'Seek my face!' and we reply, 'Your face, Lord, 1 will seek' (Ps.27:8; cf. Acts 13:1, 2).

(g) Prayer is a key to our experience of God's peace (Phil. 4:6, 7), for a burden shared with God is far more than a burden halved –it is a burden lifted and carried by God (1 Pet. 5:7).

2. Some basic principles and rules of prayer.

(a) A first principle of prayer is that we must be in fellowship with God (Prov. 15:8): reconciled to God through faith in our Lord Jesus Christ, our fellowship is with the Father and with His Son (1 John 1:3), and we may call God 'Father' (Luke 11:2; Rom. 8:15).

(b) A second rule of prayer is the practice of obedience– by putting away sin (Ps. 66:18; 1 John 1:9), by maintaining right relationships with others (Matt. 5:23, 24; 1 Pet. 3:7), and by striving to remain in Christ (John 15:7).

(c) A third rule of prayer is dependence upon the Lord Jesus Christ and His work on our behalf (Eph. 2:13) – we pray in His Name (John 14:13, 14; 15:16; 16:23, 24, 26).

(d) A fourth rule of prayer is the exercise of faith (Heb. 11:6; Jas.1:6-8) – if we believe, we will receive whatever we ask for in prayer in the name of the Lord Jesus (that is to say, in harmony with all He has revealed of God, and all that His name stands for (Matt. 21:21, 22; Mark 11:22-24; John 14:13-15). Believing prayer has the assurance that we may receive beyond all our asking (Eph. 3:20).

(e) A fifth rule of prayer is readiness for action, for faith and works go together (Jas. 2:17): having prayed, we must be ready to be the instruments often by means of which God answers our prayers (Ex. 14:15, 16; Matt. 9:37,38; cf. 10:1-16).

(f) A sixth principle of prayer is the honest desire for God's will to be done, and His Name to be glorified (Matt. 6:10; 1 John 5:14; cf. Ex. 32:11-13; Matt. 26:39).

(g) A seventh principle of prayer is sincerity: God has no time for hypocrites who make a lot of show without reality in their hearts (Isa. 29:13; Mark 12:40), but He promises to be near all who call upon Him in truth (Ps. 145:18).

3. Prayer's parts.
(The Bible prescribes no set order for the different parts of prayer, and daily circumstances will dictate a varying starting

point. However, there is a natural order, although not binding, that the Bible suggests.)

(a) **Adoration** consists in reverencing God in a spirit of worship (Ps. 89:7, 8; Isa. 6:1,2).

(b) **Praise** concerns itself with what God is, and it gives glory to God (Ps. 18:3; 145:3).

(c) **Thanksgiving** focuses upon what God has done for us (Phil. 4:6), and, no matter what our circumstances, there is always cause for thanksgiving to Him (Ps. 126:3; Eph. 1:3; 1 Thess. 5:18).

(d) **Confession of sin** is a vital part of prayer for the maintenance of our fellowship with God (1 John 1:5-10), for 'he who conceals his sins does not prosper, but whoever confesses and renounces them finds mercy' (Prov. 28:13).

(e) **Prayers and supplications** are separate, yet related (1 Tim. 2:1; Eph. 6:18): prayer has regard to the needs that are always present with us (as represented in the petitions of the Lord's Prayer - Matt. 6:9-13) and supplications have regard to specific situations where special or emergency help is required (as illustrated in Mary's petition to Jesus at the wedding in Cana – John 2:3 and Mary and Martha's message to Jesus about Lazarus – John 11:3).

(f) **Intercession** approaches God for others (Col. 4:12): we are to pray for all men and women without distinction of race, nationality or social position (1 Tim. 2:1, 2). We are to do so when they are in need or are rebellious (Ex. 8:12, 30; 32:11-32; Num. 14:13-19; cf. Jer 15:1); when they are ill (Jas. 5:14); when they are unjustly treated, and perhaps imprisoned (Acts 12:5; Heb. 13:3); and even when they are our enemies (Matt. 5:44; Luke 23:34).

(g) Governments and rulers are not to be neglected in our intercession (1 Tim. 2:1, 2).

(h) In praying for missionaries, for example, we should pray for their deliverance from malicious enemies, acceptance with God's people, health of mind and body, the ability to speak the right words boldly at the moment of opportunity, the turning of difficult circumstances to spiritual good, God-given opportunities for preaching Christ and progress in the establishment of the

Church (Rom. 15:30-32, 3 1; 2 Cor. 1:10, 11; Eph. 6:19; Phil. 1:19; Col.. 4:3; 2 Thess. 3:1, 2).

(i)   **Dedication to God and to His will** must be the background to all our prayers (Rom. 12:1, 2; Heb. 10:7).

4.   Characteristics of prayer at its best.

(a)   Reverence (Gen. 18:25,27; Acts 9:31; 10:2; 2 Cor. 5:11; Heb. 12:28).

(b)   Humility (Ps. 10:17; Luke 18:9-14; Jas. 4:6).

(c)   Freedom and confidence (Eph. 3:12; Heb. 4:15, 16).

(d)   Agreement with Scripture (1 Thess. 4:3; 1 Tim. 2:1-3; 1 John 5:14, 15).

(e)   Definiteness (1Chron. 4:10; Eph.1:16-23; 3:14-21; Phil. 1:3-11; Col. 1:9-12).

(f)   Intelligence (1 Cor. 14:15;cf. Neh. 1:1-11).

(g)   Earnestness (Luke 11:5-13; Mark 7:24-29; Jas. 5:17, 18).

(h)   Persistence (Gen. 32:26; 1 Thess. 5:17).

(i)   Submission to God (Matt. 26:39, 42, 44; Mark 14:35, 36, 39; Luke 22:42; Rom. 12:1,2).

(j)   Fasting (Neh. 1:4; Matt. 4:2) - some situations are dealt with satisfactorily only by prayer and fasting (Acts 13:1-3; 14:21-23).

5.   Our chief Helper in prayer is the Holy Spirit.

(a)   In the gift of the Holy Spirit (Acts 2:38), God has provided a perfect Counsellor who is with us forever (John 14:16), and who testifies with our spirit that we are God's children, helping us cry, 'Abba, Father' (Rom. 8:15, 16; cf. Gal. 4:6).

(b)   He prompts us to pray by reminding us of our Lord Jesus Christ's words and promises (John 14:26), and He urges us to pray according to the will of God that they reveal.

(c)   He also prompts our concern for individuals (Rom. 10:1; cf. 9:1, 2), so that we know it to be sin if we do not pray for them (1 Sam. 12:23).

(d)   When the Holy Spirit excites our feelings, He also enables us to give utterance to them, in the right manner – and He intercedes for us according to God's will (Rom. 8:26, 27).

(e)   Prayer is to be in the Spirit (Eph. 6:18; Jude 20): praying in the Spirit, we depend upon Him as we ask for the things we know to be right and in accord with God's will (Matt. 6:9-13; Luke 11:2-4), and the result is a renewed experience of God's peace, and an attitude of submission to God's will, no matter how He may choose to answer our prayers (2 Cor. 12:7-10; Phil. 4:6, 7).

(f) We must never forget that the Holy Spirit is a Person whom we both grieve (Eph. 4:30) and quench by sin (1 Thess. 5:19).

(g) By the Spirit's help we can fulfil our Lord's instruction that we should always pray and not give up (Luke 18:1; Rom. 8:26; 1 Thess. 5:17).

---

67. THE STATE

Question: **What is the relationship of Christians to the state and what should be their attitude towards human authorities?**

Answer: **The relationship of Christians to the state is determined by the understanding the Bible gives of God's establishment of those in authority. The duty of Christians is to uphold all rightful authority and to strive to be good citizens, demonstrating by their exemplary conduct that their true citizenship is in heaven. On those infrequent occasions when the state demands obedience contrary to God's commands, their duty then is to obey God.**

1. God's establishment of those in authority.

(a) There is no authority except from God, and He has established those that exist (Rom. 13:1).

(b) God confers upon individuals the right to govern (1 Kings 19:15; 2 Kings 8:7-13; Jer. 27:6; John 19:11).

(c) Human rule is temporary, however, whereas God's rule is eternal (Dan. 4:31), and He installs and removes human sovereigns and rulers (Dan. 2:21), and at any moment He can bring their dominion to an end (Dan. 7:12).

(d) God is like a potter who can do what He likes with the clay (Rom. 9:21; cf. Prov. 8:15, 16; Isa. 26:13-16; Jer 18:6); He can move the hearts of rulers who have no faith and allegiance to Him so that they accomplish His purposes (2 Chron. 36:22, 23; Ezra 1:1-4; Isa. 44:28; 45:1).

(e) There are various institutions of government ordained for our common good (1 Pet. 2:13, 14). (Within every people or nation, permanently settled in a geographical area, there needs to be a public authority with the power of ultimate decision that demands obedience, and is capable of enforcing its legislative and executive measures for the protection of all, both from internal and external enemies - cf. Acts 17:26.)

(f) There are supreme civil authorities, whether sovereigns, emperors, dictators, presidents or central governments (1 Pet. 2:13).

(g) There are also local civil authorities, such as governors and local government officials (1 Pet. 2:14).

(h) These different sorts of authority are God's servants for the benefit of good citizens (Rom. 13:4).

(i) They are established by God to punish those who do wrong and to commend those who do right (1 Pet. 2:14) – they are not, therefore, a terror to those who do good but to those who do wrong (Rom. 13:3).

(j) They have the right to bear the sword – that is to say, to punish, and to execute God's punishment on the wrong-doer (Rom. 13:4; cf. Acts 16:22, 23, 37; 22:24; 2 Cor. 11:23, 25); they are entrusted by God with the office of avenger and righter of wrongs (1 Kings 19:16, 17, Isa. 10:5-11).

(k) The state, for its necessary support and maintenance, has the right to command the payment of taxes and revenues, and to expect respect and honour (Rom. 13:6, 7) - it is, in fact, God's servant in attending to such duties (Rom. 13:4).

(l) Whoever, therefore, resists the civil authorities in their God-given duties resists what God has established, and rebels bring God's judgment on themselves (Rom. 13:2).

2. The plain duty of Christians, therefore, is to uphold proper authority and to be good citizens.

(a) We are to be subject to every authority instituted among us (1 Pet. 2:13), respecting the most prominent people in the state and honouring all who hold public office (Rom. 13:7), in order to keep a clear conscience (Rom. 13:5).

(b) Our submissiveness is to express itself, whenever possible, in honest subjection and obedience to the laws and instructions of the state (Tit. 3:1).

(c) We are to honour everyone and in particular the supreme state authority (Rom. 13:7; 1 Pet. 2:17).

(d) We are neither to curse those in authority (Ex. 22:28) nor to harm them (1 Sam. 24:6; 2 Sam. 1:14).

(e) We are to pray for all those in authority that we may live peaceful and quiet lives in all godliness and holiness (1 Tim. 2:2).

(f) We are to pay taxes to the government without complaint (Mark 12:13-17; Rom. 13:6, 7).

(g) We are to be good citizens by speaking evil of no one, avoiding quarrelling, acting with gentleness and showing perfect courtesy to everyone (Tit. 3:2).

(h) We are to be ready to do whatever is good (Tit. 3:1).

(i) While it is true that we hold a dual citizenship (Phil. 3:20), we are given no reason whatsoever for neglecting our civil responsibilities to the state (Rom. 13:1-7).

(j) Our desire to fulfil these duties is a direct consequence of our experience of God's salvation (Tit. 3:1-7).

(k) While the state can sometimes make unreasonable demands, our proper duties to it will not infringe God's rights (Mark 12:17).

3. When the state or other authorities command anything that is contrary to God's commandments, it is the duty of Christians to obey God.

(a) Rulers and civil authorities are always in danger of being intoxicated by power: they may attribute merit to themselves (Isa. 10:5-14), deify themselves (Ezek. 28:1-5), elevate themselves against God (Isa. 14:13, 14), and even go so far as to offend Him by blasphemy (Dan. 11:36).

(b) It is as well to remember, therefore, that the authority God entrusts to us is never absolute, but is limited by moral obligations – for example, while in the Old Testament owners were given authority over their slaves, God's law regulated its exercise by carefully stating the rights of slaves (Ex. 21:1-6, 26, 27; Deut. 15:12-18).

(c)   Civil and other authorities sometimes choose to listen to the malicious accusations of enemies of the gospel who argue that Christian preaching is a political crime or that Christians are the cause of trouble (Acts 17:6; cf. 19:26, 27; 24:5).

(d)   Religious authorities sometimes persecute Christians (Luke 12:11), and in the days of the early Church it was the high priests who commanded the apostles not to speak and teach in the name of Jesus (Acts 4:18; 5:27, 28, 40).

(e)   The apostles' response provides the classic answer when Christians are commanded to stop doing what God has plainly commanded: 'We must obey God rather than men!' (Acts 5:29).

4.   In usual circumstances, the fulfilment by Christians of their obligations to the state will be an essential part of their Christian testimony that commends both them and the gospel to the powers that be.

(a)   Christians are God's workmanship, created in Christ Jesus to do good works that God prepared in advance for them to do (Eph. 2:10).

(b)   We are urgently exhorted to bear fruit in every good work (Col. 1:10), to try to be always kind (1 Thess. 5:15), and to do good to everyone (Gal. 6:10).

(c)   We may rest assured that those who do right will generally receive the commendation of those in authority (1 Pet. 2:14).

(d)   We are to live in society as the servants of God (1 Pet. 2:16).

(e)   We are submit ourselves to every human authority for the Lord's sake (1 Pet. 2:13).

(f)   By our good citizenship we are to put to silence the ignorant criticisms of foolish people (1 Pet. 2:15).

---

68.   SOCIAL RESPONSIBILITY

Question: **What are the principles that should guide the Christian in the exercise of social responsibility and involvement in social action?**

Answer: **The Christian's responsibility for society is plainly taught in the Bible, and often indirectly.   Social action on behalf of any who are in need is demanded by the rule: 'Love your neighbour as yourself.'   The description of Christians as 'the salt of the earth' implies the beneficial effect their behaviour should have upon society.**

1.   The pattern God Himself has set.

(a)   God gave male and female a body as well as a soul, and He provided for the well-being of both (Gen. 1:27-30).

(b)   We may say that God inaugurated social action in the provision He made for Adam and Eve after their disobedience –'The LORD God made garments of skin for Adam and his wife and clothed them' (Gen. 3:21); and the provisions of His law underlined its importance (e.g. Ex. 22:25; Lev. 19:9, 10; 23:22; Deut. 15:11; 24:12-15).

(c)   God loves the world (John 3:16), and He causes His sun to rise on the evil and the good, and sends rain on the righteous and the unrighteous (Matt. 5:45).

(d)   God's wrath is declared against extortion, robbery, oppression, and racial discrimination (Jer. 22:13; Ezek. 22:23-31, especially verses 29 and 31; Amos 2:6-8).

(e)   God does not forget people's dishonest dealings at the expense of the helpless (Amos 8:4-14).

(f)   God forbids favouritism on the grounds of class, money and privilege (Lev. 19:15; Gal. 3:28; Jas. 2:1-13).

(g)   God has shown us what is good and what He requires of us as members of society; He requires us to act justly, to love mercy and to walk humbly with Him (Micah 6:8; cf. Amos 5:24).

2.   **God confirmed this pattern of social responsibility in the example of His Son, our Lord Jesus Christ.**

(a)   Our Lord Jesus Christ went around doing good (Acts 10:38).

(b)   He cared for all whose need confronted Him (Matt. 8:28-34; Luke 7:11-17).

(c)   He was friendly with outcasts (Matt. 9:9-13; Mark 2:13-17; Luke 7:39; 15:2; 19:7).

(d)   He healed those who were ill (Matt. 11:1-6; Luke 7:21).

(e)   He fed the hungry (Matt. 14:14-21; Mark 6:30-44; Luke 9:10-17; John 6:1-13).

(f)   He taught the importance of good works: 'Let your light shine before men, that they may see your good deeds and praise your Father in heaven' (Matt. 5:16).

(g)   He spoke of His disciples' function as light and salt in the world (Matt. 5:13-15).

3.   **We have the example of the early Church.**

(a)   The early believers had everything in common (Acts 2:44).

(b)   They sold their possessions and goods, and gave to those who had need (Acts 2:45; 4:32, 34, 35).

(c)   They sought to look after widows and others in difficulty and there were no needy persons among them as a consequence (Acts 4:34; 6:1).

(d)   The early churches collected gifts for the impoverished Jerusalem Christians (Acts 24:17; Rom. 15:26; 1 Cor. 16:3).

4.   **We have the teaching of the apostles.**

(a)   They took up our Lord's emphasis upon the continuing debt we have to love one another - 'he who loves his fellow man has fulfilled the law' (Rom. 13:8; cf. Mark 12:28-34; Jas. 2:8).

(b)   They taught that Christians do not cease to be earthly citizens because they have become citizens of heaven; rather they ought to be better citizens (Phil. 1:27; 1 Pet. 2:13-17).

(c)   They instructed Christians to do good to all people, especially to those who belong to the family of believers (Gal. 6:10), to be kind to each other and to everyone else (1 Thess. 5:15).

(d)   They made it plain that Christians are not to be afraid of exposing evil (Eph. 5:11).

(e)   They emphasised the importance of diligent work and honest dealings so that none would have just grounds for criticising believers' behaviour (Eph. 4:28; 2 Thess. 3:10-13).

5.   Guidelines for Christian social involvement.

(a)   We are to be good citizens (Matt. 17:24-27): we have duties to the state and society as well as having a duty to God, and each must be fulfilled (Matt. 22:15-22; Rom. 13:1-7; 1 Tim. 2:1, 2; 1 Pet. 2:17).

(b)   We are to keep before us the priority of meeting people's spiritual need (e.g. Luke 4:18, 19), and the unique trusteeship of the gospel our Lord Jesus Christ has committed to us (Matt. 28:18-20; 1 Thess. 2:4).

(c)   By upholding the priority of the gospel, we do not neglect social action - in fact, where the gospel is genuinely received, it changes people's lives so that they influence society for good (Luke 19:8; John 8:11).

(d)   Our commitment to the gospel, however, is not a commitment demanding callous indifference to people's material and physical needs - we must be willing to share not only the gospel but our very selves with them too (1 Thess. 2:8; cf. Matt. 25:34-40; 1 John 3:16-18).

(e)   We are never to make our spiritual responsibilities an excuse for neglecting practical and social needs - this was the mistake of the priest and the Levite in the story our Lord Jesus told of the man who fell into the hands of robbers and who was helped by the good Samaritan (Luke 10:30-37).

(f)   When, however, we are involved in meeting people's material, physical and social needs, we must encourage them and ourselves to realise the importance of the right spiritual relationship with God we all need (Mark 2:5, 11).

(g)   We must not minimise the distinctive contribution we are able to make to social betterment by living the Christian life as we ought in all its aspects – especially within our home, among our neighbours, and at our daily employment (Eph. 5:22-6:9).

(h)   As we show that we care about right relationships and that the individual counts and really matters, we make a contribution that the world desperately needs - it was in this way, for example, that Christianity brought about the freedom of slaves (see, for example, Paul's letter to Philemon and the new attitudes it encouraged).

(i)   Our primary concern should be with those social needs with which we are personally confronted day by day (Luke 10:30-37; Rom. 15:25, 26).

(j)   When we are rightly involved in social action of any kind, we need to review periodically our involvement – and sometimes even to withdraw for a while to accomplish such a review – to ensure that proper priorities are being maintained (John 6:15; Acts 6:1-4).

(k)   Love for God and love for people are never in conflict: loving God as we ought, we love our neighbour also (Luke 10:27, 28).

---

69. WORK

Question: What does the Bible teach about work?

Answer: Work was an original purpose of God for humanity, but Adam's rebellion against God marred human experience of His purpose in it so that all too often we find our work a burden rather than a pleasure. Work is part of God's scheme for the support of the human race, and properly fulfilled it brings its own rewards.   While to avoid work is folly, life is not to be filled exclusively with work – God makes provision for rest and recreation.   Christians should bear witness to their faith by the quality of their work.

1.   There are many varieties of work.

(a)   Work has taken a variety of forms from the beginning of God's creation (Gen. 4:2; 9:20).

(b)   The Old Testament speaks of God filling people with His Spirit, giving them skill, ability and knowledge in all kinds of crafts, to be metal workers, carvers and embroiderers (Ex. 31:2-11).

2.   Work was an original purpose of God for humanity.

(a)   Men and women are appointed by God as His 'deputies' to co-operate with Him in the continuing work of harnessing and utilising the resources God provides in His creation (Gen. 1:27, 28).

(b) Men and women were commanded to subdue the earth, and to have rule over it (Gen. 1:28; Ps. 8:3-8) – a command clearly implying the necessity for work.

(c) Before the fall, we see Adam happily at work (Gen. 2:15).

(d) The principle of work is written into the whole of God's creation (Prov. 6:6-11).

(e) It is always assumed that work constitutes part of God's pattern for human beings (Ex. 20:9, 10; Ps. 104:23).

(f) Work in all its different forms is a provision of God's wisdom for people (Isa. 28:24-29).

(g) But God is not said to have commanded Adam to work, and the implication is present that it was a pleasure for him to work prior to the fall (Gen. 2:15; cf. 3:17-19).

(h) God intends that men and women should find enjoyment in their work (Eccl. 5:18-20); since the fall, there is often more pleasure in work itself than in the achievements of our work (Eccl. 2:10, 11).

(i) There is no disgrace in manual work; its dignity is insisted upon (Eph. 4:28; 1 Thess. 4:11) and our Lord Jesus Christ set an example by working as a carpenter (Mark 6:3).

(j) Work for all is a sign of God's blessing; sometimes unemployment in a nation may be a sign of God's judgment (Zech. 8:9-13).

3.   Human rebellion against God marred human experience of God's purposes in the principle of work.

(a) The curse that followed the fall was not the curse of work, but the pain and hardship connected with it by reason of the curse upon the ground (Gen. 3:17-19; 5:29).

(b) As a consequence of sin, and the disorder following in its wake, work all too often becomes a burden rather than a pleasure (Gen. 3:17-19).

(c) Daily work can become pointless and empty in meaning when performed without God (Ps. 127:2).

(d)   There is a futile element in human work because, although people who work may achieve something in life, their motive tends to be envy of their neighbour (Eccl. 4:4).

(e)   Work has sometimes been an instrument of exploitation and oppression (Ex. 1:11 -14; Jas. 5:4-6).

(f)   People's lives can be made bitter by hard labour (Ex. 1:14).

4.   The purpose that may be discerned behind the principle of work.

(a)   The great incentive for daily work is our daily bread as the fruit of it (Prov. 16:26).

(b)   Daily work is the means of building the home and sustaining it (Prov. 24:27).

(c)   Daily work is part of God's scheme for the support of the human race (Prov. 27:25-27).

(d)   By our work we are to make some return to our parents (1 Tim. 5:4). Such provision may not always be necessary, but it is a denial of the Christian faith not to provide for any member of our own family who may be in need (1 Tim. 5:8).

(e)   Our employment is not to be merely a means of gaining things for ourselves (Luke 3:11; Acts 20:35; Rom. 12:13).

(f)   Giving to those who are poor and not so well off as ourselves has a constant emphasis in the teaching of our Lord Jesus Christ (Matt. 19:21; Luke 14:13), and the early Church practised our Lord's teaching (Acts 2:44, 45; 4:32).

(g)   The apostle Paul set an example of working, not only for his own support, but also for the benefit of those who were serving God with him (Acts 20:34); he also laid emphasis upon the provision of help for the poor (Rom. 15:26, 27; 2 Cor. 8 and 9; Gal. 2:10).

(h)   We should not work for ourselves alone, but with the definite object of being able to help others (Eph. 4:28), since those who are unable to work are entitled to aid.

5.   Work, properly fulfilled, brings its rewards.

(a)   Work brings the satisfaction of peaceful sleep, a benefit not to be despised (Eccl. 5:12).

(b)   Work, well done, is worthy of a reasonable wage (Matt. 10:10; Luke 10:7; 1 Tim. 5:18).

(c)   God chooses to reward people for good work, whatever their position or status in life (Eph. 6:8).

(d)   Diligence in daily work brings reward (Prov. 22:29; 27:23-27); whereas laziness in daily work breeds dissatisfaction (Prov. 13:4).

(e)   Ability eventually outruns privilege in employment, insofar that a diligent and wise employee will gain by conscientiousness what others may possess by birth or some special privileged relationship (Prov. 17:2).

6.   Life is not to be all work.

(a)   Work brings some reward, but too much work, or a total concern with work, can destroy its benefits (Eccl. 2:10, 11, 24; 4:6).

(b)   People can make an idol of their work and their achievements with disastrous consequences - for example, the rich fool in the parable (Luke 12:16 -21).

(c)   Our daily work is not to be motivated by the desire to wealthy for this can plunge us into ruin and destruction (1 Tim. 6:9, 10).

(d)   It is better to have small earnings when they are gained with a restful mind, than to gain a large income by worry and anxious work (Eccl. 4:6).

(e)   There is great gain in godliness with contentment; and godliness happily acknowledges the principle of rest that is so clearly written into God's commandments (1 Tim. 6:6).

(f)   The cycle of work goes hand in hand with the cycle of rest: the fourth commandment safeguards the principle that our life is not to be all work (Ex. 20:8-11).

7.   The folly of avoiding work.

(a)   Idleness is condemned (2 Thess. 3:11).

(b)   Individuals who do not work destroy themselves (Eccl. 4:5).

(c)   Not to have proper work to do is a person's undoing if this state of affairs arises from laziness (Prov. 21:25).

(d)   Idleness destroys character (Prov. 18:9).

(e)   God will judge the slacker, and He makes no distinction between employer and employee (Col. 3:23-25).

(f)   None who are able to support themselves are entitled to be supported by others (2 Thess. 3:10).

8.   Employers and employees.

(a)   Employers are to pay wages willingly and on time (Lev. 19:13; cf. Deut. 24:14, 15); and to withhold proper wages is sin in God's sight (Jas. 5:4).

(b)   Employers are to remember their responsibility to be fair and just to those whom they employ, never forgetting that, if they are Christian believers, they are to view themselves as having Christ Himself as their Heavenly Employer (Col. 4:1).

(c)   Employers are not to misuse the power put in their hands; and they are to refrain from using threats (Eph. 6:9).

(d)   Employers are to be as conscientious and responsible towards those who work for them as they expect employees to be towards employers (Eph. 6:9).

(e)   Christian employees are to do their work, not with the idea of currying favour, but as a sincere expression of their devotion to the Lord (Eph. 6:5-8; Col. 3:22).

(f)   Whatever Christians do, they are to put their whole heart and soul into it, as work done for the Lord Jesus Christ, and not for human employers alone (Col.. 3:23).

(g)   Christians are to know that their real reward, a heavenly one, will come from the Lord, since they serve the Lord Christ, and not just their human employers (Col.. 3:24).

9.   Christians should bear witness to their faith by the quality of their work.

(a)   Knowing God through Jesus Christ makes a difference to the whole of life (Rom. 14:7, 8): therefore, daily employment will be marked by this difference too.

(b)   We are not to be conformed to the world's view of work, but we are to be transformed by the renewal of our mind, that we may prove what is God's will in our daily employment, as in everything else (Rom. 12:2).

(c)   Our daily work must be seen as included within the sphere of the good works that God has prepared for us to do (Eph. 2:10): our primary calling is to come to the Lord Jesus Christ as repentant sinners and to believe on Him, and then to be set apart for God's possession (1 Cor 1:2, 9); but our secondary calling is to discover those good works for which God has both fitted and chosen us (Eph. 2:8-10).

(d)   The principle of our acting as salt and light in society must certainly have particular reference to the sphere of our daily employment (Matt. 5:13-16).

(e)   We are to earn our own living (2 Thess. 3:12), making the maximum use of our resources and talents, whether they are large or small (Matt. 25:14-30).

(f)   Our daily work is to be characterised by good behaviour (1 Pet. 3:16).

(g)   We are to do our work quietly and efficiently (2 Thess. 3:12).

(h)   It is important to be engaged in what may be described as 'doing something useful' (Eph. 4:28).

(i)   Paul set an example of honest work by his tent making, and the importance of such work featured in his teaching (Acts. 18:3; 1 Thess. 2:9; 2 Thess. 3:7-10).

(j)   In all our work we are to see ourselves as serving the Lord (Rom. 12:11, Col. 3:22-24).

(k)   Work should be an act of worship - done 'as to the Lord' (Eph. 6:5-8).

(l)   We must take care not to discredit the faith whether by our standards of work or by our attitude to it (1 Thess. 4:11, 12).

(m)   The governing attitude and principle of the whole of the Christian life is that we should do all to the glory of God, and this goal must comprehend our daily employment (1 Cor. 10:31).

70. LEISURE

Question: **What does the Bible teach about leisure?**

Answer: **The principle of rest and leisure is inherent in God's institution of the Sabbath, and the fourth commandment safeguards the principle that human life is not to be all work.**
The purpose of leisure is recreation and refreshment. The knowledge that God intends all His gifts to be received, used, and rejoiced in increases the Christian's appreciation and enjoyment of leisure. In a world marred by the fall, Christians have to exercise discernment to ensure that their leisure enhances their appreciation of goodness, righteousness and truth, and genuinely refreshes them for renewed service of God in the world.

1. **The basis for any consideration of the subject of leisure.**
(a) Leisure is free time; time in which we are at liberty to choose our activity; the time available for other things after our daily work.
(b) The fundamental basis with which we begin and upon which we build is that everything God made is good (1 Tim. 4:4; cf. Gen. 1:31).
(c) We must not fail to acknowledge that every good and perfect gift comes from God (Jas. 1:17).
(d) God has provided in His creation satisfaction for men and women's bodies and joy for their hearts (Acts 14:17).
(e) God has richly provided us with a host of pursuits for our enjoyment (1 Tim. 6:17).
(f) The good things of God's creation are intended by Him to be thankfully enjoyed by those who believe in Him and know the truth (1 Tim. 4:3).
(g) The creative and artistic gifts of men and women, as with all the other gifts given to them by God, are to be received gratefully (1 Tim. 4:3-5).

(h)   But the fall means that these gifts can be abused and misinterpreted (1 Tim. 4:1-5), and the principles of goodness, righteousness and truth, uniformly laid down in the Bible, apply (Eph. 5:9).

(i)   Furthermore, there is a right time for everything (Eccl. 3:1-8); and there is a right and a wrong time for relaxation or leisure (Eccl. 10:16-18)

2.   The essential principle behind leisure.

(a)   God rested on the seventh day, after His creative activity (Gen. 2:2).

(b)   On the pattern and basis of God's own 'rest,' it would seem to have been God's purpose for men and women from the beginning to have one day in seven for rest and recreation, for God blessed the seventh day and made it holy (Gen. 2:2, 3).

(c)   The principle of rest and leisure, as necessary and essential for us, is inherent in the institution of the Sabbath (Gen. 2:3; Ex. 20:8-11).

(d)   The fourth commandment safeguards the principle that human life is not to be all work (Ex. 20:8-11).

(e)   While the objective of the 'Sabbath' principle in its application to animals is simply that of resting their bodies, for human beings the purpose is, in addition, recreation and refreshment (Ex. 23:12).

(f)   We need leisure and time to rest (Mark 6:31).

3.   The use of leisure.

(a)   The early Christians chose to change from the Jewish Sabbath (Saturday) to the Christian Sunday so as to combine the day of rest with the day they met together to remember the Lord Jesus Christ's death and resurrection (Acts 20:7; Rev. 1:10).

(b)   The principle remains that the Sabbath was made to benefit people and not people to benefit the Sabbath (Mark 2:27).

(c)   Worship of the Lord on a Sunday is part of Christians' leisure because it is something they want to do: the Lord's Day is a day when believers choose to delight themselves in the Lord, instead of following selfish and unhelpful inclinations (Isa. 58:13, 14).

(d)   There are many different views of pleasure and leisure: for example, it is fun for a fool to do wrong (Prov. 10:23).

(e) The writer of Ecclesiastes sought to put human pleasures to the test, and found them to be meaningless (Eccl. 2:1-11); people's wild pursuit of pleasure sometimes leads them into trouble (Dan. 5:l-6).

(f) The leisure of the lazy can be their ruin (Prov. 21:25).

(g) Leisure is not doing nothing, but, having time at our disposal, choosing to do with it what we will. Thus, for Christian believers, one of the most profitable uses of our leisure is enjoying fellowship with God's people (Ps. 16:3), and we can say, 'Better is one day in your courts than a thousand elsewhere' (Ps. 84:10).

(h) Believers' delight is in the law of the Lord, and in the works of the Lord, and this pleasure leads them to study them (Ps.1:2; 111:2).

(i) However leisure time may be utilised, it should be used positively for, if the principle behind the Sabbath - so far as people's bodies and minds are concerned - is that of refreshment, any leisure that debilitates is unhelpful, and outside of God's purpose (Ex. 23:12).

4. Principles to govern the use of leisure.

(a) Any realistic consideration of leisure recognises that the world in which we live offers many 'pleasures' that compete for our attention and involvement (1 Pet. 4:3).

(b) We must always remind ourselves that sin offers short-lived pleasure; therefore not every offer of pleasure is to be pursued (Heb. 11:25).

(c) The desire for pleasures can be an unhelpful source of strife within ourselves (Jas. 4:1), not least when they are of a purely sensual kind (Mark 7:21, 22).

(d) We are warned that in the last days people will be lovers of pleasure rather than lovers of God (2 Tim. 3:4).

(e) Pleasure sought for pleasure's sake proves empty and unsatisfying (Eccl. 2:10, 11).

(f) Our approach to leisure, therefore, must be thoughtful and self-controlled – that is to say, we must know what we are doing and why (1 Pet. 1:13).

(g) We have to learn to discriminate so as to reject what is wrong and choose what is right (Isa. 7:15).

(h)   The Christian knows a better way than drinking and overindulgence to obtain satisfaction and joy – the fullness of the Spirit (Eph. 5:18-20).

(i)   Our use of leisure time is not to be contrary to the principle of our making the best use of our time (Eph. 5:15, 16; Col. 4:5).

(j)   The time we have at our disposal, after we have done our daily work and given ourselves opportunity for rest and necessary tasks, should include fruitful service for God – the latter is a right use of our leisure, and properly entered into proves a means of refreshment (Phil. 1:22; cf. John 4:6, 8, 31-34).

(k)   We need to have the shortness of life brought constantly before us so that we gain a heart of wisdom to use life properly (Ps. 90:12).

(l)   Living in a world where entertainment is automatically assumed to have a place in people's leisure, and in their times of resting, we need to relate Christian principles to it. Moral considerations are as relevant to the use of leisure time as to anything else: the Christian is to seek to do everything to the glory of God (1 Cor. 10:31).

(m)   Whatever we do, we are to do everything in the name of the Lord Jesus, thanking God the Father through Him (Col. 3:17); at all times we are to clothe ourselves with the Lord Jesus, and not to think about how to gratify the desires of the sinful nature (Rom. 13:14).

(n)   We will often find, not least in the sphere of entertainment, that while much is permissible, not everything is beneficial (1 Cor. 6:12; 10:23); we enjoy liberty as Christians, but we recognise that not everything is constructive and helpful.

(o)   We must not allow any pastime to make us its slave (1 Cor. 6:12).

(p)   In our leisure, as in everything else, we should not merely go our own way, but our actions and activities should have in view the good of others too (Rom. 15:1-3).

(q)   We are to keep in our thoughts all that is true and noble, all that is right and pure, all that is lovely and admirable, whatever is morally excellent and praiseworthy - this positive and straightforward directive provides us with tremendous scope, but with a reliable yardstick to apply (Phil. 4:8).

(r)   Our leisure activities must not be moulded by the desires of our old ways before we were Christians, but must conform to the objective of holiness in every part of our life (1 Pet. 1:14-19).

(s)   In our leisure activities we should abstain from the desires of our sinful nature, for they are always at war with our souls (1 Pet. 2:11).

(t)   Activities that include or tend towards debauchery, lust, drunkenness, orgies, carousing, and detestable idolatry are ruled out for the Christian (1 Pet. 4:3).

(u)   Our former companions may think it strange that we will no longer plunge with them into the same flood of dissipation, and, as a result, they may heap abuse on us (1 Pet. 4:4).

(v)   Our aim to live no longer by evil human desires but according to the will of God will influence every use to which we put our time (1 Pet. 4:2), for we make it our goal to please the Lord (2 Cor. 5:9), in whose presence we always are (Ps. 139:1-12; Heb. 13:5).

---

71. GUIDANCE

Question: **What does the Bible teach about guidance and the will of God?**

Answer: **The Bible teaches that the basic secret of guidance is commitment to the will of God, both before and after it is known and discovered. The will of God in general is given to us in the Bible and the unique instruction it provides. The particular will of God for our lives is discovered and worked out as we present our bodies to Him as a living spiritual sacrifice, and continue to do so, striving after daily obedience to His Word.**

1.   The choice before us.
(a)   Human desires or the will of God? Our wishes or God's will (1 Pet. 4:2)?

(b)   Rather than living for God's will, we have all lived much of our life according to our human desires; as Christians we should live the rest of our earthly life for the will of God (1 Pet. 4:2).

2.   The truth concerning our own will.

(a)   Our own will is always prone to evil; the things that our bodies and minds find congenial are often in marked contrast to what God wants for us (Eph. 2:3).

(b)   As Christians, we should aspire not to do our own will, but God's; wanting our own will to coincide always with His (Luke 22:42; John 5:30).

3.   Christians find within themselves a desire for God's will.

(a)   Our new life or spiritual nature demands that we seek to do God's will (Phil. 2:12, 13).

(b)   That we desire to follow the will of God is the result of His grace in our life through our Lord Jesus Christ (Eph. 2:8-10).

(c)   God's great mercy to us, rightly considered and meditated upon, stimulates us to seek the will of God, irrespective of the cost involved (Rom. 12:1, 2).

(d)   Even as our body desires food for its health, our soul requires obedience to God's will for its well-being (John 4:34).

4.   The Lord Jesus is our example of obedience to God's will.

(a)   He came with the sole purpose of doing the Father's will (Heb. 10:7-9).

(b)   He frequently spoke of His determination to seek not His own will but the will of the Father (John 5:30; 6:38).

(c)   Knowing the will of the Father, He spoke of it with assurance and He acted in perfect co-operation with it (John 6:39, 40).

(d)   At every crisis, obedience to God's will was foremost (Matt. 26:42).

(e)   The doing of God the Father's will was His food (John 4:34).

5.   Fundamental truths regarding God's will.

(a)   As we consider God's will with our limited human minds, there are two parts to it: there is that which is declared or published and that which is secret or hidden. God's declared or published will includes those events that have already taken place that are revealed to be His will - for example, the death of our Lord Jesus Christ to deliver us from our sins (Gal. 1:4) – and the whole of His written Word in which He tells men and women what to do. God's secret or hidden will, through which all things are ordered and done according to His plan and decision, concerns those things that are not revealed to us (Eph. 1:11).

(b)　The published will of God relates to the whole of our lives: we should do all of it (Col. 4:12); and this is God's requirement (Acts 13:22).

(c)　God's will is good, pleasing and perfect (Rom. 12:2).

(d)　God's will is presented to us supremely in the Lord Jesus Christ, and the dynamic for doing it, which we so desperately need, is found in Him alone, and our union with Him (1 Thess. 5:18).

6.　The fundamental importance of God's will in our life.

(a)　What God looks for most is obedience to His will. He could say of David, '1 have found in David son of Jesse a man after my own heart; he will do everything I want him to do' (Acts 13:22).

(b)　Obedience to the will of God is more important than mere outward profession (Matt. 7:21); God requires not lip service to His will, but action – for example, the parable of the two sons (Matt. 21:28-32).

(c)　Any profession of Christ's Lordship or religious activity, without obedience to God's will, are worthless to God, and are rejected by Him (Matt. 7:21-23).

(d)　Obedience to the will of God is the condition and proof of a right relationship to our Lord Jesus Christ (Matt. 12:50; Mark 3:35).

(e)　God wants us to be filled with the knowledge of His will (Col. 1:9).

(f)　Knowing God's will is the secret of achieving important goals: first, living as the Lord wants; secondly, doing what pleases Him; thirdly, producing in our lives all kinds of good deeds, and, fourthly, growing in our knowledge of God (Col. 1:10).

7. **Examples of God's published will.**
   First, with regard to our salvation.

(a) It is not the will of the Father that one of those who trusts in our Lord Jesus Christ should perish (Matt. 18:14).

(b) The will of the Father is that the Son should not lose any of all those He has given Him, but that the Lord Jesus should raise them all to life on the last day (John 6:39, 40).

(c) By God's will all believers are made holy through the sacrifice of the body of Jesus Christ once for all (Heb. 10:10).

   Secondly, with regard to our growth in holiness.

(d) The will of God for our life may be summed up in the one word 'sanctification' (1 Thess. 4:3, 7).

(e) It is God's will that by doing good we should silence the ignorant talk of foolish people against Christianity (1 Pet. 2:15).

(f) It is God's will that, as Christian believers, we should always be joyful, pray constantly, and be thankful in all circumstances (1 Thess. 5:16-18).

(g) It is God's will that we should appreciate our need and obligation to be filled with the Spirit at all times (Eph. 5:17-20).

8. **Relating ourselves to God's will.**

(a) Our purpose in life, like that of our Lord Jesus Christ, should be to do the will of the Father (John 6:38).

(b) The will of God determines our place and function in the Church of Christ, and the direction of our life (1 Cor. 12:11; Eph. 2:10).

(c) Doing the will of God means obeying the instructions given in His Word (1 Thess. 4:1, 2).

(d) We should be testing and approving what God's will is for our life (Rom. 12:2).

(e) The will of God should be the determining factor in all our plans and schedules (Rom. 15:32).

(f) Knowing that God's will determines the things that happen to us, we should submit to them in a Christ-like manner (1 Pet. 3:17).

(g) There may be, therefore, a battle within us for the submission of our will to God's (Matt. 26:42) for the will of God often runs contrary to our natural feelings.

(h)   In every circumstance, and in circumstances that are beyond our control, Christians may say, with confidence, 'The Lord's will be done' (Matt. 26:42; Acts 21:14).

(i)   The will of God should be sought and obeyed in small things as well as in large (Phil. 4:6; 1 Thess. 5:16-18).

9.   Discovering God's will.

(a)   When we really choose to do God's will, God never leaves us in ignorance of it (John 7:17).

(b)   He wishes to equip us with everything good for doing His will (Heb. 13:21).

(c)   The knowledge we need of God's will does not come from human wisdom with its proneness to pride (1 Cor. 1:20; 2:5, 6, 13; 3:19).

(d)   Our knowledge of God's will comes from the illumination of the Holy Spirit: He gives the wisdom and understanding that enable us to know God's will (Col. 1:9).

(e)   The will of God in general and also on particular issues is given to us in the Bible (Matt. 12:50; Mark 3:35; 1 Thess. 4:1; cf. Luke 8:21; Rom. 2:18).

(f)   The precise will of God for our individual lives, however, may be known only as we present our bodies as a living sacrifice, holy and acceptable to God (Rom. 12:1, 2); to be in harmony with God's will we must first give ourselves to God and then to others (2 Cor 8:5).

(g)   This dedication involves our refusal to be conformed any longer to the patterns of this world, and our willingness to be transformed by the renewal of our minds (Rom. 12:2).

10.   Prayer has an important place both in our discovering God's will and our submission to it.

(a)   The Lord Jesus Christ taught that God's will is to figure in our prayers to our Father (Matt. 6:10).

(b)   Our prayers should centre around our being filled with the knowledge of God's will in all spiritual wisdom and understanding, so that we may live a life worthy of the Lord, fully pleasing to Him, bearing fruit in every good work, and growing in the knowledge of God (Col. 1:9, 10).

(c)   Expressed another way, prayer should be directed at our standing firm in all the will of God, mature and fully assured (Col. 4:12).

(d)   Praying in this fashion, we may be sure that God will both hear and answer (1 John 5:14, 15).

(e)   Prayer may be regarded as the surrendering of our wills to God's will (2 Cor 12:7-10).

(f)   Prayer's true motive is the desire for God's will to be done and His Name to be glorified (John 17:1).

(g)   All our requests to God should be subject to His will (Rom. 1:10).

11.   How we should do God's will when we know it.

(a)   We should do what God wants from our heart: this means doing God's will with our eye on His approval, rather than people's (Eph. 6:6).

(b)   When we know God's will, we should live it out to the full (Phil. 1:12-14, 22; 2:17).

12.   The practical outworking of God's will.

(a)   Doing God's will means accomplishing the work He has chosen for us, whatever that may be (John 4:34).

(b)   Our obedience to God's will is bound to mean giving ourselves to God's people in very practical, and often costly, ways (2 Cor. 8:5).

(c)   Doing God's will is closely associated with His working in us what is in accordance with His good purposes (Phil. 2:12, 13; Heb. 13:21).

(d)   Suffering of some kind may often be in God's will for us (1 Pet. 4:19); our Lord's experience is an example (Matt. 26:42).

(e)   Sometimes God takes something away from us that He may give it back to us for good; but we cannot be sure that it will be so (Philem. 15).

(f)   When God's will includes suffering, it is fundamentally important that we should continue to do good and that we should commit ourselves to our faithful Creator (1 Pet. 4:19).

(g)   We sometimes need great patience to persist in doing the will of God in order to receive what He has promised (Heb. 10:36).

(h) But we may have the glorious assurance that where there is a will of God, there is a way of God: consider the example of God's will in the lives of Joseph and Moses.

13. Finally, the blessing God's will is to us when we do it.

(a) When we do God's will we live for ever, in marked contrast to the world around that passes away, together with all the desires we associate with it (1 John 2:17).

(b) The nearest approach to heaven on earth is the doing of His will as it is done in heaven (Matt. 6:10).

(c) The will of God is always identical with what is good, pleasing and perfect (Rom. 12:2).

(d) When we know God's will we are in a position to choose what is best (Rom. 2:18).

(e) Our spiritual life and our Christian joy are fed and enriched, as we are obedient (Ps. 40:8; John 4:34).

(f) When the will of God is the objective of our life, we discover tremendous peace (Phil. 4:6, 7).

(g) As we do the will of God we receive what He has promised (Heb. 10:36).

---

72. THE FAMILY

Question: How important is the family and what is its function?

Answer: **The family begins with a husband and wife, living in a permanent marriage union, with children as the usual and natural consequence of that union. The principal function of the family is the procreation, preservation, and education of children and this makes it the primary unit of society. The family antedates all other human relationships and societies.**

1. The family requires a high view of marriage as its foundation.

(a) Marriage has its basis and norm in God's act of creation, and is the original form of human fellowship (Mark 10:6, 7).

(b)   When marriage takes place a fresh pattern of life is established. A new family begins as a man leaves his mother and father and is united to his wife, the two becoming one flesh (Gen. 2:24; Mark 10:8).

(c)   It is good for a man to have a wife (Gen. 2:18; Prov. 18:22), and but one wife (Gen. 2:24; Mark 10:6-8; 1 Cor 7:2-4).

(d)   A husband is the head of the wife as Christ is Head, and Saviour too, of the Church (Eph. 5:23),

(e)   A husband's principal duty is to love his wife (Col. 3:19), and to love her as he loves himself (Eph. 5:28, 33).

(f)   A husband should be faithful to his wife (Prov. 5:19; Mal. 2:14-15), respecting her (1 Pet. 3:7), and avoiding all harshness or bitterness in his actions (Col. 3:19).

(g)   A husband should comfort his wife (1 Sam. 1:8), consult her (Gen. 31:4-16), and be quick to praise and show his appreciation of her (Prov. 31:28, 29).

(h)   A wife is the principal helper of her husband (Gen. 2:18).

(i)   A wife's foremost duty is submission to her husband (Gen. 3:16; Eph. 5:22, 24; 1 Pet. 3:1).

(j)   A wife should love (Tit. 2:4), honour (Eph. 5:33), and obey her husband (1 Cor. 14:34; Tit. 2:5), always striving to fulfil her marital duty to him (1 Cor. 7:3-5, 10).

(k)   A prudent wife is a gift from the Lord (Prov. 19:14), her husband's crown (Prov. 12:4), and a priceless treasure (Prov. 31:1-31).

(l)   Children are a gracious gift from the Lord to a husband and wife (Gen. 33:5; Ps. 127:3; 1 Sam. 1:27), and as such enhance and deepen the marriage relationship.

2.   The harmony of husband and wife is essential for the well-being of a family.

(a)   That disharmony in any area of married life can be disastrous and detrimental to a family's welfare is one of the reasons why a Christian should seek to have a Christian partner (1 Cor. 7:39; 2 Cor. 6:14).

(b)   Husband and wife are to be sensitive and thoughtful of the sexual needs of each other (1 Cor. 7:3-5).

(c) For the physical relationship to cement their unity and harmony, husband and wife must be faithful to one another in their heart as well as physically (Matt. 5:27, 28).

(d) The original happiness of marriage has been sadly shattered by the corruption of the human heart (Mark 7:20-23).

(e) Selfish disagreement, especially as it expresses itself in nagging, ruins harmony (Prov. 19:13; 25:24; 27:15).

(f) Unhappy marriage causes a total breakdown in happiness (Prov. 12:4).

3. Parental duties.

(a) Parents should love their children (Tit. 2:4), showing their love both in compassion (Ps. 103:13) and in careful discipline (Prov. 3:11, 12; Heb. 12:7).

(b) Parents should pray for their children, praying generally for their spiritual welfare (Gen. 17:18; 1 Chron. 29:19), and specifically for their well-being when tempted (Job 1:5) or unwell (2 Sam. 12:16; Mark 5:23; John 4:46, 47, 49).

(c) Parents should provide for their children (Job 42:15; Isa. 1:2f).

(d) They should save up for them and be prepared to spend everything they have, if necessary, for their welfare (2 Cor 12:14, 15).

(e) They should know how to give good gifts to their children (Matt. 7:9-11).

(f) Parents should educate their children (Eph. 6:4), seeing themselves as their proper and primary instructors (Prov. 4:1-5, 10-12).

(g) They should instruct them in God's ways (Deut. 31:12-13), with the assurance that, as their children are trained up in the way that they should go, when they are old they will not turn from it (Prov. 22:6).

(h) They should teach their children spiritual truth from the Scriptures, for children may share the promises of God (Acts 2:39). The Scriptures are able to make them wise for salvation through faith in Jesus Christ (2 Tim. 3:15).

(i) They should teach their children most of all by example, remembering our Lord's solemn warning that if we cause a child who believes in Him to sin that it would be better to have a millstone hung around our neck, and to be drowned in the depths of the sea (Matt. 18:6).

(j) Parents should discipline their children (Deut. 8:5).

(k) Children need discipline because folly is deep-rooted in their hearts (Prov. 22:15; 29:17); to neglect discipline is to throw away the family's security (Prov. 13:24; 22:6).

(l) Parental discipline, however, is to be careful and loving, and fathers in particular are instructed to be watchful lest they make their children resentful or discourage them (Col.3:21; Eph. 6:4).

(m) While discipline is never pleasant at the time, its fruits are good (Heb. 12:10, 11).

(n) The experience children have of true human fatherhood should make it easy for them to appreciate God's greater Fatherhood (Matt. 7:9-11; Heb. 12:5-11).

4. Children's duties.

(a) Children should love their parents, not forgetting to be demonstrative in their love when appropriate (Gen. 46:29).

(b) Children should respect their parents (Lev. 19:3), honouring both their father and mother (Ex. 20:12). They should respect their parents' possessions as they do other people's (Prov. 28:24).

(c) To treat parents with mockery or disrespect merits condemnation (Gen. 27:12; Prov. 30:17).

(d) The commandment to honour parents is obligatory (Mark 10:19); any instruction that cuts across it is hypocrisy and transgression (Matt. 15:4-9; Mark 7:10 -13).

(e) Children should obey their parents (Eph. 6:1), listening deliberately to their advice and instruction (Prov. 6:20; 23:22).

(f) The ultimate prosperity of children may greatly hinge upon their obedience to their parents (Deut. 4:40).

(g) Children are to strive to obey their parents in everything (Col. 3:20).

(h) Children, when adults, should provide, where necessary, for their parents, since they have a continuing responsibility towards them (Matt. 15:5, 6; Mark 7:11-13).

(i) They must learn to do what is their Christian duty, and repay those who have brought them up (1 Tim. 5:4; cf. John 19:26, 27).

5. **The common duties of the family in which all the members need to share.**

(a) Love – the primary duty of the members of any family is love (1 Cor.13; 1 John 5:1).

(b) Helpfulness – the life of the family is made harmonious by deliberate co-operativeness but made difficult by quarrelsomeness (Prov. 18:19).

(c) Mutual forbearance - the members of the family are to be forgiving of one another (Gen. 50:16-21; Matt. 18:21-22).

(d) Submission – all members of the family must accept the need for the proper and firm management of household life, and the necessity, therefore, for the parents to give direction (Prov. 31:27, 28; 1 Tim. 3:4, 5).

(e) Concern for unity – all need to see that they contribute by their behaviour and attitudes to the unity or disunity of the family, and that unity must be the goal always (Gen. 45:24; Ps. 133:1).

(f) Worship – the worship of God together, with the home seen as a place where God's presence may be known, brings immeasurable help to the family (Josh. 8:35; 1 Cor. 16:19).

(g) Concern for others – the individual family unit is to look outside of itself and is to care for needy relatives, and especially grandparents (1 Tim. 5:3, 4), so that grandchildren become the crown of the old (Prov. 17:6).

6. **The Christian family has the benefits of the gospel that add immeasurably to its happiness and security.**

(a) God is known to be the Giver of every good gift the family enjoys (Jas. 1:17).

(b) God's Word becomes the final authority and guide so that the family has wise and consistent direction (2 Tim. 3:16, 17).

(c) Parents and children should pattern their behaviour on the kingdom of heaven (Phil. 1:27; 3:20).

(d) The Holy Spirit makes love possible and effective in the most difficult of circumstances (2 Tim. 1:7)

(e) Husbands love their wives after the pattern of Christ's love (Eph. 5:25).

(f) Wives submit themselves to their husbands as part of their submission to the Lord (Eph. 5:22).

(g) Children obey their parents with the desire to please the Lord by so doing (Eph. 6:1; Col. 3:20).

(h) Elderly relatives are cared for as part of Christian duty (1 Tim. 5:4).

(i) Relationships within the family are seen in the context of our relationship with God: a right relationship with God demands a right relationship with those to whom we are closest (1 Pet. 3:7).

(j) Marriage and the family are held in the highest possible honour because God honours them (Heb. 13:4).

---

73. EDUCATION

Question: What does the Bible teach about education?

Answer: **Education aims at developing individuals' aptitude for every kind of learning, so that they are well informed, quick to understand and competent to serve.   Education begins in the home, and all who teach children remain delegates of those children's parents, and nothing releases parents from their basic responsibility for the teaching and discipline of their own children.   The principal lesson to be taught is that the fear of the Lord is the beginning of wisdom.**

1.   **Education is a subject worthy of study.**

(a) We are to attribute all that is good in this world to God (Jas. 1:17): the study of everything that is good, therefore, is a worthy pursuit. Both the natural processes of the earth and the course of historical events are governed by God's wisdom (Isa. 28:23-29; 31:2); therefore by a proper understanding of these fruits of God's activity we are caused to acknowledge Him more worthily.

(b) God has given men and women special responsibilities in His creation that demand the education of their minds (Gen. 1:28; Ps. 8:5-8).

(c)   God has given all kinds of abilities to men and women that need to be discovered, drawn out, and used (Ex. 31:3-5).

(d)   The intellect is not to be despised: more can be done by proper education than by authoritarianism and force (Eccl. 9:17, 18).

2.   The aims of education.

(a)   The first aim of education is the imparting of understanding or insight (Prov. 4:1, 7); and basic to this understanding or insight is the truth that 'the fear of the LORD is the beginning of wisdom' (Prov. 1:7).

(b)   The second aim of education is knowledge – the person who has understanding or insight seeks knowledge (Prov. 15:14).

(c)   Knowledge is constantly gained by those who have understanding, to be used at the appropriate time in the future (Prov. 10:14).

(d)   Knowledge helps an individual to discern what is best, and then to make the right choices (Phil.1:9, 10).

(e)   The third aim is wisdom – that is to say, the ability to use knowledge in a way pleasing to God and helpful to others (Prov. 2:1-6; 14:33).

(f)   Those who possess wisdom do not profess to know everything, but they are always ready to take advice, and show a willingness to learn from any who will teach them (Prov. 13:10).

(g)   The truth that education is not speedily achieved is generally recognised (Dan. 1:4, 5): our Lord Jesus Christ is said to have grown in wisdom, as part of His human development from boyhood to manhood (Luke 2:40, 52).

(h)   The aims of the educative purpose may be expressed as follows: to enable people to show aptitude for every kind of learning, to be well informed, quick to understand, and qualified to serve (Dan. 1:4).

3.   The education of children.

(a)   Children are a gift from God (Ps. 127:3-5; 128:3, 4; cf. Gen. 11:30; 17:16).

(b)   Children are necessarily limited in their understanding (1 Cor. 14:20).

(c)   Children are naturally restricted in their outlook (1 Cor. 13:11).

(d)   Children are easily swayed (Eph. 4:14).

(e)   A basic factor in our approach must spring from the knowledge that folly is bound up in the heart of a child, and this must always be borne in mind (Prov. 22:15).

(f)   Children are to be viewed not only as immature, but as sinful by nature (Ps. 51:5).

(g)   God-centred education should begin from the earliest days of a child's life, training it in the way that it should go (Prov. 22:6).

(h)   Such education and training must include careful discipline (Prov. 22:15; 29:17).

(i)   The administering of discipline is not to be abhorrent for true discipline is a mark and proof of love (Heb. 12:5-11).

(j)   To withhold discipline can all too easily mean setting a child's course for destruction (Prov. 19:18).

(k)   Education begins in the home, for parents are to give their children instruction (Prov. 4:1), providing them with sound teaching (Prov. 4:2). We must not lose sight of the parental responsibility for the education of children: parents may delegate parts of their responsibility, but other teachers are to be regarded as their delegates.

(l)   Parents are commanded to instruct their children (Gen. 18:19; Ex. 10:2; 12:26,27; 13:14-16; Deut. 4:9, 10; 6:6-9; 11:19; Isa. 38:19).

(m)   In particular, parents are to be diligent in the religious or spiritual education of their children (Deut. 6:6-9), seizing casual as well as formal opportunities.

(n)   Parents are to give their children God's commands so that they may be careful to do all the words of the law (Deut. 32:46); the way of wisdom should be heard first from parents' lips, and in their parents' lives children should find living examples to follow (Prov. 4:11, 12).

(o)   By their actions parents are to prompt the right sort of questions from their children that will then enable the parents to instruct the children in the mighty redeeming acts of God (Ex. 12:26, 27; 13:14-16).

(p)   Education, whether provided by parents or others, requires wise teachers: the lips of the wise spread knowledge (Prov. 15:7, 12).

(q)   Wise teachers reprove (Prov. 15:12), and are refreshing in their candour and clarity (Prov. 18:4).

(r)   Wise teachers have insight and discernment to recognise the character and intentions of those whom they teach, and they know how to draw out the best from them (Prov. 20:5).

4.   The requirements for success in education.

(a)   To arrive at wisdom by way of understanding and knowledge, we have to begin by recognising that discipline is necessary (Prov. 23:13, 14; 29:15).

(b)   Open rebuke is better than hidden love (Prov. 27:5).

(c)   The second requirement is that correction should be heeded (Prov. 10:17): progress comes through teachableness, and teachableness includes the readiness to accept rebuke.

(d)   If people are often reproved, and still choose to resist, they will suddenly be destroyed - without remedy (Prov. 29:1).

(e)   To love discipline and correction is to love knowledge (Prov. 12:1); the prudent heed correction (Prov. 15:5, 32).

(f)   A rebuke goes deeper into a person of understanding than a hundred lashes upon the back of a fool (Prov. 17:10).

(g)   Character benefits, and is made attractive, by receiving constructive criticism with genuine pleasure (Prov. 25:12).

(h)   The third requirement is that those under instruction should be receptive (Prov. 12:15): the wise know that they can always increase their knowledge (Prov. 1:5; 18:15).

(i)   Application to instruction, and concentration upon it, are to be urged upon those who are receiving it (Prov. 23:12).

(j)   Education requires attentiveness to instruction (Prov. 4:1, 13; 17:27, 28) – wisdom is a long-term investment (Prov. 19:20).

(k)   The fourth requirement is that knowledge must be practically applied (Prov. 19:27).

(l)   The purpose of having an understanding mind is to be able to do successfully what has been committed to us to accomplish in life, including the ability to distinguish between right and wrong (1 Kings 3:9).

5.   The value of education.

(a)   Education is a grace and honour (Prov. 1:8, 9), in that the properly educated are attractive in character, a profitable addition to anyone's acquaintances.

(b)   Education benefits individuals no end: those who obtain wisdom love themselves and prosper (Prov 19:8).

(c)   Education is satisfying, because it gives the individual hopes for a happy future (Prov. 23:13-18).

(d)   Education is better than material wealth (Prov. 16:16): wealth can be deceptive, whereas education of the right sort foils its deception (Prov. 28:11).

(e)   Wise speech comes from true education, and when people can use their tongues wisely, they have overcome one of the main causes of friction and trouble in human relationships (Prov. 15:7, 21; 16:23).

(f)   Goodwill on the part of all right thinking people, and success, come as the results of education because of the understanding, knowledge, and wisdom it provides (Prov. 13:15,16; 21:22; 24:3-6).

6.   Basic to the whole subject of education, from the biblical viewpoint, is the truth that proper education is based upon the fear of the Lord.

(a)   Ideally, education should be God-centred (Prov. 1:7; 9:10).

(b)   The purpose of God-centred education is the reverencing of God: this is the duty of every person (Eccl. 12:13).

(c)   Wisdom, counsel and understanding, in the fullest sense, belong to God (Job 12:13); the truly wise are those to whom God has graciously imparted wisdom (Matt. 12:42; Acts 6:10; 7:10; Jas. 3:17; 2 Pet. 3:15).

(d)   True wisdom stems from the fear of the Lord (Job 28:28; Prov. 1:7; 9:10).

(e)   As Christianity is the only true religion since the God who has revealed Himself in Jesus Christ is the only true God, the only possible means of an entirely profitable education is Christian discipline and instruction (Eph. 6:4).

(f)   To educate fallen men and women, we must remember their fallen nature: they are darkened in their understanding and separated from the life of God because of the ignorance that is in them, due to the hardening of their hearts (Eph. 4:18).

(g)   If education is divorced from God's revelation, it can soon become impoverished and unproductive (1 Cor. 1:17; 2:4;

2 Cor. 1:12), and, at its worst, both foolish and devilish (1 Cor. 1:19-25; Jas. 3:15-16).

(h) Wisdom, without a reverence for God, easily becomes a source of human pride (Isa. 5:21), and, having no anchor in God, it is doomed to failure (Isa. 19:11-15).

(i) When people deny God, they become futile in their thinking (Rom. 1:21, 22).

(j) We need to be aware of the limitations of human intellect, even at its very best (Eccl. 8:17; 12:12).

(k) The fear of the Lord is the beginning of wisdom (Prov. 1:7).

(l) Where there is a reverence for God, God is pleased to prosper the whole course of an individual's education, irrespective of the teachers who may be involved (Dan. 1:17).

---

74. SEX

Question: What does the Bible teach about sex?

Answer: **Sex is a gift of God, and a key to its proper appreciation is a right understanding of marriage. As with all of God's gifts to us, the gift of sex can be abused. Self-knowledge, therefore, is to govern a Christian's attitude to sex; and this knowledge means the control of the thought-life and the recognition of the dignity of the Christian's body as the temple of the Holy Spirit. God's call to sanctification is the test of all behaviour between the sexes.**

1. Sex is a gift of God.

(a) Sex is a creation of God (Gen. 1:27; Matt. 19:4; 1 Tim. 4:3).

(b) Sex, as created by God, was good (Gen. 1:31; 1 Tim. 4:3, 4).

(c) God's primary purpose in the creation of sex was the procreation of children (Gen. 1:28): that is to say, the coming of children was intended to be always a cause of joy (John 16:21).

(d) Sexual desire is one of the reasons, therefore, that men and women come together in marriage (1 Cor. 7:9).

(e)   To fulfil this desire within marriage is right, but outside of marriage is wrong (1 Cor. 7:8, 9).

2.   We must appreciate the importance of marriage.

(a)   Marriage is a gift and calling of God to some and not to others (1 Cor 7:7, 17).

(b)   Marriage has higher ends than merely the fulfilment of the sexual desire: one of its pre-eminent purposes is the bearing of children (Ps. 127:3-5; 1 Tim. 5:14) and their rearing in the discipline and instruction of the Lord (Eph. 6:4) - for this reason among others, marriage for the Christian is to be to someone who belongs to the Lord (1 Cor. 7:39).

(c)   Marriage is further intended for the mutual help of husband and wife by means of friendship and companionship (Gen. 2:18, 20).

(d)   Marriage is to be entered upon not in passionate lust but in holiness and honour (1 Thess. 4:4, 5).

(e)   Marriage is to be received with thanksgiving, as with all of God's gifts (1 Tim. 4:3, 4).

(f)   Marriage has special enjoyment and meaning for those who believe and know the truth (1 Tim. 4:3; Eph. 5:22-33).

(g)   Marriage is consecrated by the Word of God and prayer (1 Tim. 4:3-5).

(h)   When a man and woman come together they are one flesh (Eph. 5:31; note also 1 Cor. 7:16); thus those who are married cease to have exclusive rights over their own bodies (1 Cor. 7:1-6).

(i)   Within marriage the full enjoyment of the sexual relationship is encouraged within the bounds of self-control and holiness (1 Cor. 7:3-6).

(j)   The marriage bond is indissoluble (Gen. 2:24; Matt. 19:3-9; Mark 10:3-9; Eph. 5:31): what God has joined together, no one should dare to separate (Matt. 19:6).

(k)   Marriage should be honoured by all (Heb. 13:4): to violate the sanctity of marital intercourse is great wickedness and sin against God (Gen. 39:9; 1 Thess. 4:3-6; Heb. 13:4).

3. **We must also appreciate the honourableness of the unmarried state.**

(a) The unmarried state is recognised to be God's call to some (Matt. 19:10-12; 1 Cor. 7:7).

(b) Celibacy or virginity is a gift of God to some, even as marriage is to others (1 Cor. 7:7, 17).

(c) There are definite advantages in the unmarried state so far as service for God is concerned: undivided attention to the Lord is possible in a manner that is impossible to the married (1 Cor. 7:32-35).

(d) The unmarried should dedicate themselves to Christ (1 Tim. 5:11) - their first pledge is to Him (1 Tim. 5:12).

4. **Self-knowledge is to govern a Christian's attitude to sex.**

(a) The Christian's old nature is corrupt through deceitful desires (Eph. 4:22): its sinful desires are at war against the soul (1 Pet. 2:11), and the danger attaching to these desires is never to be overlooked (1 Cor. 9:27).

(b) Christians' new self is in conflict with the old; and they are to live according to the new and not according to the old (Eph. 4:17-24).

(c) Satan's temptations centre especially on the sexual urge (1 Cor. 7:5): sexual desires are a particular source of temptation in youth (2 Tim. 2:22).

(d) The recognition of this problem inherent in human nature means that the body is to be disciplined and subdued (1 Cor. 9:27).

(e) Knowledge of human nature makes plain that physical desire and attraction are often confused with love, whereas they are by no means the same (2 Sam. 13:1-20); and physical desire, mistaken for love, once acceded to, frequently leads to lack of respect and hatred (2 Sam. 13:15).

(f) Of ourselves we cannot control the passion of our sinful hearts and flesh (Rom. 7:19, 20, 24); only by our living according to our new life in the Holy Spirit can we overcome them (Gal. 5:16).

5. **The control of the thought-life.**

(a) We have all sinned with regard to sex, in thought if not in deed, at some time (John 8:1-9).

(b)　Sin begins with the thoughts (Matt. 5:28; Mark 7:21-23).

(c)　Evil thoughts, sexual immorality, theft, murder, adultery, greed, malice, deceit, lewdness, envy, slander, arrogance and folly come naturally and easily to our heart (Mark 7:21).

(d)　Jesus condemned as adultery of the heart the adulterous desire, even if no adulterous designs attach themselves to the desire (Matt. 5:27, 28).

(e)　We need to be ruthless in dealing with those situations and temptations that would lead us astray sexually (Matt. 5:27-30).

(f)　We need to fill our thoughts with things that are true, noble, right, pure, lovely, admirable, excellent and praiseworthy (Phil. 4:8), rather than occupying ourselves at all with things that are shameful (Eph. 5:12).

6.　God's warnings with regard to the misuse of sex.

(a)　We are solemnly warned that God will punish all who abuse sex (1 Thess. 4:6): the adulterer and all the sexually immoral He will judge (Heb. 13:4).

(b)　All who live according to evil human desires and not according to the will of God will give account to God who is ready to judge the living and the dead (1 Pet. 4:2-5).

(c)　No immoral or impure person has any inheritance in the kingdom of Christ and of God (Eph. 5:5, 6).

7.　The Christian's body.

(a)　Christians are not to regard their bodies as their own – they have been bought with a price (1 Cor. 6:19, 20).

(b)　Christians are to have a reverence for the body: it is a temple of the Holy Spirit (1 Cor. 6:19).

(c)　Christians are to honour God with their bodies (1 Cor. 6:20).

(d)　The body is to be continually offered to God as a living sacrifice (Rom. 12:1).

(e)　By immorality we sin against the body (1 Cor. 6:18), and against Christ (1 Cor. 6:15, 17).

8.　Principles are laid down in the Bible to govern and guide man-woman relationships.

(a)　Christians are to know how they should behave with regard to sex, whether married or unmarried (1 Thess. 4:3-5).

(b)   Christians' attitude to sex will often surprise non-Christians, and especially those who knew them before they became Christians (1 Pet. 4:3, 4).

(c)   Christians are to recognise that satisfying physical desires, whether good or bad, is not the most important thing in life–more important is their heavenly citizenship (1 Pet. 2:11).

(d)   Christians must not be deceived by those who try to make them think that Christian standards are too high (Eph. 5:5, 6).

(e)   Perfect propriety is to characterise the Christian's relationships with those of the other sex (1 Tim. 5:2).

(f)   Considerateness is to dominate Christian men's relationship to women, treating them with respect as sometimes physically weaker (1 Pet. 3:7; 1 Tim. 5:2).

(g)   Christians are to be wise and careful in their relationships with those of the other sex (Eph. 5:15).

(h)   Christians should beware of foolishness in their approach to members of the other sex (Eph. 5:15-17).

(i)   Christians should beware of silly talk or levity about sex, because such leads all too often to foolish actions (Eph. 5:3-5).

(j)   Christians should beware of allowing their emotions to be excessively roused – this is part of Paul's argument against strong drink (Eph. 5:18).

(k)   Sexual temptation is to be avoided where possible (2 Tim. 2:22): it is no disgrace to run away from sexual temptation - it is exemplified and commanded (Gen. 39:12; 2 Tim. 2:22).

(l)   There is to be nothing impure in the Christian's experience of sex (1 Thess. 4:7).

(m)   Self-control is to be exercised ruthlessly before marriage: if this is impossible, then marriage should take place (1 Cor. 7:9, 36) - it is recognised that the sexual urge is more powerful in some than in others (1 Cor. 7. 8-9, 36-39).

9.   The general principles of Christian conduct taught in the Bible must be applied also to sex.

(a)   Christians must not allow their attitude to sex to be governed by the moral climate of their day (Eph. 4:14-24); they are not to form close associations with those who reject Christian teaching on the subject (Eph. 5:7), and they must be ready to speak out against wrong views of sex (Eph. 5:11).

(b)   Christians should endeavour to learn from the Bible what is pleasing to God with regard to sex (Eph. 5:10, 17; 1 Pet. 4:2).

(c)   Christians are called to sanctification: their use of sex is to be consistent with holiness (1 Thess. 4:7).

(d)   There is a right time and place for everything we need to do (Eccl. 3:1-8).

(e)   There are circumstances where it is necessary to refrain from things that are right in themselves (1 Cor. 7:29-31).

(f)   Every kind of evil between the sexes should be avoided (1 Thess. 5:22).

(g)   Whatever Christians would wish others to do to them, they should do to others (Matt. 7:12).

(h)   Christians should not provoke others to envy by reason of some special relationship (Gal. 5:26).

(i)   The well-being of Christians' souls will be a guide to their proper attitude and response to evil desires (1 Pet. 2:11).

(j)   The Holy Spirit is given to enable Christians to gain victory over sin in the body (Rom. 8:13; Gal. 5. 23; 2 Tim. 1:7). As the Holy Spirit's help is sincerely sought, His help is given (Luke 11:13).

(k)   The right attitude to sex is maintained as Christians are filled with the Spirit, have sincere and spiritual fellowship with one another, and endeavour at all times and everywhere to give God thanks for His gifts (Eph. 5:18-20; read these verses in the light of the earlier verses of the chapter).

75. GIVING

Question: **What does the Bible teach about giving?**

Answer: **Giving, modelled upon the Old Testament tithe, supports and furthers God's work and purposes for His people in the world. It is to be regular, systematic and according to how God has prospered us. However, the New Testament does not lay down the principle of the tithe, but presupposes that our giving will more than equal it because of the inward compulsion of the Holy Spirit moving us to respond to God's generosity with joyful and grateful liberality.**

1. **Any consideration of Christian giving must begin with God's giving.**

(a) Every good and perfect gift comes from God the Father (Jas. 1:17).

(b) When God gives, He gives with a wonderful generosity, e.g. in His blessing of creation (Gen. 1:22, 28; cf. Ps. 104), in His promises to His people (Gen. 17:1-22; 22:17; Ex. 1:7, 20; 32:13), in His provision of rich prosperity (Deut. 28:11) and salvation (Ps. 5:7; 31:19; 51:1).

(c) God's giving is limitless - He has given us His Son, and in His Son He gave Himself (John 1:14; 3:16; Acts 20:28; 2 Cor. 9:15).

(d) Our Lord Jesus Christ, though rich beyond all telling, became poor for our sakes, so that we through His poverty might become rich (2 Cor. 8:9): He gave His life as a ransom for many (Matt. 20:28), and His flesh for the life of the world (John 6:32, 33, 51; cf. Luke 22:19).

(e) He makes us rich with every spiritual gift (1 Cor 1:5-9), with a variety of spiritual gifts (1 Cor 12:1-11), the gifts of His ascension (Eph. 4:7-13).

(f) God's giving is part of the outflow of His love towards us (1 John 3:17).

(g) He gives to us that we may be in a position to give and be generous in our own giving (2 Cor 9:11).

2. **Tithing was the basic pattern of giving in the Old Testament.**

(A tithe is a tenth part, and it may have to do with the ancient custom of counting by tens, a system made easy by the ten fingers and toes common to human beings.)

(a) The Jews were instructed to tithe their cereal and fruit crops and their livestock (Lev. 27:30-33).

(b) Underlying the tithe was the basic idea that the earth is the Lord's and everything in it (Ps. 24:1).

(c) Tithing came to mean an expression of thanksgiving to God for His generosity (Gen. 28:20-22).

(d) The Jews paid their tithes to the Levites (Num. 18:20-24), or later to the Levites who served as priests (cf. Heb.7:5), in return for the service they rendered at the Tent of Meeting (Num. 18:21), and as compensation for their lack of landed possessions.

(e) Payment was made in Jerusalem (Deut. 12:5, 6, 11, 17, 18) and then each third year in their home communities instead of Jerusalem for the relief of local need (Deut. 14:28-29; 26:12).

(f) The Levites, in turn, were required to give one tenth of the tithe to the priests (Num. 18:26, 28; Neh. 10:38, 39).

(g) In times of spiritual decline the people sometimes neglected to pay their tithes, so that Hezekiah, for example, found it necessary to call authoritatively for their payment (2 Chron. 31:4-12).

(h) Nehemiah discovered a similar position of neglect (Neh. 13:11, 12).

(i) Malachi was obliged to rebuke the people for robbing God by withholding tithes and offerings (Mal. 3:7-12).

(j) In the Old Testament, as in the New, giving is no substitute for justice, mercy and walking humbly with God (Micah 6:8; Matt. 23:23; Luke 11:42; 18:9-14).

(k) If we ask, Is tithing an obligation under the new covenant? the New Testament maintains an eloquent silence on the matter (for example, see 1 Cor. 9:13).

Bible Answers

3.   The New Testament has much to say about the proper characteristics of Christian giving.

(a)   It will be, above all, a reflection of God's dealings with us (Matt. 15:32, 33), and an outflow of the giving of ourselves to the Lord (2 Cor. 8:15).

(b)   It will be according to our ability (Acts 11:29), in keeping with our income (1 Cor. 16:2).

(c)   At the same time it will be undeterred by our means, whether large or small, because giving will be counted a privilege (2 Cor. 8:3, 4).

(d)   It will be regular, systematic, and without fuss or ostentation (1 Cor. 16:2; cf. Matt. 6:2-4).

(e)   It will sometimes be costly (Luke 21:4), frequently generous beyond measure (2 Cor. 8:2), and to the limit of our resources (2 Cor. 8:3) - in fact, it will set no limits (1 John 3:16).

(f)   It will be joyful, cheerful, ungrudging, an act of the will, without external pressure, and a matter of individual determination (Luke 21:4; 2 Cor. 8:2-4, 8; 9:5, 7).

(g)   It will look for nothing in return (Luke 14:12-14), and it will seize every possible opportunity (2 Cor. 9:11).

(h)   It will be seen as one of the reasons why we go to work, earn money and have possessions - we gain in order to give away (Eph. 4:28).

4.   The secret of generous giving is correct motivation.

(a)   The desire to respond to the grace and generosity of God, and our thanksgiving to God for the gift of His Son, and the love we feel for Him (2 Cor. 8:7-9; 9:15).

(b)   The desire to acknowledge that God Himself is our true wealth rather than the sum total of our material possessions, as the world would have us think (Ps. 16:2; 73:25; 2 Cor. 6:10).

(c)   The desire to be a good steward of what God has given us (Rom. 14:12; 1 Pet. 4:10).

(d)   The desire to show our love for God by love for others (1 John 5:1-2), as we respond to Him in good deeds by the generous use of our material resources (1 Tim. 6:18).

(e)   The desire to provide help and relief for those who are in need, especially fellow-Christians (Acts 11:29; 1 Cor. 16:1; 2 Cor.

8:4; Gal. 6:10): we share our surplus so that their deficit may be met, and on occasions vice versa (2 Cor. 8:14, 15; Eph. 4:28; 1 Tim. 6:18).

(f) Our desire to be faithful in supporting God's work by providing adequate and generous financial assistance for those who serve Christ in the gospel at home and overseas (1 Cor. 9:1-14; Gal. 6:6; 1 Tim. 5:17).

5.   There are inevitable consequences of proper giving.

(a) God is pleased by our generous giving (2 Cor. 9:7): it is a spiritual sacrifice (Heb. 13:16).

(b) God more than makes up to us what we give (2 Cor. 9:8; Phil. 4:15-19).

(c) God is thanked and praised for our giving by those who benefit from it (2 Cor. 9:13), and so He is honoured (2 Cor. 8:19).

(d) God encourages us by it too: it is a proof of our faith by our works (Jas. 2:14-18), and evidence of God's grace at work in us (2 Cor. 8:1).

(e) By giving in a way that pleases God, we lay up for ourselves a good foundation for the future (1 Tim. 6:19).

(f) We discover too in the present a unique happiness (Acts 20:35) and unexpected blessings (Mal. 3:10).

---

76. PRIDE

Question: What is pride?

Answer: The pride we have in view is that which shows itself in our having too high an opinion of ourself.   It constitutes sin because it leads us to think we can be independent of God as well as superior and often indifferent to others.

1.   The nature of pride.

(a) It comes from within our heart (Mark 7:22; Luke 9:46, 47): it is described as being part of a person's inmost thoughts (Luke 1:51), and arrogance of heart (Ps. 131:1; Isa. 9:9; Dan. 5:20).

(b) It is our seeing ourselves as different from others in some respect, and feeling superior (1 Cor. 4:7); it is a false sense of our own importance (Matt. 26:33; Mark 14:29).

(c) It is an inappropriate love of self (2 Tim. 3:2), and the exaltation of self (Luke 18:9-14).

(d) It is our departing from our proper position before God and others (Jude 6), thinking of ourselves more highly than we ought (Rom. 12:3).

2.   Forms of pride.

(a) It may take the form of pride in appearance (Mark 12:38; 1 Pet. 3:3).

(b) It may take the form of pride in position or prestige (Mark 9:33-37; Luke 9:46-48; Mark 12:38, 39; 1 John 2:16).

(c) It may take the form of pride in power (Lev. 26:19, 20; Ezek. 30:6; cf. Acts 8:18, 19).

(d) It may take the form of pride in achievements and success (2 Chron. 26:15, 16).

(e) It may take the form of pride in possessions (2 Kings. 20:13; Luke 12:13-21).

(f) It may take the form of pride in knowledge (1 Cor. 8:1) and of intellect (Isa. 5:21).

(g) It may take the form of pride in abilities and spiritual gifts (1 Pet. 4:10-11; cf. 1 Cor. 12:4-11).

(h) It may take the form of pride in people, and the human relationships we possess (1 Cor. 3:21).

(i) It may take the form of pride in spiritual blessing (2 Cor. 12:7).

3.   The expression of pride.

(a) It expresses itself in attitudes (Eccl. 7:8), in excessive self-confidence (Matt. 26:33-35; Mark 14:29-31; Luke 22:33), in an unwillingness to take advice (Prov. 13:10), in contempt for others (Ps. 123:4), in presumptuous planning for the future (Jas. 4:13-16), and in arrogance (Prov. 8:13).

(b) It expresses itself in our eyes: we may have haughty eyes (Prov. 6:17; 21:4), and such may first be demonstrated in regard to our parents (Prov. 30:17).

(c)   It expresses itself in our objectives and ambitions: pride always wants more of that of which it is proud (Hab. 2:4, 5), which is another way of saying that it is greedy.

(d)   It expresses itself in words (1 Sam. 2:3; Luke 9:46), particularly in boasting (Isa. 10:12, 13) and exaggeration (Dan. 4:1; 2 Pet. 2:18; Jude 16).

(e)   It expresses itself in actions and reactions: it does not rejoice in the success of others (1 Cor. 13:4); it prompts anger and violence (Gen. 4:6ff).

4.   The effects of pride.

(a)   It encourages arrogance (Prov. 21:24).

(b)   It makes us brag about one person at the expense of another (1 Cor. 4:6); it lifts us up to a false sense of our own importance (1 Tim. 3:6).

(c)   It brings quarrels and dissension in its wake (Prov. 13:10; 28:25).

(d)   It breeds a false self-confidence (Matt. 26:33-35; Mark 14:29-31; Luke 22:33).

(e)   It makes us foolishly feel we can be independent of everyone, including God (Psa. 10:4; Hos. 7:10).

(f)   It provides a false sense of security (Obad. 3, 4).

(g)   It leads to contempt and rejection of God's Word (Jer. 43:2).

(h)   It leads to self-deception (Jer. 49:16); the pride of our heart deceives us (Prov. 26:12; Obad. 3).

(i)   It becomes an obstacle to our worship of God, and acceptance with Him (Gen. 4:3-5; Jas. 4:6).

(j)   It cuts us off from God because it constitutes part of our inner defilement (Mark 7:20-23).

(k)   It ultimately brings both a fall (1 Cor. 10:12) and disgrace (Prov. 16:18; cf. 18:12).

5.   Examples of pride in the Bible.

(a)   The angels who did not keep their own position (Jude 6; cf. Isa. 14:12-15).

(b)   Pharaoh, who was proud in his dealings with the Israelites (Neh. 9:10).

(c)   Hezekiah, who was too proud to show his gratitude to God for His goodness to him (2 Chron. 32:25).

(d)   Nebuchadnezzar, who was proud of his might and majesty (Dan. 3:1-30; 4:30; 5:20).

(e)   Belshazzar, whose heart was proud in that he refused to humble himself (Dan. 5:22, 23).

(f)   Haman, who desired respect and homage for himself (Esth. 3:5).

(g)   Moab, whose pride was seen in arrogance and empty boasting (Isa. 16:6).

(h)   Tyre, whose pride was in its achievements and commerce (Isa. 23:8, 9).

(i)   Edom, whose pride deceived it so that it felt it was not vulnerable from attack (Obad. 3).

(j)   Babylon, whose pride led it to be defiant against the Lord (Jer. 50:29-32).

(k)   Assyria, whose pride gave it a sense of superiority over all others (Ezek. 31:3, 10, 11).

(l)   Israel, whose pride was intoxicating and without justification (Isa. 28:1; Hos. 5:5, 9).

(m)   Judah, whose pride caused it not to give glory to God (Jer. 13:15-19).

(n)   The Pharisees, whose pride caused them to trust in themselves that they were righteous and to despise others (Luke 18:9-14).

(o)   The teachers of the law, whose pride was seen in their delight in outward show and public acknowledgement (Mark 12:38-40).

(p)   Peter, who felt he was stronger than others and able to withstand temptation (Matt. 26:33-35; Mark 14:29-31; Luke 22:33).

(q)   Herod Agrippa, who thought he could take glory to himself that was God's alone (Acts 12:21-23).

(r)   The Laodiceans, whose pride made them blind to their spiritual poverty (Rev. 3:17).

6.   The guilt of pride.

First, it causes us to sin against God.

(a)   It is declared to be sin (Prov. 21:4).

(b)   When we are proud we have lost sight of our indebtedness to God, that we have nothing good that we have not received (1 Cor. 4:7).

(c)   We ascribe to ourselves the success that we really owe to God (Judg. 7:2).

(d)   We refuse to hear God's words and follow the stubbornness of our hearts (Jer. 13:10).

(e)   We think we can be independent of God when, in fact, the opposite is the case (Jer. 13:8-11).

(f)   We trust not in God but in ourselves, believing that we can build our life on what we think we can accomplish and control ourselves (Ps. 52:1; 75:4; 94:3, 4).

Secondly, it causes us to sin against others.

(g)   Puffed up, we take pride in one person over against another (1 Cor. 4:6).

(h)   Conceited, we ignore and despise those whom we think inferior to us (Rom. 12:16; cf. Luke 18:9).

(i)   Proud, we think little of the interests of others and are often inconsiderate of them (Ps. 10:2; Prov. 21:24).

7.   The condemnation of pride.

(a)   One of the factors that should make us condemn our pride is that it is Satan's principal sin (1 Tim. 3:6; Rev. 13:5).

(b)   God has no pleasure in our foolish pride (Jer. 13:15; Zeph. 3:11).

(c)   Pride is part of those characteristics that mark people out as opposed to God (2 Tim. 3:2-4).

(d)   God hates pride (Amos 6:8; Jer. 13:9) and He resists the proud (Jas. 4:6; 1 Pet. 5:5).

(e)   Pride makes God's judgment inevitable (Jer. 13:15-17), so that He will put an end to it (Ps. 18:27; Isa. 2:12; 13:11; 23:9; Jer. 13:9).

(f)   Those who walk in pride, God is well able to abase (Dan. 4:37).

8.   The cure of pride.

(a)   Its cure begins when we realise that there is no place at all for pride in ourselves before God (1 Cor. 1:29).

(b)   Its cure proceeds as we see ourselves as sinners, and individually as 'the worst' of sinners (1 Tim. 1:15), in stark contrast to how we once viewed ourselves (Luke 18:11,12; Phil. 3:4-6).

(c)   Its cure is about to be effected when we abandon all claims to self-righteousness and depend utterly and completely on Jesus

Christ for both salvation and righteousness before God (Phil. 3:7-11), so that we then glory in Jesus Christ (Phil. 3:3), and in His Cross (Gal. 6:14).

(d)   The cure must never be taken for granted, for the danger of pride will not be removed until we are changed perfectly into our Lord's likeness (2 Cor. 12:7; Phil. 3:21).

(e)   Pride is kept under control as we realise that the only wise and legitimate pride is pride in the Lord (1 Cor. 1:31): paradoxically, having humbled ourselves before God, we can boast in Him (Jer. 9:23, 24), in His divine intervention and help in the past, and in the assurance we have of the same benefits in the future (1 Chron. 29:11; Ps. 5:11; 32:11; 89:17).

(f)   The cure of pride is assisted by our being mindful of the proverbs of Scripture concerning it (1 Kings 20:11; Prov. 25:14; 27:1).

(g)   Its cure is further assisted by attentiveness to the words of Scripture that warn against pride and encourage instead the pursuit of humility (Jas. 4:6; 1 Pet. 5:5).

(h)   If we do not allow pride to be cured now, it will be finally cured at the Day of Judgment: God has a day reserved for the proud and lofty (Isa. 2:12, 17; Mal. 4:1), and His judgment is directed at the extinction of all false pride (Dan. 4:37; Matt. 23:12).

(i)   Safety for the Christian lies in the active pursuit of humility, following the example of our Lord Jesus Christ without compromise (Phil. 2:1-13).

---

77. WRATH

Question: What is wrath?

Answer: Wrath is our reaction of indignation and displeasure at the deeds, words or intentions of others. It is not always sinful in that wrath may be a just reaction to wrong but it is frequently sinful either because selfishness prompts our anger or because our anger, though justly stirred, runs away with itself and leads to wrong words and actions.

1. **Wrath and anger.**

(a) Wrath describes passionate rage that boils up suddenly in an angry outburst, sometimes to disappear almost as quickly, but at other times to become a lasting bitterness.

(b) Wrath and anger are almost synonymous words in the Bible. In the New Testament wrath comes from a Greek root that means 'to boil up' or 'to well up' and originally denoted violent movement. Wrath, therefore, indicates a rage that quickly bursts forth, often uncontrollably, and as quickly disappears. Anger, however, describes an angry attitude and temper that lasts and is nursed.

(c) Wrath and anger are especially sins of the tongue (2 Cor. 12:20; Jas. 3:3-18), but they find their place on our tongues and in our actions because they are cherished in our hearts (Eccl. 7:9; Amos 1:11).

2. **Wrath and anger are not always out of place and sinful.**

(a) We ought to be angry when good is put aside and evil exalted, and we have examples in the Bible of just and holy anger:

  (i) Moses was angry at the Israelites' lack of trust in God (Ex. 16:20), and at their apostasy in making a golden calf (Ex. 32:19, 22);

  (ii) David was angry at the unjust rich man about whom Nathan told him, not realising at first that it was at himself his anger was rightly directed (2 Sam. 12:5);

  (iii) Nehemiah was angry at the abuses that had taken place in Jerusalem (Neh. 5:6);

  (iv) Paul's spirit was deeply distressed, to the point of anger, in Athens when he witnessed its idolatry (Acts 17:16).

(b) We have evidence too of God inducing a proper anger in His people for good purposes (Rom. 10:19; 2 Cor. 7:11).

(c) Our Lord Jesus Christ was angry at people's indifference to human need (Mark 3:5), and His wrath was the revelation of God's.

(d) God's holy and just wrath and anger are described in the Bible in various aspects:

  (i) God's wrath is slow (Ps. 103:8; Isa. 48:9; Jonah 4:2; Nah. 1:3);

(ii)   God's wrath is righteous (Ps. 58:10, 11; Rom. 2:5-8; 3:5, 6; 9:18, 20, 22; Rev. 16:6, 7);

(iii) God's wrath is perfectly controlled - e.g. our Lord's clearing the temple of traders was not done on impulse, but the night before He inspected the temple (Mark 11:11).

3. But more often than not we do wrong to be angry because of the selfish motives and attitudes that prompt our anger (Jonah 4:4).

(a) Pride – and especially hurt pride – promotes anger (Gen. 4:3-5; 2 Kings 5:11, 12; Esth. 3:5; Dan. 3:13).

(b) Unwillingness to accept rebuke spurs on anger (2 Chron. 26:19).

(c) Jealousy kindles anger (1 Sam. 17:28; Acts 5:17, 18).

(d) Resentment encourages anger (Luke 4:28).

(e) Selfishness sparks off anger (1 Kings 21:4).

(f) Touchiness provides ready opportunity for anger (Gen. 40:1-3).

(g) Malice is the companion often of anger (Gen. 27:41, 45; Col. 3:8).

4. Wrath and anger do harm and easily lead to other sins.

(a) When we lose control of ourselves on account of wrath or anger sin crouches at the door (Gen. 4:7).

(b) Like a wind or hurricane that arises swiftly or unexpectedly or a fire that gets out of control, wrath and anger can do immeasurable harm (Ps. 124:3; Eccl.10:4) and mischief (Prov. 6:34; 15:1; 16:14), besides being overwhelming (Prov. 27:4).

(c) They tear families apart (Amos 1:11).

(d) They show on our face (Gen. 4:5).

(e) They have physical repercussions (Acts 7:54)– to harbour anger or resentment is as bad for the body as it is for the soul (Prov. 14:30).

(f) They mar prayer and fellowship with God (1 Tim. 2:8).

(g) They spoil Christian fellowship and the life of the church (2 Cor. 12:20).

(h) They give the devil a foothold that he will use to his own evil advantage (Eph. 4:26, 27).

(i)   They can be the first step even to murder, and they can certainly constitute the spirit of murder for murder is only anger full-grown (Matt. 5:21, 22).

(j)   They are accompanied frequently by quarrelling and harsh words (Prov. 15:18; Eph. 4:31).

(k)   They lead often to cruelty and injustice (Gen. 49:7; 2 Chron. 16:10; Prov.14:17; 27:4).

(l)   They issue all too often in strife and contention (Prov. 21:19; 29:22; 30:33), violence (Dan. 2:12) and murder (Gen. 4:8; 49:6; Ex. 2:11, 12; Matt. 2:16-18).

5.   The condemnation of wrath and anger.

(a)   They are a characteristic of fools (Prov. 12:16; 14:17,29; 27:3, 4; Eccl. 7:9).

(b)   They provide sufficient grounds for terminating friendship, since keeping friendship with someone whose temper is uncontrolled can lead us in the same direction (Gen. 49:6; Prov. 22:24).

(c)   They reveal the state of a person's heart (Luke 6:45).

(d)   They are acts of the sinful nature, and are opposed to God's Spirit (Gal. 5:20).

(e)   They never bring about the righteous life God desires (Jas. 1:19, 20).

(f)   They are a violation of the sixth commandment (Matt.5:21, 22).

(g)   They bring their own punishment (Job 19:29, Prov. 25:28).

(h)   They are frequently an infringement of God's prerogative of judgment for wrath and anger so easily make us take judgment into our own hands (Rom. 12:19).

(i)   They put us in danger of God's judgment (Matt. 5:22).

6.   The Christian attitude to wrath and anger.

(a)   We recognise wrath and anger, arising from bitterness, as belonging to the old life we once lived before our conversion, and that they are among the many things which we are to get rid of (Eph. 4:31).

(b)   We are to be slow to become angry (Ps. 37:8; Prov. 15:18; 16:32; 19:11; Tit. 1:7; Jas. 1:19).

(c)   Aiming at the avoidance of wrath and anger, we also try to placate those who are carried away by wrath and anger, where it is right and possible to do so (Prov. 15:1, 18; 16:32; 29:8, 11).

(d)   Our aim when anger is justifiable is neither to allow it to cause us to sin (Eph. 4:26), nor to give Satan a foothold by means of it (Eph. 4:27).

---

78. ENVY

Question: What is envy?

Answer: Envy is basically ill-will occasioned by looking at someone else's superior position or advantages. It is sinful because, besides indicating discontent with God's providence, it is contrary to love for our neighbour in that love rejoices at the good of others.

1.   The characteristics of envy.
(a)   Envy begrudges the honour and advantages others enjoy (Gen. 26:14).
(b)   It fails to see God's providence in the provision of gifts, honours and abilities (Deut. 8:17, 18; Prov. 30:8, 9).
(c)   It is sad at the happiness of others (Luke 15:25-30).
(d)   It makes us hostile to those who have never injured us (Gen. 37:3, 4).
(e)   It seeks the destruction of others rather than their welfare (Matt. 27:18; Mark 15:10).
(f)   It may even break through every restraint in order to bring about the ruin of the person who is envied (Gen. 4:3-8).

2.   The incitement of envy.
(a)   It is stimulated by the attractiveness and commendation given to the virtues of others (1 John 3:12; cf. Gen. 4:3-8).
(b)   It is stirred up by the success of others (1 Sam. 18:8, 9; Dan. 6:3, 4; Acts 13:45; 17:4, 5).
(c)   It is prompted by pride (1 Tim. 6:3-5).
(d)   It is encouraged by the existence of both bitterness (Jas. 3:14) and malice (Tit. 3:3) in our hearts towards others.

3.   The prevalence of envy.

(a)   It was behind Adam and Eve's first rebellion, for by means of the encouragement of envy Satan caused them to lose their enjoyment of unspoiled fellowship with God (Gen. 3:1-6).

(b)   It was envy that brought about the first shedding of blood in human history (Gen. 4:3-8).

(c)   It is one of the evil things that is characteristic of the human heart and that defiles us before God (Mark 7:20-23; Jas. 3:14).

(d)   It is often the explanation why people work so hard to succeed, in that they envy their neighbours and want to surpass them (Eccl. 4:4).

(e)   It is behind most coveting (1 Kings 21:1-4).

(f)   It can fill a life, together with other forms of wickedness that go with it (Rom. 1:29).

4.   The condemnation of envy.

(a)   God hates envy (Prov. 3:31, 32).

(b)   Envy is a characteristic of the world, as it chooses to live without reference to God (1 Cor. 3:3; Tit. 3:3).

(c)   In terms of the great conflict there is between light and darkness, envy and jealousy belong to the darkness (Rom. 13:12-13).

(d)   Envy is an evidence of a corrupted mind (Rom. 1:28, 29), and is an act of the sinful nature in contrast to the fruit of the Spirit (Gal. 5:19-23).

(e)   Envy is the opposite of fellowship: moved by envy, we want to have what others have; in fellowship, however, we desire to share with others what we ourselves possess (Mark 14:3-9).

(f)   Envy is the opposite of love (1 Cor. 13:4; 1 John 3:11, 12) so that it makes us unlike God (1 John 4:8).

(g)   Envy makes us like Satan, whose work we further when we allow it to rule our hearts and actions (John 8:44; 1 John 3:12).

5.   The dangerous consequences of envy.

(a)   It is more cruel and destructive than anger (Prov 27:4).

(b)   It is like a cancer, doing harm to both the body and the mind (Prov. 14:30).

(c)   It ruins spiritual appetite (1 Pet. 2:1, 2) and fellowship with God (Ps. 66:18).

(d)   It quickly leads to slander of every kind (1 Pet. 2:1, 2).

(e)   It breeds a destructively critical spirit (Dan. 6:3, 4; Acts 17:5).

(f)   It gives birth to unwarranted suspicion and anger (1 Sam. 18:8, 9).

(g)   It can give vent to itself in spiteful actions (Gen. 26:14, 15).

(h)   It can suddenly escalate into disorder and every evil practice (Gen. 37:11; Acts 7:9; Jas. 3:16): conspiracy (Gen. 37:18), mockery (Gen. 37:19), thoughts of murder (Gen. 37:20), violence (Gen. 37:23), cruelty (Gen. 37:24), betrayal (Gen. 37:25-28), lies (Gen. 37:32) and immeasurable hurt to others (Gen. 37:34).

---

79. LUST

Question: What is lust?

Answer: Lust is either uncontrolled, overmastering desire or desire willingly allowed to go beyond what is lawful and legitimate. Lust is sinful because it puts pleasure before pleasing God, and it places self-gratification before the good of others.

1.   The distinction between desire and lust.

(a)   Desires – whether physical, mental, spiritual or sexual – were given by God to male and female at their creation and were wholly good (Gen. 1:31; 1 Tim. 4:3, 4; Jas. 1:17).

(b)   Sin, however, acting like a poison, mars all human desires, and left to itself would use them to increase the corruption that is in the world (2 Pet. 1:4).

(c)   Desire is necessary, for example, if appetite is to ensure that the body is fed (Matt. 4:2), and if the human race is to be continued by procreation (Gen. 3:16; Heb. 13:4).

(d)   Our Lord Jesus Christ had an eager desire to eat the Passover with His disciples (Luke 22:15), and Paul had a desire to depart and be with Christ (Phil. 1:23): these desires were wholly commendable.

(e)   Our desires, however, can so easily be set on evil things and then they become lusts (1 Cor. 10:6).

(f)   Desire becomes lust when its object is unlawful (Ex. 20:14; 2 Sam. 11:3, 4).

(g)   Desire becomes lust when it gains control of us rather than our controlling it (1 Thess. 4:5) - thus looking becomes covetousness (Josh. 7:21), eating becomes gluttony (Phil. 3:19), attraction leads to mental adultery (Matt. 5:27, 28), and burning sexual desire becomes immorality (2 Sam. 11:2-4).

2.   The source of lust.

(a)   Desires – both good and bad - find their origin in our heart (Ps. 37:4; Matt. 15:19, 20; Rom. 1:24, 29). (In Biblical language, the heart covers the whole of our inward life – our thinking, feelings and will.)

(b)   Lust is part of our nature as fallen men and women, and that nature may be described as being corrupted through deceitful lusts (Eph. 4:22).

(c)   Lust springs from the evil desires of our mortal bodies that demand satisfaction in unlawful, and therefore sinful ways (Rom. 6:12).

(d)   Lust finds its home in our sinful nature that pleads for the gratification of its desires (Rom. 13:14; Gal. 5:16).

(e)   Lusts reflect the connection of fallen men and women with the devil (John 8:44).

(f)   Lust is a manifestation of the sin that dwells in men and women and that controls them (Rom. 7:7, 8).

3.   Lust's characteristics and objectives.

(a)   Lust is deceitful in that it promises happiness but it brings misery (Eph. 4:22).

(b)   Lust shows itself in uncontrolled passion (1 Thess. 4:5) leading to sexual immorality and sometimes depravity and perversion (Rom. 1:29; Jude 7).

(c)   Lust reveals itself in covetousness whether of money (Acts 20:33), other people's material possessions (Ex. 20:17), or another person's body (Prov. 6:25; Matt. 5:28).

(d)   Lust's pre-eminent stimulus is what comes to men and women through their eyes (1 John 2:16): Eve, for example, was tempted by what she saw of the tree in the middle of the garden (Gen. 3:6), and Achan was tempted by what he saw among the spoils of the city of Jericho (Josh. 7:21).

(e)   Lust finds itself stirred by what it sees, whether in the form of another person's attractiveness (2 Sam. 11:2-4; Job 31:1; Matt. 5:28) or in terms of the attractions and pleasures of the world (Matt. 4:8; Luke 8:14).

(f)   Lust can be stimulated by harmful friendships and bad company (2 Tim. 2:22).

(g)   Lust keeps company with sins such as debauchery, drunkenness, orgies, carousing and detestable idolatry (1 Pet. 4:3).

(h)   Lust is linked often with obscenity, foolish talk or coarse joking (Eph. 5:3, 4).

(i)   Lust desires our surrender to it (1 Thess. 4:4, 5) through its strong enticements (Jas 1:14; Jude 16).

(j)   Lust listens only to what it wants to hear (2 Tim. 4:3): those who follow after their own evil desires choose to scoff at all presentations of truth that might make them uncomfortable (2 Pet. 3:3).

4.   Lust's consequences.

(a)   Lust never stands still: once conceived it gives birth to sin; and sin, when it is full-grown, gives birth to death (Jas. 1:15).

(b)   Lust degrades the body (Rom. 1:24; 1 Cor. 6:18-20).

(c)   Lust corrupts the good things of life (2 Pet. 1:4).

(d)   Lust breeds inward conflicts and outward strife (Jas. 4:1).

(e)   Lust chokes the influence of God's Word in an individual's life (Mark 4:19).

(f)   Lust leads to transgression and wronging another person (1 Thess. 4:5, 6).

(g)   Lust makes us the world's friend and God's enemy (Jas. 4:4): God demands our total obedience and love from the whole heart (Deut. 6:5).

(h)   Lust brings upon itself the judgment of God (1 Thess. 4:6): it merits His wrath (Col. 3:6).

5.   The antidote to lust.

(a)   The only effective antidote to lust is the grace of God that brings salvation and that teaches us to say 'No' to ungodliness and worldly passions, and to live self-controlled, upright and godly lives in this present age while we await the return of Jesus Christ (Tit. 2:11-13).

(b)   Realising that the Lord Jesus gave Himself for us to redeem us from all wickedness, and to purify for Himself a people that are His very own (Tit. 2:14), prompts gratitude (Rom. 12:1, 2) and the desire to live for Him and not for ourselves (2 Cor. 5:15).

(c)   We say 'No,' therefore, to worldly passions (Tit. 2:12); we flee evil desires, if necessary, and pursue righteousness (2 Tim. 2:22); we put off our old self with its wrong desires and put on the new self, created to be like God in true righteousness and holiness (Eph. 4:22-24).

(d)   We aim at living self-controlled lives (Tit. 2:12): godly people are not passionless, but controlled in their desires (Gal. 5:22-24).

(e)   We find strength for these things from knowing that they please God and are His will (1 Thess. 4:3; 1 Pet. 4:1-3).

(f)   We find power for doing what is right through the new life the indwelling Holy Spirit gives us (Gal. 5:16).

(g)   We find daily encouragement from God's very great and precious promises to persevere in proving the reality of the antidote that His salvation provides against lust (Heb. 13:20, 21; 2 Pet. 1:4).

---

80. GLUTTONY

Question: **What is gluttony?**

Answer: **Gluttony is excessive eating, so that we live to eat rather than eating to live. It is sinful because by it we make a god of our stomach, and harm both our body and our usefulness to others.**

1.   Gluttony in general.

(a)   The Greek word for 'gluttony' in the New Testament represents someone who eats too much (Matt. 11:19; Luke 7:34).

(b)   Food and drink can become a foolish preoccupation of life (Luke 21:34).

(c)   Gluttony is greedy overindulgence in food – or eating for eating's sake (Prov. 23:20).

(d)   Gluttony goes beyond what is enough (Prov. 25:16), in that more is eaten than the body requires for satisfaction (Ps. 78:29, 30); and special occasions are often thought of as an opportunity for excess (Prov. 23:1-3).

(e)   Gluttons tend to eat too frequently, and at the wrong times (Eccl. 10:16); they eat not for strength but for the enjoyment of excess (Eccl. 10:17).

(f)   Gluttony pays undue attention to the desire for food, and allows the desires of the sinful nature to dominate life (Rom. 13:13, 14).

(g)   Gluttony is accompanied in many instances by excessive drinking, and is to be regarded as equally detrimental as drunkenness (Deut. 21:20; Prov. 23:20, 21).

2.   The effects of gluttony.

(a)   Gluttony leads to our surrender to our natural appetites with their bias to excess and sin.   Cravings naturally characterise fallen human nature (Eph. 2:3), and because of sin those desires can often be deceitful (Eph. 4:22), and Satan may endeavour to lead us astray, if he can, by the natural appetite we have for food (Matt. 4:3).

(b)   Gluttony causes drowsiness and sleep at the wrong times (Prov. 23:20, 21).

(c)   Gluttony leads to laziness and idleness (Eccl. 10:16-18).

(d)   Gluttony brings about the dulling of our senses (Prov. 23:21) so that we can become oblivious of moral and spiritual issues (Amos 6:4-7), and lacking in all spiritual alertness (Luke 21:34-36).

(e)   Gluttony can prove a great snare because lack of awareness of spiritual and moral issues brings tragic consequences (Gen. 25:29-34; Heb. 12:16, 17).

(f)   Gluttony can produce associated evils (Deut. 21:20; Ps. 141:4), including bragging about shameful excess (Phil. 3:19).

(g)   Gluttony can prove ruinous in its influence upon others (Prov. 28:7; Eccl. 10:16, 17).

(h)   Gluttony tends to lead to a feeling of self-sufficiency and independence of God (Deut. 32:15; Prov. 30:8, 9; Isa. 22:13).

(i)   Gluttony injures health in that the body becomes heavy and plump (Deut. 32:15).

(j)   Gluttony can be the first step to poverty (Prov. 23:21).

(k)   Gluttony has ruin as its end (Phil. 3:19), and self-indulgent people can be described as dead while alive (1 Tim. 5:6).

(l)   Esau (Gen. 25:29-34), Eli's sons (1 Sam. 2:12-17) and the rich man called Dives (Luke 16:19-31), are illustrations of some of the sad effects of gluttony

3.   The sinfulness of gluttony.

(a)   Gluttony is, in effect, waste of food, and waste of food is contrary to God's intention (Lev. 23:22; John 6:12).

(b)   Gluttony ignores truths and obligations God has plainly revealed. For example, gluttons forget that it is not mere food that gives life (Deut. 8:3); gluttons fail to see that God is concerned with the daily practicalities of life (1 Cor. 10:31), and they certainly do not seek God's blessing on their eating (1 Tim. 4:4, 5).

(c)   Gluttony is frequently part of a hedonistic approach to life, that is to say, the theory of ethics in which pleasure is regarded as the chief good or the proper end of action (Isa. 22:13; Luke 12:19; 1 Cor. 15:32).

(d)   Gluttony is a form of slavery because by it we make ourselves slaves of food rather than servants of God (1 Cor. 6:12, 13); instead of ruling our bodies, our bodies rule us (Rom. 13:13, 14).

(e)   Gluttony makes a god of food and of the stomach (Phil. 3:19).

(f)   Gluttony is a manifestation of worldliness, of loving the world rather than God in that lavish and expensive eating habits are something of which we can be foolishly proud (1 John 2:15-17; cf. Phil. 3:19).

(g)   Gluttony often offends the principle and commandment that we should love our neighbour as ourselves. Gluttony is frequently the sin of those who live only for themselves (Luke 16:19), so that while they eat, others whom they could help go hungry (Luke 16:19-21).

(h)   Gluttony causes us to sin against the body, forgetful that it is a wonderful gift of God (Ps. 139:14).

(i)   God judges gluttony (Num.11:33,34; Ps. 78:25-31), and we will all be judged for our use of the body (2 Cor. 5:10).

4.   Correctives for the avoidance of gluttony.

(i)   A proper perspective and sense of priorities.

    (a)   One day God will put an end to food and to the stomach (1 Cor. 6:13).

    (b)   There are deeper dimensions to human life than physical hunger (Deut. 8:3): the food we more urgently need is what nourishes spiritual life.

    (c)   The needs of the body are not as important as the requirements of the soul (Matt. 9:1-8; Mark 2:1-12; 1 Cor. 5:5).

    (d)   God's kingdom is not a matter of eating and drinking but of the righteousness, peace and joy that the Holy Spirit gives (Rom. 14:17).

    (e)   For those who know God, eating and drinking are not secular activities: whether they eat or drink, they want to do everything to the glory of God (1 Cor.10:31).

    (f)   True satisfaction is found neither in food nor in other physical pleasures but in doing God's will (John 4:34).

(ii) An understanding of the proper place of food in human life.

    (a)   Food is a necessity for life: everyone needs to take nourishment of proper and sufficient quantity to maintain physical life and well-being (1 Tim. 6:8); food is meant for the stomach, and the stomach for food (1 Cor. 6:13).

    (b)   All of God's creatures depend on Him for food (Ps. 104:27, 28), and we are encouraged to pray for our daily bread (Matt. 6:11), and to regard it as a proper objective of our daily work (Eccl. 6:7; 2 Thess. 3:10).

    (c)   Food is good since God created foods to be received with thanksgiving by those who believe and know the truth (1 Tim. 4:4, 5).   He desires that we should enjoy His gifts (1 Tim. 6:17), for His goodness is illustrated to us in terms of the good things He has given us to eat (Deut. 32:13, 14).

    (d)   Health, however, does not depend on living upon delicacies (Dan. 1:5-16).

    (e)   Food should be eaten principally for the sake of maintaining strength (Eccl. 10:17), and while enjoyment of eating is lawful, slavery to that enjoyment is not (1 Cor. 6:12).

(iii) An appreciation of the Christian teaching concerning his body.

   (a)   The body is the sphere or activity in which we do either good or evil (2 Cor. 5:10).

   (b)   The body is fearfully and wonderfully made (Ps. 139:14) but sadly can be the subject of abuse (Phil. 3:19).

   (c)   Our use of the body should be determined by what God has done for us in Jesus Christ (Rom. 12:1, 2; 1 Cor. 6:12-14, 20): the body is not meant for lust but for the Lord (1 Cor. 6:13).

   (d)   The body is the instrument, in which, and by which, we may honour Christ (Phil. 1:20).

   (e)   The highest dignity is given to our bodies as Christians in that our bodies have become temples of the Holy Spirit, whom we have received from God (1 Cor. 6:19).

   (f)   Hence Christians are to know how to control and manage their own body in holiness and honour (1 Thess. 4:3, 4).

(iv) A rightful maintenance of self-discipline.

   (a)   Restraint is to be put upon a big appetite (Prov. 23:2), so that enough is eaten rather than too much (Prov. 25:16).

   (b)   Part of the fruit of the Spirit is self-control (Gal. 5:23).

   (c)   Fasting may find a place in this self-discipline and God's people throughout the centuries have set an example of fasting: David (2 Sam. 12:16, 22; Ps. 109:24), Nehemiah (Neh. 1:4), Esther (Esther 4:16), Daniel (Dan. 9:3), the disciples of John (Matt. 9:14), Anna (Luke 2:37), Cornelius (Acts 10:30), and the early Christians (Acts 13:2).

   (d)   It is important to remember, however, that Christianity brought an end to ritual fasting (Mark 2:18-22).

   (e)   Our Lord Himself fasted (Matt. 4:2), and gave instruction concerning it (Matt. 6:16-18).

   (f)   Fasting is linked, therefore, with prayer in special situations (Acts 14:23). It is part of worship (Luke 2:37;

Acts 13:1-3) and a symbol of self-humbling before God (Ps. 35:13; 69:10).

(g) Fasting, however, is never to be a matter of display, but is to be in secret (Matt. 6:16-18).

(v)   A genuine concern for the needs of others.

(a) We avoid gluttony by exercising a proper concern for the material needs of others (1 Tim. 6:17, 18).

(b) We are to be generous and share our food with those who are hungry (Prov. 22:9).

(c) We should discipline our intake of food so that we can assist the poor (Isa. 58:6, 7).

(d) We are not to neglect the needs of people's bodies to be fed (Jas. 2:16; cf. Matt. 25:42).

(e) Even in the way we eat, we are to have the good of others in view before our own (1 Cor. 10:31-33).

(vi)   The pursuit of the true satisfaction God intends for us.

(a) Christians know that there is a better way to joy and happiness than excess in the satisfaction of physical appetites: they are to find it in the continuous experience of God's Spirit filling their life (Eph. 5:18).

(b) A Christian's 'food' should be to do the Father's will (John 4:34; cf. 2 Cor. 5:9).

---

81. AVARICE

Question: What is avarice?

Answer: Avarice is the love of money and greed for gain, the opposite of contentment.   It is sinful because it is a form of idolatry in that money and what it may secure becomes our god, leading us not only to dishonour God our Creator but also to neglect and abuse other people.

1.   Avarice defined.

(a) One of the principal features of human life is the amassing of earthly property (Matt. 6:19-21).

(b)   Avarice is the love of money and greed for gain (1 Tim. 3:3).

(c)   Avarice means that we never have enough (Hab. 2:5).

(d)   Avarice is the opposite of contentment with what we already possess (Heb. 13:5).

(e)   Avarice is not limited to material possessions: its focus, for example, can be upon power (3 John 9) or sexual immorality (2 Pet. 2:14).

(f)   Avarice often takes the form of covetousness (Josh. 7:20, 21).

(g)   Avarice is laying up treasure upon earth to the total neglect of being rich toward God (Luke 12:21).

(h)   Avarice can become the attitude of a whole nation in that everyone is greedy for unjust gain (Jer. 8:10).

2.   How avarice manifests itself.

Avarice manifests itself in opinions and viewpoints

(a)   **The meaning of life.** Avarice finds the meaning of life in the acquisition of money and possessions, encouraged by false ideas about them and what they can provide (Luke 12:18, 19).

(b)   **Profit.** Avarice always keeps the personal profit motive to the fore, so that all actions and enterprises are looked at from the viewpoint of personal advantage (Tit. 1:11).

(c)   **Security.** Avarice regards wealth as the principal symbol of security (Jas. 5:2, 3).

(d)   **Happiness**. Avarice views wealth as the main source of happiness (Luke 12:18, 19).

Avarice manifests itself actions

(e)   **Stinginess.** Avarice can make us mean in our dealings with others (Prov. 28:22).

(f)   **Selfish luxury and pleasure.** Avarice can, on the other hand, make us lavish and self-indulgent in personal enjoyment of luxury and pleasure (Jas. 5:5; Luke 16:19).

(g)   **Dishonesty.** Avarice can prompt us to seek wealth by dishonest or unworthy means (Ezek. 22:27; 1 Pet. 5:2).

(h)   **Indifference to the rights of others.** Uncontrolled longing for possessions can cause us to set aside the rights of others, especially if we are in a position of power or influence (Amos 2:6; Luke 16:19-21).

(i) **Division.** The desire for wealth can divide relatives and spoil relationships (Gen. 13:5, 6), and especially is this the case in families over wills and inheritances (Luke 12:13).

(j) **Injustice.** Greed can lead to injustice, e.g. employers giving insufficient wages in order to increase their profits (Jas. 5:4).

(k) **Violence**. Striving for unlawful wealth can lead to violence and even murder (Ezek. 22:27; Mic. 6:12).

Avarice shows itself in attitudes of mind

(l) **Arrogant complacency.** Wealth easily breeds a harmful complacency (Prov. 18:23; 28:11), and the false conviction that the future is in our hands (Jas. 4:13-17).

(m) **Gloating satisfaction.** Wealth is simply hoarded often and gloated over (Luke 12:18, 19; Jas. 5:2, 3).

(n) **Anxiety.** Satisfied as an avaricious person may be with wealth, its preservation brings anxiety (Eccl. 5:12).

(o) **Discontent.** Those who love wealth will never be satisfied by it (Eccl. 5:10), and their eyes will always be greedy (1 Sam. 2:29; cf. 2:12-17).

3. The sinfulness of avarice.

(a) It breaks the first great commandment: 'Love the Lord your God with all your heart, and with all your soul and with all your mind' (Matt. 22:37).

(b) Avarice causes us to give our hearts to material treasures, and to be so devoted to our possessions that we cease to love God (Matt. 6:21, 24).

(c) Avarice is a form of idolatry in that money becomes our god (Col. 3:5).

(d) Avarice denies the truth that our proper and true happiness is in having the Lord as our God (Ps. 144:15), and having Him as our helper (Ps. 146:5; Heb. 13:5, 6).

(e) It breaks the second great commandment: 'Love your neighbour as yourself' (Matt. 22:39).

(f) Avarice causes us to hoard money and possessions selfishly rather than to use them for personal good and the benefit of others (Jas. 5:2-4).

(g)   The love of money proceeds from the love of self (2 Tim. 3:2), and always has personal gain in view even in the discharge of seemingly honourable tasks (Tit. 1:11).

(h)   It ravages human relationships.   Greed occurs in a group of four nouns that comprehensively describe the power of sin in spoiling human relationships: wickedness, evil, greed and depravity (Rom. 1:29).

(i)   It hurts other people as, for example, by neglect (Luke 16:19, 20) or by example —for instance, if parents take the alluring road to wealth they may find their family overwhelmed by the evil ways of the world (Gen. 13:10-13; cf. Gen. 19:12-26).

(j)   Avarice is the first step to all kinds of sin (1 Tim. 6:10).

(k)   Greed is linked frequently in the Bible with sexual immorality and idolatry, in that greed in one form quickly leads to greed in another, so that people end up worshipping the objects of their greed (1 Cor. 5:9-11).

(l)   It is behind many of the acts of the sinful nature, all of which are in direct opposition to God's will for men and women (Gal. 5:19-21).

(m)   It finds deceit easy in that greed may be the real motivation of what seem to be good and kind actions (1 Thess. 2:5; 1 Pet. 5:2; 2 Pet. 2:3).

(n)   It is the most obvious form of worldliness, in that two of its pre-eminent characteristics are the desire to buy everything that appeals to us, and the pride that comes from wealth and importance – such love of the world is the opposite of love for God (1 John 2:15, 16).

4.   The folly of avarice.

(a)   The happiness and enjoyment avarice promises are often illusory (Eccl. 2:8-11, 26; Luke 19:2).

(b)   Wealth is a totally insufficient source of security for the future, because God may not give us the opportunity to enjoy it (Eccl. 6:2).

(c)   Avarice loses sight of the temporary hold we have on all our material possessions (Prov. 27:24; Luke 12:20).

(d)   It forgets, too, that even our earthly hold of them is subject to circumstances over which we have no control (Jas. 5:2, 3).

(e)   It brings us into the unenviable position of not really being sure who our true friends are, although our affluence attracts many apparent friends (Prov. 14:20; 19:4).

(f)   Avarice makes the big mistake of thinking that our lives consist in the abundance of our possessions (Luke 12:15).

(g)   Avarice fails to recognise that there are many important things money cannot achieve: wealth can take care of our burial but not our destiny thereafter (Luke 16:23), so that it cannot save us from eternal separation from God; material wealth will be of no use on the Day of Judgment (Isa. 10:1-3).

(h)   Avarice can cost us our eternal well-being (Matt. 16:26), in that our pursuit of money leads us to forget that our greatest need is to be rich before God (Luke 12:19, 20).

(i)   Avarice can mean that we possess immense outward wealth and at the same time know an inner poverty (Prov. 28:22).

(j)   Avarice shuts us out of God's kingdom (Matt. 19:23, 24, Mark 10:23-25, Luke 18:24, 25).

(k)   Avarice brings God's judgment, in that if we are thinking all the time about getting rich we will be punished (Prov. 21:13; 28:20; Jas. 5:1).

(l)   The proceeds of avarice will be evidence against us on the day of judgment so that wrongly accumulated wealth will prove to be a liability rather than an asset: the store of accumulated wealth becomes, in effect, a store of divine wrath from which God will draw on the day of judgment (Jas. 5:3).

(m)   Those whose lives are governed by avarice may be compared to cattle feasting themselves while, all unknowingly, they are living in the shadow of the day of their slaughter (Jas. 5:5).

5.   Proper correctives to avarice.
The corrective of an eternal perspective

(a)   The danger of wealth is that it may be limited to this world alone (1 Tim. 6:17-19).

(b)   The true value of material possessions is seen when we appreciate that at the judgment of the world they will all disappear (Rev. 18:11-19).

(c)   Our view of wealth is determined by what we consider to be true currency (2 Cor. 6:10), in that there is a prosperity that has nothing to do with this world's wealth (Rev. 2:9).

(d) Real wealth does not consist in the abundance of our possessions but in the state of our soul, upon whether or not we are rich toward God (Luke 12:15-26; cf. Ps. 73).

(e) The knowledge of God's salvation through Jesus Christ is more profitable than wealth and more relevant to our basic need (Acts 3:6).

(f) True wealth is spiritual wealth such as pardon (Eph. 1:7), peace with God (Rom. 5:1), the support of God's Spirit (John 14:16) and the assurance of heaven (John 14:2, 3).

(g) Christians may appear poor but in reality they possess everything worthwhile and they have better things awaiting them in the life to come (2 Cor 6:10; Heb. 10:34).

The corrective of the Bible's warnings given by means of sad examples of what avarice has caused men and women to do: things happened to people in the past as examples and were then written down as warnings for us (1 Cor. 10:11)

(h) Avarice has made people turn away from following the Lord Jesus Christ (Matt. 19:22).

(i) It has caused them neglect human need on their doorstep (Luke 16:19-21).

(j) It has made them think that all is well with them when the opposite has been the case (Luke 12:19).

(k) It has prompted people to betray friends (Matt. 26:15, 16).

(l) It has made employers exploit their employees (Jas. 5:4).

(m) It has been behind lies and the practice of deceit (Acts 5:3, 4, 8).

The corrective of the genuine pursuit of Christian discipleship.

(n) Our Lord's chosen lifestyle involved the forfeiture of financial security (Luke 9:58), and He warned His disciples against all active striving for the increase of material possessions as a means of true security (Luke 12:15).

(o) Christians are not to be lovers of money (1 Tim. 3:3), and those who assume Christian leadership must be outstanding examples of those who neither love money nor are greedy for it (1 Tim. 3:3, 8; Tit. 1:7).

(p)   Christians are to live with the assurance that their material needs are of concern to God and they are encouraged to bring them to God day by day as they pray (Matt. 6:11; Luke 11:3).

(q)   Christians' aim must be contentment (Heb. 13:5).

The corrective of putting wealth to use.

(r)   God can make us wealthy (1 Sam. 2:7), and there is no sin in material prosperity providing it is acquired honourably and used wisely (2 Cor. 9:8).

(s)   If material wealth is used rightly it can add to our heavenly wealth which is much more important (Matt. 6:19-21; Luke 12:33, 34).

(t)   Used to benefit others, our possessions are a means of showing our love not only to others but also to God Himself (1 John 3:17, 18).

---

82. SLOTH

Question: What is sloth?

Answer: Sloth is laziness and unhelpful inactivity, the opposite of hard work, diligence and self-discipline. It is sinful because it abuses time, wastes life and leads to neglect of our duty to God, our neighbour and our own well-being.

1.   **Sloth's characteristics.**

(a)   **Laziness.** Sloth is laziness and disinclination to action, exertion or labour; and, persevered in, it amounts to a slow death (Prov. 21:25).

(b)   Sloth can be displayed in many different spheres of life: in the home (Eccl. 10:18), the garden (Prov. 24:30, 31), daily employment (Prov. 20:4), the exercise of responsibility for others (Isa. 56:9-12), and in the care of our soul (2 Pet. 1:5-11).

(c)   **Inactivity.** Sleep is a mark of the lazy (Prov. 6:10, 11; 19:15; 24:33, 34): lazy people get little further than a door swinging on its hinges (Prov. 26:14).

(d) **Soft options.** Sloth makes a habit of the soft or easy choice (Prov. 20:4): it encourages people to stay at home when they ought to be out and doing (Prov. 22:13).

(e) **Lack of resolution.** Sloth describes the situation of individuals who for one reason or another do not have the resolution to act: for example, they lack discipline to get down to hard work or to begin something that needs to be done (Prov. 6:6-11).

(f) **Excuses.** Sloth encourages people to make excuses for their laziness: for example, they suggest that they are not at their best in the morning (Prov. 26:14) or that they cannot do anything well if they are hurried (Prov. 26:15, 16).

(g) **Pessimism.** Sloth meets difficulties everywhere (Prov. 15:19), and some of them are quite exaggerated and imaginary (Prov. 26:13).

(h) **A world of wishing.** Sloth causes people to live in a world of wishing: they seldom move from the will to the deed (Prov. 21:25, 26).

(i) **Dissatisfaction.** Laziness results in dissatisfaction with life (Prov. 13:4).

(j) **Conceit.** Sloth is accompanied often by conceit: lazy people think they are more intelligent than seven others who can give reasons for their opinions (Prov. 26:16).

(k) **Blind to itself.** Sloth is sometimes completely unaware of itself (Prov. 26:16); slothful people believe their own excuses (Prov. 22:13), and shirkers deceive themselves into imagining that they are realists (Prov. 26:13).

2.   Sloth's consequences.

(a) Laziness has its price (Prov. 12:24).

(b) **Self-indulgence.** Sloth leads to physical softness, and following the dictates of natural desires (Prov. 20:4).

(c) **Untidiness of life.** Sloth breeds a general untidiness of life (Prov. 15:19).

(d) **Deficient convictions.** Lazy people are too lazy to develop and possess genuine convictions; they may pretend that they are simply open-minded, although laziness is the principal cause of their lack of personal conviction (Prov. 26:16).

(e) **Apathy.** Sloth makes people apathetic about the most necessary duties (Prov. 12:27; 26:15).

(f) **Mischief.** Sloth leads all too easily to unhelpful and harmful activity, such as meddling in other people's affairs (2 Thess. 3:11) and gossip (1 Tim. 5:13).

(g) **Unfinished tasks and lack of achievement.** Sloth makes people miss their opportunities: for example, failing to sow at the right time, they have no harvest to gather (Prov. 20:4); they put things beyond their reach by laziness (Prov. 13:4).

(h) **Disappointment.** Disappointment is the inevitable accompaniment of laziness (Prov. 13:4; 21:25).

(i) **Gradual deterioration.** Sloth is a creeping, spreading disease (Prov. 19:15), so that a little laziness quickly becomes habitual (Prov. 6:10, 11).

(j) **Poverty.** Sloth can lead to various forms of poverty (Prov. 6:10, 11), especially material need (Prov. 20:4; 21:25) and hunger (Prov. 19:15; 24:33, 34).

(k) **Bondage or wrongful indebtedness to others.** Sloth leads people to bondage in that they live at the expense of others and put themselves in their debt, frequently in a way that will prove detrimental to them (Prov 12:24).

(l) **Uselessness.** Sloth is synonymous with a somewhat expensive uselessness (Prov. 18:9).

(m) **Destructiveness.** Lazy people's sluggishness eventually overwhelms them (Prov. 24:30-34). When God's gifts and benefits are not properly used, they may be lost (Luke 19:26).

(n) **Ruin.** Lazy people's ease is their own undoing and ruin (Prov. 21:25; 24:30, 31; Eccl. 10:18).

3. Sloth's sinfulness.
The abuse of time

(a) Sloth makes people bad stewards of time, in that time is short (1 Cor. 7:29), and is to be used to the full (Col. 4:5).

(b) Slothful people forget that every day is a day God has made for good purposes (Ps. 118:24).

The waste of life

(c) Human existence should mean fruitful service (Phil. 1:22).

(d) Life is to be used for daily work with cheerfulness and purpose (Col. 3:23).

The contradiction of God's image in which we were made

(e) God is always working (John 5:17), and His Son set us an example in that He went about doing good (Acts 10:38).

(f) Our Lord's earthly life was the complete opposite of sloth: His food was to do the Father's will (John 4:34).

The neglect of duty to God, our neighbour and ourselves

(g) By sloth we neglect to serve God with the wholeheartedness that alone satisfies Him (Deut. 1:34-36; Josh. 14:8, 9, 13, 14; Matt. 25:26).

(h) By sloth we neglect to serve our neighbour with the diligence such service requires (Luke 10:29-37; 16:19-21; 2 Cor. 8:16).

(i) By sloth we neglect our duty to ourselves in that our spiritual well-being requires diligence (2 Pet. 1:5-8), as does our usefulness in the exercise of our God-given gifts (1 Pet. 4:9-11).

4. **Correctives to sloth.**
   A Christian understanding

(a) Sloth is contrary to Christian instruction (2 Thess. 3:6), and the apostles set a deliberate example of avoiding all idleness (2 Thess. 3:7-9).

(b) Christians are not to flag in zeal but rather are to serve the Lord with spiritual fervour (Rom. 12:11).

(c) Christians are to make good use of the time between now and the Lord Jesus Christ's second advent (Matt. 25:1-30), making sure that they fulfil the ministry He has given to them (Col. 4:17).

(d) Christians are to serve the Lord in the new way of the Spirit (Rom. 7:6).

A proper stewardship of time

(e) There are many evil pressures encouraging the misuse of time, so that proper stewardship is all the more important (Eph. 5:16).

(f) The shortness of life's opportunities should make us wise in the use of our time (Ps. 90:12).

(g) There is a right time for everything (Eccl. 3:1-8).

An appreciation of the purpose of life

(h)   Whatever our hands find to do, we should do with all our might (Eccl. 9:10).

(i)   We may be sure that God has a programme of good works for us to fulfil at every stage of life (Eph. 2:10).

A proper place for, and control of, sleep and relaxation

(j)   Restful sleep is a gift from God (Ps. 127:2), and it is intended that sleep should be the reward of a diligent worker (Eccl. 5:12).

(k)   Our Lord practised temporary withdrawal from normal activity (Matt. 14:13, 23), and called upon His disciples to do the same (Mark 6:31).

(l)   There is a right and wrong time both for sleep and relaxation, and wisdom knows the difference (Eccl. 10:16, 17).

An understanding of the place of diligence in right living

(m)   The ant is an example of diligence: ants have no leader, chief, ruler, but they store up their food during the summer, getting ready for winter (Prov. 6:6-8).

(n)   Diligence is necessary if we would gain understanding and wisdom (Prov. 17:24).

(o)   Diligence should characterise our activity no matter how uncertain we are of the future (Eccl. 11:6).

(p)   All the responsibilities that come to us in life are to be exercised diligently (Rom. 12:8; Col. 3:17).

(q)   Diligence brings its own reward and wealth (Prov. 12:27; 13:4).

83. LOVE

Galatians 5:22: 'The fruit of the Spirit is love.'

Question: What is the love required of us?

Answer: **The love required of us is a totally unselfish love, a matter of will and action, expressed in service of the undeserving as much as of the deserving, based upon the pattern of the love set forth in the Cross of our Lord Jesus Christ.**

1. God is the source of love.
(a) Love comes from God (1 John 4:7).
(b) God is love (1 John 4:8,16), and is called 'the God of love' (2 Cor. 13:11).
(c) Love characterises every aspect of God's relationship to His people (Hos. 2:19).
(d) God has demonstrated His love to us: He sent His one and only Son into the world (John 3:16; Rom. 8:32; Col. 1:13) —He sent Him to be the atoning sacrifice for our sins (Rom. 5:8; Gal. 2:20; 1 John 4:9, 10).
(e) God the Father has lavished the greatest possible love upon us as believers by letting us be called His children (Eph. 1:4, 5; 1 John 3:1; Jude 1).
(f) We both know and rely upon the love God has for us (1 John 4:16).
(g) God has given us the Spirit of love to live within us (Gal. 5:22; 2 Tim. 1:7).
(h) God pours out His love into our hearts by the Holy Spirit (Rom. 5:5) - His love holds us captive (2 Cor. 5:14).
(i) Our love for God is the response of gratitude (Luke 7:47; 1 John 4:19).
(j) We are to show to the world that we are God's children, and Christ's disciples, by the display and practice of love (John 13:35; 1 John 3:14; 4:7).

(k)   The love of Christ's people for others for His sake is something quite different from the love with which the world is familiar (John 13:34).

2.   The priority of love.

(a)   Love has priority over spiritual gifts (1 Cor. 13:1-3).

(b)   To be specific, love has priority over the gift of tongues (1 Cor. 13:1).

(c)   Love has priority over the gift of prophecy (1 Cor. 13:2).

(d)   Love has priority over the gift of knowledge and teaching (1 Cor. 13:2, 8) - knowledge without love so easily puffs us up with a sense of our own importance (1 Cor. 8:1).

(e)   Love has priority over the special gift of faith that can accomplish miracles (1 Cor. 13:2; cf. 12:29; Mark 11:22-24).

(f)   Love has priority over the special gift of generous giving (1 Cor. 13:3; cf. Rom. 12:8).

(g)   Love has priority over complete dedication to an ideal, even if that dedication involves death for its sake (1 Cor. 13:3).

(h)   Love's priority is seen in that it is to be the foremost aim of all Christians, whereas this is not true of God's other gifts (1 Cor. 14:1; cf. 12:27-31).

(i)   Besides being part of the fruit of the Spirit, love takes first rank among that fruit (Gal. 5:22; cf. Rom. 15:30; Col. 1:8; 3:14).

(j)   Love's priority is seen in that our Lord Jesus Christ has given love as a new commandment (John 13:34; 1 John 4:21): it is one of the first commandments we receive after we have come to faith in Him (1 John 3:23; cf. Matt. 28:20).

(k)   Love is the one continuing debt we owe to one another (Rom. 13:8).

(l)   Its priority is all the greater when we realise that the true love we express to others is really love expressed to Jesus Christ Himself (Matt. 25:31-40).

3.   The foremost characteristics and activities of love.

(a)   Patience (1 Cor. 13:4).

(b)   Kindness (1 Cor. 13:4): love strives to be honest (Mark 10:21), and in speaking the truth endeavours to do so without unnecessary offence (Eph. 4:15).

(c)   Joy (1 Cor. 13:6).

(d)   Patience (1 Cor. 13:7): love makes allowances for people (Eph. 4:2), and covers over a multitude of sins (1 Pet. 4:8).

(e)   Faith: the outflow of genuine faith is love (Gal. 5:6; 1 Thess. 3:6; 5:8; 1 Tim. 1:14).

(f)   Hope (1 Cor. 13:7).

(g)   Endurance (1 Cor. 13:7), after the pattern of our Lord's love for His disciples (John 13:1).

(h)   Service: love is active in good deeds (Heb. 10:24), prompt in willing service (Gal. 5:13), and anxious to fulfil God's law towards a neighbour (Rom. 13:10).

(i)   Generosity (2 Cor. 8:8-12, 24): love goes out of its way to share and meet another's need (1 John 3:16, 17).

(j)   Constructiveness: love builds up (1 Cor. 8:1), unites believers (Col. 2:2), and binds all other virtues together in perfect unity (Col. 3:14).

(k)   Reflective of God's love: love shows kindness even to its enemies (Matt. 5:43-45; Luke 6:27, 35), always endeavouring to show to others the love the Lord Jesus has shown to us (John 13:34).

4.   Opposites of love.

(a)   Envy (1 Cor. 13:4).

(b)   Boastfulness (1 Cor. 13:4).

(c)   Pride (1 Cor. 13:5).

(d)   Rudeness (1 Cor. 13:5).

(e)   Selfishness (1 Cor. 13:5).

(f)   Irritability and touchiness (1 Cor. 13:5).

(g)   Resentment (1 Cor. 13:5).

(h)   Maliciousness (1 Cor. 13:6).

(i)   Hatred (1 John 3:11-18).

5.   The consistent aims and objectives of love.

(a)   Love aims at growth (Phil. 1:9), that it may increase and overflow (1 Thess. 3:12; 2 Thess. 1:3).

(b)   Love aims at being non-selective in its objects and to love everyone in the same way (Phil. 2:2) - Christian love encompasses all other Christians as members of the family of believers and others as neighbours (Gal. 6:10).

(c)   Love aims at sincerity and genuineness (Rom. 12:9; 2 Cor. 6:6; 1 Pet. 1:22; 1 John 4:18).

(d)   Love aims at consistency: its objective is to live a life of love, following Christ's example (Eph. 5. 2); it wants to love deeply (1 Pet. 4:8).

(e)   Love aims at building others up in the things of God (1 Cor. 8:1), with no thought of self-interest (Rom. 15:1-4).

(f)   Love's objective is to follow the pattern of Christ's love even if that involves personal sacrifice (John 13:34; Eph. 5:2, 25).

(g)   Love's objective, therefore, is to do everything with love (1 Cor. 16:14).

6.   The permanence of the priority of love.

(a)   It is basic to all Christian ethics (1 John 2:7).

(b)   It remains the principal test of a person's profession of being a Christian (1 John 2:9, 10; cf. John 13:35).

(c)   It never ends or fails (1 Cor. 13:8).

(d)   When spiritual gifts pass away, and are unnecessary, love will remain (1 Cor. 13:8-12).

(e)   Faith, hope and love are the principal priorities of the Christian life, but the greatest of these is love (1 Cor. 13:13).

---

84. JOY

Galatians 5:22: 'The fruit of the Spirit is ... joy.'

Question: What is the joy required of us?

Answer: The joy required of us is not the seldom-found result of an agreeable set of circumstances but an inward joy springing up within us, irrespective of what our circumstances or difficulties may be.   It is a gift of God through our Lord Jesus Christ, and is one of the principal consequences of the experience of salvation.

1. **Defining joy.**

(a) Joy is virtually synonymous with gladness or delight (Matt. 5:12; Luke 1:14), and has to do with our heart (Ps. 16:9; 33:21; Acts 2:26, 46; 14:17) or soul or spirit (Luke 1:47), that is to say, our innermost being (John 7:38).

(b) God Himself is the author of the joy our heart or soul needs to know, and it is His gift to believers (Rom. 15:13; 1 Thess. 3:9).

(c) Christian joy has God as its object (Ps. 9:2; 33:21; 149:1; Joel 2:23) – God Himself becomes our joy and delight (Ps. 43:4).

(d) Joy focuses its attention on God – His power, His holiness and His mercy (Luke 1:49, 50) – and on what He may always be relied upon to do (Luke 1:51-55); it finds its rest in His character and attributes (Rev. 19:6, 7).

(e) Christian joy is always joy in God's saving acts (Isa. 44:23) – His salvation is its supreme joy (Rev. 19:7).

(f) The distinctive feature of Christian joy is that it is joy in God through our Lord Jesus (Rom. 5:11; cf. 1 Cor. 1:31; Phil. 3:3; 4:4, 10) – He has been the anticipated joy of the ages, in that Abraham and others rejoiced at the thought of seeing His day (John 8:56; cf. 1 Pet. 1:10-12).

(g) God the Holy Spirit conveys this joy in Christ to the individual believer's soul (John 7:38; cf. Luke 10:21; Rom. 14:17; Gal. 5:22; 1 Thess. 1:6) – a joy that is a foretaste of heaven (1 Pet. 4:13; Jude 24).

(h) Christian joy is a secure joy: since it does not find its source in human beings, men and women cannot take it away (John 16:22).

(i) Christian joy is a glorious joy for it already has something of heaven's touch upon it (1 Pet. 1:8, 9).

(j) Christian joy is an inexpressible joy since it is incapable of adequate declaration or explanation by words (1 Pet. 1:8).

(k) Christian joy is an everlasting joy (Isa. 35:10; 51:11).

2. **Defining some of the foundations of Christian joy.**

(a) Christian joy is the joy that the gospel of our Lord Jesus Christ provides (Luke 2:10, 11; 1 Thess. 1:6; 1 John 1:1-4): for example, the joy of being found by the Heavenly Father through the Good Shepherd (Luke 15: 7, 10, 32), or the joy of finding Christ and His kingdom as a treasure without price (Matt. 13:44-46).

(b)   Christian joy is the joy of faith (Ps. 33:21; Acts 16:34; Phil. 1:25) – faith and joy in a crucified (Gal. 2:20; 6:14), risen (Matt. 28:8; John 16:20-22) and ascended Saviour (Luke 24:50-53), whom we have not yet seen, but believing in Him we are filled with inexpressible joy (1 Pet. 1:8).

(c)   Christian joy is the joy of salvation (Ps. 51:12; Isa. 35:10; 51:11; Hab. 3:18; Acts 8:39; 13:48), with the special joys that salvation brings of forgiveness (Ps. 51:1-12; cf. Eph. 1:7), reconciliation to God (Rom. 5:11), justification through faith (Rom. 5:1, 2), and acceptance with God (Jude 24).

(d)   Christian joy is the joy of a new life (Rom. 6:4; 2 Cor. 5:17; cf. Luke 19:6-9).

(e)   Christian joy is the joy of fellowship with the Father and with His Son Jesus Christ (1 John 1:3, 4; cf. John 14:21, 23).

(f)   Christian joy is the joy of fellowship with one another (Ps. 133:1; 2 Cor. 2:2) because that fellowship is based on fellowship with the Father and the Son (1 John 1:1-7).

(g)   Christian joy is the joy of future and glorious prospects – of rewards (Matt. 5:12; 25:21, 23), but most of all looking forward to sharing God's glory (Rom. 5:2) and participation in our Saviour's triumph (Heb. 12:2; cf. Phil. 2:9-11; 2 Tim. 2:11, 12).

(h)   One important way of defining Christian joy is that it is Jesus Christ's joy in us (John 15:11).

3.   The joy our Lord Jesus Christ exhibited.

(a)   He possessed a full and unique joy (John 15:11; 17:13).

(b)   His joy expressed itself in praise and thanksgiving (Luke 10:21).

(c)   He was full of joy through the Holy Spirit (Luke 10:21).

(d)   His joy was to do the Father's will (Ps. 40:8; John 4:34).

(e)   He endured the Cross, despising the shame, for the joy that was set before Him (Heb. 12:2).

(f)   His prayer for His disciples to His Father was that they should have the full measure of His joy within them (John 17:13).

(g)   Christian joy at its best, therefore, is the Lord Jesus sharing His joy with us to the full as He completely shares our life (John 17:13; cf., 14:21, 23; Rev. 3:20).

4.   How joy expresses itself.

(a)   It expresses itself in contentment and pleasure in ordinary everyday things (Acts 2:46) because God is recognised as the source and author of all that is good and all in which we can rejoice (1 Thess. 3:9; 1 Tim. 4:4; 6:17; Jas. 1:17).

(b)   It expresses itself in praise and thanksgiving (Ps. 27:6; 33:1; Luke 1:46, 47; 10:21; Acts 2:46, 47; Rev. 19:7).

(c)   It expresses itself in singing (Ps. 5:11; 9:2; Isa. 12:6; 35:10; 44:23; 49:13) as the Holy Spirit aids that expression through psalms, hymns and spiritual songs (Eph. 5:18-20).

(d)   It expresses itself in confidence in God and in His supplies of strength (Neh. 8:10), so that Christian joy not only survives difficult circumstances but almost seems to thrive on them (Matt. 5:12; Acts 5:41; Col. 1:11), because of the joyful perspective of faith that God uses every difficulty and obstacle to mature and perfect the development of His Son's character in us (Rom. 5:3; Heb. 12:11; Jas. 1:2, 3).

(e)   Joy expresses itself in confident prayer (John 16:24).

(f)   Joy expresses itself in Christian fellowship (Rom. 12:15; 2 Tim. 1:4; 2 John 12).

(g)   Joy expresses itself in generous giving (2 Cor. 8:2).

5.   The maintenance of the Christian's joy.

(a)   There is no doubt that God intends that it should be maintained (1 Thess. 5:16), and outward trials (1 Pet. 1:6), and earthly considerations that affect ordinary human happiness (Hab. 3:17,18; Ps. 73:25, 26; Phil. 4:11-13; 2 Cor. 6:10; Heb. 13:5, 6) should make no difference since the One in whom our joys are found is always the same (Heb. 13:8).

(b)   Joy is maintained as faith grows (Phil. 1:25).

(c)   Joy is maintained as hope abounds (Rom. 15:13): we are ever to have before us our living hope (1 Pet. 1:3, 4) and the prospect of our sharing Christ's glory (1 Pet. 4:13).

(d)   Joy is maintained as identification with the Lord Jesus is practised (1 Pet. 4:13; cf. Col. 1:24).

(e)   Joy is maintained as we continually rediscover the perfection of God's peace through the exercise of prayer (Ps. 34:5; John 16:24; Rom. 15:13; Phil. 4:6, 7).

(f)   Joy is maintained as we honestly face obstacles and challenges to our faith, with the help of the Holy Spirit day by day (Acts 13:52; Eph. 5:18-20).

6.   Obstacles and impediments to Christian joy.

(a)   Failure to progress in the faith (Phil. 1:25).

(b)   Neglect of practical righteousness (Matt. 5:6).

(c)   Not taking the trouble to seek peace in human relationships (Rom. 14:17; cf. Matt. 5:9).

(d)   Breakdowns in loving each other as commanded by our Lord Jesus Christ (John 15:10-12).

(e)   Unbelief (Phil. 1:25; 1 Pet. 1:6, 7).

(f)   Disobedience (John 15:10, 11).

(g)   The neglect of prayer (John 16:24).

(h)   Broken fellowship with God and His people in anyway (1 John 1:1-7).

(i)   Unconfessed sin (Ps. 51:3, 8, 9, 12; 1 John 1:5-10).

(j)   All that grieves the Holy Spirit (Eph. 4:30), for His ministry is the key to our experience of our Saviour's joy.

---

85. PEACE

Galatians 5:22: 'The fruit of the Spirit is ... peace.'

Question: What is the peace required of us?

Answer: The peace required of us is peace in the sense of peaceableness. The peaceableness, however, is the direct consequence of our discovery of peace with God through our Lord Jesus Christ, and the disposition this new relationship with God brings.

1.   The priority of peace with God, and the way to it.

(a)   The world has lost true peace because of human sin: there is no peace for the wicked (Isa. 48:22; 57:21).

(b)   Fallen rebellious men and women do not know the way of peace (Rom. 3:17).

(c)   When we lack peace, we soon forget what real happiness and prosperity are like (Lam. 3:17).

(d)   God alone can give His creatures true peace (Ps. 4:8).

(e)   In order to provide peace for His creatures, God had to make the great provision of a Saviour (Luke 2:9-14).

(f)   No peace with God was possible without the just demands of His wrath against our sins being satisfied, and God accomplished this by the death of His Son upon the Cross (Rom. 5:1; Col. 1:20).

(g)   Christians are those who, like all people by nature, were once enemies of God, but whom God has reconciled to Himself (Rom. 5:11; Eph. 2:16).

(h)   The Lord Jesus Christ, therefore, came into the world to guide our feet into the way of peace (Luke 1:79), and His saving work is the sole foundation of our peace (Eph. 2:14-17).

(i)   Justified by faith, we have peace with God through our Lord Jesus Christ (Rom. 5:1)– peace follows upon faith (Mark 5:34; Luke 7:50; Rom. 15:13).

(j)   Peace, therefore, is inseparable from the experience of God's grace in Christ (Gal. 1:3; 1Thess. 1:1).

(k)   Peace is God's free gift to His people (Num. 6:26), and He delights in their enjoyment of it (Ps. 29:11; 147:14).

(l)   God's peace is like a river (Isa. 48:18); it is a peace that transcends all understanding (Phil. 4:7).

(m)   The Lord Jesus Christ, our Saviour and Lord, is the Guarantor and Guardian of our peace (Isa. 9:6), and He can give us peace at all times and in every way (2 Thess. 3:16).

(n)   His peace is quite different from what the world provides, for it can quieten troubled hearts and drive away anxious fears (John 14:27).

(o)   Obedience to God, and in particular to His commandments, is a key to the maintenance of our experience of God's peace (Ps. 119:165; Isa. 48:18).

(p)   The active pursuit of righteousness is a second condition of the maintenance of our peace (Ps. 85:10; Rom. 12:17, 18).

(q)   The third condition is maintained fellowship with God (Ps. 73:21-28), especially as that fellowship expresses itself in prayer (Phil. 4:6, 7).

(r)   The peace we know with God, and from God, brings the obligation to know too peace with one another, whatever our race, colour or background – this was one of the purposes for which our Lord Jesus Christ died (Eph. 2:14).

2.   The peaceableness that flows from finding our peace with God and the peace He gives.

(a)   When we lack peace with God, and thus inner peace, we also lack peace in our personal relationships (Jas. 4:1-4).

(b)   Finding in our Lord Jesus peace with God, however, we also find a meeting place and harmony with one another, whatever may have been our divisions of race, colour, class or circumstances beforehand (Eph. 2:14-18).

(c)   Peace or peaceableness is part of the outflow of spiritual and eternal life as our minds are controlled by the Holy Spirit (Rom. 8:6).

(d)   Peaceableness is a consequence of having the salt of the gospel in our life (Mark 9:50) - all our relationships are significantly affected for the good (Rom. 14:17-19).

(e)   Peaceableness is the outworking of love (Col. 3:12-15; 1 Thess. 5:13), and love is not easily provoked (1 Cor. 13:4, 5).

(f)   Reconciled to God, we are able to benefit from God's heavenly wisdom, and peaceableness is a fundamental aspect of that wisdom (Jas. 1:5; 3:17, 18).

(g)   Reconciliation to God brings a commitment to righteousness (1 Pet. 2:24), and peace is the regular fruit and gift from God when we persevere in doing what is right (Rom. 14:17; Jas. 3:18; cf. Isa. 32:17).

(h)   Reconciliation to God is synonymous with membership of God's family, and God carefully disciplines the characters of His spiritual children to make them more peaceable (Heb. 12:11).

(i)   Filled with the Spirit (Eph. 5:17) – a further great gift of reconciliation - we develop His fruit of peaceableness in our characters (Rom. 8:6; Gal. 5:22).

(j)   Peace and peaceableness are fundamental aspects of the kingdom of God (Rom. 14:17), so much so that the Lord Jesus said, 'Blessed are the peacemakers' (Matt. 5:9).

3.   The expression of peaceableness.

(a)   Peaceableness expresses itself in the determination to maintain a clear conscience (1 Pet. 3:10-16), and this resolve involves the regular and genuine pursuit of practical righteousness (Heb. 12:14) – peacemakers so sow peace that they raise a harvest of righteousness (Jas. 3:18).

(b)   Peaceableness expresses itself in the active pursuit of good works (Jas. 3:17), even in the face of opposition from those who regard themselves as our enemies (Matt. 5:43-48; 1 Pet. 2:20; 3:13, 14).

(c)   Peaceableness expresses itself in forbearance (2 Tim. 2:22-24), mercy (Jas. 3:17) and gentleness (1 Pet. 3:15; Tit. 3:2), especially where correction has to be given to others (2 Tim. 2:25).

(d)   Peaceableness expresses itself in considerateness (Tit. 3:2; Jas. 3:17), kindness to everyone (2 Tim. 2:22, 24), and respect for all without discrimination or prejudice (1 Pet. 3:15).

(e)   Peaceableness expresses itself in the active pursuit of peace, even if it means relinquishing our rights (Gen. 13:8; 21:22-24) – although that does not mean pretending problems do not exist but rather dealing with them peaceably (Gen. 21:25-32).

(f)   Peaceableness expresses itself by coming between contending parties and trying to make peace (1 Sam. 25:18-35; Matt. 5:9).

(g)   Peaceableness expresses itself particularly in the words and language we employ (Prov. 18:6, 7), seeking that our words should be honest and truthful (Prov. 16:13), apt and wise (Prov. 25:11, 12), gentle and restrained (Prov. 15:1; 17:27), and sometimes few (Prov. 11:12, 13).

(h)   Peaceableness expresses itself in the home (Prov. 17:1), for a lack of peace there brings misery (1 Sam. 1:3-7).

(i)   Peaceableness in marriage has as its secret the concentration of each partner upon his or her duties to the other rather than what he or she may expect from the other as a matter of right (Eph. 5:22, 25).

(j)   Peaceableness for parents means being sensitive and realistic in their demands and expectations of their children (Eph. 6:4).

(k)   Peaceableness within the church fellowship means striving always for peace and agreement (Col. 3:15; 1 Thess. 5:13; Heb. 12:14).

4.   Appreciating peaceableness by identifying its opposites.

(a)   Envy (Prov. 14:30; Gal. 5:21; 1 Tim. 6:4; Jas. 3:14-17).

(b)   Jealousy (Mark 10:37,41; 2 Cor. 12:20; Gal. 5:20).

(c)   Pride and conceit (Gen. 4:4, 5; Ps. 131:1; Jas. 4:1-6).

(d)   Arrogance (2 Cor. 12:20).

(e)   Selfish ambition (Jas. 3:14, 16, 17).

(f)   False loyalties (1 Cor. 1:10-13).

(g)   Uncontrolled desires, such as coveting (Jas. 4:1-3).

(h)   Hatred (Gal. 5:20).

(i)   Irresponsible behaviour, especially that brought about by drunkenness (Esth. 1:12; Gal. 5:21; 1 Tim. 3:3).

(j)   Harshness (Prov. 15:1).

(k)   Slander, gossip and malicious talk (2 Cor. 12:20; 1 Tim. 6:4; Tit. 3:2; 1 Pet. 3:10-12).

(l)   Unhealthy interest in controversies and arguments (1 Tim. 6:4; 2 Tim. 2:23).

(m)   Quarrelling (1 Cor. 1:11; 2 Cor. 12:20; 1 Tim. 3:3; 6:4).

(n)   Factions, dissensions, and conspiracy (Esth. 2:21; 2 Cor. 12:20; Gal. 5:20).

(o)   Some activities lead to peace, and others do not (Luke 19:42; Rom. 14:19): those that lead to peace are to be pursued, and those that do not are to be fled from without argument (2 Tim. 2:22).

5.   The fundamental importance of peaceableness.

(a)   God is slow to anger (Jonah 4:2), and His spiritual children should be the same (Matt. 5:9).

(b)   Peaceableness characterised the life and ministry of our Saviour (Zech. 9:9; Matt. 21:5; John 12:14, 15), and His mind is to be in us (Phil. 2:5), and His example ever before us (1 Pet. 2:21-23).

(c)   God the Holy Spirit desires peaceableness as part of His fruit in our life (Gal. 5:22).

(d)   Our experience of spiritual joy is intimately linked with our pursuit of righteousness and peace (Rom. 14:17).

(e)   Furthermore, a heart at peace gives life to the body (Prov. 14:30).

(f)   Peaceableness is one of the conditions of God's presence and of His blessing upon us (2 Cor. 13:11) – and often we will find Him making up to us in spiritual peace what we may appear to have lost in preserving neighbourly peace (Gen. 13:14-18; 1 Pet. 3:9).

(g) The body of Christ, the Church, can function properly only as it knows peace (1 Cor. 14:33): without peace there can be no mutual edification (Rom. 14:19).

(h) Peaceableness helps to bind God's people together in unity (Eph. 4:3).

(i) Peaceableness is sometimes used by God to win surprising victories, victories that might not have been won in any other way (1 Sam. 24:17; Prov. 25:15; 1 Pet. 3:15, 16).

(j) Peaceableness is a matter for active pursuit in the Christian life (1 Pet. 3:10, 11).

---

86. PATIENCE

Galatians 5:22: 'The fruit of the Spirit is ... patience.'

Question: What is the patience required of us?

Answer: **Of the two Greek words translated often as patience that chosen to describe this aspect of the fruit of the Spirit is the one used of God's patience, forbearance and steadfastness. It particularly expresses restraint in the face of opposition. Our patience, like God's, is to be the outflow of love, shown to everyone, and demonstrated most of all in forgiveness. The patience God has shown us is to be reflected directly in the patience we show to others.**

1. God is patient.

(a) Patience – slowness to anger – was part of God's amazing revelation of His character to His people in the Old Testament (Ex. 34:6; Num. 14:18; Neh. 9:30); it was a fact of certain knowledge among them (Jonah 4:2).

(b) The same truth concerning God's patience is presented to us in the New Testament (Rom. 9:22; 1 Tim. 1:16; 1 Pet. 3:20; 2 Pet. 3:15): He is rich in patience (Rom. 2:4).

(c)   God's patience has been seen throughout history, most of all in His dealings with Israel (Judg. 3:7,9, 12, 15; Rom. 10:21), in spite of all her spiritual adultery and backsliding (Hos. 2:14-23; Amos 4:6-11).

(d)   God's patience is regularly linked with His constancy and faithfulness (Num. 14:18; Ps. 86:15; Jonah 4:2), goodness and tolerance (Ex. 34:6, 7; Rom. 2:4).

(e)   God's patience is not in opposition to His righteous wrath: His patience means that His wrath's operation is postponed until something takes place in men and women that justifies the postponement; if, however, a change does not take place, then wrath executes its judgment and punishment (Num. 14:18).

(f)   God's patience allows the development of either obedience or disobedience, resulting either in deliverance or destruction (1 Pet. 3:20); and the potential of wrath necessarily increases with the patience shown (Rom. 9:22).

(g)   God's patience is seen in that He longs and waits to be gracious to us (Isa. 30:18).

(h)   It is plain, therefore, that God's patience should lead people towards repentance (Rom. 2. 4), and they should be urged not to abuse God's patience and the opportunity it gives for finding salvation (2 Pet. 3:15).

(i)   We may find God's patience difficult to understand, particularly when the implementation of His justice seems to be delayed (Psa. 35:17; Jer. 15:15); one of the reasons for this problem in our minds is our very human concept of time (2 Pet. 3:8).

(j)   We are called to be like God in those of His attributes that we can reflect and share, and this includes, therefore, His patience (Matt. 5:48).

2.   God has provided examples of patience.

(a)   The foremost example is our Lord Jesus Christ who displayed amazing patience with His disciples: in their slowness to understand (Mark 4:10-20), in their worldly-mindedness (Mark 10:35-45), and in their desertion of Him in His hour of need (Matt. 26:56; Mark 14:50; 16:7).

(b)   The supreme example of His patience was His conduct in His trial and crucifixion (Matt. 26:59-68; 27:27-50; 1 Pet. 2:21-25).

(c)   His continuing patience is seen in His present dealings with men and women: Paul knew himself to be an example of the Lord Jesus Christ's limitless patience that bore with him as a persecutor until it won him over – a boundless patience that continues towards people today (1 Tim. 1:13-16).

(d)   Abraham (Gen. 22:17,18; Heb. 6:15), the prophets (Jas. 5:10), Job (James 5:11), and so many of our spiritual forebears are models of patience (Heb. 11:13); and the things that happened to them are examples to help us (1 Cor 10:11).

(e)   The example of patience the apostle Paul was to Timothy helps us too (2 Tim. 3:10).

3.   The patience God has shown us is the patience we are to show to others.

(a)   The pattern of God's dealings with us is to be the pattern of our dealings with others (Matt. 5:7; Luke 6:36).

(b)   Our patience must most of all be shown in forgiveness (Matt. 18:23-35).

(c)   Our patience must be the expression of love (1 Cor 13:4).

(d)   Our patience is to be evident in our relationships to everyone, whether we are warning, encouraging or helping them (1 Thess. 5:14).

4.   The necessity of patience.

(a)   It is essential to a life worthy of our calling as Christians, enabling us to preserve the unity the Spirit gives, for patience encourages the peace that binds us together (Eph. 4:1-3; Col. 1:10, 11).

(b)   It is an essential part of a Christian's spiritual 'dress' or 'clothing' (Col. 3:12).

(c)   It is a necessary condition of claiming God's promises (Heb. 6:12).

(d)   It is a priority in the teaching of, and preaching to, others (2 Tim. 4:2).

(e)   It is a key to victory in the battle against the world, the flesh and the devil (1 Pet. 2:11; 5:8-10; see the repeated use of the verb 'stand' in Eph. 6:11, 13, 14).

(f) It is an essential part of a Christians' testimony, when persecuted or unjustly treated, that they patiently refuse to retaliate (1 Pet. 2:18-23; 3:13, 14).

5. The rewards of patience.

(a) It can bring people to an experience of salvation (2 Pet. 3:15).

(b) It yields a rich harvest (Jas. 5:7).

(c) It adds attractiveness to character (Gal. 5:22).

(d) It marks us out as true servants of God (2 Cor. 6:4-6).

6. The achievement of patience.

(a) First and foremost, we must focus our attention upon the example God has given us in His Son Jesus Christ (Heb. 12:1-3).

(b) We should pray for patience, realistically facing up to the challenges to it (Col. 1:10, 11).

(c) We are to make it a deliberate objective (Col. 3:12).

(d) As we grow in the grace and knowledge of our Lord Jesus Christ (2 Pet. 3:18), so the fruit of the Spirit in patience grows.

---

87. KINDNESS

Galatians 5:22: 'The fruit of the Spirit is ... kindness.'

Question: What is the kindness required of us?

Answer: **The kindness required of us is the outflow of love in goodness and forgiveness, after the pattern of God's kindness to us. Such kindness is sympathetic, down-to-earth in practical concern and help, and uninfluenced by the merits or gratitude of those to whom it is extended.**

1. The nature of kindness.

(a) Kindness is linked with compassion (Eph. 4:32); it follows upon compassion in the spiritual garments Christian believers are to wear (Col. 3:12).

(b) Kindness is love in action (Eph. 2:6, 7; 4:32; Tit. 3:4).

(c)   Kindness is the reaction of love with goodness towards those who may ill-treat it (1 Cor. 13:4): it is goodness in action (2 Cor 6:6).

(d)   Kindness is love in practice, doing good to others (Luke 6:35).

(e)   Kindness is almost synonymous with forgiveness (Eph. 4:32; Col. 3:12, 13).

(f)   Kindness is uninfluenced by the gratitude or ingratitude of those to whom it is extended; it does not stop when it gets no return (Luke 6:32-35.

2.   The declared opposites of kindness.

(a)   Bitterness (Eph. 4:31, 32).

(b)   Anger (Eph. 4:31, 32).

(c)   Slander and malice (Eph. 4:31, 32; 1 Pet. 2:1-3).

(d)   Deceit (1 Pet. 2:1-3).

(e)   Hypocrisy (1 Pet. 2:1-3).

(f)   Envy (1 Pet. 2:1-3).

3.   The fundamental example of kindness.

(a)   God Himself is the supreme example of kindness: His kindness never fails (Ps. 18:50; Isa. 54:8; Jer. 9:24) and we are instructed to take note of it (Rom. 11:22).

(b)   God is rich in kindness, a truth displayed in His tolerance and patience to the ungrateful and the wicked (Luke 6:35; Rom. 2:4).

(c)   God's kindness is seen in the way in which He delays the Judgment, giving men and women an opportunity for repentance (Rom. 2:4).

(d)   Salvation is the fruit of God's kindness exercised through our Lord Jesus Christ (Tit. 3:4): not only has He saved us from the punishment of sin but He has raised us up with Christ and made us to sit with Him in the heavenly places (Eph. 2:4-6).

(e)   Furthermore, in the ages to come, He is going to show the incomparable riches of His grace towards us in Christ Jesus, so that Christians are examples of how wonderful God's kindness is (Eph. 2:7).

(f)   Everything the Lord Jesus Christ said and did revealed God's kindness. When He said, 'My yoke is easy (Matt. 11:30), 'easy' is an adjective derived from the noun 'kindness' used in

Galatians 5:22. The burdens the Lord Jesus Christ puts upon us when we become His disciples are never too much for us; to serve Him is to find ourselves experiencing His kindness.

(g) God's kindness does not come to an end (Ruth 2:20).

(h) We should not presume, however, upon God's kindness (Rom. 2:4), for His kindness does not mean that He will not punish the guilty (Rom. 11:22); rather God's kindness should lead us towards repentance (Rom. 2:4).

4. The outworkings of kindness (Luke 6:35).

(a) Kindness means loving our enemies, and doing good to those who hate us (Luke 6:27).

(b) Kindness involves blessing those who curse us, and praying for those who ill-treat us (Luke 6:28).

(c) Kindness means that if people strike us on one cheek, we turn to them the other; if they take our coat, then we let them have our shirt as well (Luke 6:29).

(d) Kindness finds expression by giving to everyone who asks us for something, and when someone takes what is ours, not demanding it back (Luke 6:30),

(e) Kindness works by doing to others as we would have them do to us (Luke 6:31).

(f) Kindness is not loving only the people who love us but loving our enemies and doing good to them, lending and expecting nothing back (Luke 6:32-36).

(g) Kindness refrains from judging others (Luke 6:37).

(h) Kindness is marked by generous giving (Luke 6:38).

(i) Where kindness is at work, after the pattern of our Lord Jesus Christ, people are not irritated, upset or annoyed unnecessarily; burdens are not unsympathetically placed upon them (Matt. 11:29, 30).

(j) Where kindness is really at work, its expressions are the same to all, even when the people showing kindness may themselves be under strain (2 Cor 6:3-10).

5. The necessity of kindness in the Christian.

(a) God requires kindness to others: it is a condition of pleasing Him, and of walking humbly with Him (Micah 6:8), and without it the Lord has a controversy with us (Hos. 4:1, 2).

(b)   Kindness is a proof of our new birth, of our possession of the divine nature, for in genuine kindness we reveal the same attitude as our heavenly Father (Luke 6:27, 35).

(c)   Kindness is a characteristic of the new self that is renewed in knowledge after the image of its Creator (Col. 3:10); it is an essential part of the spiritual clothing of God's people to be put on deliberately (Col. 3:12).

(d)   Kindness is one of the marks of God's servants (2 Cor. 6:6).

(e)   Kindness has a converting power (Rom. 2:4; 1 Pet. 2:12).

(f)   The measure of kindness we use towards others is what we may expect God to use towards us (Luke 6:38).

---

88. GOODNESS

Galatians 5:22: 'The fruit of the Spirit is ... goodness.'

Question: What is the goodness required of us?

Answer: When we affirm that God is good, we are declaring that He is all that He as God ought to be. The goodness required of us is that we should always strive to live as the members of God's family ought to live, with high moral standards and actively practising good works. The basic content of the Christian's life is to be goodness.

1.   God's goodness.

(a)   God is good (2 Chron. 30:18; Ps. 86:5; 106:1; 107:1; 118:1), and He alone is worthy of that description (Matt. 19:17; Mark 10:18).

(b)   His goodness is seen in that His love endures forever (1 Chron. 16:34).

(c)   His goodness is displayed in creation (Gen. 1:4, 10, 12, 18, 21, 25, 31; 1 Tim. 4:4).

(d)   His goodness is demonstrated in all His works (Ps. 104:24-30; 119:68; Acts 14:17).

(e)   His goodness is witnessed to by His gifts (Neh. 9:20; Ps. 85:12; Luke 1:53; 11:13; Jas. 1:17).

(f)   The commandments and directions God gives are good (Ps. 119:39; Mark 3:4; Rom. 7:12; Heb. 6:5).

(g)   God's promises are good (1 Kings 8:56), not least in the salvation (Heb. 9:11; 10:1) and hope (2 Thess. 2:16) He grants to those who believe on His Son Jesus Christ.

(h)   God's message to people in Jesus Christ is good news (Rom. 10:15).

(i)   God's will and purposes for our lives are good (Ps. 84:11; Rom. 12:2) and the work He begins in Christians' lives at their new birth is 'a good work' (Phil. 1:6).

(j)   Even when God needs to discipline Christians it is always for their good (Ps. 119:67,71; Heb. 12:10).

(k)   There is no limit to God's goodness and the good He gives to His spiritual children in Christ (Rom. 8:32; Eph. 1:3).

(l)   Goodness finds its model and example in our Lord Jesus Christ (1 Pet 2:19-24), who is the visible image of the invisible God (Col. 1:15): He went around doing good (Acts 10:38).

2.   God's goodness teaches us truth about ourselves.

(a)   Goodness is the test of a person's life (Matt. 7:15-20; Luke 6:43-45), and God judges everyone by the same standard of goodness (Rom. 2:9-11).

(b)   By nature no one consistently does good (Rom. 3:12): evil things rather than good things are the more natural fruit of human lives (Matt. 12:34).

(c)   The more we know ourselves, the more we know that good does not naturally live in us (Rom. 7:18).

(d)   Even though we may possess the desire to do good, we are not able to do it; instead of doing the good we want, we find ourselves doing the evil we do not want to do (Rom. 7:18, 19).

(e)   The call God gives to salvation, therefore, is not based upon a person's goodness but entirely upon God's grace (Rom. 9:11-16; Eph. 2:8): God has shown how much He loves us in that while we were still sinners the Lord Jesus Christ died for us (Rom. 5:7, 8).

(f)   God's goodness should make us continually thankful (Ps. 118:29), so that we recognise that the only proper response to it is the offering of ourselves to Him (Rom. 12:1).

(g)   Real goodness begins when we hear God's message of salvation, retain it in a good and obedient heart, and persist until fruit is born (Luke 8:8, 15) – the fruit of the Spirit that includes goodness (Gal. 5:22, 23).

3. Defining goodness.

(a)   Goodness is to act justly, to love mercy and to walk humbly with God (Micah 6:8).

(b)   Goodness is genuine obedience to the law of God (Ps. 34:14, 15; 37:27).

(c)   Goodness is the outflow of love (Gal. 5:22; 1 Cor. 13:1-7).

(d)   Goodness is the putting aside of our own will and pleasure so as to please our neighbours for their good in order to build them up in the faith (Rom. 15:2).

(e)   Goodness is the opposite of wrong and evil (1 Thess. 5:15; 1 Pet. 3:11; 3 John 11), disobedience (Tit. 1:16), self-seeking (Rom. 2:7, 8) and insincerity (Jas. 3:17).

(f)   Goodness always helps rather than harms (Luke 6:9; Acts 9:36), delights in giving rather than receiving (Matt. 7:11; Acts 20:35; 2 Cor. 9:8), and concerns itself with the need that requires to be met rather than with the merits of the person in need (Luke 6:33; Gal. 6:10).

(g)   Real goodness is consistent goodness (Tit. 2:10), flowing from a life full of the Holy Spirit and of faith (John 7:38, 39; Acts 11:24).

4. Goodness in us is the fruit of the Spirit.

(a)   The word translated 'goodness' in 'the fruit of the Spirit' (Gal. 5:22) conveys the idea of moral excellence and belongs with righteousness and truth to 'the fruit of the light' (Eph. 5:9).

(b)   The fruits of the Christian life are all fruits of goodness (Matt. 7:17-20).

(c)   Born again by God's Spirit into His family, we find within ourselves new desires for goodness (2 Thess. 1:11).

(d)   Goodness is a reflection of our heavenly Father's character being reproduced in us (Matt. 5:45; 3 John 4, 11).

(e)   Practical goodness is part of the transformation to be expected of converted men and women (Eph. 4:28).

(f)   Christians should be full of goodness (Rom. 15:14), being wise about what is good but innocent about what is evil (Rom. 16:19).

(g)   Goodness is essentially living and behaving in the world as true servants of God (1 Pet. 2:15, 16).

(h)   One of the principal demonstrations of goodness is submission to others: to civil authorities (1 Pet. 2:13-17), to employers (1 Pet. 2:18-25), of wives to husbands (1 Pet. 3:1-6), of children to parents (Eph. 6:1-3), and to one another (Eph. 5:21; 1 Pet. 3:8).

(i)   Goodness responds to opposition and suffering with patience (1 Pet. 2:20), and does not allow anything to put it off from pursuing the right course (1 Pet. 3:6).

(j)   Goodness on the part of Christians is God's chosen answer to people's unjust opposition to Christian witness (1 Pet. 2:15; 3:1-6).

(k)   Our lives are meant to bear fruit in every good work (Col. 1:10).

5.   Goodness and good works.

(a)   True worship of God and good works go together (Matt. 5:16; 1 Tim. 2:10).

(b)   Good works have no place in the obtaining of salvation (Eph. 2:8, 9; Tit. 3:5) but they are a principal evidence of our experience of it (Jas. 2:17): we are born again to do good works God has prepared in advance for us to do (Eph. 2:10).

(c)   Works cannot be divorced from words, and goodness shows itself in speech (Matt. 12:34; Luke 6:45; 2 Thess. 2:17), speech that builds others up (Eph. 4:29) and avoids speaking evil (Tit. 3:1, 2).

(d)   Goodness never pays back wrong for wrong but always tries to be kind (1 Thess. 5:15), not only to fellow-Christians but to everyone (Gal. 6:10).

(e)   Our income is intended to enable us to be rich in good works (1 Tim. 6:17, 18), so that there should be a harvest of good works in our lives as we wisely use what God has given us (2 Cor. 9:8-11).

(f)   Goodness is displayed in all kinds of good deeds such as bringing up children well, showing hospitality, doing menial tasks for others, helping those in trouble, and being ready to do whatever is good whenever the opportunity presents itself (1 Tim. 5:10; Tit. 3:1).

(g)   Good works do not have to be forced upon goodness; rather they are spontaneous and willing (Philem. 14).

(h)   God has provided the Scriptures so that by the instruction they provide we may be thoroughly equipped for every good work (2 Tim. 3:16, 17), for the wisdom they impart from above ensures a harvest of good deeds (Jas. 3:17, 18).

(i)   God provides strength and encouragement to persevere in good works (2 Thess. 2:16, 17; Heb. 13:20, 21).

(j)   Good works honour God: they make the teaching about God our Saviour attractive in the eyes of the world (Tit. 2:9, 10), and they compel people to praise our Father in heaven (Matt. 5:16).

(k)   It is not surprising, therefore, that the Christian should be eager to do good (1 Pet. 3:13).

---

89. FAITHFULNESS

Galatians 5:22: 'The fruit of the Spirit is ... faithfulness.'

Question: What is the faithfulness required of us?

Answer: Faithfulness is our proper response to God's faithfulness, and an outworking of living faith in Jesus Christ. Faithfulness is loyalty, reliability and dependability. It expresses itself in unswerving loyalty to God at any cost. It means fulfilling our duties and responsibilities to others, irrespective of how convenient or easy these obligations may be. Faithfulness is the principal virtue our Lord Jesus Christ chooses to reward.

1.   **Faithfulness is an outstanding feature of God's character** (Isa. 49:7; 1 Cor. 1:9; 10:13).

(a)   He is the faithful God who keeps His covenant of love with those who love Him and keep His commands (Deut. 7:9).

(b)   He does not lie (Num. 23:19; Tit. 1:2).

321

(c)   His faithfulness is unfailing (2 Tim. 2:13), great (Lam. 3:23) and incomparable (Ps. 89:8).

(d)   His faithfulness is immeasurable (Ps. 36:5), certain (Ps. 89:2; Isa. 54:10), and everlasting (Ps. 89:33; 119:90).

(e)   His faithfulness is revealed in nature's order and balance (Gen. 8:22; Jer. 33:20-22).

(f)   His faithfulness shows itself in the fulfilment of His promises to His people (Josh. 21:43; Isa. 25:1; Ezek. 37:11-14).

(g)   His faithfulness has been gloriously expressed to us in our Lord Jesus Christ (John 1:14; 13:1; 14:6; Rev. 19:11).

2.   Faithfulness is an essential aspect of Christian character.

(a)   It is part of the fruit of the Spirit, and that fruit is the sum of Christian character (Gal. 5:22, 23).

(b)   Character is the test of a person's religion (Matt. 7:15-20; Luke 6:43-45), and is the one thing we cannot borrow, lend or escape for it is the real 'us' (Prov. 9:12; cf. 14:10).

(c)   Faithfulness arises from what a person is through and through – it does not occur accidentally (Luke 16:10).

(d)   Faithfulness needs to be valued, and meditated upon in the heart, if it is to show itself in conduct (Prov. 3:3).

(e)   Faithfulness should extend to trustworthiness in everything (1 Tim. 3:11).

(f)   The person who is faithful with very little will be found faithful with much (Luke 16:10).

(g)   Without faithfulness our characters are deficient of an essential quality (Jas. 1:2-4).

(h)   Christian character, however, is not produced in a moment (Rom. 5: 3,4): many of the testings that God permits, He overrules so as to develop faithfulness on our part (Jas. 1:2-4).

3.   Faithfulness has relevance to our speech and our general use of words.

(a)   Faithful speech is honest, direct, and unambiguous (Matt. 5:37); when we say either' Yes' or 'No' we must mean what we say (2 Cor. 1:18).

(b)   Faithful speech is strictly truthful and avoids exaggeration (Jas. 5:12).

(c)   Faithful speech is the opposite of lying, false witness and evasive speech (Prov. 14:5; Hos. 4:1, 2).

(d)   Faithful speech rebukes when such is necessary, but with kindness and love (Ps. 141:5; Prov 27:6).

(e)   It is not enough to protest loyalty with our lips and then to deny it by our conduct (Prov. 20:6).

(f)   Since it is characteristic of God to be always faithful to His promises, so must we be faithful to the promises we make (Matt. 5:48; 2 Cor. 1:17-20; Heb. 10:23).

4.   Faithfulness is to mark our relationship to God.

(a)   Genuine faith in God must always lead to faithfulness to Him (Hab. 2:4).

(b)   God requires our total loyalty (Luke 16:13), and our foremost expression of faithfulness must be to Him (Acts 11:23).

(c)   Faithfulness itself, even more than the fruits of faithfulness, is that for which God looks (Matt. 24:4-26; 25:21, 23; Rev. 2:10), and if it is absent He has a controversy with us (Hos. 4:1, 2; 6:4-7).

(d)   Christians are called of God to show faithfulness to Jesus Christ His Son (Eph. 1:1; Col. 1:2), a faithfulness that must be steadfast and consistent (Acts 11:23).

(e)   We are to be faithful in doing the will of God no matter what the obstacles (Heb. 10:36), even in the face of death (Rev. 2:10).

(f)   Our faithfulness is of infinite value to God (1 Pet. 1:7), and it causes us to find favour and a good name in His sight (Prov. 3:4).

(g)   Our faithfulness to God is very much influenced by our appreciation of His faithfulness to us (Heb. 10:23).

(h)   Fortunately, our lack of faithfulness does not nullify the faithfulness of God (Rom. 3:3; 2 Tim. 2:13); God is willing to heal our faithlessness when we return to Him in repentance (Hos. 14:4).

5. **Faithfulness is to mark all our other relationships.**

A. **Husbands and wives**

(a) Husbands should be completely faithful to their wives (Prov. 5:15-20; 1 Tim. 3:2, 12), a faithfulness that should extend to their thoughts (Ex. 20:17; Matt. 5:27, 28).

(b) A faithful husband loves his wife as he loves his own body (Eph. 5:28), and finds his sole satisfaction in her (Prov. 5:15-20).

(c) A faithful husband behaves towards his wife with consideration, treating her with respect and honour, recognising her more limited physical powers (1 Pet. 3:7).

(d) A faithful husband strives to love his wife as Christ loves the Church (Eph. 5:25-33).

(e) Wives are to be consistently faithful to their husband's interests (Prov. 31:12).

(f) A faithful wife helps her husband play his part in the community (Prov. 31:23).

(g) A faithful wife can be completely trusted by her husband, and her affection for him will fill him with delight at all times (Prov. 5:19; 31:11).

(h) A faithful wife is her husband's pride and joy (Prov. 12:4).

B. **Parents and children**

(a) Faithful parents are careful in the training of their children, recognising that the course their children adopt in later life depends upon the training they initially receive at home (Prov. 22:6), and so they give their children instruction and good precepts from their earliest age (Prov. 4:1-4).

(b) Faithful parents diligently discipline their children because they love them (Prov. 13:24).

(c) Faithful parents not only teach their children the way of wisdom but they lead them along straight paths (Prov. 4:11), conferring upon them for life the benefit of godly example (Prov. 20:7).

(d) Faithful parents teach their children about the past dealings of God with His people, appreciating their responsibility for the generations that are to follow (Ps. 78:5, 6).

(e)   Faithful children obey their parents on the strength of the commandment, 'Honour your father and mother' (Ex. 20:12; Eph. 6:2).

(f)   Faithful children listen to their father and do not despise their mother when she is old (Prov. 23:22).

(g)   Faithful children do not regard the property of their parents lightly, and avoid the snare of imagining that what is wrong outside the family is permissible within it (Prov. 28:24).

(h)   Faithful children appreciate that they have duties as well as rights: they are careful, therefore, in their treatment of their parents, and make necessary provision for them (Prov. 19:26).

C.   Employers and employees

(a)   Faithful employers do not withhold proper wages (Jas. 5:4).

(b)   Faithful employers are conscientious and responsible towards those who serve them as they expect them to be in their work for them (Eph. 6:9).

(c)   Employees are to be faithful to their employers (Tit. 2:9, 10).

(d)   Faithful employees do not steal (Tit. 2:10); rather, they should be so reliable, for example, in handling money entrusted to them, that they do not need to be checked up upon (2 Kings 12:15).

(e)   Faithful employees are never rude or insolent to their employers (Tit. 2:10).

(f)   Faithful employees render to their human employers service as if it were to the Lord Jesus Christ Himself (Eph. 6:5-8), and in this way, by their behaviour at work, they make the teaching about God our Saviour attractive (Tit. 2:10).

D.   Christian fellowship

(a)   We are to be faithful brothers and sisters to one another in God's family because of our common relationship to the Lord Jesus Christ (Col. 1:2).

(b)   We must be always eager to believe the best of one another (1 Cor. 13:7).

(c)   Where wrong needs to be put right, we must be faithful in speaking the truth to one another in love (Prov. 27:6; Eph. 4:15, 25).

(d)   We must stand by one another, even when trouble may result (Heb. 10:33).

(e) We must be faithful in our exercise of the gift of hospitality (3 John 5-8).

(f) We must serve one another all the better because of our relationship in Christ (1 Tim. 6:2).

(g) To be faithful to one another we must make time, and seize opportunities, to meet with other Christians so as to encourage and help one another (Heb. 10:25).

(h) We must be faithful to the spiritual leaders God gives us, so that they may fulfil their task joyfully and not sadly (1 Thess. 5:12, 13; Heb. 13:7).

6. Faithfulness also finds expression in our service of God, and the use to which we put all He has given us.

(a) Faithfulness is a primary qualification for service and office in the body of Christ, the Church (1 Tim. 3:11; 2 Tim. 2:2).

(b) God is to be served with faithfulness (Josh. 24:14; Matt. 24:45; Heb. 3:1, 2, 5, 6): we cannot serve two masters (Luke 16:13).

(c) God entrusts us with a stewardship, and it is required of stewards or trustees that they should be found faithful (1 Cor. 4:2).

(d) If, for example, our service is the communicating of God's Word in any way, we are to speak that Word faithfully, as in the sight of God (Jer. 23:28; 2 Cor. 2:17), renouncing all that is underhand or insincere (2 Cor. 4:2), ensuring that we pass God's Word on accurately and faithfully (Josh. 11:15; Acts 20:27).

(e) We are to serve God faithfully by keeping and upholding the faith (2 Tim. 4:7), earnestly contending for the faith that was once for all entrusted to God's people (Jude 3).

(f) Whatever service we render to others, we are to render it faithfully (3 John 5).

(g) We serve God faithfully as we use our money and material possessions in the interests of His kingdom (Luke 16:10, 11), recognising that all we own is a gift from Him (1 Chron. 29:14).

7. Faithfulness has great importance in respect of rewards.

(a) God gives His own reward to faithfulness (1 Sam. 26:23).

(b) The true standard of reward is faithfulness to opportunity rather than length, honour or seeming importance of service (Matt. 20:1-16).

(c)   The Lord knows the truth about our faithfulness (Rev. 2:13, 19).

(d)   A faithful individual will be richly blessed (Prov. 28:20).

(e)   The Lord Jesus will reward His faithful servants on His return (Matt. 24:46, 47): equal gifts, if used with unequal faithfulness, will be unequally rewarded (Luke 19:12-27); unequal gifts, used with equal faithfulness, will be equally rewarded (Matt. 25:14-30).

(f)   A crown of righteousness awaits the servants of Christ who have kept the faith and been faithful in service (2 Tim. 4:7, 8): significantly, those who are described as being in the closest proximity to the Lord Jesus Christ in heaven are those who have proved themselves faithful (Rev. 17:14).

(g)   We should be watchful concerning our faithfulness, lest we lose our reward (2 John 8).

8.   The Bible provides many examples of faithfulness.

(a)   Abraham was found faithful in his heart to the Lord (Neh. 9:7, 8; Gal. 3:9).

(b)   Moses was faithful to the tasks God committed to him of caring for God's people (Num. 12:7; Heb. 3:2, 5).

(c)   Joseph was faithful to his Egyptian master at great cost to himself (Gen. 39:2-20) and then also to the keeper of the prison (Gen. 39:22, 23).

(d)   David was faithful to Saul in spite of all the injustices he suffered at his hands (1 Sam. 22:14).

(e)   Daniel was faithful both to God and to his human employer, the king of Babylon (Dan. 6:4, 10).

(f)   Shadrach, Meshach and Abednego were outstanding examples of faithfulness to God as they obeyed His commandment (Ex. 20:5; Dan. 3:28).

(g)   Ruth's answer to Naomi is a classic example of faithfulness (Ruth 1:16, 17).

(h)   Paul sought to be faithful in not holding back any truth God wanted His people to receive from him (Acts 20:20, 27).

(i)   Silas was a faithful brother in his service of both Peter (1 Pet. 5:12) and the apostle Paul (Acts 15:40; 1 Thess. 1:1).

(j)   Onesimus was faithful in his relationship to his fellow-Christians (Col. 4:9).

(k)   Tychicus was faithful in serving others for Christ's sake (Eph. 6:21).

(l)   Timothy was faithful to the apostle Paul in the tasks delegated to him (1 Cor. 4:17; Phil. 2:19-22).

(m)   Antipas was faithful in his witness to the Lord Jesus even though it meant martyrdom (Rev. 2:13).

(n)   The remembrance of those who have been faithful to God in the past inspires us to faithfulness (Heb. 11:4-40; 12:1, 2).

(o)   We do well to imitate the faith and faithfulness of godly leaders who have both helped us and have been an example to us in the past (Heb. 13:7).

9.   Faithfulness may bring its own costly consequences.

(a)   Faithfulness may bring reproach and persecution, as it did to our Lord Jesus Christ (Rom. 15:2, 3).

(b)   There is great blessing, however, in hardship or persecution that come as a result of faithfulness to Christ (Matt. 5:11, 12).

(c)   Even our lives may be put in jeopardy by faithfulness (Dan. 3:14-21; Rev. 2:13).

(d)   Suffering on account of faithfulness to God and to others, because it is God's will, will bring its own experience of His help (2 Tim. 1:8; 4:17), and it is, of course, only by God's mercy and help that faithfulness can be achieved (1 Cor. 7:25).

---

90. GENTLENESS

Galatians 5:22, 23: 'The fruit of the Spirit is … gentleness.' (Gentleness here is the Greek word *prautes*. It can be translated as gentleness or as meekness, in the older and more favourable sense of the word.)

Question: What is the gentleness or meekness required of us?

Answer: The gentleness or meekness required of us is an inward attitude that enables us to be in a position of submission to God's will, irrespective of difficulty, and to treat others with gentleness, humility,

courtesy, and consideration. **(Gentleness and meekness are not commonly appreciated or admired qualities, for, in their contemporary use, they carry a suggestion of spinelessness or weakness.** **Gentleness is the alternative to meekness in many translations, but it is not entirely satisfactory.** **Aristotle defined meekness as the happy medium between excessive anger and excessive angerlessness.** **Gentleness, humility, courtesy, considerateness and meekness - put together - best express the Greek word** *prautes***.)**

1. **The nature of gentleness and meekness.**

(a) Gentleness is part of love's outflow (1 Cor. 4:21).

(b) Gentleness and meekness are frequently linked in the New Testament with patience (Eph. 4:2; Col. 3:12, 13), and humility (Matt. 11:29; Eph. 4:2; Col.. 3:12).

(c) They are gifts of the Spirit, and a fruit of the wisdom from above that God gives (Jas. 3:13).

(d) They are a duty laid upon us by God as an essential part of the life to which He has called us in Christ (Eph. 4:2; Col. 3:12).

(e) Gentleness may be thought of as part of Christians' essential clothing (Col. 3:12), that they must never be without (Tit. 3:2).

(f) Submission to the will of God is the most important aspect of meekness (Jas. 4:10; 1 Pet. 5:6).

(g) Meekness strives to choose God's will before self-will (Matt. 26:39; Mark 14:36; Luke 22:42).

(h) Even if submission to God means becoming as the scum of the earth and the refuse of the world, meekness accepts obedience to God's will, and strives to act in a manner pleasing to Him (1 Cor. 4:13) - cf. the example of Stephen (Acts 7:60).

(i) Meekness cries to God in prayer, and reverently accepts His answer whatever it may be (Heb. 5:7).

(j) Meekness goes hand in hand with confident waiting upon God (Ps. 147:6; 149:4; 1 Pet. 2:21-23) —it causes people to counsel themselves, 'Be still before the LORD, and wait patiently for Him' (Ps. 37:7).

(k) Meekness discovers the unique peace that comes from submission to God's will (Ps. 131:1, 2).

(l)   Mary is an example of meekness before God: '1 am the Lord's servant ... May it be to me as you have said' (Luke 1:38).

(m)   Consideration for others is the second most important aspect of gentleness and meekness – humble before God, we learn to be gentle in our dealings with others (1 Pet. 5:5, 6).

(n)   Gentleness is synonymous with courtesy towards everyone (Tit. 3:2).

(o)   Gentleness is unassuming (Zech. 9:9; Matt. 21:5) and makes us approachable (Matt. 11:29).

(p)   Gentleness and meekness are marks of servants of God (Isa. 42:1-4; 53:7, 2 Tim. 2:24, 25), of those who genuinely strive to walk in the Lord Jesus Christ's footsteps (1 Pet. 2:21-24).

(q)   Gentleness is much more concerned to serve God than to advance personal status (Num. 12:3; Phil. 2:5-8).

(r)   Gentleness is an indispensable characteristic of the ideal teacher (Matt. 11:29; 2 Tim. 2:25).

(s)   It is also a vital factor in the exercise of discipline (1 Cor. 4:21), and in the spirit in which the erring or wayward Christian is to be sought out and brought back into fellowship (Gal. 6:1).

(t)   Moses exhibited meekness and gentleness to a remarkable degree, more than all his contemporaries (Num. 12:3), and, significantly, he was described by God as His faithful servant (Num. 12:7).

2.   The gentleness and meekness of our Lord Jesus Christ.

(a)   Gentleness was a promised characteristic of the Messiah in the Old Testament prophecies (Isa. 42:1-4; Zech. 9:9).

(b)   Gentleness and meekness were two of the foremost characteristics that our Lord Jesus Christ exhibited during His earthly life (2 Cor.10:1), and were part of His own self-description (Matt.11:29).

(c)   Submission to the will of God the Father was an important aspect of our Lord's meekness (Heb. 10:7).

(d)   His food was to do the will of the Father and to finish His work (John 4:34).

(e)   He provided a perfect example of submission in the Garden of Gethsemane when He prayed, 'Not my will, but yours be done' (Luke 22:42).

(f) It was also displayed in His submission to the wrongs inflicted upon Him as He discharged His ministry as God's suffering Servant: 'He was oppressed and afflicted, yet he did not open his mouth' (Isa. 53:7); He did 'not shout or cry out, or raise his voice in the streets' (Isa. 42:2).

(g) When insults were hurled at Him, He did not respond with retaliation; His response was to entrust Himself to Him who judges justly (1 Pet. 2:23).

(h) But the second important aspect of our Lord's gentleness was His consideration for others, and especially His unassertiveness and His tenderness to the weak and needy (Isa. 42:2, 3) – e.g. His dealings with the Samaritan woman (John 4:1-26), the woman taken in adultery (John 8:1-11), and Zacchaeus (Luke 19:1-10).

(i) He encouraged men and women to come to Him on account of His gentleness (Matt. 11:29).

(j) His consideration for the disciples was marked by gentleness: for example, He was concerned for them when they were tired (Mark 6:31), and when they were troubled and needed comfort (John 14:1-3).

3. **Gentleness and meekness may be better understood by appreciating some of the opposite features of human behaviour with which they are contrasted.**

(a) Self-assertiveness or arrogance (1 Pet. 3:15).

(b) Jealousy and selfish ambition (Jas. 3:13, 14).

(c) Shouting, brawling and quarrelsomeness (Isa. 42:2; Matt. 12:19; 2 Tim. 2:24, 25).

(d) Self-justification and self-defence (Isa. 42:2; Matt. 12:19).

(e) Resentment (2 Tim. 2:24, 25).

(f) Abrasiveness (Matt. 11:29, 30).

(g) Anger (Jas. 1:19-21).

(h) Violence and being warlike (Matt. 21:5).

(i) Aggressiveness (1 Cor. 4:21).

(j) Unnecessary sternness in the application of discipline (1 Cor. 4:21; 2 Tim. 2:25).

4.   **The practice and expression of gentleness and meekness.**

(a)   Their practice is to be continuous, like the wearing of clothes (Col. 3:12); they are to be actively pursued (1 Tim. 6:11).

(b)   They express themselves in believing submission to God's will, even when we cannot understand what God may be doing (Job 1:21; Acts 20:22-24; 21:10-14; 1 Pet. 4:19).

(c)   They express themselves in submissive listening and obedience to the instruction of God's Word, even if that obedience involves the acceptance of rebuke and the need for repentance (Jas. 1:21).

(d)   They express themselves in respect for all people, not for whom or what they are, or what their attitude may be in return (Tit. 3:2; 1 Pet. 3:15).

(e)   They express themselves in restraint when provoked (2 Tim. 2:25).

(f)   When authorities or others ask for an account of a Christian's profession of faith, it is to be given with meekness and gentleness, even though injustice that has been suffered might prompt indignation or hurt (1 Pet. 3:15, 16).

(g)   They express themselves in tenderness in dealing with those who need to be corrected (Isa. 42:3; 2 Tim. 2:25), so that correction is given without arrogance, impatience or anger, and the endeavour to give no unnecessary offence (Gal. 6:1).

(h)   They express themselves in accepting the example of the Lord Jesus as the only acceptable norm for obedience to God and the service of others (2 Cor. 10:1; Phil. 2:5-8).

5.   **The importance of gentleness and meekness.**

(a)   Meekness finds its place among the Beatitudes: 'Blessed are the meek, for they will inherit the earth' (Matt. 5:5).

(b)   Gentleness makes us true helpers of others after the pattern of our Lord Jesus Christ (Matt. 11:29), for rather than antagonising people we may win them over to what is right by love's expression through gentleness (2 Tim. 2:25).

(c)   The humility that comes from meekness is a necessary condition for knowing God's guidance (Ps. 25:9).

(d)   Meekness is a condition of receiving God's blessing (Ps. 37:11).

(e)   The Lord causes gentleness and meekness to prosper —He crowns the humble with salvation (Ps. 149:4).

(f)   While it may be a mystery and a paradox to the unbelieving world, meekness is a secret of happiness (Ps. 37:11; Matt. 5:5).

---

91. SELF-CONTROL

Galatians 5:22, 23: 'The fruit of the Spirit is … self-control.'

Question: What is the self-control required of us?

Answer: The self-control required of us is self-mastery, so that through the help of the Holy Spirit, we are not under the power or dominion of any sin or habit, but we willingly use our Christian freedom to serve Christ by serving others.   It is different from the rest of the fruit of the Spirit because it relates not so much to our relationship to God or others but to our duty to ourselves.

1.   Areas in which self-control is most obviously relevant.

(a)   Self-control is relevant to the whole of human life (1 Thess. 5:6, 22).

(b)   Eating (Prov. 23:20; 25:16).

(c)   Drinking (Eccl. 10:17; Rom. 13:13)– drunkenness leads to uncontrolled actions and excess (Eph. 5:18).

(d)   Sex (Tit. 2:5): sexual intercourse is a good gift of God that is meant to be exercised in marriage alone (Mark 10:6, 7), and even then it is a precious benefit to be enjoyed in a manner consistent with self-control (1 Cor. 7:1-6).

(e)   The exercise and satisfaction of our desires (1 Pet. 2:11; 4:4; cf. Matt. 14:4; Mark 6:18), and the enjoyment of human pleasures (Matt. 14:6, 7; Mark 6:21-23).

(f)   Occasions of temptation (Mark 14:37-40, 66-72): sometimes the self-controlled Christian will know that the wisest course is to flee from it (2 Tim. 2:22; Jas. 1:14).

(g)   The estimate we have of ourselves, and the exercise of pride (Rom. 12:3, 16; cf. Phil. 2:3).

(h) Weaknesses of temperament – for example, a tendency to be cowardly (Mark 6:26; Matt. 14:9; 2 Tim. 1:6-8).

(i) The expression of our feelings: for example, if insulted it is fools who show their irritation straightaway; whereas it is the prudent and self-controlled who keep their feelings out of sight (Prov. 12:16).

(j) Temper (Ps. 37:8; Eph. 4:26; 1 Thess. 5:14).

(k) The use of the tongue (Matt. 14:6, 7; Mark 6:22,23; Jas. 3:1, 2), and in the promises we may make (Ex. 8:8, 15; Eccl. 5:2; Matt. 14:6, 7; Mark 6:22, 23).

(l) Resistance to worldly pressures to live with a wholly materialistic outlook (1 Tim. 6:6-10): it is only by self-control that we can avoid the sin of coveting (Acts 20:33; Rom. 7:7, 8; 13:9, 10), and ensure that our treasure is in heaven rather than on earth (Matt. 6:19-21; cf. John 6:27).

(m) The use of time (Eccl. 3:1-8; Eph. 5:15, 16; Col. 4:5).

(n) Spiritual experience: our calling to freedom must not mean indulgence of our sinful nature (Gal. 5:13); our spiritual joy and exuberance must not lead to excess (Eph. 5:18-20); and our exercise of spiritual gifts must not be selfish but for the edifying of the whole body of Christ (1 Cor. 14:12, 26-33, 40).

2.   Opposites of self-control.

(a) Undisciplined living with all its sad consequences (Prov. 21:25; 26:14; Eccl. 10:18; 1 Pet. 1:13, 14; 4:3, 4).

(b) Sexual immorality, impurity and debauchery (Gal. 5:19) – all illustrations of a lack of control of the body and its sexual appetites.

(c) Idolatry, of which covetousness is a form (Gal. 5:20; Col. 3:5) – a lack of control over our eyes and what they may prompt us to want, and a lack of discipline with regard to the acquisitive spirit contemporary society encourages (1 John 2:15, 16).

(d) Hatred, jealousy, and envy (Gal. 5:20, 21) - all failures to control the wrongful feelings that our sinful nature prompts.

(e) Discord, selfish ambition, dissensions and factions (Gal. 5:20) – these all arise from the failure to control self and its display in forceful and selfish feelings or points of view.

(f) Fits of temper (Gal. 5:20) - failure to control our anger and our tongue.

(g)   Drunkenness and orgies (Gal. 5:21) - failure to control thirst and sexual desires.

3.   What self-control means in practice.

(a)   It is essentially self-mastery or dominion over oneself (Rom. 6:13, 14), leading to an orderly life (Eph. 5:15).

(b)   It means coming to terms with the truth about our body and ourselves: we are weak in our natural selves (Mark 14:38; Rom. 6:19; 8:1), sinful (Rom. 8:3), and inclined to think about how we may gratify the desires of our sinful nature (Rom. 13:14; Gal. 5:13).

(c)   It means making our body our slave rather than allowing it to be our master (1 Cor. 9:27).

(d)   It means being sufficiently honest with ourselves to appreciate that self-discipline must begin with our mind and our thoughts (Phil. 4:8; 1 Pet. 1:13; cf. Matt. 5:28).

(e)   It means having before us clear goals, so that we live our lives with purpose and a clear sense of direction (1 Cor. 9:24-27).

(f)   It means having an eye to the good of others as well as our own: our Christian freedom is not to please ourselves but to choose to please others for their good, following the example of our Lord Jesus (Rom. 15:1-3).

(g)   It means recognising the place of watchfulness (Matt. 26:41; Mark 14:38) and not overestimating our strength (1 Cor. 10:12).

(h)   It means recognising the place of prayer, and giving time to it (Matt. 26:41; Mark 14:38; 1 Pet. 4:7).

(i)   It means honest and drastic action often with regard to known sources of temptation (Matt. 5:29; 18:8, 9; Mark 9:43-47), giving no room for the gratification of the desires of our sinful nature (Rom. 13:14) - in other words, the readiness to say 'No' to ungodliness and worldly passions (Tit. 2:12).

(j)   It means being like an athlete in our approach to life, recognising the need for personal strictness (1 Cor. 9:25; 2 Tim. 2:5).

(k)   It demands perseverance (2 Pet. 1:6).

(l)   It means being inwardly strong through the resources of Jesus Christ (Phil. 4:13; 2 Tim. 1:7; 2:1).

4.   **The necessity and priority of self-control.**

(a)   It is an essential part of godliness that, sadly, will be despised in the last days (2 Tim. 3:1-5).

(b)   It is an essential qualification for holding office in the Church of God (1 Tim. 3:2; Tit. 1:8).

(c)   It is linked with righteousness (Acts 24:25), one of the principal priorities of Christian living (1 Pet. 2:24).

(d)   It is part of our present experience of God's salvation (Tit. 2:12-14).

(e)   It is the climax of the fruit of the Spirit (Gal. 5:23), and is relevant to every age-group (Tit. 2:2, 5, 6, 12).

(f)   It is part of the freedom to which our Lord Jesus Christ calls us (John 8:36; Gal. 5:1, 13) – a freedom purchased at tremendous cost (Gal. 3:13).

(g)   Without self-control we are an easy target for Satan (1 Cor. 7:5; Eph. 4:26, 27).

(h)   Without self-control we may bring harm to others as well as to ourselves (Mark 6:20-28; cf. 2 Sam.11:1-17; 12:15).

(i)   It is essential if we are to maintain and safeguard the value of our Christian testimony and service of the Lord Jesus (1 Cor. 9:25-27).

(j)   It is part of our conformity to the likeness of our Lord Jesus Christ (Rom. 8:29): His whole life was disciplined so as to fulfil the Father's will (Luke 9:51; John 4:34); He was disciplined in prayer (Mark 1:35; Luke 11:1), in the face of temptation (John 6:15; Luke 22:39-46), and tremendous ill-treatment (1 Pet. 2:23).

(k)   We shall be judged with regard to our exercise of self-control (Acts 24:25; 1 Cor. 9:25-27).

---

92. CHRISTIAN DISCIPLESHIP

Question: **What is Christian discipleship?**

Answer: **Christian discipleship is our response to the call of Jesus Christ to follow Him.   It involves a counting of the cost and a total commitment to Him, so that the whole of our life is given to making God's kingdom our primary concern.**

1. **The cost and conditions of discipleship.**

(a) 'Disciple,' the Greek word for 'apprentice' or 'learner,' is the word used most often in the New Testament – some 250 times – to describe members of Christ's kingdom (Luke 11:1; 14:26-33).

(b) Disciples of the Lord Jesus were not called 'Christians' until the establishment of the church in Antioch (Acts 11:26), and then it was but a nickname.

(c) Discipleship constitutes our answer to the call of Jesus Christ to follow Him (Matt. 4:19; Mark 1:17; 2:14; 10:21; Luke 9:59; John 1:43), in the light of His death and resurrection on our behalf (Matt. 28:18-20; Acts 9:1-22; Rom. 12:1, 2; Phil. 3:1-11).

(d) No one, however, should be allowed to embark upon discipleship without first appreciating the cost (Matt. 19:21; Luke 18:22) - our Lord went to great trouble to underline its demands (Luke 14:25-33).

(e) The love we have for people, and the desire we may have that they should become disciples, must not mean that we neglect to make them count the cost (Mark 10:21).

(f) The basic principle is that we cannot serve two masters; if we try to do so, the results are bound to be unfortunate (Matt. 6:24; Luke 16:13).

(g) For some, the cost may relate particularly to wealth, since discipleship involves the abandonment of every idol that would take Christ's place in a person's life (Matt. 19:21; Mark 10:21; Luke 18:22).

(h) The home is not to assume priority over discipleship of Christ (Luke 18:28-30).

(i) Discipleship begins with a renunciation, and it is not intended that the act of renunciation should be left until later (Matt. 19:21; Mark 10:21; Luke 18: 22).

(j) Looking back is no more possible for the disciple than it is for someone who flees persecution (Luke 17:31, 32, cf. Gen. 19:17, 26), or for anyone who puts a hand to the plough and looks back (Luke 9:62; cf. 1 Kings 19:20, 21), or for the athlete whose focus is on the finishing tape ahead (Phil. 3:13, 14).

(k) Discipleship means, secondly, a sincere acknowledgement of the Lordship of Christ (Matt. 7:21-27; Luke 6:46; 13:26-27).

(1) Discipleship means, thirdly, a life of devotion to Christ – the relationship we have to Him has priority over every other relationship (Matt. 12:49,50; Mark 3:34,35; Luke 8:21).

(m) Devotion to Christ may bring reproach from people but it is something of tremendous value to Him (Matt. 26:10; Mark 14:6).

(n) Discipleship means, fourthly, the acceptance of the principle of dying to self (John 12:23-26).

(o) Our Lord Jesus Christ set a pattern for all disciples to follow: if we cling to our life we will lose it; but if we give it up for Him, we will find it, that is to say, save it and keep it for eternal life (Matt. 10:39; 16:25; Mark 8:35; Luke 9:24, 17:33; John 12:25).

(p) Only when this principle of dying to self is genuinely accepted can there be a true readiness for trials and persecution (Matt. 5:10-12; Mark 9:49; cf. 8:34-37).

(q) Only when disciples are willing to die daily to self will they be ready to serve others for Christ's sake without reservation or personal choice (Matt. 20:26-28; Mark 10:42-45).

(r) Discipleship means, fifthly, the discipline of instruction (Matt. 10:23-25; Luke 6:40).

(s) Discipleship means doing the will of the Father, and to this end the Word of God must be both listened to and obeyed (Matt. 12:48-50).

2. The proof of discipleship.

(a) The proof of which our Lord spoke most often is the proof of obedience (Matt. 7:21, 24-27; 12:50; Mark 3:35; Luke 6:46-49; 8:21; 11:28).

(b) It is by our obedience to Christ that we show our love for Him, so that disobedience is equal to an absence of love (John 14:21, 24).

(c) True obedience to Christ will frequently incur the world's hatred (John 15:18-25).

(d) The proof of discipleship is seen often, therefore, in the correspondence between the world's reaction to the ministry of Christ's disciples and the reaction our Lord Jesus Christ Himself received in the course of His own ministry as He obeyed the Father (John 15:20).

(e) Fruitfulness is picked out as a proof of discipleship (John 15:8) – there are different levels of fruitfulness (Matt. 13:8, 23; Mark

4:8, 20; Luke 8:8, 15), and it is not achieved all at once (Luke 8:14, 15).

(f) When disciples abide or remain in Christ by means of obedience, they become spiritually fruitful (John 15:5), so that fruitfulness becomes a legitimate test of any profession of discipleship (Matt. 12:33; Luke 6:43, 44).

(g) Chastisement – or bearing in mind the picture of fruit, pruning – is a necessary part of discipleship calculated to make us more fruitful (John 15:2).

(h) Love is a proof of discipleship (John 13:34, 35).

(i) Love for God is the substance of the first summary of the commandments, and love for others the substance of the second (Matt. 22:36-40; Mark 12:28,31; Luke 10:27).

(j) The love disciples exhibit is to go beyond the limits of ordinary human love (Matt. 5:46-48; Luke 6:32-35).

(k) An obvious awareness of privilege is another proof of discipleship, since we quickly learn that we did not choose Christ but that He chose us (John 15:16).

(l) Over all the work of disciples there stands the principle that having paid nothing for what we have received, we charge nothing for what we do (Matt. 10:8; Acts 3:6; 20:33-35; cf. Rom. 1:5).

(m) Humility is a further proof of discipleship (Mark 9:35; cf. Matt. 11:28-30, Phil. 2:5-11).

(n) Greatness in the sight of God involves humble service (Mark 9:35): it expresses itself in our willingness to take upon ourselves the function and attitude of a servant (Matt. 20:26-28; Mark 10:43-45; Luke 22:26, 27).

(o) Our Lord warned against the desire for status (Luke 14:11; cf. Mark, 10:15, 16).

(p) Like a young child, we should be unassuming and humble (Matt. 18:1-5).

(q) Disciples, wanting to walk in Christ's footsteps, willingly wash one another's feet (John 13:14, 15).

(r) A final proof of discipleship is faithfulness – those who stand firm to the end will be saved (Matt. 24:13).

(s) The parables of the talents and pounds (or silver minas) emphasise the need for faithful service during this present period of history, prior to the Lord's return (Matt. 25:14-30; Luke 19:12-27).

3.   The aims of discipleship.

(a)   A principal, all-comprehending aim, is Christlikeness of character (Matt. 10:24, 25; Luke 6:40), the character outlined in the Beatitudes (Matt. 5:3-12), and summed up in the fruit of the Spirit (Gal. 5:22, 23).

(b)   The aim of discipleship is to share in the work of the Lord Jesus whether in terms of what we are – for example, as salt (Matt. 5:13) and light (Matt. 5:14-16) – or in terms of what we do – for example, in evangelism (Luke 5:10), harvesting the spiritual harvest (Matt. 9:37, 38; John 4:35-38), preaching the kingdom of heaven (Matt. 10:5-15), serving others (John 13:1-17), and making disciples (Matt. 28:19, 20).

(c)   The aim of discipleship is to glorify the Father on earth by completing the work He gives us to do (Matt. 5:16; John 17:4).

(d)   The aim of discipleship is to express such unity as Christ's disciples that the world knows that the Father sent the Son into the world to show His love (John 10:16; 17:20-23).

(e)   In essence, the aim of discipleship is to bear witness to our Lord Jesus Christ (Luke 24:48; Acts 1:8), and to His pre-eminence in God's purposes, both in creation and redemption (Acts 3:20-22; Col.. 1:15-20).

4.   The benefits of discipleship.

(a)   First, a spiritual relationship to God through His Son Jesus Christ (Mark 3:32 -35) – eternal life is to know God the Father and Jesus Christ whom He sent (John 17:3).

(b)   Secondly, a personal attachment to Christ that shapes the whole of life (Mark 2:18-22, John 21:19, 22) – we are one with Him in His death, resurrection and ascension (Rom. 6:1-4; Eph. 2:6, 7).

(c)   Thirdly, a discovery of God's purposes for our life (Rom. 12:1, 2; 2 Cor. 5:9, 15).

(d)   Fourthly, a sharing of a wonderful fellowship (Mark 3:13-15; Luke 12:32; Acts 1:14; 2:42; 1 Pet. 5:9, 13).

(e)   Fifthly, a learning of the way to joy – the Beatitudes, for example, emphasise that disciples possess the secret of true happiness or joy (Matt. 5:3-12).

(f)   Joy is the result of discovering the kingdom of heaven (Matt. 13:44).

(g) Disciples' joy is not in what they have achieved, but in what God has done for them through His Son (Luke 10:20).

(h) Our Lord Jesus desires that His own joy should be in His disciples, and that their joy should be complete (John 15:11; 17:13).

(i) Sixthly, a freedom from the besetting worries of human existence: as we seek first God's kingdom and His righteousness, food, clothing, housing and everything else we need will be given us, without our needing to be anxious about them (Matt. 6:33-34).

(j) Seventhly, a joyful anticipation of heaven (John 14:1-3; 17:24), and the reward the Lord Jesus will give His faithful disciples (Matt. 16:27).

(k) As our Lord Jesus was not of this world, so too disciples are no longer of this world; as He was exalted because of His faithful obedience, so His faithful disciples will be exalted (2 Tim. 2:12) –the joy of disciples' spiritual inheritance cannot be measured (1 Pet. 1:4; cf. Ps. 16:11).

---

93. OBEDIENCE

Question: **What does the Bible teach concerning obedience?**

Answer: **Obedience is doing everything God commands, of which our Lord Jesus Christ is the perfect example. The Christian life begins with obedience and continues by means of it. It is the proof both of new birth and discipleship, and it constitutes the secret of the happiness the Christian enjoys, no matter how costly obedience may be.**

1. **The Bible defines obedience.**
(a) Obedience is doing everything God commands (Ex. 19:5; Deut. 5:9, 10; Josh. 22:2; Jer. 7:23).
(b) The Scriptures, God's Word, are to be the rule of our whole life (2 Tim. 3:16, 17).
(c) Obedience is our practical response to the Word of God (Matt. 13:23; Gal. 5:7; Jas. 1:22-25).

(d)   Christian obedience is our coming to Christ, hearing His words, and putting them into practice (Luke 6:47; John 8:51).

(e)   Obedience is closely associated with a sensitive conscience, that is constantly educated and informed by the Holy Spirit by means of the Scriptures, and is consistently obeyed (Acts 23:1; 24:16; 2 Cor. 1:12; 2 Tim. 1:3).

(f)   Obedience is synonymous with walking with God (Gen. 6:9) and loving God (1 John 5:2).

2.   Our Lord Jesus Christ is the perfect example of obedience.

(a)   Obedience was the foremost characteristic of His earthly life (Heb. 10:7).

(b)   He obeyed the Father's commands and remained in His love (John 15:10).

(c)   His perfect obedience in accepting even death (Phil. 2:8) made possible our acceptance with God, and our fellowship with Him, as we believe in the Lord Jesus Christ as the Son of God and Saviour (Rom. 5:14-19; 8:1).

(d)   His obedience to the Father should be the pattern of ours (John 15:10).

3.   Obedience has an important place both in the beginnings of the Christian life and in its continuance.

(a)   Under the new covenant obedience is God's gift to enable His people to enjoy His favour, rather than a necessary condition to be achieved before His favour may be enjoyed (Jer. 31:33, 34; 32:40).

(b)   The Christian life begins with obedience (John 6:29; Acts 26:19; 1 Pet. 1:22), having as its first object the pattern of teaching presented in the gospel (Rom. 6:17), summarised in the words, 'Repent and believe the gospel' (Mark 1:15; Acts 2:38).

(c)   Discipleship begins with an act of obedience (Matt. 9:9; Mark 2:14).

(d)   We are chosen, redeemed and sanctified with our obedience to Jesus Christ in view (1 Pet. 1:2).

(e)   It is as a result of our new relationship to God by new birth that we are called upon to obey Him (1 Pet. 1:14).

(f) Obedience is God's work in us, as a consequence of the new birth, for God works in us to will and to act according to His good purpose (Phil. 2:13, 14).

4. The priority of obedience.

(a) Obedience has from the beginning of creation been an indispensable obligation, since God has every right to command His creatures, and has made known His requirements (Gen. 2:15-17).

(b) The results of Adam's failure to obey indicate its priority: by his failure to obey the whole of humanity was involved in guilt, condemnation and death (Rom. 5:19; 1 Cor. 15:22).

(c) The old covenant required obedience as a condition of God's favour (Ex. 19:5; 1 Kings 3:14; 2 Kings 21:8. Neh. 1:5).

(d) Obedience sums up our whole duty to God (Deut. 10:12, 13; Eccl. 12:13) and is commanded (Deut. 13:4; Ps. 119:4).

(e) Obedience is more important than isolated acts of service to God, religious observances and externals (1 Sam. 15:22; 1 Cor. 7:19).

(f) Obedience is our principal means of pleasing God (1 John 3:21, 22).

(g) Where obedience to God clashes with obedience to human authorities, God is to be obeyed (Acts 5:29).

(h) Obedience is the condition of our remaining in our Lord Jesus Christ's love (John 15:10), and enjoying a personal relationship to Him (Matt. 12:50).

(i) Obedience is a prerequisite of unbroken fellowship with the Father and the Son (John 14:23, 24; 1 John 1:3, 7).

(j) Obedience is the means of our growing in holiness (Luke 1:6).

5. Practical implications of obedience.

(a) Obedience involves devoting ourselves to the study and observance of God's Law (Ezra 7:10).

(b) Obedience demands a change in the pattern of our life compared with what it was before our conversion (1 Pet. 1:14): obedience to God is the opposite of the service of sin (Rom. 6:17).

(c) Obedience includes loving God's children (1 John 5:2).

(d) Obedience requires holiness in all we do (1 Pet. 1:15, 16).

(e)   Obedience results in practising the humility our Lord Jesus exemplified (John 13:12-17; Phil. 2:5-8).

(f)   No matter how difficult or complicated a problem or a decision, the first course of action to be followed is that of obedience to God (Phil. 2:12, 13).

(g)   Obedience to God demands obedience within family relationships: submission to one another out of reverence for Christ (Eph. 5:21); the submission of a wife to her husband (Eph. 5:22); and the obedience of children to their parents (Eph. 6:1-3).

(h)   Obedience to God expresses itself in obedience within the fellowship of the local church, as we follow the direction of our spiritual teachers (Phil. 2:12), and as we obey them and submit to their authority (Heb. 13:17).

(i)   Obedience to God includes giving the obedience He commands to the governing authorities (Matt. 22:21; Rom. 13:1-7; 1 Pet. 3:13, 14; Tit. 3:1, 2).

6.   Characteristics of obedience.

(a)   Obedience recognises God's supreme authority to command (1 Sam. 3:10; Acts 9:5,6).

(b)   Obedience springs from a delight in the law of the Lord and meditation on it (Ps. 1:2; 119:104,105,129).

(c)   Obedience is diligent (Heb. 6:11) and persevering (Heb. 10:36).

(d)   Obedience is rendered even when apprehension concerning the results of it exist (Acts 9:10-19).

(e)   Obedience is uncompromising and wholehearted (Matt. 6:24; John 15:14).

(f)   Obedience, once practised, is taught and communicated to others (Matt. 5:19).

7.   The significance of obedience when found in the life of an individual.

(a)   Obedience is the proof of discipleship (John 10:27), and is never burdensome to the true believer (1 John 5:3).

(b)   Obedience results from spiritual birth (Eph. 2:10).

(c)   Obedience proves the reality of our knowledge of God (1 John 2:3).

(d) Obedience demonstrates our love for God (Dan. 9:4; John 14:15, 21, 23, 24; 2 John 6).

(e) Obedience indicates that we live in Christ and that He lives in us (1 John 2:6; 3:24).

(f) Obedience provides a measure of our fruitfulness as Christians (Matt. 13:23; Mark 4:20; Luke 8:15; John 15:10, 14, 16).

(g) Obedience marks us out as faithful (Rev. 12:17).

8. Obedience's incentives.

(a) Faith prompts and sustains obedience (Heb. 11:8), with right views of the Lord Jesus Christ constituting the secret of faith (Heb. 12:2).

(b) Meditation upon the value of our Lord's friendship encourages obedience (John 15:14).

(c) The consideration of God's goodness stimulates obedience (1 Sam. 12:24; Ps. 26:3; Rom. 12:1).

(d) The knowledge of the encouragements God gives serves to energise obedience: happiness (Luke 11:28; Jas. 1:25), joy (John 15:1-11), God's blessing (Mal. 3:10-12), confidence before God in prayer (1 John 3:21, 22), spiritual stability (Luke 6:46-49), everlasting life (John 8:51; Rev. 2:10) and a generous reward (John 12:26; Col. 3:23, 24).

---

94. CHRISTIAN WITNESS

Question: What is Christian witness?

Answer: Christian witness is the privilege and duty that arises from the experience of God's salvation in Jesus Christ. Commanded by God, and world-wide in its scope and intention, its purpose is to set forth God's saving acts in the death and resurrection of our Lord Jesus Christ, in accordance with the Scriptures, and in dependence upon the Holy Spirit.

1. Witness is both a privilege and a duty arising from the experience of God's salvation.

(a) Witness is the spontaneous and natural consequence of an experience of our Lord Jesus Christ's power (Mark 5:20; Luke 8:39; John 4:29).

(b) Those who love God's salvation delight to say 'The LORD be exalted' (Ps. 40:16).

(c) A sense of compulsion lies behind Christian witness - we cannot help speaking about what we believe and know about Jesus Christ (Acts 4:20; 2 Cor. 4:13).

(d) The Lord Jesus Christ's love compels us to witness (2 Cor. 5:14).

(e) Reconciled to God, through the atoning work of Christ, we find ourselves entrusted with the message of reconciliation (2 Cor. 5:18-20).

(f) Christian witness finds its impetus in the personal experience of salvation (Isa. 12:2-4; 2 Tim. 1:11, 12).

2. Witness is expected and commanded by God.

(a) All who know, believe and understand that the Lord is both God and Saviour are commissioned to be His witnesses (Isa. 43:10, 11).

(b) Testimony to the Lord Jesus Christ is to be given openly and unashamedly (Luke 12:8, 9; 2 Tim. 1:8).

(c) The Word of life is to be held out by all Christians (Phil. 2:16).

(d) Witness is to be given courageously and fearlessly (Phil. 1:14).

(e) This witness, however, is to be given with gentleness and with respect for the individuals to whom it is addressed (1 Pet. 3:15).

(f) At any time, as opportunity provides, we are to be ready to witness (1 Pet. 3:15); if we do not aim at witnessing at every proper opportunity, as commanded (Col. 4:5), we will probably not witness at all (Eccl. 11:3, 4).

(g) Our witness should be consistent and constant, for the success that may attend it can never be predicted (Eccl. 11:6; Heb. 10:23).

(h) Our witness should be plain and clear like a city on a hill (Matt. 5:14), and effective like salt (Matt. 5:13).

(i) Restraint should be removed from our lips when there is opportunity for witness (Ps. 40:9).

(j) To conceal our testimony to God's faithfulness and salvation is sinful (Ps. 40:10).

3. **Witness is to be world-wide in its scope and concern.**

(a) Witness should begin with our family and our immediate acquaintances (Mark 5:19; Acts 16:31).

(b) Ideally, corporate Christian witness should have an echoing and spreading effect throughout a whole neighbourhood and area (1 Thess. 1:8).

(c) The scope of Christian witness is to be the world (Isa. 12:2-4; Acts 1:8), and it is God's ordained means of spreading the gospel to all nations (Matt. 28:19, 20).

4. **Witness cannot be separated from the life and conduct of the individual Christian and the local church.**

(a) Witness of life and speech go together but the priority of witness of life must never be forgotten (Phil. 2:14-16; 1 Pet. 3:1, 2).

(b) Witness must be confirmed by the evidence of a forgiven and purified life (Ps. 26:6, 7; 51:1-19).

(c) The truth of Christian witness is demonstrated by the good effects it has upon people's lives (1 Cor. 1:6) in distinctive Christian character and conduct (Matt. 5:13).

(d) Good conduct, even in the face of provocation and opposition, constitutes essential Christian witness (1 Pet. 2:12).

(e) The witness of our life must support the witness of our lips (1 Thess. 1:6-8; 1 Pet. 3:1).

(f) The corporate life of God's people – especially in their display of Christian love – is fundamental to their witness (Phil.2:14-16; 1 Pet. 1:22; 2:9).

5. **Witness is, nevertheless, primarily by our words or speech.**

(a) Christian witness requires the witness of words (1 Pet. 3:15).

(b) With the great end of redemption as the confession 'Jesus Christ is Lord,' it is clearly our duty to bear testimony to this truth now (Phil. 2:11).

(c) Witness involves the confession of our mouth that 'Jesus is Lord' (Rom. 10:9), a confession we are to make before the world (Matt. 10:32; Luke 12:8).

(d) In giving witness we tell of the glory of God's kingdom and we speak of His might (Ps. 145:11), and how both are made known so wonderfully in Jesus Christ (Acts 8:12).

(e)   The witness of words cannot help but sometimes find expression in song (1 Chron. 16:8, 9; Ps. 9:11; 18:49; 40:3; Isa. 12:4, 5; Eph. 5:19).

6.   Witness requires the power of the Holy Spirit to be effective.

(a)   Power for witness is given by God (Acts 1:8).

(b)   Witness needs not only words, but also the power of the Holy Spirit to give those words deep conviction (1 Thess. 1:5).

(c)   Effective witness depends completely on the enduement and power of the Holy Spirit (Luke 24:48, 49; 1 Cor. 12:3).

7.   The central subject of witness is what God has achieved through the work of His Son, the Lord Jesus Christ.

(a)   Witness is the making known of God's deeds among the people (1 Chron. 16:8; Ps. 9:11; Isa. 12:4; Jer 51:10; 1 Pet. 2:9-10).

(b)   At its simplest, witness is proclaiming how much Jesus has done for sinners (Mark 5:19, 20; Luke 8:39).

(c)   It is the proclaiming of the good news of Jesus Christ (1 Cor. 1:6; 15:15; 1 John 1:1-4).

(d)   It focuses on the death of Christ, His resurrection from the dead, and the message of light and life which springs from these saving events (Acts 26:23; 1 Cor. 15:1-4).

(e)   Central to all that is stated is the message of Jesus Christ and His death upon the Cross (1 Cor. 2:2; Gal. 6:14).

8.   What God has achieved through the work of His Son, Jesus Christ, is described in the Bible as 'the Word of God.'

(a)   The good news of Christ is identical with the Word of the Lord that abides forever (1 Pet. 1:24, 25); the gospel of salvation through Christ is the Word of truth (Eph. 1:13).

(b)   All Scripture is inspired by God and is able to make men and women wise for salvation through faith in Jesus Christ (2 Tim. 3:15-17).

(c)   The principal theme of the whole of the Word of God is that Christ, the Messiah, had to suffer and then rise again on the third day, and that through what He accomplished repentance and forgiveness may be preached to people everywhere (Luke 24:45-48).

(d) This assurance explains the early Church's concern to preach the Word of God with boldness (Acts 4:29-31).

(e) Preaching the Word was the priority of the early Church (Acts 6:2-4), in that the whole evangelistic programme of the early Church is summed up in expressions relating to the preaching of the Word of God (Acts 13:5, 7, 44, 46, 48, 49; 14:25, 15:7; 15:35, 36; 16:6, 32; 17:11, 13; 18:11; 19:10).

(f) The progress of the early Church in witness is described in terms of the spread of the Word of God (Acts 6:7; 12:24; 19:20).

(g) Witness and evangelism go forward as the Word of the Lord spreads and is honoured (2 Thess. 3:1).

(h) To preach the Word of God is to preach Christ, for He is the Incarnate Word of God (John 1:1; Rev. 19:13) — by Him God has spoken to us (Heb. 1:2), and all the Scriptures speak of Him (Luke 24:27).

(i) It was for the Word of God and the testimony they maintained that the martyrs were – and are – killed (Rev. 6:9).

9. Christian witness, therefore, is according to the Word of God and from the Word of God.

(a) Christian witness is the declaration of God's attested truth (Luke 24:44-48; 1 Cor. 2:1).

(b) It begins with the great proclamation that God has spoken, first, in the Old Testament (Heb. 1:1), and, secondly, in a unique and final manner by His Son Jesus Christ (Heb. 1:2).

(c) Christian witness to the Lord Jesus Christ is according to the pattern of sound teaching given us in God's Word (2 Tim.1: 8, 13).

(d) Christian witness emphasises that everything that happened in the life of the Lord Jesus Christ was according to the Old Testament Scriptures (Acts 26:22, 23; 1 Cor. 15:3, 4; Heb. 1:1-14).

(e) Christian witness bears testimony to what the Scriptures declare concerning the death and resurrection of Jesus, and the repentance and forgiveness to be preached in consequence (Luke 24:46-48).

(f) Christian witness consists of teaching and preaching the good news of Christ (Acts 5:42; 15:35) so that the Word of God is presented in its fullness (Col.1:25). Once the truths of the good news have been taught (2 Cor. 5:17-19), the appeal by preaching can be made to people's wills, on Christ's behalf, 'Be reconciled to God' (2 Cor. 5:17-19).

(g) Christian witness, therefore, is not a matter of eloquence or superior human wisdom, but rather the simple declaration of God's Word (1 Cor. 2:1), so that the hearers may confirm the truth of what has been said by their private examination of the Scriptures (Acts 17:11).

(h) Christian witness may be summed up as bearing witness to the Word of God and the testimony of Jesus Christ (Rev. 1:2).

10. Christian witness requires recognition of the carefulness with which the Word of God should be handled and used.

(a) We must handle the Word of God honestly, always refusing to use deception, or to distort it (2 Cor. 4:2).

(b) As we witness by setting forth the truth plainly, we commend ourselves to people's consciences in the sight of God (2 Cor. 4:2).

(c) The Word of God is the Spirit's sword (Eph. 6:17).

(d) It is the instrument God uses to bring spiritual life to men and women (Jas. 1:18; 1 Pet. 1:23).

11. Our witness is inevitably and vitally linked with our knowledge of, and obedience to, God's Word.

(a) We are to be instructed in the Word (Acts 2:42; Gal. 6:6).

(b) By constant use of the Scriptures, we should be skilful in our use of them (Eph. 6:17; Heb. 5:13,14).

(c) We should do our best to present ourselves to God as those who are approved, workers who do not need to be ashamed, and who correctly handle the Word of truth (2 Tim. 2:15).

(d) We are to let the Word of God dwell in us richly (Col. 3:16).

(e) When the Word of God is at work in our lives we impart it to others (1 Thess. 2:13; cf. 1:7, 8).

12. **The Holy Spirit adds His power to the Word of God when it is faithfully proclaimed.**

(a) The secret of witnessing to the Word of God with boldness and effectiveness lies in being filled with the Spirit (Acts 4:31).

(b) Desiring above everything else to witness to our Lord Jesus Christ, the Holy Spirit delights to bear witness to the Word of God's grace in Christ when it is faithfully declared (John 15:26; Acts 14:3).

(c) As genuine witness to Christ is given, according to the Word of God, the Holy Spirit adds His own spiritual power to it (1 Cor. 2:4).

(d) When the Holy Spirit does this, faith is awakened by the message that comes through the Word of God (Rom. 10:17), and as the Word of God is received, those who receive it are brought to living faith in Christ and membership of His Church (Acts 2:41; cf. 2:22-36).

(e) The confidence of Christian witness, therefore, is not in plausible words or subtle argument but in the power of the Word of God and the Holy Spirit (1 Cor. 2:1-5).

---

95. PERSONAL EVANGELISM

Question: How are we to fulfil our responsibilities in personal evangelism?

Answer: We are to see ourselves as workers together with God, understanding what is His unique work in bringing a person to saving faith in Jesus Christ, and what is our part.

As we present the gospel to all to whom God gives us the opportunity, we are to look expectantly for those evidences of the Holy Spirit's activity in their lives that the Bible leads us to expect.

1. **Essential truths should influence all our thinking and acting when endeavouring to lead others to faith in our Lord Jesus Christ.**

(a) Such activity is pleasing to God: there is more joy in heaven over one sinner who repents than over ninety-nine who do not need to repent (Luke 15:7).

(b) It is by means of this activity that the Christian Church grows and multiplies (Acts 2:47; 6:7; 9:31; 12:24).

(c) The New Testament assumes that all Christians will be ready to engage in making the gospel known to others (Matt. 28:19; Phil. 2:14-16; Col.. 4:5; 1 Pet. 3:15).

(d) To endeavour to lead others to Christ is part of loving our neighbours as ourselves (Luke 10:27; 2 Cor. 5:14; John 1:40-42).

(e) We know that God does not want anyone to perish but everyone to come to repentance (2 Pet. 3:9).

(f) We are in conflict all the time with the devil as we endeavour to do this task (Eph. 6:12): he has blinded the minds of unbelievers, so that they cannot see the light of the gospel of the glory of Christ (2 Cor. 4:4). We do not despair, however, for we know that the work is God's (Acts 16:14; Gal. 1:14-16; 1 Pet. 1:1, 2).

(g) We are workers together with God in this task (1 Cor. 3:5-9; 2 Cor. 6:1).

(h) We work not for time but for eternity (Dan. 12:3).

(i) Our supreme motive is the glory of God (1 Cor 1:30, 31; 10:31).

2. **We must be clear as to what God alone can do, and what we, therefore, cannot do.**

(a) Conviction of sin is the work of God the Holy Spirit (John 16:8-11).

(b) God alone can give repentance to people - it is His gift (Acts 5:31; 11:18).

(c) Only God can draw men and women to His Son (John 6:44).

(d) God alone can reveal Jesus (Acts 9:3-5; 2 Cor. 4:6).

(e) It is God's unique prerogative to bring about new birth (John 1:12, 13; 3:3, 5).

3. **We must be clear as to what God requires of us by way of preparation for this work.**

(a)   We need an awareness of our own dependence upon the Lord Jesus for salvation (Gal. 2:20; 1 Tim. 1:15).

(b)   We must know the Scriptures.
   (i)   They alone equip us effectively (2 Tim. 3:16, 17).
   (ii)   Only the Scriptures contain the truth people need in order to be saved (2 Tim. 3:15).
   (iii) The Scriptures bring about conviction of sin (Acts 2:37).
   (iv)   By the Spirit's power, the Scriptures bring about new birth, regeneration (1 Pet. 1:23).
   (v)   The Scriptures are the means the Spirit uses to give saving faith (Rom. 10:17).
   (vi)   To help people by means of the Scriptures requires diligent study and growth in understanding on our part (2 Tim. 2:15).

(c)   We need an understanding of the desperately urgent plight of people without Christ (Matt. 9:36).
   (i)   They are lost (Luke 19:10).
   (ii)   Their need should touch our emotions (Acts 20:31).

(d)   We must be in earnest when we engage in this work.
   (i)   We should know great sorrow and unceasing anguish in our hearts for people without Christ (Rom. 9:1, 2).
   (ii)   We should long in our hearts for the salvation of others (Rom. 10:1).

(e)   The whole of our life needs to be open before God, and cleansing should be sought for all known sin (Ps. 51:10-13; 2 Tim. 2:20, 21).

(f)   We must be filled with the Holy Spirit (Acts 6:5; Eph. 5:18; cf. Acts 8:12, 29, 39; 1 Cor . 2:4).

4. **We must be clear as to what God requires of us by way of co-operation in this work.**

(a)   Although the work of conversion is essentially God the Holy Spirit's work, He calls us to work with Him in achieving it (Acts 26:17, 18).

(b)   God has given us all that is necessary for performing the task: the authority of Jesus, His commission to preach, the message of salvation (symbolised in baptism), the commandments of Jesus and His presence with us by the Spirit (Matt. 28:18-20).

(c) Our responsibility is to make known the Word of God (Acts 16:14; Rom. 10:14-17).

(d) We should endeavour to make it known to all without being influenced by any kind of prejudice (Gal. 6:10; cf. Luke 14:21-23; 1 Cor. 1:26-29).

(e) We should urge people to seek God (Isa. 55:6, 7; Luke 13:23-25), to repent (Matt. 4:17; Acts 17:30), to turn from their sins (Matt. 18:3), and to believe on the Lord Jesus Christ (Acts 16:31).

(f) In doing these things we must be willing to show people real and genuine friendship, that will often be costly in time, energy and much more besides (Luke 10:29, 33-35; 2 Tim. 2:10).

(g) We are to be ready to do this work at any time and anywhere (2 Tim. 4:2; 1 Pet. 3:15).

   (i) This work begins where we are and extends to wherever God may call us (Acts 1:8).

   (ii) Whether in our homes (Acts 18:26), or in public places (John 4:7-26; Acts 17:17), on board ship (Acts 27:21-25) in prison (Acts 16:30, 31; Phil. 1:12, 13; 4:22), in the open air (Acts 16:13, 14) or from house to house (Acts 20:20), we are to be ready to make the Lord Jesus Christ known.

(h) We co-operate with God by means of prayer.

   (i) James tells us that we do not have because we do not ask God (Jas. 4:2).

   (ii) The reality of our concern will be seen in our prayers for the salvation of others (Rom. 10:1).

   (iii) We may ask God to do the things that He alone can do (Acts 4:29-31).

5.   We need to be clear as to the essential facts of the gospel that must be taught and explained before any response should be anticipated.

(A)   The gospel that has to be understood

(a) The appointed time, concerning which the prophets in the Old Testament had spoken and to which the people of God had looked forward, has come. Through Christ God has visited and redeemed His people (Acts 2:16-21).

(b) This act of God, intervening in human history, is to be seen in the life of Jesus Christ, the Messiah, sent by God, rejected, put to death by men, and raised up by God on the third day (Acts 2:32, 36).

(c) By His death and resurrection Jesus Christ has conquered sin and death and opened the kingdom of heaven to all believers. In no one else is salvation to be found (Acts 4:12).

(d) Proofs of God's present power in the world are to be found in the resurrection of our Lord Jesus Christ and the evidence of the Holy Spirit's working in the Church (Acts 4:33; Rom. 1:4; Eph. 1:19, 20).

(e) This is but the beginning of God's kingdom. The Lord Jesus Christ will come again as Judge, and God's kingdom will be finally established (Acts 3:20, 21; 17:30, 31; 2 Thess. 1:6-10).

(f) Therefore all people everywhere should repent and be baptised in the name of Jesus the Messiah for the forgiveness of their sins, and thus receive the gift of the Holy Spirit (Acts 2:38).

(B) Fundamental to a person's understanding of the gospel is appreciation, therefore, of at least the following truths:

(a) Christ's coming and death were by God's set purpose and foreknowledge and were no accident (Acts 2:23; 1 Pet. 1:20).

(b) Jesus is the Christ, the Son of God (John 20:31; Acts 9:20).

(c) Christ's purpose in coming into the world and in dying upon the cross was to save sinners (Gal. 2:20; 1 Tim. 1:15).

(d) Christ's resurrection was God the Father's declaration of Christ as His Son and evidence of His satisfaction with His work (Rom. 1:4).

(e) To enter into the benefits of Christ's work – to know forgiveness, the gift of God's Spirit and a place in His kingdom – repentance and open confession of Christ are required (Acts 2:38).

(f) Christians recognise their personal sinfulness (Rom. 7:24; 1 Tim. 1:15).

(g) Christians know their personal indebtedness to Christ in that He gave His life a ransom for them (Mark 10:45; Gal. 2:20; 1 Pet. 2:24).

(C)   **The benefits promised by the gospel.**

(a)   Reconciliation with God (2 Cor. 5:18-21).

(b)   Justification (1 Cor. 1:30; 6:11).

(c)   Deliverance from condemnation (John 3:18; Rom. 8:1; 1 Cor. 11:32).

(d)   Belonging to the people of God (Acts 2:41, 47; 1 Cor. 1:2; 6:1, 2; 16:1, 15; 1 Pet. 2:4-10).

(e)   Membership of the kingdom of God (1 Cor. 6:9-11; Col. 1:13).

(f)   The gift of the Holy Spirit (Acts 2:38; 1 Cor. 2:12; 6:19).

(g)   Eternal life (John 3:16; 11:25, 26).

(h)   The resurrection of the body (1 Cor. 6:14; 15:53, 57).

6.   **We need to adhere to the principles that are always to govern our presentation of the gospel.**

(a)   We are to act towards people in the light of what the Bible says about the unconverted and unregenerate.

   (i)   They are dead in their transgressions and sins (Eph. 2:1).

   (ii)   Their minds are blinded by Satan (2 Cor. 4:4).

   (iii) They are lost (Luke 19:10).

   (iv)   They are slaves of sin (John 8:34).

(b)   We are always to think of the other person's good rather than of our own (1 Cor. 10:32, 33).

(c)   We are to be direct and straightforward in our presentation of the gospel and its demands, never allowing our presentation of the truth to be influenced by people's reactions (2 Cor. 4:2).

(d)   We are to be direct and forthright in speaking of sin (Mark 7:20-23; Acts 24:25).

(e)   We are to aim at speaking clearly to people, i.e. in terms that they can understand (Col. 4:4).

(f)   Graciousness, gentleness and respect are to characterise our words (Col. 4:6; 1 Pet. 3:15).

(g)   Love, in all its aspects, is to be dominant in our approach (1 Cor. 13).

(h)   We are to deal with people from the Scriptures (Acts 8:30-35; 2 Tim. 3:15), our confidence being not in our skill of presentation but in the power of God's truth (1 Cor. 2:1-5), knowing that the message of the Cross will be the power of God to those who are to be saved (1 Cor. 1:18).

(i)   We are to act in the assurance that if people really seek God, they will find Him (Matt. 7:7,8; Acts 10:1-8, 30-33, 44-48).

(j)   We are not to hesitate to give our personal testimony (Acts 22:1-16; 26:12-23; 1 Tim. 1:15; 1 Pet. 3:15).

(k)   We are to depend all the time upon God the Holy Spirit.

    (i)   We need to be sensitive to His promptings (Acts 16:6-8), and there may be occasions when He urges us to be very direct in our approach (Acts 8:30).

    (ii) The work we do is valuable only as it is done with a demonstration of the Spirit's power (1 Cor. 2:4).

    (iii) If the Holy Spirit is at work, we know that He will complete His work (Phil. 1:6).

7.   There are certain things we are to look for in dealing with people whom we would lead to the Lord Jesus Christ.

(a)   Conviction of sin (Acts 2:37).

(b)   An awareness of God's holiness (Isa. 6:5; Luke 5:8).

(c)   The deflation of pride (Jas. 4:6).

(d)   A submission to what God says (Jas. 4:7).

(e)   A resistance to those considerations and obstacles that would turn aside a person from having dealings with God (Jas. 4:7).

(f)   Readiness to use the means God has given us of drawing close to Him (Jas. 4:8).

(g)   Eagerness to hear the Word of God (Acts 16:14).

(h)   Prayer (Acts 9:11; 10:2; Jas. 4:8).

(i)   Changing attitudes, habits and actions (Jas. 4:8).

(j)   Sorrow for sin (Jas. 4:9).

(k)   A humility before God (Jas. 4:10).

(l)   When these things are present we may be sure that God is at work in people's lives and we may encourage them to call upon the name of the Lord Jesus for salvation (Rom. 10:13), knowing that He will lift them up (Jas. 4:10)

---

96. THE MISSIONARY TASK AND MISSIONARY MOTIVES

Question: What is the missionary task, and what are the considerations and motives that demand our involvement in missionary enterprise?

Answer: The missionary task is to make disciples of all nations. The Bible presents many motives for supporting and engaging in missionary work, prominent among which are concern for God's glory, obedience to our Lord's commission, the desperate need of men and women without Christ, the adequacy and purpose of the atonement, and the coming again of our Lord Jesus Christ.

The Missionary Task

1. **Our Saviour's commission to us is to make disciples of all nations** (Matt. 28:18-20).
   (a) As the ministry of reconciliation is exercised (2 Cor. 5:18-20), and the fragrance of the knowledge of Christ spread everywhere (2 Cor. 2:14), men and women will receive the gospel, take their stand upon it, hold it fast, and be saved by it (1 Cor. 15:1-11); they are then to be made disciples (Matt. 28:19).
   (b) The most common description of Christians in the Acts of the Apostles is 'disciples' (Acts 6:2, 7).
   (c) The task of missions is to make disciples (Acts 14:21), that is to say, to secure the obedience of men and women in word and deed to Christ (Acts 6:7; Rom. 15:18; cf. Acts 8:36-39; 9:18).

2. **The whole world, therefore, is our concern.**
   (a) Starting from home to the ends of the earth is our sphere of operation (Acts 1:8).
   (b) The scope of our endeavours is to take in 'all who are far off' (Acts 2:39).
   (c) The world is to be thought of as a plentiful harvest field (Luke 10:2).

(d)   Pentecost was an illustration of the scope of missions: all – no matter what nationality - heard the good news of Christ in their own language (Acts 2:6-11).

(e)   Our commission is to preach the gospel to every creature, no matter what human barriers and prejudices have to be overcome in the process (Acts 10:1-48, and especially 10:28, 34).

(f)   The obligation that is upon us is to preach the gospel to all (Rom. 1:14, 15; Luke 10:5, 6).

3.   Priorities have to be determined and recognised in the furtherance of the missionary task.

(a)   Our Lord's primary attention, for example, was directed towards the Jews (Matt. 10:5, 6), although this in no way implied that the gospel was not to go to the Gentiles: it was merely a question of priorities in the early days.

(b)   Those among the Jews who had not heard His message were a priority to our Lord Jesus Christ (Mark 1:37,38; Luke 4:42-44).

(c)   The aim of missions must always be to preach the gospel where the name of Christ is as yet unknown (Rom. 15:20).

4.   The conversion of whole families is a priority in missionary work.

(a)   The household is to be the objective (Luke 10:5): if we aim only at the children, we may delay the founding of the church for a generation.

(b)   The conversion of whole households is to be looked for and expected (Acts 10:24, 33, 44; 16:15, 31-34; 18:8).

(c)   The first church in a place may well be a house-church (Acts 16:14, 15; Philem. 2).

Missionary Motives

5.   The glory of God.

(a)   Our desire is to be that God should be praised in all things (1 Pet. 4:11).

(b)   Our concern for God's glory should be a consuming passion (John 2:17).

(c)   Our chief purpose in life is to glorify God (1 Cor. 10:31).

(d)   The great end of the plan of redemption is the glory of the Father (Eph. 1:6, 14; Phil. 2:11).

(e)   God is honoured when people are caused to praise and thank Him (Ps. 50:23)– for no reason do they praise Him more than for His salvation (Luke 2:10-14, 20).

(f)   God is glorified when redeemed men and women bring glory to Him on account of His mercy to them (Rom. 15:8-12).

(g)   Our Lord Jesus brought glory to the Father on earth, by completing the work the Father gave Him to do (John 17:4) – we should have the same objective.

6.   The command of our Lord Jesus Christ.

(a)   We are to go into the entire world and preach the gospel to all creation (Mark 16:15).

(b)   We are to go and make disciples of all nations (Matt. 28:19).

(c)   This was the final command of our Lord Jesus – a command He gave with impressive authority (Matt. 28:18-20).

7.   The trust that the gospel is in itself.

(a)   The gospel is a trust (1 Thess. 2:4).

(b)   Its value cannot be overestimated (Gal. 1:8, 9).

(c)   It is a ground of universal joy, and it demands to be proclaimed (Luke 2:10, 11, 17, 18).

(d)   The message of God's love is so great that it must not be kept secret (John 3:16; 2 Cor. 5:14).

8.   The experience we ourselves have of salvation.

(a)   Knowing the joy of God's salvation, we feel compelled to teach transgressors God's ways, and to encourage sinners to return to the Lord (Ps. 51:12, 13).

(b)   Our experience of God's salvation puts us under an obligation to declare it to others (Rom. 1:14-16).

9.   The constraint of Christ's love.

(a)   Knowing Christ's love for us, we find ourselves motivated by His love for others to reach them with the gospel (2 Cor. 5:14, 15).

10.   The need of those who are without Christ.

(a)   Men and women without Christ are without hope and without God in the world (Eph. 2:12).

(b)   They do not know God, and their lives are governed by their passions (1 Thess. 4:5).

(c)   Their main concerns are what to eat, drink and wear, not knowing the love of a heavenly Father (Matt. 6:31, 32; Luke 12:29, 30).

(d)   They are often influenced and led astray to mute idols (1 Cor. 12:2).

(e)   The sorrows of those without Christ increase because of the false gods they follow (Ps. 16:4).

(f)   They are spiritually blind and imprisoned (Isa. 42:6, 7).

(g)   Compassion for people's harassed souls is a powerful missionary motive (Matt. 9:36).

(h)   It is part and parcel of loving our neighbours as ourselves (Luke 10:27).

11.   The adequacy of the atonement.

(a)   Christ is the atoning sacrifice for our sins, and not for ours only but also for the sins of the whole world (1 John 2:2).

(b)   The death of Christ was not for the Jewish nation only, but for the gathering together of all the children of God scattered throughout the world (John 11:51, 52).

(c)   By His blood Christ ransomed people for God from every tribe, tongue, people and nation, and He has made them to be a kingdom and priests to serve God (Rev. 5:9, 10).

12.   The revealed and declared purposes of God concerning the Church.

(a)   God's purpose from the beginning has been to bless all the nations of the earth through the obedience of Abraham (Gen. 22:17, 18).

(b)   His purpose is that all nations will flow to Zion, the new Jerusalem (Isa. 2:2).

(c)   Throughout the Scriptures God has given assurance of His purpose to call the nations of the world to faith in Himself (Mal. 1:11).

(d) His purpose is to take out of all nations a people for His name (Amos 9:11, 12; Jer. 12:14-16, Isa. 45:22; Acts 15:14-18).

(e) The Father has promised the nations as His Son's inheritance (Ps. 2:8).

(f) The knowledge that God is going to call men and women to Himself is a powerful missionary motive (Acts 2:38, 39; 18:9, 10).

13. The desire to please Christ, and to receive His commendation.

(a) It is right for us to want the Lord Jesus Christ to be satisfied as He sees the fruit of all that His sufferings have accomplished (Isa. 53:11).

(b) In communicating the gospel our desire is to please God who tests our hearts (1 Thess. 2:4).

(c) The parables of the pounds (or silver minas) and the talents encourage us to work with an eye to our Master's commendation, as we fulfil the great task He has assigned us (Luke 19:11-27; Matt. 25:14-30; cf. 2 Cor. 10:18).

(d) Knowing what it means to fear the Lord, and to want to please Him, we try to persuade others (2 Cor. 5:11).

14. The judgment that is to come.

(a) The truth that Christians must stand before the judgment seat of Christ is not to promote fear but the desire to please Him now, so that we may be pleasing to Him then (2 Cor. 5:9, 10).

(b) The certainty of judgment is a great incentive to urgent preaching (2 Tim. 4:1, 2).

(c) The judgment will be a time of misery for those who have rejected the Lord Jesus Christ (2 Thess. 1:8, 9; Rev. 1:7).

(d) Those who have disobeyed the truth and obeyed wickedness will experience God's wrath and eternal punishment (Rom. 2:8; Jude 14, 15; Rev. 20:15).

15. The return of the Lord Jesus Christ.

(a) The return of the Lord Jesus Christ is a missionary motive because the gospel is to be preached to all nations and throughout the whole world as a testimony to all nations, before the end (Mark 13:10; Matt. 24:14).

---

97. MISSIONARY WORK

Question: **What governing concept should we have of missionary work?**

Answer: **Missionary work is essentially God's work, by which our Lord Jesus Christ's ministry and work are continued, and in which He requires our active co-operation and hard work.**

1. Missionary work is the Lord's work.

(a) God assigns the workers to their tasks (1 Cor. 3:5).

(b) God gives the spiritual increase (1 Cor. 3:7).

(c) God makes the appeal through His ambassadors (2 Cor 5:20).

(d) God shines into the hearts of men and women with the light of the gospel (2 Cor 4:6).

(e) God calls men and women to faith in His Son (Acts 2:39).

(f) God opens the hearts of individuals so that they respond to the message of the gospel (Acts 16:14).

(g) God gives to men and women the gift and privilege of turning from sin and receiving eternal life (Acts 11:18).

(h) God opens the door of faith to people (Acts 14:27; cf. 15:4, 12).

(i) God adds day by day to the Church those who are being saved (Acts 2:47).

(j) The task of missions is to work together with God (2 Cor. 6:1).

2. Missionary work is the continuation of the Lord Jesus Christ's ministry and work.

(a) The Church is to continue what the Lord Jesus began to do and teach (Luke 10:16; Acts 1:1-3).

(b) While the whole emphasis is to be upon teaching and preaching, a concern for the whole person is to be shown by missions (Luke 10:8, 9).

(c) Concern for the whole person means that there is a place for the healing ministry in missions, but such a ministry must be clearly given in the name of Jesus Christ (Acts 4:9, 10).

3. **The example and principles established by our Lord Jesus should be followed carefully.**

(a) Fundamental principles were laid down in the sending out of the twelve (Mark 6:8-13; Matt. 10:1, 5-14; Luke 9:1-6), as too in the sending out of the seventy (Luke 10:1-12).

(b) There are occasions in the Acts of the Apostles where we can see Paul following the pattern set by our Lord Jesus Christ (Acts 13:51; 18:6, 7).

4. **Missionaries are God-appointed.**

(a) The Lord appoints His messengers (Luke 10:1).

(b) The Lord assigns the tasks to which they are called (1 Cor. 3:5).

(c) The Lord chooses His instruments for His special tasks (Acts 9:15, 16).

(d) The Lord indicates to churches the individuals to be set apart for the work to which He has called them (Acts 13:2).

5. **God gives specific commissions to individuals to fulfil.**

(a) Peter was entrusted, for example, with the gospel to the Jews, and Paul with the gospel to the Gentiles (Gal. 2:7-9; Acts 22:17-21).

(b) Some may be assigned to planting, others to watering; some to laying foundations, others to building upon foundations already laid (1 Cor. 3:5-10).

6. **Missionary work is a matter of partnership.**

(a) First, it is to be undertaken in partnership with God (1 Cor. 3:7, 9; 2 Cor. 6:1).

(b) Secondly, it is to be undertaken in partnership with other missionaries, and other missions (Luke 10:1; Acts 20:4; Rom. 16:1-4; 1 Cor. 3:7-10; Gal. 2:9).

(c) Thirdly, it is to be undertaken in partnership with the local church or churches (Phil. 1:5).

    (i) The church is to be regarded as the sending or directing agency under the guidance of the Holy Spirit (Acts 13:2-4);

    (ii) Missionaries are to be committed to the grace of God by the churches that confirm their call (Acts 14:26);

(iii) The whole church is to be behind the missionary enterprise of its members (Acts 15:22, 25), and involved and interested in all that God does with and through them (Acts 14:27);

(iv) Missionaries are to work in close partnership with the church or churches that, under God's direction, send them forth (Acts 14:26);

(v) Missionaries have a responsibility to report to the churches what God has done with them and through them (Acts 15:4,12; cf. Acts 14:27).

7. Different contributions are necessary in missionary endeavour.

(a) There are different kinds of gifts, service and working, but it is the same God who is the source of them all (1 Cor. 12:4-6).

(b) Some missionary work is foundation laying, while other is building upon a foundation already laid (1 Cor. 3:10).

(c) Some missionary work is planting, while other work is watering what another has planted (1 Cor. 3:8).

8. Missionary work requires hard work and sometimes suffering.

(a) A harvest field requires workers (Luke 10:2).

(b) 'Work' and 'labour' are words frequently used by Paul to describe missionary enterprise (2 Cor. 11:23; Phil. 1:22; Phil. 2:30; cf. Acts 15:38).

(c) Missionary work involves identification and accommodation to other people and their ways (Luke 10:8; 1 Cor. 9:19-23).

(d) Missionary work means sacrifice, hardship and suffering (2 Cor. 4:6-18; 6:3-10; 11:23-29; cf. Acts 9:16).

(e) Missionary work often meets with great opposition, sometimes because it conflicts with vested interests - the gospel is to be proclaimed nevertheless (Acts 16:19-24; 1 Thess. 2:2).

(f) Opposition is no reason for not fulfilling the missionary task – it is to be anticipated (Luke 10:3).

(g) We should be willing to endure anything for the sake of winning the elect (2 Tim. 2:10).

98. MISSIONARY STRATEGY

Question: What are the first principles of missionary strategy?

Answer: The first principles of missionary strategy are God's wisdom in choosing to save people by the preaching of His Son's gospel, and the priority, therefore, of the teaching and preaching of God's Word for the birth and establishing of witnessing churches.

1. **God's wisdom in choosing to save people by the preaching of His Son's gospel.**

(a) While to us who are being saved the message of the cross is the power of God, to those who are perishing the preaching of the cross is foolishness (1 Cor. 1:18).

(b) It pleases God through the foolishness - in the world's eyes - of what is preached in the gospel, to save those who believe (1 Cor. 1:21).

(c) Human ways of thinking may be quite different or contrary to God's strategy (1 Cor. 1:26-31).

(d) Missionary work is carried on, not according to worldly, material considerations but according to eternal values (2 Cor. 4:16-18).

2. **The concept of progress that should be uppermost is the growth and multiplication of the Word of God.**

(a) The main task of missions is to proclaim the Word (Acts 17:10-13), to deliver the essential truths (1 Cor. 15:3, 4), so that, hearing the preaching of the good news of Christ, men and women may come to faith (Rom. 10:14-17).

(b) Missionary progress is to be thought of in terms of the growth and increase of the Word of God (Acts 6:7; 12:24; 19:10, 20).

(c) In asking for prayer for himself and his fellow-missionaries, Paul significantly urged his friends, 'Pray for us that the message of the Lord may spread rapidly and be honoured, just as it was with you' (2 Thess. 3:1).

3. **Missionary endeavour must concentrate on teaching the Word of God.**

(a) Our task is to teach disciples all that the Lord Jesus has commanded them to be and do (Matt. 28:19, 20).

(b) Fulfilling the task of teaching disciples all that the Lord Jesus Christ requires of them (Matt. 28:19, 20), according to God's word, involves, of necessity, providing disciples with the Scriptures in their own tongue.

(c) The emphasis of the apostles was upon teaching:

 (i) The Jewish authorities directed their opposition at the apostles' speaking and teaching in the name of Jesus (Acts 4:18);

 (ii) Miraculously released from prison, Peter and John were found in the temple courts teaching the people once more (Acts 5:25);

 (iii) The apostles taught in Jesus' name so effectively that the hostile authorities said that they had filled Jerusalem with their teaching (Acts 5:28);

 (iv) Every day in the temple and at home the apostles did not stop teaching and proclaiming the good news that Jesus is the Christ (Acts 5:42);

 (v) Following the Council at Jerusalem, Paul and Barnabas returned to Antioch and remained there, 'where they and many others taught and preached the Word of the Lord' (Acts 15:35);

 (vi) Having received the assurance from the Lord that He had many people in Corinth whom He was going to call, Paul continued there for eighteen months, 'teaching them the Word of God' (Acts 18:11);

 (vii) At the end of the Acts of the Apostles we find Paul confined to his lodgings, but he 'preached the kingdom of God and taught about the Lord Jesus Christ' (Acts 28:31).

(d) A right balance is clearly necessary between teaching and preaching (Acts 8:5, 25, 35, 40; 15:35; 28:31).

(e) The apostolic pattern was to entrust Christian teaching to reliable people who, in turn, would be qualified to teach others (2 Tim. 2:2).

4.   Witness should be established in key centres.

(a)   In the Mediterranean, Paul operated from Antioch, the third city of the Roman Empire (Acts 11:25-30; 12:25; 13:1-3; 14:24-28).

(b)   Paul spent eighteen months in his second missionary journey in Corinth, which was one of the largest commercial centres of the Roman Empire (Acts 18:1-18).

(c)   He had a long stay in Ephesus, the capital of the province of Asia and the centre of trade for Asia Minor (Acts 19:1-41).

(d)   Missionary work is clearly to take in the villages and the rural areas together with the cities and towns (Mark 1:35-39; Luke 10:1; Acts 8:5, 25, 40).

(e)   Key cities and centres, however, are the obvious starting point in any new area: when, for example, the gospel came to Europe, the first preaching point was 'Philippi, a Roman colony and the leading city of that district of Macedonia' (Acts 16:12).

5.   A simple course of strategy should be followed.

(a)   Work should begin with those who are most disposed to listen, with the intention of working out into the community from such beginnings:

    (i)   Thus, in a Jewish situation, the apostles preached first of all in the temple courts (Acts 5:20, 25), and Paul's first approach, where there were any Jews in the community, was to endeavour to preach the gospel in the synagogues (Acts 9:20; 13:5; 17:1, 2, 10, 17; 18:4, 5).

    (ii)   Where there was no synagogue, Paul's first approach was to preach to any Gentiles who sought to follow the Jewish religion, and any who were at all religious, and thus accustomed to thinking of God and His claims (Acts 16:13; 17:22-34).

(b)   A clear order of priorities, so far as spheres of witness in a community were concerned, seems to have been followed:

    (i)   First, religious meeting places were a prime approach, and these were usually Jewish synagogues in the early years of gospel preaching (Acts 18:4, 5; 19:8);

    (ii)   Secondly, meeting halls were used when religious meeting places were not available (Acts 19:9);

(iii)   Thirdly, public places, such as market-places, where people congregated, were utilised where the opportunity presented itself (Acts 17:17);

(iv)   At the same time, and sometimes as an only possible means, the homes of believers and interested unbelievers were used (Acts 5:42; 18:7; 20:20).

6.   Missionary work combines church planting with disciple-making.

(a)   As men and women are brought to faith and discipleship, they are to be brought together regularly for instruction in God's Word, fellowship and the breaking of bread (Acts 2:42), and for common action, where necessary (Acts 6:2).

(b)   Believers are to be taught to gather together on the Lord's day for the breaking of bread, and the ministry of the Word (Acts 20:7-12).

(c)   As believers are brought together in fellowship, they are to be encouraged to realise how much they belong to one another in Christ (Acts 9:2, 19, 26) and they are to be taught to love Christians everywhere (Acts 9:17; 1 John 3:17-19).

(d)   Believers are to be taught the priority of prayer and the ministry of the Word (Acts 6:4).

(e)   Believers are to be taught concerning the qualities and character they are to look for in the people they appoint to serve as elders and deacons (Acts 6:1-6; 1 Tim. 3:1-13; Tit. 1:5-9).

7.   The key to world-evangelisation is witnessing churches.

(a)   Believers are to be taught that whatever circumstances affect their lives, and wherever they may have to go, they are to preach the Word (Acts 8:4).

(b)   Once established, a church is to become a sending-church: see, for example, the church at Antioch (Acts 11:19-30; 13:1-3; 14:26-28).

(c)   The testimony of lip and the transformation of life of those who have newly experienced God's delivering power are two of the most powerful means of drawing attention to the gospel and of bringing people to faith (Acts 3:9-16; 4:4; 9:20-22).

(d)   Young churches are to be taught to shine like stars in their communities, by the quality of their corporate life, thus enabling them to hold out the word of life effectively (Phil. 2:15, 16).

(e)   The transformation of lives through the gospel is a most powerful means of spreading its message through the whole of an area, and beyond (1 Thess. 1:7-10).

8.   Spiritual leaders are to be looked for and encouraged within the newly emerging churches.

(a)   It is to be expected that the Holy Spirit will give spiritual gifts of leadership to young churches as He does to churches that have been longer established (Acts 13:1-4).

(b)   The lack of education people may have and their ordinariness must not influence our assessment of what the Holy Spirit can do through them - for example, Peter and John (Acts 4:13).

(c)   It is to be expected that the Holy Spirit will raise up in the young churches men and women of equal spiritual gifts to those He used to bring the gospel to them (Acts 13:1-4; 15:35).

(d)   The appointing authority for spiritual leaders - or better, the recognising body, for it is the Holy Spirit who raises up spiritual leaders - is the church, not the missionaries (2 Cor. 8:19, 23).

9.   Missionary advance must go hand in hand with church-consolidation.

(a)   Sustained periods of teaching and preaching are to be the pattern of missionary work (Acts 18:11; 19:8-10).

(b)   The aim of missions is to proclaim the gospel fully (Rom. 15:19), to declare to new converts all that will be helpful to them (Acts 20:20), the whole will of God (Acts 20:27). This means sharing with them the moral demands of the gospel (1 Thess. 4:1-8), and warning and preparing them for the hardships that may well be before them as a consequence of their faith in the Lord Jesus Christ and their obedience to Him (Acts 14:22).

(c)   The work of missions is to build up spiritual infants in Christ to make them spiritually mature (1 Cor. 3:1-3; Col. 1:28,29).

(d)   The strengthening of young churches, therefore, is as necessary as starting work in new areas, and at times it may have a greater priority (Acts 14:21-23; 18:18-23).

(e)   Believers are to be firmly established in the faith, and they are not to be left in an untaught state (Acts 8:14-17); no effort is to be spared to this end (1 Thess. 3:1-3, 10).

(f)   The task of missions is to see newly-founded churches shepherded and directed in their affairs by elders from among their own number (Acts 14:23), and such spiritual leaders profit from being called together and exhorted regarding their duties and warned of the dangers to which they may be prone (Acts 20:17-35).

(g)   Young churches need to be visited for the purpose of their encouragement (Acts 15:36; 20:2): they need to be reminded of truths they already know (Rom. 15:15), and guided on important issues where more experienced Christians and churches have discerned God's will (Acts 16:4, 5).

10.   The proper relationship of missionaries to new believers must be appreciated.

(a)   The relationship of missionaries to converts must be that of fellow-believers, brothers and sisters in God's family (Acts 15:36).

(b)   Missionaries are to be in partnership with the Christians they see established as a fruit of their labours (Acts 13:1-3; cf. 2 Cor. 8:23; Philem. 17).

(c)   Missionaries are directed by the Spirit through the united conviction of the local church – whether the sending church or the receiving church (Acts 13:1-4).

(d)   Missionaries should be subject to the teaching, ministry and discipline of the local church, even if it is a young church (Acts 13:1-4).

(e)   Missionaries should teach converts, by example, to live according to the Scriptures (1 Cor. 4:6).

(f)   Missionaries should reproduce themselves in the people among whom they serve, so that they themselves can move on, knowing that the church will continue with a spiritual ministry (Acts 13:1-4).

(g)   The work of missions is not to make converts or churches dependent upon missionaries (1 Cor. 3:4-7).

(h)   Converts and churches should be taught to appreciate that the missionaries' objective is not to bind them in allegiance to themselves but to the Lord Jesus Christ (2 Cor.. 11:2).

11.   Literature has an important place in church consolidation.

(a)   Paul's letters in the New Testament bear witness to the place and importance of literature dealing with Christian doctrine and conduct.

(b)   Young Christians, particularly from pagan backgrounds, need literature to guide them (Acts 15:19-31).

---

99. HIDDEN FACTORS IN MISSIONARY ENTERPRISE

Question: What are the hidden factors we must take account of in missionary enterprise?

Answer: First, the Holy Spirit is the agent of God's new creation in Christ – the Church – and His power is essential.   Secondly, we engage in a spiritual work when we engage in missionary work and our dependence upon God, expressed in prayer and the activity of faith, must be real.

1.   The Holy Spirit is the Agent of God's new creation in Christ – the Church.

(a)   The Holy Spirit's activity in God's new creation is all-important:

   (i)   He puts the redeemed in possession of the results of the Father's love and the mediation of Christ (2 Cor. 3:8, 9; John 7:37-39);

   (ii)   Justification takes place in the name of the Lord Jesus Christ and by the Spirit of God (1 Cor. 6:11; 1 Pet. 1:2);

   (iii)   Through the Spirit the redeemed are brought into the one body, the Church, this act being described as a baptism (1 Cor. 12:13);

   (iv)   The Spirit is the Author of the new birth (John 3:5, 6).

(b)   The Holy Spirit is directly associated with the extension of God's new creation – the Church (Matt. 28:19; cf. Acts 1:4, 8).

    (i)   He ensures that messengers are raised up and workers sent forth to proclaim the gospel (Matt. 9:38; cf. Acts 13:2, 4; 16:6, 7, 10; 20:28);

    (ii)   He accompanies the preaching of the gospel with His power (1 Pet. 1:12);

    (iii)   He shows people their need of salvation by convicting them of sin (John 16:8-11);

    (iv)   He testifies about Christ (John 15:26), and by His influence men and women are enabled to say 'Jesus is Lord' (1 Cor. 12:3);

    (v)   For the care of the Church the Spirit raises up overseers or pastors (Acts 20:28);

    (vi)   He allots varying gifts to Christians (Rom. 12:6-8);

    (vii)   In each Christian the Spirit desires to display His power in a particular way, for some useful purpose (1 Cor. 12:4-11);

    (viii)   The Spirit's purpose is to equip God's people for work in Christ's service, for the building up of the body of Christ (Eph. 4:11-13).

(c)   Not surprisingly, the Lord Jesus, therefore, taught the apostles that they were dependent upon the Holy Spirit for the fulfilment of their commission (Acts 1:4, 5, 8).

(d)   Missionary work should be marked by power (Luke 10:17-19), and we need at every stage to acknowledge our dependence upon the Holy Spirit.

2.   When we engage in the work of missions, we engage in a spiritual battle.

(a)   The work of missions is part of a great spiritual battle (2 Cor. 10:3, 4).

(b)   Missionary work is in open conflict with the god of this world who has blinded the minds of unbelievers to keep them from seeing the light of the gospel of the glory of Christ (2 Cor . 4:4).

(c)   Opposition and indifference, therefore, are not to take us by surprise (Luke 10:10, 11; 2 Cor. 4:3, 4).

3. **Dependence upon God is to characterise missionary enterprise.**

(a) It is to be clear to all that missions and missionaries depend upon God (Luke 10:4).

(b) This fundamental principle is not to be interpreted, however, to the detriment of the responsibility of Christians to support missionary work: those who give themselves completely to the work of the gospel may be expected to live by the gospel (Luke 10:7; 1 Cor . 9:1-18).

(c) Furthermore, dependence upon God does not rule out missionaries being self-supporting where that would seem the more appropriate and honourable practice (Acts 18:3; 20:34).

4. **Our confidence in missionary work is in the Lord, not in the converts.**

(a) God begins the good work in people's lives, and He will bring it to completion at the day of Jesus Christ (Phil. 1:6).

(b) Missionaries may have confidence in God about their converts' obedience to God (2 Thess. 3:4).

5. **The priority of prayer.**

(a) Missionary endeavour is to be born in prayer, and carried through by prayer (Acts 4:23-31).

(b) Paul's prayers for the churches indicate the priority he himself gave to it in his endeavours (Eph. 1:16-23; 3:14-21; Phil. 1:3-11; Col. 1:9-12).

6. **Missionary work involves acting according to faith.**

(a) We are called to work, believing that the Lord Himself will work with us (Matt. 28:20; Mark 16:20; Luke 10:1).

(b) The assurance we have, by faith, that God's purposes shall be fulfilled gives us the necessary grace to persevere (Acts 18:9-11).

7. **Missionary work is momentous in its importance and consequences.**

(a) The kingdom of God comes near men and women by means of missionary endeavour (Luke 10:8-12).

(b)   The response men and women give to the missionary representatives of Christ is the response they give to the Lord Jesus Christ Himself (Luke 10:16).

---

100. SUPPORTING MISSIONS

Question: How are we to support missionary work?

Answer: We are to support missionary work wholeheartedly and generously, by finance and prayer, as part of our worship of God.

1.   **Some preliminary considerations.**
(a)   Giving people the gospel means giving them our very selves in service – there is no room for half-heartedness (1 Thess. 2:8).
(b)   Christians in churches that have been brought into being and blessed through the gospel should provide the wherewithal for others to labour in new and emerging churches (2 Cor. 11:8).
(c)   Those who come to faith are to be taught to have a sense of responsibility for one another in every way, both spiritually and materially (Acts 4:32-37).
(d)   Missionary service should not be a burden to those who are served by it (1 Thess. 2:9; 2 Thess. 3:7-9).
(e)   Missionaries have a right to be supported (1 Cor.. 9:4-13): those who proclaim the gospel should get their living by the gospel, according to the Lord's command (1 Cor. 9:14).
(f)   A basic principle of missions is that it is more blessed to give than to receive (Acts 20:35).
(g)   The whole of the local church is involved in the sending forth of a missionary, under the direction of the Holy Spirit (Acts 13:1-4).
(h)   God's people should be encouraged to have a sense of responsibility and of partnership in missionary enterprise (Phil. 1:3-5; 4:15).
(i)   A truly worshipping church is a missionary-minded church (Acts 13:2).

(j)   A missionary-minded church happily sees its most gifted members called and set apart for missionary service (Acts 13:1-4).

2.   Supporting missions by finance.

(a)   The tribes, in the Old Testament period, were required to give from their inheritance a certain portion for the use of those who were set apart for God's service (Josh. 21:1-3; cf. 1 Cor. 9:13, 14; Gal. 6:6).

(b)   Giving is part of our honouring God and fearing His name (Mal. 1:6-8).

(c)   Our giving proves the reality of our faith and obedience to the gospel (2 Cor. 9:13).

(d)   Giving is the privilege of everyone (1 Cor. 16:2), by tithes and by offerings (Mal. 3:10).

(e)   To share what we have with others is a spiritual sacrifice pleasing to God (Heb. 13:16); there is a fellowship of giving and receiving (Phil. 4:15).

(f)   We should give so that there is an abundance in God's storehouse (Mal. 3:10).

(g)   When it comes to giving, it is best to say little, and do much (Mal. 1:14).

(h)   Giving is part of our missionary partnership (Phil. 4:15), and properly used it brings many expressions of thanksgiving to God (2 Cor. 9:12).

(i)   Giving should be regular and systematic (1 Cor. 16:2), according to how we have decided for ourselves (2 Cor. 9:7) and promised (2 Cor. 9:5); our giving is to be cheerful (2 Cor. 9:7), loving (1 Cor. 13:3), according to our ability (Acts 11:29), and in keeping with our income (1 Cor. 16:2).

(j)   Our giving should be in the light of God's indescribable gift of His Son to us (2 Cor. 9:15).

(k)   The more God enriches us, the more scope we should find for generous giving (2 Cor. 9:11); our gifts should not be grudgingly given but willingly (2 Cor. 9:5).

(l)   The Lord watches the giving of His people, and He does not despise any gift: the value of our gifts is in proportion to what we have left, and what it has cost us to give (Mark 12:41-44; Luke 21:1-4).

(m) Giving is not to be influenced by the difficulties of the times: the difficulties serve to provide an even greater opportunity of proving God (Mal. 3:10).

(n) We are foolish if we say we cannot afford to give and to be generous (Prov. 22:9; cf. Deut. 15:9, 10; Prov. 19:17; 28:27; 2 Cor. 9:7,8).

(o) When we fail to give, we work hard with little profit; we eat, but never have enough; we drink, but we are always thirsty; we clothe ourselves, but we are never warm; we earn a wage but it goes nowhere (Hag. 1:6).

(p) Generous giving to meet the needs of others brings blessing from God (Prov. 22:9; Hag. 1:5, 7, 9-11).

(q) As we meet the needs of others God meets ours (Mal. 3:10-12; 2 Cor. 9:6-11; Phil. 4:18, 19).

(r) In giving to God's work at home and abroad, sparse sowing means sparse reaping, and generous sowing means generous reaping (2 Cor. 9:6).

(s) In distributing our money set apart for others, we need to recognise that we do not always know who needs help most, but others do: we should happily leave its distribution to those who know the needs better (Acts 4:34-37; cf. Acts 5:1-11; 1 Cor. 16:1-4).

3. Supporting missions by prayer.

(a) Missionary concern is seen in prayer to God (Rom. 10:1).

(b) We should begin by praying for governments and world leaders, that they may be enabled to maintain peace and order so that the preaching of the gospel may go forward, according to God's pattern and will (1 Tim. 2:1-4).

(c) Paul's prayer requests guide us in the kind of petitions we should bring to God on behalf of missionaries:

   (i)   Deliverance from malicious unbelievers (Rom. 15:30, 31; 2 Thess. 3:2);

   (ii) Acceptance with God's people (2 Cor. 1:11; Rom. 15:31).

   (iii) Health of mind and body (Rom. 15:32; 2 Cor. 1:8-11).

   (iv) The ability to speak the right words fearlessly at moments of opportunity (Eph. 6:19);

   (v)   The turning of difficult circumstances to good use in the interests of the gospel (Phil. 1:19);

(vi)   God-given opportunities for proclaiming the good news of the Lord Jesus Christ (Col. 4:3);

(vii)   Progress in the establishment of the Church through the Word (2 Thess. 3:1).

(d)   Paul's prayers for the young churches guide us in the kind of petitions we should bring to God on behalf of the Christian believers among whom and alongside whom our missionaries work (Eph. 1:16-23; 3:14-21; Phil. 1:3-11; Col. 1:9-14).

(e)   Our support by prayer should be unceasing (Eph. 1:16).

BIBLE DEFINITIONS

ADOPTION is an act of God by which He bestows on those who are justified in Christ, the status or standing of God's sons and daughters (John 1:12). They are made members of His family, and possess all the privileges of that family. The Holy Spirit is the Spirit of adoption because by the miracle of new birth He makes believers the sons and daughters of God and enables them to call God their Father and to have the feelings towards God that go with the relationship (Rom. 8:15).

ADVOCATE is a title given to both our Lord Jesus Christ and the Holy Spirit. The word carries the idea of calling alongside someone to help, and in the context of a law court was used for the counsel for the defence. In the references to the Holy Spirit in John's Gospel, where the word is translated 'Counsellor', 'Helper' would be sometimes the most apt translation (John 14:16, 26; 15:26; 16:7). In 1 John 2:1, where it is used of the Lord Jesus Christ, it may be translated 'Advocate', 'One who speaks in our defence', indicating its more legal use.
Advocates do two things: first, they stand and plead on behalf of their clients; secondly, they advise their clients how to speak when called upon to do so. Our Lord Jesus Christ acts for believers in the first sense: He appears in God's presence on our behalf, interceding there by His presence and on the basis of His finished work on the Cross (Heb. 7:25).
The Spirit acts for believers in the second sense. He comes alongside us as we pray, for example, and puts pleas and words into our mouths (Rom. 8:26-27).

ALIENATED describes the condition of people in relation to God before reconciliation. They are cut off or separated from the life of God through sin and ignorance (Eph. 4:18). The evil in their lives makes them God's enemies (Col. 1:21).

ANGEL OF THE LORD. This unique individual appears in the Old Testament as a messenger of God, but constantly acts and speaks in a way that implies that He is Himself God. Divine titles are given to

Him, together with worship (Gen. 16:10-13; 18:13, 14, 19, 25, 33; 22:11; 48:15, 16; Ex. 3:2, 6, 14; 13:21; 14:19; 23:20; Josh. 5:13-15; Judg. 6:11; 13:3ff). As the Old Testament revelation unfolds, this angel or messenger of the Lord is called the Son of God, the Messiah (Isa. 42:1-4; Mal. 3:1). Many hold, with justification, that the angel of the Lord in the Old Testament was none other than the Son of God who later became flesh as Jesus.

ANGELS are created beings, who act as God's messengers (Acts 7:53; Gal. 3:19; Heb. 2:7), and as His heavenly servants (Heb. 1:14). Their presence with God always represents His glorious nature (Rev. 5:11). There are evidences of a rebellion among the angels, with Satan as their leader (Job 4:18; Matt. 25:41; 2 Pet. 2:4; Rev. 12:9).

ANTICHRISTS are enemies or opponents of the Messiah who appear in the last days. They are individuals who put forth teaching that fundamentally opposes and denies the Lord Jesus Christ (1 John 2:18, 22; 4:3; 2 John 7). Such teaching may be deceitful in that it pretends to be genuinely Christian (2 John 7-10).

APOSTATE, APOSTASY, APOSTASIZE. Apostasy is falling away from allegiance to Christ, abandoning the Christian faith (1 Tim. 4:1). An apostate is a person who, having shown all the outward signs of faith in Christ and obedience to Him, then loses all interest and even becomes hostile to Christ and His claims (Heb. 6:6).
Apostasy is persistence in sin, sinning deliberately after receiving the knowledge of the truth as it is in Christ (Heb. 10:26). It is the result often of a superficial profession of Christ (Matt. 13:5, 6, 20, 21). To 'apostasize' is to become an apostate. See Question 34.

APOSTLES. The word 'apostle' means a person sent by another. The title belongs strictly in the New Testament to the twelve apostles and Paul who joined their number later. They were chosen, called and sent forth by the Lord Jesus Christ Himself (John 6:70; 13:18; 15:16, 19; Gal. 1:6); they were His witnesses, especially of His resurrection (Acts 1:8, 22; 1 Cor. 9:1; 15:8; Gal. 1:12; Eph. 3:2-8; 1 John 1:1-3). In a particularly marked sense they knew the help of the Holy Spirit, who led them into all truth (Matt. 10:20; John 14:26; 15:26; 16:7-14; 20:22; 1 Cor. 2:10-13; 7:40; 1 Thess. 4:8). God confirmed the value and authenticity of their work by signs and miracles (Matt. 10:1, 8; Acts 2:43; 3:2; 5:12-16; Rom. 15:18, 19; 1 Cor. 9:2; 2 Cor. 12:12, Gal. 2:8).

ASCENSION. See Question 22.

ASSURANCE is the conviction Christians have from the Holy Spirit (Rom. 8:15, 16; 1 John 3:24), through their obedience to the gospel, that they are children of God and heirs of eternal life (1 John 5:13). The genuineness of this conviction is demonstrated by right belief in Christ (1 John 2:22; 5:1), God-honouring conduct, after the pattern of Jesus' teaching (1 John 2:3-6; 3:3) and love for other Christians (1 John 3:10-17; 4:7-12, 20, 21). See Question 33.

BACKSLIDE, BACKSLIDING. Backsliding describes the state of believers when their spiritual life declines and they lose their spiritual vitality through deliberate disobedience to God. It consists of faithlessly turning or drawing back from what God requires (Jer. 3:6-14; Hos. 11:7).

BAPTISED, BAPTISM. See Question 36.

BELIEVE is the verb from which we obtain the noun 'faith'. It describes belief and knowledge of God's existence (Heb. 11:6), assurance concerning His trustworthiness, active confidence in His help and the entrusting of ourselves to His care (John 3:16; Acts 16:31, 34; 27:25; Rom. 10:9, 10; 2 Tim. 1:12).

BELIEVER is the name given to those who believe in the Lord Jesus Christ as the only Saviour and acknowledge Him as Lord (Acts 2:36), and who then, as a consequence, find themselves added to His Church (Acts 2:41, 44, 47; 5:14). See **BELIEVE.**

BLASPHEMY is insulting the majesty of God. At first specific words of cursing and insult were thought of as offending in this way (Lev. 24:16; Mark 2:7), but it came to be appreciated that words that encroach upon God's sole rights are also blasphemy. This explains the false charge that religious authorities made concerning the Lord Jesus Christ (Mark 14:64). The opposite of the Holy Spirit's influence in a person's life (1 Cor. 12:3), blasphemy is characteristic of the devil and his agencies (Rev. 13:1, 5, 6).

BLOOD OF CHRIST is an expression often used in the New Testament to express the Lord Jesus Christ's death as a sacrifice for our sins. It is a particularly apt way of describing His death in view of the ceremonial offerings of the Old Testament that prepared the way for it by their symbolism (Heb.10:1-17). His blood purges our consciences of moral guilt, and provides the forgiveness that gives us peace (Heb. 9:13, 14). Its power to cleanse is continuous, enabling us to maintain fellowship with God (1 John 1:7).

BODY. The body represents many aspects of human life, besides describing an individual's purely physical being: the main characteristic of human life is that it is 'in the body' (2 Cor. 5:8). The body is the organ of a person's activity (1 Cor. 6:20; Rom. 12:1), the instrument of human experience and suffering (2 Cor. 4:10; Gal. 6:17), and the place and sphere where the sexual functions operate (Rom. 4:19; 1 Cor. 7:4).
The Christian's weak and mortal body is destined to be changed into a glorious body – like Christ's glorified body – at the resurrection from the dead at Christ's return (1 Cor. 15:44; Phil. 3:21).
The word 'body' is also used to describe the community of Christians, the Church, as the body of Christ (Rom. 12:5; 1 Cor. 10:17; 12:13, 27; Eph. 1:23; 2:16; 4:12, 16; 5:23, 30; Col. 1:18, 24; 2:19; 3:15).

BOOK OF LIFE. A pictorial expression of the truth, often expressed, that the Lord knows those who belong to Him (2 Tim. 2:19), and that their entry into the full enjoyment of eternal life is certain (Phil. 4:3; Rev. 3:5).

BORN AGAIN or 'regeneration', as it is called, is the supernatural work of the Holy Spirit by which those who are dead in trespasses and sins are made spiritually alive (John 3:3, 6, 7, 8; Eph. 2:1; Jas. 1:18; 1 Pet. 1:23). See Question 26.

CALLED, CALLING, CALLS. Calling is a unique act of God by which the elect are brought into fellowship and union with Christ (1 Cor. 1:9) so that they benefit from all the fruits of His redeeming and saving work on their behalf. It is the first step in the application of God's salvation to the individual (Rom. 8:28-30; cf. Acts 16:14). The call carries with it the grace of God sufficient to enable the individual to answer the call and to believe on the Lord Jesus Christ and be saved (Acts 16:31).This grace is, in fact, what we call regeneration. There is also the 'call' to service. It is an individual's duty to recognise that call, and for the local church, when involved at all, to recognise it too and to act accordingly (Acts 13:2; 16:10).

CHASTISEMENT is the careful and gracious disciplining and correcting of our characters by means of unpleasant circumstances and trials. God's object in chastisement is always our spiritual development and maturity (Heb. 12:5-7). A company of people, or a local church, or a single individual may be the focus of it.

CHOSEN. In the Old Testament the expression was used of the Israelites (1 Chron. 16:13; Ps. 89:3) whom God chose from the peoples of the world, not on account of any merit, to fulfil His eternal purposes in the world (Deut. 7:6, 8; Isa. 42:1; 43:20, 21).
In the New Testament it is a designation of those whom God has chosen from all the peoples of the world, and drawn to Himself through the gift of faith in His Son, Jesus Christ. It reminds Christians that their faith rests on God's grace and His work in them, and not on their own merits, and that they are chosen for God's own purposes (Eph. 1:4; 5:27; Col. 1:22).

CHRIST is a Greek word signifying 'The Anointed One' - the meaning of the word 'Messiah'. Anointing was a symbol of being set apart by God for a special task. The Jews looked for the coming of a Great One, called the Messiah, who would accomplish God's purposes for His people. Jesus accepted the title but only infrequently, for first century Jews thought mainly of the Messiah as a political deliverer, and Jesus had not come as such (Matt. 16:16, 17; Mark 14:61, 62; John 4:26; cf. Matt. 1:18; 2:4; Luke 2:11, 26).

CHRISTIAN. Christians are those who are associated with Christ and committed to Him – Christ's men and women. Believers were first called Christians in Antioch (Acts 11:26). To believe the apostolic message of the gospel was to become a Christian (Acts 26:28). To be known as a Christian, in some circumstances, became the cause of persecution (1 Pet. 4:16).

CHURCH. The word 'church' is used mainly in two ways: first, of the whole company of those redeemed through Christ (Matt. 16:18; Acts 9:31; 1 Cor. 6:4; 12:28; Eph. 1:22; 3:10, 21; 5:23ff, 27, 29, 32), and secondly, of a company of professing believers in a particular area or district (Matt. 18:17; Acts 20:28; 1 Cor. 1:2; 10:32; 11:16, 22; 15:9; 2 Cor. 1:1; Gal. 1:13; 1 Thess. 2:14, 2 Thess. 1:4; 1 Tim. 3:5, 15).

CLEANSED, CLEANSING is what we need from our sin (Ps. 51:2). It normally describes physical cleansing, but it has another meaning in the Bible. Sin pollutes the soul, and makes it an object of God's disapproval. The removal of sin, both in its condemning and corrupting influences, through the blood of Christ, is described as cleansing (Heb. 1:3). This cleansing is available continuously to Christians as they endeavour to live in obedience to God, and confess their sins with honest repentance as they become aware of them (1 John 1:7-9).

COMMUNION is sharing and participating, and is an expression of the New Testament word that we more often translate as 'fellowship'. Communion is a particularly apt word for describing the Lord's Supper because by participating in it, not only do Christians express their personal fellowship with Christ and their share in the benefits of His atoning work, but they do so in fellowship with all other Christians on account of their essential spiritual unity and identity in Christ (1 Cor. 10:16, 17).

COMMUNION OF SAINTS is another way of expressing the fellowship of Christian believers. This fellowship, or communion, is the identity, sympathy and belonging we have with all believers through our common allegiance to the Lord Jesus Christ (Eph. 4:6, 13). The more fellowship with God the Father and the Son is enjoyed, the more communion with God's people is experienced (1 John 1:3).

CONDEMNATION, CONDEMNED. Condemnation describes the result of a person's sinful condition before God. Deserving the wrath of God, a sinner is sentenced to just punishment – death (Ezek.

18:4; John 3:16-19). Through Christ, a believer's sin is adequately and finally dealt with, and all condemnation is removed (Rom. 8:1; 1 John 4:10).

CONFESS, CONFESSION. The same word is used in different ways. First, confession is the acknowledgement before God of our individual sins; and upon such confession depends our experience of His forgiveness and cleansing (1 John 1:9). Secondly, confession is our public declaration that Jesus is the Son of God and has become our Saviour and Lord, to whom we give our total allegiance (Rom. 10:9, 10; Phil. 2:11; cf. Matt. 10:32; Luke 12:8). Thirdly, confession is the witness we give to the truths of the faith (1 Tim. 6:12; Heb. 10:23).

CONSCIENCE is that part of us that registers disapproval when we go against what we know is right, and gives approval when we do the right thing. As a faithful witness, it declares the truth (Rom. 2:15; 9:1; 2 Cor. 1:12), like a trusted adviser, it prohibits evil (Acts 24:16; Rom. 13:5), and like a judge, it assesses what is deserved (Rom. 2:15; cf. 1 John 3:20, 21). Conscience on its own is not the standard of right and wrong; it needs to be instructed and informed by the Word of God and the Holy Spirit. Before we become Christians, conscience tends to be either bad or asleep. When the work of conviction begins our conscience is made sensitive, and we know we have a bad conscience before God. When we are reconciled to God, as a gift from Him, the blood of Christ cleanses our consciences (Heb. 9:14). A clear conscience (Acts 24:16) is maintained as we make every effort to do God's will and allow no sin to remain unconfessed (1 John 1:6-10).

CONTRITION is brokenness of spirit through a right appreciation of the sinful nature of sin. Our pride is properly humbled by this appreciation and we are then in a fit position to receive God's grace and forgiveness (Ps. 34:18; 51:17; Isa. 57:15; 66:2).

CONVERSION. See Question 27.

CONVICTION is the work of the Holy Spirit, who, usually through the Scriptures as they are read or preached, convicts our consciences of our sin before God, so that we are in no doubt about the justice and certainty of God's wrath upon sin, and we begin to hate sin and realise our need to turn from it (John 16:8, 9; cf. Acts 2:37; 1 Thess. 1:5, 9, 10).

CORRUPTION is used first in a physical sense of the body decaying and dying (Ps. 16:10; cf. Acts 2:27), and secondly in a spiritual sense of our state before God as a consequence of our sinful rebellion (Ps. 14:1). Left to ourselves we get worse and worse, and everything we do is spoiled by our sin.

COVENANT. A covenant is a compact or a contract. When the word is used in connection with God, it has the idea of a one-sided arrangement made by a superior party. In the covenant with Adam, for example, God placed him on probation, promising life on the condition of his obedience (Gen. 2:16, 17).
It is used particularly, however, of obligations God imposes upon Himself, for the reconciliation of sinful men and women to Him (Gen. 17:7; Deut. 7:6-8; Ps. 89:3-4; Heb. 13:20).

CREATION. The God and Father of our Lord Jesus Christ is the Creator of all things (Neh. 9:6; Ps. 90:2; Isa. 42:5; Acts 17:24, 25; 1 Cor. 8:6). God the Son and God the Holy Spirit were active in the creation (Gen. 1:2; Job 26:13; John 1:3; Col. 1:16; Heb. 1:2), and God the Father has ordained that all creation will ultimately belong to the Son (Heb. 1:2). In the final analysis, the absolute creation of all things by God is a matter for faith rather than scientific proof (Heb. 11:3). See Question 9.

CROSS. The cross was an upright stake or beam used in punishing and executing criminals, particularly by the Romans. It describes the painful form of death Jesus endured, but it is more often used as a one-word summary of the good news of salvation, that Jesus 'died for our sins'. 'The message of the cross' is 'the preaching of the gospel' (1 Cor. 1:17-19).

CURSE is a sentence of destruction called down upon an individual because of misdemeanour. In the Bible it does not refer to blasphemous language, as it may today. The Lord Jesus Christ took upon Himself the curse for our wrong-doing (Gal. 3:13). Our failure to keep God's law brings upon us the curse of God - that is to say, death (Gal. 3:10; Rom. 6:23). The Lord Jesus Christ willingly stood in our place at the Cross, taking our death upon Him. In this way He became a curse for us (Gal. 3:13).

DAY OF JUDGMENT. See **JUDGMENT.**

DEPRAVED is used to describe our corrupt human state before God as a result of sin. Men and women are said to be totally depraved, not in the sense that they are as bad as they can possibly be, but rather that sin has corrupted every part of their being, their mind, will and affections. Human hearts are full of evil and madness (Eccl. 9:3; Matt. 15:11, 15-20; Mark 7:15, 20-23), and sometimes correction only increases the desire to sin (Zeph. 3:7).

DESTRUCTION describes the eternal death, damnation and ruin that are the just punishment of the wicked (Matt. 7:13; Rev. 17:8, 11).

DEVIL See Question 43.

DISCIPLE was something of a technical term used of those who attached themselves to a particular teacher. A disciple is someone under instruction. Jesus chose the twelve, to bring them under His instruction so that they would be able to convey His teaching later to others (Matt. 28:20; cf. 2 Tim. 2:2). But many more besides the twelve were called 'disciples' (Luke 10:1ff), and the term was given generally to all professing Christians (Acts 11:26). The Lord Jesus Christ requires faithfulness and obedience to what He says as the major condition of discipleship (John 8:31).

DISOBEDIENCE can describe either deliberate or obstinate rejection of God's will (Eph. 2:2; 5:6) and the refusal to hear His words (Jer. 11:10; 35:17).

ELDERS were the spiritual leaders of the early churches, and were appointed from the earliest times (Acts 11:30). Their precise functions are not clear, although pastoral care and rule were their particular responsibilities and some had the further task of teaching and preaching the Word of God. The qualifications for elders and bishops are more or less identical (Tit. 1:6-9; 1 Tim. 3:1-7) and it is generally agreed that the two titles were interchangeable, referring to the same spiritual office.

ELECT, ELECTION. Election is God's eternal, unconditional choice of guilty sinners to be redeemed and born again of His Spirit so that they may be brought finally to His everlasting glory (Rom. 8:30; Eph. 1:3-12; 1 Pet.1:2). A believer's experience of salvation, sanctification, and glory all flow from God's election (2 Thess. 2:13, 14) something that has no regard at all to any works or merit of a believer (Rom. 11:6; 2 Tim. 1:9).

ETERNAL always conveys the idea of something that is without end (Luke 16:9; Acts 13:46), and, when used to describe God, of His having neither beginning nor end (Gen. 21:33; Isa. 26:4; Rom. 16:26; Heb. 9:14).

ETERNAL LIFE, EVERLASTING LIFE is never-ending life, the opposite of death and corruption (Rom. 6:22; Gal. 6:8). It is the gift of God, and the present possession of Christians through believing in the Lord Jesus Christ (Rom. 6:23; John 3:16; 10:28). Its essence is everlasting fellowship with God (John 17:3).

EVIL describes what is bad, and contrary to law, such as crime, sin and wrongdoing. It begins in the human heart (Matt. 9:4), and, unchecked, leads to further evil (Eccl. 8:11).

EVIL ONE is a name given to the devil because of his wicked, bad, base and vicious activities (Matt. 13:19; John 17:15; Eph. 6:16; 1 John 2:13, 14; 5:18, 19).

EXPIATE, EXPIATION. To expiate is to pay the penalty of sin, and to make amends for it. Christ is the expiation for our sins in that they were transferred to Him, and He died for them, so that He might bring us to God (1 Pet. 3:18). By giving Himself up sacrificially for us, Christ annulled the power of sin to separate us from God (Heb. 2:17; Rom. 3:25).

FAITH See Question 29.

FALL, THE See Question 13.

FATHER (See GOD) 'Father' is the distinguishing name of the first Person of the Trinity in relation to the second Person - the Son (John 14:6; 20:17; Rom. 15:6; 2 Cor. 1:3). The relationship has no like anywhere, and is beyond our understanding.

The word is used, secondly, of the relationship God the Father has with those who believe in His Son (Rom. 1:7; 1 Cor. 1:3; 2 Thess. 2:16). Such are taught by the Holy Spirit to call Him 'Father' (John 1:12; Rom. 8:15; 1 John 3:1).

The relationship that God has to men and women in general is seldom spoken of as fatherhood; the opposite is the case (John 8:44).

FELLOWSHIP is a favourite Christian word and describes our sharing as Christians in God's grace, the salvation the Lord Jesus Christ brings, and the indwelling of the Holy Spirit that is the spiritual birthright of all believers. The fellowship we have with one another, therefore, springs from the fellowship we have with the Father, Son and Holy Spirit (1 John 1:3). Fellowship with God is a relationship in which we receive from, and respond to, all three Persons of the Trinity in a relationship of friendship (John 14:23; Rom. 5:5; 8:16; Eph. 4:30). Such fellowship is the life of heaven begun on earth (1 Pet. 1:8).

FLESH is used to describe an important part of our bodies, and as such no blame is attached to it (1 Cor.15:50; Luke 24:39). It is also used to describe the sinful and corrupt nature of men and women. It then represents the lower part of our human nature, where our natural desires have unhindered scope, leading to all kinds of sin (Rom. 7:18; Gal. 5:19-21; Eph. 2:3). In those who have been born again, the deeds of the flesh are put to death as the Holy Spirit is obeyed. But in those who are not Christians, the flesh dominates (Rom. 8:4-9, 12, 13).

FORGIVENESS is God's cancelling the sinner's debt and guilt on the basis of Christ's death for sinners (Micah 7:19; Matt. 26:28; Mark 14:24; Eph. 1:7). The conditions are repentance and faith in the Lord Jesus Christ (Acts 2:38; 5:31; 10:43; 1 John 1:9).

GENTILES was, to begin with, a term for 'nations'. The Jews knew themselves to be different and distinct from other nations and races and they used this term to describe all such people. In the New Testament the term usually has foreigners, like the Romans, or those speaking Greek in mind, and now it covers all who are not of Jewish race.

GLORY is used of God Himself to sum up the perfection of all that He is and all that He does, not least His grace, power and righteousness - the latter revealing especially how far short men and women fall of His standards (Rom. 1:23; Eph. 1:17; Jude 24).
The word is also used to describe the eternal happiness that Christians are to enjoy in the life to come (Rom. 8:18, 21; 1 Pet. 5:1, 10).

GOD is Spirit (John 4:24): invisible (1 Tim. 6:15, 16; John 1:18), personal (Ex. 3:14), great beyond human estimation (Isa. 40:18; 45:6; Rom. 11:33-34), life-giving (Gen. 1; John 5:26; Acts 17:25) and supremely powerful (Ps.115:3; Isa. 40:15, 17).
There is but one God (Deut. 6:4), but one in three Persons, Father, Son and Holy Spirit (Matt. 28:19; 2 Cor. 13:14).
Although no one has ever seen God the Father (John 1:18), God has given clues to His existence in creation (Gen. 1:1; Ps. 19:1; Acts 17:24; Rom. 1:18-20), in the nature of men and women (Ps. 139:14; Rom. 2:14, 15), and in the glorious revelation of Himself in the Person of His Son, Jesus Christ (2 Cor. 4:6; John 1:14, 18; 14:9; Col. 1:15-17; 1 John 1:1-3).
Added to these evidences, there is the witness of the Bible (2 Tim. 3:16), and of those who have found God (Acts 4:20; 1 John 5:20).

GOD (god) is a word used of divine beings generally, and of the one true God, the God and Father of our Lord Jesus Christ. It is also used of idols who are so-called 'gods', and of Satan who is the god of this world (2 Cor. 4:4). In using this term to describe idols and evil spirits the Bible does not acknowledge their deity - the opposite is the case – but it recognises the false worship that people foolishly give to them.

GODHEAD is an expression standing for the very being of God, or His essential nature; an alternative word is deity (Acts 17:29; 2 Pet. 1:3, 4).

GOOD WORKS are the good deeds and actions that are to be produced in Christians' lives following upon their experience of justification (Eph. 2:10). Even as the health of a tree is shown by its fruit, so too the health of Christians is shown by their good works (Matt. 5:16; 7:15-20). They necessarily contain imperfections but they are pleasing to God because they arise from living faith in Christ. Good works are worthless, however, as a means of justification and for gaining merit before God (Eph. 2:9; Tit. 3:5).

GOSPEL means 'good news' - the good news concerning God's Son Jesus Christ. The good news is that Christ died for sinners, and that through repentance and faith in Him sinners can be made right in God's sight, and receive the gift of the Holy Spirit and everlasting life.

GOSPELS – The four gospels – Matthew, Mark, Luke and John – are the books in which the story of our Lord Jesus Christ's life and teaching is found. They are not so much biographies of Jesus as written copies of the apostles' teaching and preaching, putting the emphasis on the events through which God's salvation is made available to men and women – the 'good news' after which the gospels are named. According to the four gospel writers, there is but one gospel – the gospel of Jesus Christ, the Son of God - delivered to, and preached by, the apostles (Acts 2:42; 1 Cor. 15:1-4).

GRACE is the undeserved love of God to men and women revealed in Christ, giving them through Him help and countless gifts and benefits that they could never merit (Rom. 3:24; 5:15; 6:1; Eph. 1:6; 2:5, 7, 8).

GUILT is the deserving of punishment because of law-breaking or failure to do something required. All, since the first rebellion in the Garden of Eden (Rom. 5:12), are guilty before God since all have sinned and fall short of His glory (Rom. 3:23) and are accountable to Him (Rom. 3:19). Salvation rescues us from guilt of sin (Eph. 1:7), since the sacrifice of our Lord Jesus Christ completely dealt with it, assuring us of God's perfect forgiveness (Heb. 10:4, 18).

HEART covers the whole of our inward life: our thinking, feeling and will (Matt. 13:15). Sin has its roots in the heart (Matt. 15:19, 20) and it is in our hearts, therefore, that God's work of salvation begins (Matt. 13:19; Rom. 2:15; 2 Cor. 3:3; Heb. 8:10) so that we believe on His Son in our heart (Acts 15:9; Rom. 10:9, 10).

HEATHEN Used in the Bible, the word means 'nation'. As the only people in the Old Testament to whom God had revealed Himself in a covenant relationship, the Jews regarded other nations as completely separate and different. All other peoples, not having the covenant relationship with God, were the heathen. The term describes men and women everywhere who are without the true knowledge of God.

HEAVEN See Question 49.

HELL See Question 50.

HOLINESS, HOLINESS OF GOD. Holiness is a term that above all others expresses the perfection of God's character. He is entirely free from moral evil, and possesses infinite purity. He is absolutely distinct from all His creatures, and is exalted above them in immeasurable majesty. The idea behind the words 'holy' and 'holiness' is that of being cut off, separated, or set apart. God sets apart His people from other peoples, and He calls them to separate themselves from all that displeases Him and is contrary to His will. He calls them to be like Himself (1 Pet. 1:15, 16).

HOLY GHOST is another way of describing the Holy Spirit. Both 'Spirit' and 'Ghost' are translations of the same word in the New Testament. 'Spirit' is a better word than 'Ghost' for other uses are inclined to mislead us or to be unhelpful.

HOLY SPIRIT. The Holy Spirit is the Lord (that is to say, God) and the Giver of life, the third Person of the Trinity, to be worshipped and glorified with the Father and the Son (Matt. 28:19; 1 Cor. 12:4-6; 2 Cor. 13:14; Eph. 4:4-6). He is most commonly presented to us as the Executor of God's purposes, whether in creation (Gen. 1:2; Job 26:13), revelation (2 Tim. 3:16; 2 Pet. 1:21) or redemption (Luke 1:35; John 3:5, 6; Acts 2:24; 1 Cor. 12:3). He is the gift of the Father and the Son to believers to live within them (John 14:16; 15:26; 16:7). He gives them spiritual life (Gal. 5:25; Eph. 2:1), assures them of their spiritual relationship to God as His children (Rom. 8:16), and communicates to them the benefits of the gospel (Rom. 5:5; 15:13). See Questions 23, 24.

HOPE, as used in the New Testament, does not suggest clinging to a mere possibility, but rather the happy and confident expectation of enjoying some unseen and future promise of God. The living hope of the resurrection from the dead and the inheritance to follow are examples (1 Pet. 1:3-4).

IMMORTALITY is deathlessness, and is part of God's unique character. Christians receive it as a gift, but God Himself is the source (1 Tim. 6:16). Immortality is not merely the survival of the soul after the death of the body, but the self-conscious existence of the whole person, body and soul together, in a state of eternal happiness (1 Cor. 15:53, 54).

IN CHRIST is a characteristic description of Christians, signifying the spiritual union that all Christians have with Christ, from which springs their experience of all the benefits of His finished work and the knowledge of Him living within them by the Holy Spirit (John 15:4, 5; Rom. 8:9-11; 1 Cor. 1:30; 2 Cor. 5:17; Gal. 2:20; Phil. 1:1).

INCARNATION The word comes from Latin, meaning 'becoming-in-flesh', and describes the amazing truth of Christ, the Son of God, becoming flesh (John 1:14). In the Old and New Testaments Christ is declared to be both God and man (Ps. 2; 22; 45; 72; 110; John 1:1-3, 14; Col. 2:9). His perfect deity and perfect humanity are essentials of the Christian faith (1 John 2:22-25; 4:1-6; 5:5-12; 2 John 7), although these glorious truths are beyond the understanding of the human mind (1 Tim. 3:16). See Question 19.

INFINITE describes what is boundless, endless and very great. It is used frequently of God because no limit can be placed upon His majesty and glory. He is far greater in His being and perfection than we can know or think.

INHERITANCE. In the Old Testament the land of Canaan, promised to Abraham and his descendants, was called the 'inheritance' (1 Kings 8:36).

In the spiritual sense, the Lord Himself is said to be His people's inheritance (Jer. 10:16) and the Lord speaks of His true people as His inheritance (Deut. 4:20; 32:9; Ps. 2:8).

In the New Testament the 'inheritance' is the kingdom of God with all its benefits (Matt. 25:34; 1 Cor. 6:9; Gal. 5:21; 1 Pet. 1:3, 4). As the children of God through faith in Christ, believers are to share God's treasures and our Lord Jesus Christ's glory (Rom. 8:17).

INIQUITY is persistent wickedness and disobedience to God's laws (Isa. 53:6; Rom. 6:19; Tit. 2:14).

INSPIRED, INSPIRATION The word used in the New Testament for 'inspired' means 'God-breathed' (2 Tim. 3:16). The Scriptures came about not by the impulse of the writers themselves, but through their being moved by the Holy Spirit to speak from God (2 Pet. 1:21). The responsibility of such individuals was to transmit what they received (1 Pet. 1:10-12). The authority of the Bible springs from its divine inspiration (2 Tim. 3:16, 17). The Holy Spirit creates the conviction in the hearts of Christians that the Scriptures are the Word of God and assures them of their truth (1 Cor. 2:4, 5; 1 Thess. 1:5; 2:13).

INTERCESSION is the continuing work of our Lord Jesus Christ in heaven for Christian believers. On the grounds of His sacrifice on their behalf, He unfailingly claims every spiritual benefit for them, secures forgiveness for all their sins and makes their worship and service acceptable to God (Rom. 8:34; Heb. 7:27; 9:24; 13:15; 1 John 2:1).

A different kind of intercession is the Holy Spirit's work in Christians by which He disposes, teaches and helps them to pray according to God's will. The Spirit gives both the inclination and the ability to pray (Rom. 8:26, 27).

ISRAEL was the name given by God to the patriarch Jacob (Gen. 32:28; 35:10) and to all his descendants, and then to the whole nation. In the New Testament it is used also of Christians, whether Jews or Gentiles, as the Israel of God, the new people of God (Gal. 6:16) for whom circumcision is a matter of a change of heart, not a cutting of the body as in circumcision (Rom. 2:29).

JESUS is the Greek form of the Hebrew name Joshua, meaning 'God is salvation' or 'God is the Saviour'. In obedience to God's command, it was given to the Son of God when He became man, as a symbol of God's promise that He would rescue God's people from the guilt and power of their sins (Matt. 1:21; Luke 1:31; 2:21).

JEWS. The title 'Jew' was used first for members of the tribe of Judah or of the two tribes of the Southern Kingdom (2 Kings 16:6; 25:25). Later it was used of any Hebrew who returned from the Captivity. Now it covers the entire Hebrew race anywhere in the world (Esth. 2:5; Matt. 2:2).

JUDGE, THE Sometimes God the Father is spoken of as the Judge (Heb. 12:23), and sometimes the Lord Jesus Christ (Acts 10:42; 2 Tim. 4:1, 8). God the Father has fixed a day on which He will judge the whole world in justice by Christ the Judge whom He has appointed (Acts 17:31).

JUDGMENT, JUDGMENT DAY. Judgment is God's punishment that must rightly fall upon sinners (Rom. 2:2). All will appear before Christ, the Judge whom God has appointed (Matt. 25:31-46; John 5:22,27). The perfect justice of God and the undeniable guilt of all will be plain and beyond dispute (Gen. 18:25; Acts 17:31; Rom. 2:5, 6). Those justified through faith in Christ will be acquitted from the guilt of sin and will receive rewards according to their faithfulness (Rom. 5:1; 1 Cor. 3:9-13; 2 Tim. 4:8); the unbelieving will receive their final condemnation (Rom. 2:8; 2 Thess. 1:8, 9; Jude 15; Rev. 20:15).
The day of judgment is the day when Christ returns (1 Thess. 5:4; Heb. 10:25; 1 Cor. 3:13), when all these things will take place. See Question 46.

JUDGMENT SEAT. Both Greek and Roman judges sat on a raised platform or seat in a public place where justice was seen to be done. Because of the absolutely fair and public nature of the last judgment, the picture is taken up to illustrate the judgment day when the Lord

Jesus Christ will publicly and justly judge all people (Rom. 14:10; 2 Cor. 5:10).

JUST describes those who are upright or righteous in that they conform to the laws of God and human authorities; this is possible to us only through the new birth (1 John 2:29). It is used of God Himself to describe the perfect fairness of His judgment of individuals and nations (Ps. 7:11; 2 Tim. 4:8). It is used of the Lord Jesus Christ, who is the perfect standard of obedience and uprightness (Matt. 27:19; Acts 7:52; 1 Pet. 3:18).

JUSTIFICATION, JUSTIFY. See Question 31.

KINGDOM, KINGDOM OF GOD, KINGDOM OF HEAVEN.
The kingdom of God or the kingdom of heaven, is spoken of in two ways: first, as that of which Christians are members because the Lord Jesus Christ, through the new birth (John 3:3, 5), actively rules as King in their hearts; and secondly, as that which they possess as an inheritance in the future (Matt. 25:34; Luke 22:16; 2 Tim. 4:18; Heb. 12:28).

LAMB is a picture used of the Lord Jesus Christ to set Him forth as the One promised in the Old Testament to obtain deliverance for others from God's judgment by the sacrifice of Himself for sin (John 1:29; 1 Pet. 1:19). In the Old Testament the lamb was the principal sacrificial animal, and all such sacrifices looked forward to the one sacrifice that would deal with sin once and for all – the sacrifice of Jesus as the Lamb of God (Heb. 10:1-14). While meekness characterised Jesus as the Lamb of God in His earthly ministry (Isa. 53:7; 1 Pet. 2:22, 23), the symbol is used in the Book of Revelation to express His position as the Conqueror and the Mighty One (Rev. 5:6; 7:14ff; 12:11).

LAST DAY, LAST DAYS. The Last Day is usually a reference to the Lord Jesus Christ's second coming (John 6:39, 40, 44, 54) and the events that will then occur, principally the judgment and the resurrection of the dead.
The last days are sometimes thought of as beginning with the birth of Christ (Heb. 1:2) in that God's new and final order of things through

the redeeming work of His Son, and the consequent birth of the Church, then came into operation.

The last days also describe the period of history immediately preceding the second coming of Christ (2 Tim. 3:1), the great event that will mark the completion of the present age.

LAW is used to describe the whole of the Scriptures (Josh.1:8; Ps 119:97) and more particularly the law of God, as summed up in the Ten Commandments (Ex. 20:1-17). It is the law of God that makes us aware of our sin against Him (Rom. 3:20) and thus causes us to realise our need of the salvation achieved by the Lord Jesus Christ for sinners (Gal. 2:15, 16, 21). See Question 16.

LORD describes God, and is the word used in the Greek translation of the Old Testament to render the name of God, 'Jehovah' or 'Yahweh'. It is used regularly of Christ, meaning that He is the divine Lord, having the highest place of all, worthy of our worship, service and obedience (Acts 2:36; 1 Cor. 16:22; Phil. 2:9-11; Col. 3:24). It is also used of the Holy Spirit (2 Cor. 3:18).

Significantly, references to the LORD God in the Old Testament are applied to Christ in the New Testament (Isa. 40:3; cf. Matt. 3:3; Isa. 44:6; Rev. 1:17).

LOST describes the condition of men and women who live without Christ and are therefore without the hope and assurance of eternal life. Like lost sheep, they are separated from the Shepherd they need (Matt. 10:6; Luke 15:4; 19:10). The lost need to be found and saved through Christ, or else they will perish (Matt. 18:12-14; John 3:16).

LOVE is the foremost characteristic of God, together with His holiness (1 John 1:5; 4:8). It is a love that is utterly independent of the merits of those loved, a truth perfectly illustrated in the Cross, when Christ died for us, while we were yet sinners (John 3:16; Rom. 5:8). Christ perfectly expressed God's love for us (2 Cor. 5:14; Eph. 2:4; 3:19; 5:2).

Christian love is the fruit of the Holy Spirit's presence in Christians (Gal. 5:22). Love for God shows itself in obedience to His commandments (John 14:15, 21, 23; 15:10; 1 John 2:5; 5:3; 2 John 6). Love for others is seen in seeking their best interests, irrespective of the response received (Rom. 15:2; 1 Cor. 13; Gal. 6:10).

MEDIATOR, MEDIATION. A Mediator, literally, is a go-between. He intervenes or mediates between two parties to produce peace by removing disagreement.

The Lord Jesus Christ is the one Mediator who can reconcile God and people (1 Tim. 2:5). Being both God and man, He was uniquely qualified to mediate. He voluntarily stood between the offended God and offending sinners, in order to deliver them as He took upon Himself the wrath of God they deserve.

By Christ's unique sacrifice for sins peace between God and men and women was made possible. Christ Himself is our peace (Eph. 2:14).

MERCY is warm affection demonstrated to the needy, helpless and distressed. In sending our Lord Jesus Christ to be the Saviour of sinners, God's amazing mercy was shown (Luke 1:78; Tit. 3:5). His mercy, according to His unfailing love, is seen in the manner in which He blots out penitent sinners' transgressions (Ps. 51:1).

MESSIAH means 'Anointed' and was the name given to the coming deliverer promised in the Old Testament. The word indicated that the deliverer or saviour was to be specially consecrated for his tasks, in the same way as a king or a priest might be. Among the Greeks the title Messiah was translated 'Christos', or 'Christ'.

Jesus accepted the title (Matt. 16:16) but He used it cautiously to describe His mission, for many Jews looked upon the Messiah as merely a political deliverer rather than a spiritual Saviour. He always emphasised the sufferings that had to be His as the Messiah before He could enter upon His glory (Matt. 16:16, 20, 21).

MIND represents our ability to think, our understanding - and the word 'understanding' often translates the Greek word for 'mind' in the New Testament. The mind of those who are unregenerate is described as blinded (2 Cor. 3:14; 4:4), darkened (Eph. 4:18), alienated (Col. 1:21), puffed up (Col. 2:18), corrupt (1 Tim. 6:5), and defiled (Tit. 1:15). Regeneration brings a new awakening of the mind to love God, to understand His will and to do it (Rom. 12:1, 2; Eph. 4:23; 1 Pet. 1:13).

MIRACLE. A miracle is an act or work of supernatural origin or character that would not be possible by ordinary or natural means. Jesus' deeds of power were miracles in this sense (Matt. 13:54, 58; Luke 19:37).

NEW BIRTH See Question 26.

NEW COVENANT, NEW TESTAMENT. The word 'testament' means 'covenant' rather than our contemporary word 'testament'. The term 'New Testament' came into general use in the later part of the second century to describe these twenty-seven writings that fall into four divisions: the four gospels, the Acts of the Apostles, twenty-one letters and the Book of Revelation.

The great message of the New Testament is that God's promises of redemption have been fulfilled in the life, death and resurrection of Jesus. His blood has secured the provision of a new covenant, according to God's will and purpose, so that all who believe and obey the gospel become God's people and members of Christ's Church.

OBEDIENCE, OBEY. Obedience is the obeying of God's voice in His commandments (Josh. 22:2; Ex. 19:5; Jer. 17:23; Deut. 5:10). The revelation God has given us in the Scriptures is to be the rule of our whole life (2 Tim. 3:16, 17). The Lord Jesus Christ is the perfect example of obedience (John 15:10; Heb. 10:7).

Obedience is, in effect, our response to God's Word (Matt. 13:23). It is almost identical with a sensitive conscience, constantly educated and informed by the Holy Spirit through the Scriptures, and consistently obeyed (Acts 23:1; 24:16; 2 Tim. 1:3).

Obedience is God's work in Christians, as a result of the new birth, for God inspires both the will and the deed, for His own good pleasure (Phil. 2:13, 14; 1 Pet. 1:2, 14).

By obedience we please God (1 John 3:22), remain in the Lord Jesus Christ's love (John 15:10), maintain our fellowship with God (John 14:23-24; 1 John 1:3, 7), grow in holiness (Luke 1:6; 1 Pet. 1:14-16), and show our love for God (1 John 2:5).

OFFERING. Sacrifices and offerings are linked in the Old Testament (Ps. 40:6; Heb. 10:5). The 'sacrifices' were animal offerings and the 'offerings' non-blood offerings like the first fruits of crops. The word 'offering' carried with it the idea of drawing near. It was that with which a people drew near to God. Human sin is such that we cannot approach God without some preparation - the offerings bore witness to this truth.

Leviticus chapters 1-7 describe the sacrifices and offerings. They are of considerable significance because the Lord Jesus Christ fulfilled their deepest significance by the one offering of Himself, opening up the way for us into God's presence by His blood (Heb. 10:10, 19-22).

OLD TESTAMENT. The word 'testament' means 'covenant' rather than our contemporary word 'testament'. The term 'Old Testament' came into general use in the later part of the second century to describe the writings we know by that title.

The thirty-nine books were arranged by the Jews in three divisions: the Law, the Prophets and the Writings. They deal particularly with the promises, or covenant, that God made with Israel. They are the record of the out-working of God's redemption on behalf of His people, and they always looked forward to the spiritual redemption to take place in the future with the coming of the Messiah.

OMNIPOTENCE means possessing all power, and is characteristic, therefore, of God who alone can do anything so that no purpose of His can be frustrated (Job 42:2). There is no power higher than God's (Ps. 135:6; Rev. 1:8). His limitless power is expressed in the title 'the LORD Almighty' (Isa. 1:9; 5:9; Rom. 9:29; Jas. 5:4).

OMNIPRESENCE means being everywhere at the same time and is an ability and quality possessed only by God (Ps. 139:7-12; Amos 9:2-4).

OMNISCIENCE means possessing all knowledge and wisdom and is a characteristic of God alone. Nothing can escape God's knowledge (Ps. 139:2, 3, 6; 145:7). He alone is the all-wise God (Rom. 16:27).

PARADISE is an oriental word, first used by the Persians of an enclosed garden or park. It was taken over by the Greeks and expressed the idea of a place of supreme happiness above the earth. Our Lord used it of the heavenly home to which a believer's spirit goes at death (Luke 23:43).

PASSOVER was the name given to the feast appointed by God to keep in memory the deliverance of the Israelites from Egypt (Ex. 12). It was so called because the Lord 'passed over' or 'spared' the Israelites when He punished the Egyptians. The Israelites had to offer up a lamb or a young goat in order that the destroying angel might pass over them. The Passover lamb is a picture of Christ, and He is called 'our Passover' because His death has saved us from the judgment of God's wrath that we deserve (1 Cor. 5:7).

PEACE is harmony with God restored, made possible by the reconciliation God has accomplished through the death of His Son, Jesus Christ (2 Cor. 5:20, 21), into which we enter by faith (Rom. 5:1). This peace brings with it glorious access to God (Rom. 5:2).

PENTATEUCH is the name given to the first five books of the Bible (Genesis, Exodus, Leviticus, Numbers, Deuteronomy), the actual word itself meaning a five-volumed book. In the Old Testament, the Pentateuch is described as the law (Josh. 8:34; Neh. 8:2) or the book of the law of God (Josh. 24:26; Neh. 8:18), and sometimes as the book of Moses (Ezra 6:18; Neh. 13:1), in view of his responsibility for writing down God's revelation and the record of His dealings with the Jewish people.
In the New Testament also these first five books are associated particularly with God's law (Matt. 12:5; Luke 2:23, 24; 16:16; John 7:19; Gal. 3:10) and with Moses (Mark 12:26; Luke 2:22; 20:28; John 7:23).
The period covered by the Pentateuch is from the creation to the beginning of Joshua's leadership, after the death of Moses.

PERISH means to die, with all the consequences of death, and in particular eternal separation from God - the opposite of everlasting life (John 3:16)

PERSEVERANCE describes the New Testament teaching that once we are truly saved, we remain saved forever (John 6:39; 10:27-29; 2 Tim. 4:18). However, God requires us to live the Christian life with exertion, diligence and watchfulness (John 8:31; Phil. 2:12, 13; 2 Pet. 1:11). The strength to persevere in the faith is from God alone (Phil.

1:6). Believers hold fast to the end because they are shielded by the Lord's power (1 Pet. 1:5; cf. 1 Cor. 1:8).

PRAYER is not simply making requests of God, but rather conversation with God. In prayer God makes Himself known to our soul, often revealing His glory and His love. Christians must endeavour to pray always in the way God has established – in the name of the Lord Jesus Christ and with the help of the Holy Spirit. Through Christ Christians have confidence to come before God (Heb. 10:19) and by the Holy Spirit they are enabled to offer true prayer (Rom. 8:9, 26, 27). See Question 66.

PRESERVATION is a term used to describe God's preserving and maintaining the creation that He made, so that it continues to exist and function (Neh. 9:6). The Son and the Holy Spirit are also spoken of as having responsibility for the continuance and upholding of creation (Ps. 104:30; Heb. 1:3).

The term also describes God's preserving or keeping of believers in the Christian life, even using their trials and difficulties to strengthen them in their Christian faith (Phil. 1:6; 2:13; 2 Tim. 4:18; 1 Pet. 1:6, 7; Jude 24).

PROPHECIES, PROPHECY. Prophecy in the Bible represents the speaking forth of the mind and counsel of God. Although prophecies sometimes referred to future events, prophecy was not necessarily foretelling the future. Rather it was the setting forth of truth that could not be known by natural means. Prophecy apparently passed away when all the Bible books were available to the Christian Church. Teaching from the whole Scriptures has taken the place of the prophecy that was necessary before the complete Scriptures were available (cf. 2 Pet. 2:1).

PROPHETS spoke on behalf of God: they were individuals supernaturally instructed in God's will, and inspired and commissioned to make it known to people, with regard to both present and future events (Jer. 1:9; Isa. 51:16; 2 Pet. 1:20, 21). The Holy Spirit who inspired them caused some to write down their messages for the benefit of future generations.

PROPITIATION. To propitiate is to 'placate' or 'appease'. The reaction to sin of God's holiness is wrath, displeasure and vengeance. The purpose of propitiation is the removal of God's displeasure. By His death upon the Cross for our sins, the Lord Jesus Christ propitiated God's wrath and rendered God well disposed to His people - and this He did as the provision of God the Father's great love for sinners (1 John 4:8-10).

PROVIDENCE is God's good, kind, and unceasing activity and control of all things, working out everything in conformity with the purpose of His will (Ps. 100:5; Eph. 1:11). He permits wars, suffering, and other human tragedies and dilemmas, only as they may serve to fulfil His purposes; His final and sure purpose is that they will cease.

PSALMS means 'praises' and gives its name to the longest book in the Bible. The 150 psalms came from different authors, although many - 73 - are said to have been written by David. They were like a hymnbook for Solomon's temple. Reflecting the variety of joy and trouble God's people have known, strength and help are readily found in them by Christian believers.

RECONCILE, RECONCILED, RECONCILIATION. The idea behind the word 'reconciliation' is that of making peace again after a quarrel, the bringing together of two parties who have been estranged. The harmony that God intended in the beginning we should know with Him was completely spoiled by Adam and Eve's sin (our first parents), and our repetition of it, so that God's attitude of wrath is what we deserve. By our sin we constitute ourselves God's enemies (Rom. 5:10; Col. 1:21), because His demand for righteousness means that He is always opposed to evil.

Reconciliation, in this situation, is effected by God's dealing with the root cause of the quarrel – human sin. By the death of His Son God dealt with sin finally and effectively (Rom. 5:10, 11). God caused Christ, who Himself knew no sin, actually to be sin for sinners, so that in Christ they might be made righteous and acceptable to Him (2 Cor. 5:21). People may now be reconciled to God as they respond to God's gracious offer of salvation in Christ (2 Cor. 5:20).

REDEEM, REDEMPTION. Redemption is a term by which the Lord Jesus Christ's work for sinners may be viewed. Redemption is deliverance by purchase from captivity, bondage or death. The Biblical picture behind it is that of slavery. By nature we are slaves to sin, deserving the punishment of death (John 8:34). The price paid to purchase sinners from the slavery of sin was the death of the Lord Jesus Christ (1 Cor. 6:20; Eph. 1:7). Through Christ, believers become free from the power of sin and death, but they have a privileged obligation, as a consequence, to honour God in their bodies (1 Cor. 6:20).

REGENERATION. See Question 26.

REPENTANCE is turning from sin to God (Ezek. 33:11; Acts 3:19; 26:20), as a result of a change of mind and heart about sin.

RESURRECTION. God the Father raised Christ from the dead (Acts 2:24; 3:15; Eph.1:20; Col. 2:12), in fulfilment of the Scriptures (Ps. 16:10; cf. Acts 13:34, 35; Luke 24:44) and Christ's promises (John 2:19-22; Matt. 16:21; 20:19; Mark 9:9; 14:28). By this means He declared Jesus to be His Son (Rom. 1:4) and His acceptance of His redemptive work (1 Cor. 15:14, 17, 19), thus guaranteeing the justification of all believers (Acts 26:23; 1 Cor.15:20, 23, 49).

RESURRECTION OF THE BODY. See Question 47.

RESURRECTION OF THE DEAD. This event will take place at Christ's return (1 Thess. 4:14-16). All will rise from the dead, believers to the resurrection of life, and unbelievers to the resurrection of judgment (Dan. 12:2; John 5:28, 29; Acts 24:15; Rev. 20:11-15). The resurrection of the dead is a fundamental of the Christian message (1 Cor.15:12, 13; Heb. 6:2, 2 Tim. 2:18).

RETRIBUTION is generally recompense for evil, although sometimes for good. The wheels of God's vengeance may appear to move slowly (Eccl. 8:11) but vengeance belongs to Him, and He will righteously recompense evil (Rom. 12:19; Rev. 18:6). At His return, Christ will carry His reward with Him, to repay all according to their deeds (Rev. 22:12).

REVELATION is God's making Himself and His will known to men and women in a way that otherwise they could not themselves discover. It is God speaking to us so that we may know what He is like, and come to know Him.

God has revealed truths about Himself in His works of creation (Ps. 19:1-4; Rom. 1:20ff), His providence (Ps. 145:9; Matt. 5:45; Acts 14:16ff), and in men and women's consciences (Rom. 1:32; 2:14, 15). People everywhere may discern these truths, but they do not bring knowledge of God's salvation. God speaks to us supremely and uniquely through the Scriptures, called 'the Word of God', and through His Son, who is also called 'the Word' – the One through whom God perfectly reveals Himself to us (John 1:1; Heb. 1:1, 2).

REWARDS have nothing to do with the earning of salvation, for salvation is a free gift (Rom. 6:23; Eph. 2:8). When the gift of salvation has been received, however, God is graciously pleased to give rewards for faithful service (Matt. 19:28; Mark 10:29, 30; Luke 18:28, 29).

The parable of the talents teaches that where there is unequal ability but equal faithfulness, the reward will be the same in both cases (Matt. 25:14-30).

The parable of the pounds teaches that where there is equal ability but unequal faithfulness, the reward will be graded (Luke 19:11-27).

RIGHTEOUS, RIGHTEOUSNESS is a characteristic of God, expressing the rightness of all that He is and does (Rom. 3:5). It is used to describe, too, whatever is right in God's sight (Matt. 3:15; 5:6, 10, 20). The most important use is when it describes the right relationship people have with God when they believe in the Lord Jesus Christ (Rom. 10:10). They are made righteous in Him, that is to say, they become in Christ all that God requires them to be (1 Cor. 1:30; 2 Cor. 5:21).

SACRAMENT. A sacrament is an outward sign by which God confirms to believers' consciences His promises of goodwill towards them. The sacraments provide believers with an opportunity of declaring their devotion and allegiance to God.

The two commonly accepted sacraments of the Christian Church are baptism and the Lord's Supper. Most Protestants maintain that these are the only two because our Lord Jesus specifically established them for His people (Matt. 28:19; 1 Cor. 11:23-25). Some prefer the word 'ordinances' in place of 'sacraments', therefore, because baptism and the Lord's Supper were 'ordered' - that is to say, chosen and appointed - by the Lord Jesus Christ.

SACRIFICE, SACRIFICES. A sacrifice was an act of worship by which an offering was made to God of some object belonging to the worshipper, the purpose being to please God and to obtain His favour. The animal sacrifices of the Old Testament were intended by God to teach the method of salvation. They always had the idea of cleansing behind them and the indispensable element was the shedding of blood (Heb. 9:22, 23), but their repetition only served to point out their ineffectiveness (Heb. 10:2). Thus the sacrifices reminded people of sin, revealed the need of atonement, and prepared the way for the coming of the Lord Jesus Christ.

The expression is used of the sacrificial death of Christ, for He offered for all time a single sacrifice for sin (Heb. 10:12), achieving what the Old Testament sacrifices could never do. His sacrifice was effective once forever, guaranteeing perfect forgiveness (Heb. 9:26).

SACRIFICE, SACRIFICES (Spiritual). Christ's single sacrifice for sin for all time has completely done away with the need for animal and ceremonial sacrifices.

However God still requires sacrifices of another kind from those who are saved through Christ's one perfect sacrifice. As spiritual priests, Christians may offer to God acceptable spiritual sacrifices (1 Pet. 2:5, 9) by means of praise, thanksgiving, prayer, repentance, obedience, sharing and doing good to others (Ps. 50:14; 51:17; 107:22; 141:2; Rom. 12:1; Heb. 13:15, 16; James 1:27). By such means we worship God in the Spirit, for these are all part of the Holy Spirit's activity in the Christian (Phil. 3:3).

SAINT serves as a name for all believers, and is not given in the Bible to people of outstanding holiness and saintliness.

The word means 'separated' or 'dedicated'. Christians are called upon to separate themselves from evil (2 Tim. 2:19), and to dedicate themselves to God's service (Rom. 12:1, 2), because He has set them apart to be His own possession (1 Pet. 2:9, 10). For these reasons Christians are called 'the saints'.

SALVATION is deliverance from the guilt and penalties of sin to enjoy, instead, the unchanging favour of God forever through repentance and faith in the Lord Jesus Christ (Acts 4:12; Rom. 10:10). It is known and felt in the present by the gift of the Holy Spirit (Acts 2:38) and the forgiveness of sins (1 John 1:9), but it will be completely disclosed in the future in the full enjoyment of everlasting life and all its benefits (Acts 2:38-40; 16:30, 31; 1 Thess. 5:8, 9, 10; 1 Pet. 1:5, 13).

SANCTIFICATION. See Question 35.

SANCTIFIED, when applied either to persons or things, indicates their consecration, dedication, or inclusion in the inner circle of what is holy, because of their association with God in some way. Thus Christians, because of their relationship to God through Christ that sets them apart as His, are described as 'sanctified' – or 'saints', as the word is sometimes translated.

SATAN is the name of the prince of evil, the adversary, commonly called the devil. He is the great enemy of God and of every human being, the opposer of all that is good and the promoter of all that is evil. He has been defeated already by the Lord Jesus Christ's death and resurrection, and this defeat will be complete and clear to all at the end of this present age. See Question 43.

SAVIOUR. A Saviour is a deliverer or preserver, and as a title for the Lord Jesus Christ is especially appropriate because of His saving work on the Cross on behalf of sinners, promised by God throughout the centuries (Luke 2:11; Acts 13:23; Phil. 3:20). As the Saviour He offers forgiveness of sins on true repentance and faith (Acts 5:31), together with the gift of life and immortality (2 Tim. 1:10).

SCRIPTURES. The word means simply 'writings', and in the New Testament is used to refer to the Old Testament (Luke 24:44, 45; 1 Cor. 15:3ff). The term is often used to describe both the Old and New Testaments.

SEPARATION FROM GOD. God's holiness demands that He should be entirely separate from sin. Men and women's sins cut them off from God so that fellowship with Him is impossible (Isa. 59:2). The reality of the separation sin brings is illustrated in the cry of separation that Jesus uttered upon the cross (Matt. 27:46; Mark 15:34), when He, who knew no sin, was made to be sin for us, so that in Him we might become the righteousness of God (2 Cor. 5:21).

SIGN. A sign, like a miracle, is a work or an event that is contrary to the usual course of nature. The miracles of Jesus in John's Gospel are all described as 'signs' for besides being supernatural, they provided direct evidence of His deity, sufficient to bring people to living faith in Him (John 20:30, 31).

SIN. See Question 12.

SON, SON OF GOD was an expression Jesus rarely used, although He sometimes spoke of Himself as 'the Son' (Matt. 11:27; Mark 13:32). He is not the Son in the same sense as we may become sons and daughters of God through faith (Matt. 11:27; Luke 2:49; John 20:17). He is uniquely God's one Son – in a way no one else can be – whom He loves (Mark. 9:7; 12:6). He and the Father are one, a truth that the disciples appreciated at Jesus' resurrection (John 20:28; Rom. 1:3, 4). All the works, glory and perfection of God may be attributed to Him (John 1:3; Col. 1:16, 17; Heb. 1:2; Mark 2:5, 7). He is one with His Father; He is equal with God.

SOUL is, first, the base and centre of the inner life of a person in its varied aspects, and it can represent an individual's feelings and emotions. But, secondly, it is also the base and centre of that life that goes beyond this life. As such, the soul can receive God's salvation (Jas. 1:21; 1 Pet. 1:9). People cannot harm it, but God can give it over to destruction (Matt. 10:28). It is because it is capable of sharing in God's divine nature (1 Pet. 1:22; cf. 2 Pet. 1:4) that its worth is so tremendous – indeed nothing we possess is more valuable (Matt. 16:26; Mark 8:37).

SOVEREIGNTY is supreme authority and absolute dominion. Such sovereignty by right is God's alone. All things happen just as He decided long ago (Eph. 1:11). He rules over everything and He does what He chooses (Rom. 9:5, 18).

SPIRIT is sometimes used in place of the word 'soul' (Eccl. 12:7; Luke 23:46; Acts 7:59; 1 Cor. 5:3, 5), and is more important than the body, being that part of us that thinks, feels, wills and lives forever (Matt. 16:26; 2 Cor. 5:8; 2 Tim. 4:22).
It is also used to describe God's nature: He is Spirit, that is to say, there is nothing material in His nature (John 4:24), and He has no body.

SPIRIT OF CHRIST is a title given to the Holy Spirit, the Third Person of the Trinity (Rom. 8:9; Gal. 4:6; Phil. 1:19; 1 Pet.1:11). The title expresses the closest possible relationship between the two Persons. The Spirit was promised by the Son as well as by the Father (John 14:17, 26). It is by the Spirit that our Lord Jesus Christ lives in believers' hearts (Eph. 3:16, 17). The ministry of the Spirit has been, and is, to take of the things of Christ and make them known to us (John 16:14; 1 Pet.1:11).

TEMPTATION is used both in a good and a bad sense, and can have the meaning of testing as much as temptation. In the good sense God tests people so that they may prove themselves true (Heb. 11:17) and in this sense the Lord Jesus Christ was tested by God (Heb. 2:18; 4:15). In the bad sense it is enticement to sin, the devil's work (Matt. 4:1; 1 Cor. 7:5; Gal. 6:1; Jas. 1:13).

TESTAMENT. A testament, like a covenant, is an undertaking or engagement made between God and human beings, at God's initiative, by means of His promises.
The Old Testament communicates God's promises, relating principally to this present life, that He made to the Jews. The Old Testament was built upon the keeping of God's law.
The New Testament relates to the everlasting promises God makes in the Lord Jesus Christ throughout all the Scriptures. This testament is built on faith and not on works (John 3:16).

TESTING describes God's use of varying and difficult circumstances to make known to us our real character, and often to prove the reality and strength of our faith and obedience (Gen. 22:1, 12; Heb. 11:17; 1 Pet. 1:7; 4:12).

TRANSFIGURATION is the term used in the gospels to record what three of the apostles witnessed of Christ's glory. For a few moments the heavenly glory of Christ, that was usually hidden by the conditions of His human life, shone through His body and its clothing (Matt. 17:2; Mark 9:2). A statement by God the Father of His approval of His Son accompanied this revelation.

TRANSGRESSION is the violation of God's law, the picture behind the word being the over-stepping of the bounds laid down by the law. When we do what God's law forbids, we transgress - we step over the limits He has set (Dan. 9:11).

TRESPASS. To trespass is to make a false step, to turn aside from right and truth, to sin either against people (Matt. 6:14, 15) or against God (Rom. 5:15, 17; Gal. 6:1).

TRINITY. See Question 8.

UNJUST is used to describe those who act and behave contrary to what is right in God's sight – a description that fits us all before new birth because of our sinful nature and practice (Matt. 5:45; Acts 24:15; 1 Pet. 3:18).

UNRIGHTEOUSNESS is wrongdoing or the persistent doing of what is wrong - the characteristic of men and women as sinners (1 John 1:9; 5:17). See **INIQUITY** that is almost identical.

WASHED is a description of Christians when forgiveness of sins is thought of in terms of inward and spiritual cleansing (Acts 22. 16; 1 Cor. 6:11; 1 John 1:7-9).

WICKED describes a person or a thing that is evil, bad, base, worthless, vicious or degenerate. The lives of the wicked are governed by transgression, and the fear of God is absent (Ps. 36:1). The prosperity they appear to enjoy is a fleeting experience (Ps. 37:13).

WICKED ONE. See **EVIL ONE.**

WICKEDNESS is baseness, maliciousness and sinfulness. It is the characteristic of this present evil world (Gal. 1:4) and comes from within the human heart (Mark 7:22). Wickedness multiplies and its obvious increase will be a mark of the end (Matt. 24:10-12).

WILL is the ability we possess to decide or think for ourselves when we determine our actions. It represents the act of willing or desiring. This exercise of will is necessary to our personality and responsibility as rational beings. The will is always free, and we have the power of choice. We also have to say, however, that the will is not always good, for, since the fall of our first parents, Adam and Eve, it is diseased, impaired and prone to evil.

WORD OF GOD, THE. The expression is used in four particular senses. First, our Lord Jesus Christ is called the Word of God (John 1:1), in that God has spoken to us in His Son, giving us His final and complete revelation in Him (Heb. 1:1, 2).
Secondly, the gospel is called the Word of God (Mark 4:14; Luke 5:1; 8:11; 11:28) because it is God's message to sinful humanity (Rom. 1:16; 15:16).
Thirdly, the Old Testament Scriptures are the Word of God. Christ and the apostles spoke of the Old Testament and quoted it as God's Word (Mark 7:13; Acts 3:22-25; Rom. 1:2; 2 Tim. 3:16).
Fourthly, the Word of God taught by the Lord and the apostles is the content of the New Testament, constituting the whole Bible – the Old and New Testaments together - the Word of God. This makes the Bible the sole authority in everything that concerns faith and conduct. When the Bible speaks, God speaks. See Questions 3, 4.

WORKS (Human) i.e. deeds of men and women. We cannot gain acceptance with God by what we ourselves do or achieve (Rom. 3:20, 28; Gal. 2:16; Eph. 2:8, 9). Our acceptance by God depends upon a personal relationship to the Lord Jesus Christ. But good works are the demanded and expected result of a right relationship with God through His Son (Eph. 2:10; Tit. 2:7, 14; 3:1, 8).

WORLD is sometimes used simply to describe the world in a geographical sense (John 1:10), or the men and women of the world (John 3:16, 17). Most frequently, it refers to the life of people dominated and organised by the god of this world, Satan (2 Cor. 4:4; 1 John 2:15-17).

WORSHIP is the acknowledgement by believers of the worth-ship of God with every part of their being (Rom. 12:1, 2). Such worship is acceptable to God only as it is offered through the Lord Jesus Christ, our Mediator and great High Priest (Heb. 13:15, 16). This worship cannot be separated from practical conduct supporting what has been professed by the lips (Jas.1:27).

WRATH is the inevitable reaction of God's holiness against sin, a reaction that demands that He, the righteous Judge, will finally reckon with it (John 3:36; Rom. 1:18; 1 Thess.1:10; 5:9).

Other books of interest from Christian Focus Publications

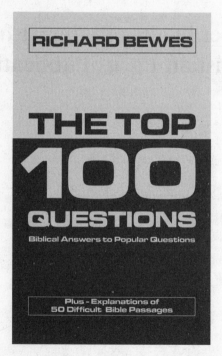

RICHARD BEWES

THE TOP
100
QUESTIONS
Biblical Answers to Popular Questions

Plus - Explanations of
50 Difficult Bible Passages

ISBN 978-1-85792-680-4

THE TOP 100 QUESTIONS
Biblical Answers to Popular Questions
RICHARD BEWES

WE'VE all had that sinking feeling when you realise that the question you have just been asked has you stumped. It has never occurred to you before and your mind races to come to a satisfactory answer, while you kick yourself for not having thought of the question before now.

As a pastor of a vibrant city church in the heart of London, Richard Bewes faces tricky questions about his faith on almost a daily basis. This book is a compilation of his Top 100 Questions, asked by people from all walks of life and religious belief, along with an appendix dealing with difficult Bible passages and questions that can arise from them.

The answers Richard offers are not pat answers to outwit the questioner, but rather, he seeks to give clear, biblical advice to genuine questions.

The book is divided into five sections:

•The Universe we Inhabit • The Truth we Believe•
•The Bible we Read • The Way we Behave • The Christ we Follow•

...the accumulated wisdom and illustration from decades of mulling over some very difficult questions – wonderfully distilled down to the key points.

Rico Tice

...provides direct, clear, concise and relevant answers to questions with which many people struggle. I learned a lot, and you will too if you buy the book!

Lindsay Brown

...gives deeply thought-out, carefully informed answers to many of the questions most troublesome to contemporary humanity.

Dallas Willard

...I'm already planning who I could send copies of the book to when it's published.

Peter Maiden

RICHARD BEWES is Retired Rector of All Souls Church, Langham Place in the heart of London's West End. He is author of some 18 books, including *The Goodnight Book* (ISBN 978-1-84550-465-6)

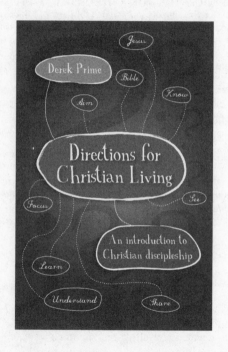

ISBN 978-1-84550-614-8

Directions for Christian Living
A Spiritual Action Plan for Growth
Derek Prime

Children and families need to know the truth about the church because children are not just the church of tomorrow, they are the church of today. Like a building, if the foundations are not solid then the whole structure is shaky. This book provides a summary of these foundations, essential knowledge for both new and established Christians. It explores the meaning of conversion, living day by day with Jesus, being filled with the Spirit, sharing our faith, talking and listening to God. Questions, Bible references and suggestions for further reading combine to make this an excellent resource for groups or for private study.

Sound biblical principles, clear instruction and helpful, practical application –vintage Prime.

Alistair Begg

After serving churches in the UK as a pastor for thirty years - first at Lansdowne Evangelical Free Church, West Norwood, in London and then at Charlotte Chapel in Edinburgh - Derek Prime has devoted himself since 1987 to an itinerant ministry and to writing.

DEREK PRIME

PRACTICAL
PRAYER

ISBN 978-1-84550-309-3

Practical Prayer

DEREK PRIME

How is your prayer Life? Or is that a touchy question?

If we are honest with ourselves we feel more than a bit awkward when questioned about our conversation times with God.

The best starting point is to be honest with God rather than shying away from the topic or putting on a show for our Christian friends. Derek Prime gives us a heartfelt and practical approach to prayer. Here are fresh, vibrant ideas to strengthen and enliven what can so often be a disappointing part of our spiritual life.

Derek uses his writing skills to simply explain the many aspects of prayer to deepen your prayer life with The Lord.

After a good introduction the 8 Chapters are helpfully divided as follows:

1. Defining Prayer; 2. Prayer & the Christian Life 3. Prayer's Potential; 4. Prayer & The Holy Spirit; 5. Method in Prayer; 6. Praying For Others; 7. Praying With Others; 8. Problems & Questions about Prayer.

After serving churches in the UK as a pastor for thirty years - first at Lansdowne Evangelical Free Church, West Norwood, in London and then at Charlotte Chapel in Edinburgh - Derek Prime has devoted himself since 1987 to an itinerant ministry and to writing.

Christian Focus Publications

publishes books for all ages

Our mission statement –

STAYING FAITHFUL
In dependence upon God we seek to impact the world through literature faithful to His infallible Word, the Bible. Our aim is to ensure that the Lord Jesus Christ is presented as the only hope to obtain forgiveness of sin, live a?useful life and look forward to heaven with Him.

REACHING OUT
Christ's last command requires us to reach out to our world with His gospel. We seek to help fulfill that by publishing books that point people towards Jesus and help them develop a Christ-like maturity. We aim to equip all levels of readers for life, work, ministry and mission.

Books in our adult range are published in three imprints.

Christian Focus contains popular works including biographies, commentaries, basic doctrine and Christian living. Our children's books are also published in this imprint.

Mentor focuses on books written at a level suitable for Bible College and seminary students, pastors, and other serious readers. The imprint includes commentaries, doctrinal studies, examination of current issues and church history.

Christian Heritage contains classic writings from the past.

Christian Focus Publications, Ltd
Geanies House, Fearn,
Ross-shire, IV20 1TW,
Scotland, United Kingdom

info@christianfocus.com